HARVARD HISTORICAL STUDIES · 143

Published under the auspices
of the Department of History
from the income of the
Paul Revere Frothingham Bequest
Robert Louis Stroock Fund
Henry Warren Torrey Fund

DEFINING GERMANY

The 1848 Frankfurt Parliamentarians
and National Identity

BRIAN E. VICK

HARVARD UNIVERSITY PRESS

Cambridge, Massachusetts, and London, England | 2002

Library of Congress Cataloging-in-Publication Data

Vick, Brian E., 1970–
    Defining Germany : the 1848 Frankfurt parliamentarians and national
identity / Brian E. Vick.
        p. cm.— (Harvard historical studies ; 143)
    Includes bibliographical references and index.
    ISBN 0-674-00911-8 (alk. paper)
    1. Deutsche Nationalversammlung (1848–1849 : Frankfurt am Main,
Germany) 2. Constitutional history—Germany—19th century.
3. Legislative bodies—Germany—Frankfurt am Main—History—
19th century. 4. Germany—Politics and government—1848–1849.
5. Civil rights—Germany—History—19th century.
I. Title. II. Harvard historical studies ; v. 143.

DD207.5 .V48 2002
320.943′09′034—dc21   2002024073

To my parents, Richard and Judy Vick
with gratitude, respect, and love

Contents

Acknowledgments

To say that this book could not have been written without the help of many might be a cliché, but it is true for all that. First I would like to express my gratitude to those who had the patience to read and comment carefully on the entire manuscript at various stages of development: Henry A. Turner, Jr., Frank M. Turner, and Piotr Wandycz of Yale University; George S. Williamson of the University of Alabama; and the two anonymous readers for the Harvard University Press. For vetting parts of the manuscript I would also like to thank Kevin Repp of Yale, Charles Lansing of Yale, and Timothy Brown of Stanford University. For their welcome suggestions and encouragement I warmly acknowledge the permanent academic fellows of the Institute for European History in Mainz, Germany, above all Director Heinz Duchhardt, Ralph Melville, Claus Scharf, and Martin Vogt. Professor Melville helpfully provided materials and information relating to Austrian and Bohemian oppositionists, while Professor Vogt was not only willing to talk at length in his office but also helped put me in contact with Wolfgang Michalka of the Frankfurt and Rastatt branches of the German Federal Archives (to whom thanks are also due). And of course I would also like to express appreciation to Patrice Higonnet of the Harvard History Department and to the various editors at Harvard University Press, including Kathleen McDermott, Elizabeth Suttell, Aïda Donald, and Richard Audet.

Financial support came in the form of a year-long dissertation-writing grant from the Andrew Mellon Foundation and the Yale Graduate School, as well as a nine-month postdoctoral fellowship at the Institute for European History in Mainz. And most recently, the Introduction to the Humanities Program at Stanford has not only offered a secure base from which to operate but also provided a quarter's paid research leave during which I was able to accomplish much of the final stage of revision.

For research support I would like to thank the staffs at the Frankfurt branch of the German Federal Archives as well as of the various libraries where I did most of my work: Sterling Memorial Library at Yale University, Green Library at Stanford, the Mainz City Library, and the Library of the Episcopal Seminary of the Archdiocese of Mainz. And I would particularly like to thank the friendly folks in the impressive library of the Institute for European History for helping to make my stay there both pleasant and productive.

Reaching farther back into the past, I would like to thank my undergraduate history advisors, Paul Seaver and Peter Stansky of Stanford University, who with true warmth and wisdom helped guide a fledgling historian; and Brigitte Turneaure, who not only helped improve my German language skills during those years but also kept wondering aloud why I did not do more with German history, asking the pertinent question: "Wozu all das Deutsch?"—"What's all the German for?"

And reaching farthest back into the past, my deepest gratitude and appreciation go to my parents, Richard and Judy Vick. Avid readers themselves, they encouraged me to explore the world of books and to follow my intellectual interests, both as a child and later on (even when I could have been doing something more remunerative during the summers). They made it clear that a career could be a freely chosen calling, and that the life of the mind was a worthy one. It is only through their hard work and willingness to sacrifice that I have been able to pursue my dreams and to make my choices freely, more freely at any rate than they ever had the opportunity to do. Grazie, genitori.

DEFINING GERMANY

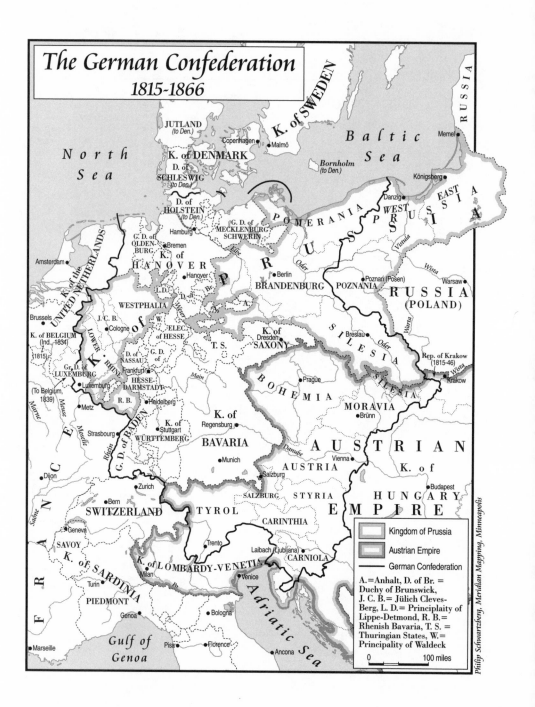

The German Confederation
1815-1866

North Sea

JUTLAND
(to Den.)

K. of DENMARK

D. of
SCHLESWIG
(to Den.)

D. of
HOLSTEIN
(to Den.)

Copenhagen
Malmö

Baltic Sea

Bornholm
(to Den.)

K. of SWEDEN

Memel

Königsberg

Danzig

WEST PRUSSIA

EAST PRUSSIA

RUSSIA

G. D. of
MECKLENBURG
SCHWERIN

POMERANIA

G. D. of
OLDEN-
BURG.

Hamburg

Bremen

K. of
HANOVER

Hanover

Elbe

Oder

Berlin

BRANDENBURG

Vistula

POZNANIA

Poznań (Posen)

RUSSIA
(POLAND)

Warsaw

Amsterdam

K. of the UNITED NETHERLANDS

Brussels

K. of BELGIUM
(Ind., 1834)

(1815)

WESTPHALIA

L.D.

D. of

Br.

Weser

A.

A.

SILESIA

Breslau

Oder

SILESIA

Wisła

Wisła

Rep. of Krakow
(1815-46)

J. C. B.

Cologne

K. of

W.

ELEC.
of HESSE

T. S.

K. of
SAXONY

Dresden

Krakow

Gr. D. of
LUXEMBURG

Luxemburg

(To Belgium,
1839)

D. of
NASSAU

G. D. of

Frankfurt

HESSE-
DARMSTADT

Main

BOHEMIA

Prague

MORAVIA

Brünn

Metz

Meuse

Marne

Moselle

R. B.

Heidelberg

K. of
WÜRTTEMBERG

Stuttgart

K. of

BAVARIA

Regensburg

Munich

AUSTRIAN

Vienna

AUSTRIA

Salzburg

K. of

Budapest

HUNGARY

EMPIRE

Strasbourg

G. D. of BADEN

Rhine

Saône

Dijon

Zurich

Bern

SWITZERLAND

Geneva

SAVOY

K. of SARDINIA

Turin

PIEDMONT

Genoa

*Gulf of
Genoa*

Marseille

TYROL

Trento

SALZBURG

STYRIA

CARINTHIA

Laibach (Ljubljana)

CARNIOLA

K. of LOMBARDY-VENETIA

Milan

Po

Venice

Bologna

Pisa

Florence

Ancona

Adriatic Sea

Danube

FRANCE

LOWER RHINE

☐ Kingdom of Prussia

☐ Austrian Empire

— German Confederation

A.=Anhalt, D. of Br. =
Duchy of Brunswick,
J. C. B.= Jülich Cleves-
Berg, L. D.= Principality of
Lippe-Detmond, R. B.=
Rhenish Bavaria, T. S. =
Thuringian States, W.=
Principality of Waldeck

0   100 miles

Philip Schwartzberg, Meridian Mapping, Minneapolis

Introduction

From his Alpine vantage just outside the Germany of Bismarck and Wagner, Friedrich Nietzsche observed that "it is characteristic of the Germans that the question 'what is German' never dies out among them."[1] Whether Nietzsche was correct to see such concern with self-definition as a truly abiding characteristic of the Germans may perhaps be debated, yet it is certain that defining the German nation has for centuries been a task fraught with difficulty. To fix its borders, to identify its constituent members, to determine its proper role in the world and its relationships with its neighbors: none of these problems has allowed of a simple solution. Indeed, attempts to define Germany and make that abstraction concrete reality have proven to be among the most contentious and portentous developments of modern European history. Even in the twentieth century, in an era of international law, collective security, and passports, efforts to settle these issues, far from ceasing, were pushed to the most radical extremes of world war, ethnic cleansing, and genocide.

At few points in the past, however, were Germany's borders, membership, and historical mission quite so open to definition as during the first half of the nineteenth century, or so openly debated as during the Revolution of 1848–1849. In the wake of the French Revolution of 1789 and the ensuing Napoleonic wars, the problem of national definition stood squarely at the forefront of educated German discourse both public and private, intimately coupled with discussions of social, cultural, and political reform and deeply implicated in the formation of group and individual identities. Yet at this early stage in the development of national ideas, conceptions of nationhood remained fluid, not as doctrinally hardened as they would later become during the classic age of nationalism in the decades leading up to the First World War. A matter of concern in the first half of the nineteenth century, the precise shape the German nation would take was also a matter of dispute.

Both the concern and the scope for disputation reached a peak in the 1848 Revolution, which at last held out the prospect of transforming such constructions of nationhood into institutional reality. March of 1848 saw the core of the German liberal-democratic opposition gather in Frankfurt to begin the process of overturning the 1815 Congress of Vienna settlement and replacing its diplomatic keystone, the German Confederation, with a German national state. Building this new Germany, however, proved unexpectedly difficult. The assembled reformers could only grope uncertainly as the familiar social, political, and national boundaries of the old Germany were engulfed in the revolution's spring torrents. When artisans, laborers, and peasants began to raise their own voices, the scholars, businessmen, and disgruntled officials of the Frankfurt Constituent National Assembly lost confidence in claiming to speak for a socially united nation of citizens. And when the constitutional struggles no longer pitted against each other the forces of the opposition and the dynasties, but rather squabbling elements within the oppositional movement itself— moderate liberals and reform conservatives, democrats and socialists—the political unity of the German nation too seemed to erode.

But what most frustrated delegates was the fact that the new nation's very borders, far from being the natural and easily discerned features of the landscape that they had assumed, had themselves sunk from view. There were territories and there were peoples, but delineating precisely where the boundaries between them were to be drawn turned out to be every bit as problematic as clarifying the new Germany's political institutions and social relations. Millions of Germans lived just outside the borders of the German Confederation, and millions of inhabitants who considered themselves something other than German lived within them. National movements among the Danes, Poles, and Italians, as well as among the Czechs and Slovenes, contested the German national movement's claims to wide swaths of territory both inside and outside the Confederation. Even when the Assembly took pains to proclaim the extension of full citizen rights to all national groups living in the new Germany, the contentiousness persisted. Borders could no longer be taken as God-given—they would instead have to be argued over, in some cases even fought over. In turn, the revolution that had thrown the borders into flux was itself called into question by those border conflicts. The Mazzinian gospel of a chiliastic "Springtime of the Nations" came to fruition in the spring of 1848, but the heavenly city could find no purchase upon contested ground.

As a consequence of these problem-plagued efforts to reconstruct the linguistically multinational German Confederation as a German national state, the 1848 Frankfurt Parliament offers a unique opportunity to study national identity among educated Germans in a phase that was crucially formative and at a time when they had the opportunity and the responsibility to make pragmatic political decisions. While wrestling with myriad other issues, delegates struggled to settle some of the most fundamental problems relating to nationhood, including Germany's precise territorial extent, the civil and cultural rights that should devolve upon the non-German-speaking and German-Jewish minorities living within those borders, and the relations the German nation so constructed should maintain with neighboring peoples. In the process they revealed much about the cultural presuppositions behind the development of German national identity, and about the nature of German nationalism in the middle of the nineteenth century. They disclosed the plasticity of the concept "Germany," but they exposed its underlying conceptual molds as well.

In order to understand the various nationality-related debates so urgently canvassed during the 1848 Revolution more fully, to grasp not just the visible patterns but also the framework beneath the fabric of debate, it is not enough to sift the evidence from 1848 alone—considerable attention must also be devoted to the parliamentarians' less voluble but no less revealing treatment of nationality in the decades prior to 1848. In the course of their prerevolutionary political and academic endeavors, the future deputies disclosed both stated and unstated assumptions about the criteria for drawing boundaries between nations and about the legal, political, and cultural relationships among connected groups in different states or distinct groups within the same states. Only by elucidating these deeper conceptions of nationhood that underlay the future Frankfurt deputies' national politics is it possible to understand the definitions of "Germany" that emerged in 1848.

The present study is the first to adopt such a dual focus and examine the Frankfurt Parliament's debates about the form, content, and mission of the nascent German national state in conjunction with the intellectual and cultural background of the preceding period in order to uncover the underpinnings of German thinking about nationality. In exploring some of the most fundamental structures of educated German national identity, this work ultimately questions many accepted truths, old and new, about German nationalism in the first half of the nineteenth century. Several of its findings may prove surprising, some perhaps controversial, others perhaps just commonsensical once pointed out. Some may surprise through their novelty, as for example the examination of such seldom-covered topics as citizenship policy, minority linguistic rights, or notions of national honor. Others of its conclusions may stimulate debate through their revisionism, as with the discussions of border-drawing policies and of Jewish emancipation, or simply through putting well-known phenomena in a new explanatory framework, as with the treatment of nationalist aggression. Ultimately it is in its broad contextualization within the realm of ideas that this work has most to offer, both in drawing on a wide array of often neglected sources and in touching on several topics of less immediate but still crucial relevance to conceptions of nationhood. For in explaining national identity in relation to ideas of liberalism, history, neohumanist education, and race, this study provides new perspectives on German nationalism and national identity during the first half of the nineteenth century.

Despite a large literature on both the early German national movement and the German 1848 Revolution, previous work offers useful points of departure for the investigation without obviating the need for it. Among the few studies devoted specifically to the nationality politics of the Frankfurt Parliament, for example, Günter Wollstein has done a masterful job of describing the Assembly's involvement with the various nationality conflicts and border disputes spawned by the revolution. He has persuasively argued the now orthodox view that all factions in Frankfurt rattled aggressively nationalist sabers and shared a vision of an expansionist, German-dominated "Mitteleuropa." By doing so he has ended decades of historical sparring between supporters of the Forty-Eighter liberals and democrats as to which group bears the most blame for such destabilizing chauvinism.[2] But the task of explaining these similarities across broad portions of the mid-century German political spectrum remains, and it raises the need to go beyond the bounds of Wollstein's study by tracing those nationalist conceptions back to their prerevolutionary breeding grounds of political theory, historical consciousness, and the romantic movement. Alongside the similarities, Wollstein has also noted the sometimes divergent approaches of Austrians and North Germans to issues such as minority rights. Searching for such smaller-scale patterns across the geographic, political, and religious landscapes thus also assumes an important part in the present investigation.[3]

Much other work on the German 1848 Revolution has recently

emerged from newer schools of social and cultural history, which by changing the objects and methods of investigation have considerably variegated knowledge of the social and political scene during the first half of the nineteenth century.[4] If such research has generally had less to say about German nationalism and the content of nationalist systems of ideas, it offers a fuller picture of the dynamics of revolutionary politics and a deeper understanding of the cultural and socioeconomic contexts in which national consciousness and national identities were formed.[5] As such it provides important background for the present study.

which authors?

In addition to an older history of ideas phase, the literature on nationalism and national movements (German and general) has also been marked in recent decades by distinct social history and cultural studies approaches, and here too the various discussions offer orientation for the present investigation. In many respects the starting point for the analysis of nationalism as ideology remains the work of the turn-of-the-century German mandarin Friedrich Meinecke and the midcentury historian of ideas Hans Kohn. Between them these scholars established the typological dichotomy of nationalisms as either political or ethnocultural. According to this scheme, political or civic-voluntarist nationalists defined the national community in purely civic terms and showed respect for individual civil rights and group cultural differences, a situation characteristic of western nations like Great Britain and France. Cultural nationalists of romantic Germany or Eastern Europe, on the other hand, emphasized submission of the individual will to an exclusive, ethnically defined community.[6] For Kohn, writing after the catastrophe of the Second World War and the Holocaust, this basic ethnocultural configuration of German nationalism was pregnant with implications for the racist nationalism and totalitarianism that were seen as its direct descendants and thus fed into the influential notion of a German *Sonderweg*, or pathologically divergent path of historical development.

Kohn → Sonderweg

For all that recent scholars of the modernization or social history school of nationalism studies often question the efficacy of categorizing varieties of nationalism according to ideology rather than socioeconomic structures, they often continue to characterize nationalist beliefs in ways that reflect the distinctions set out by Meinecke, Kohn, and other idealist historians. Anthony Smith, for example, retains certain aspects of the Kohnian civic-ethnic dichotomy even as he critiques it, while Eric Hobsbawm makes the German case an exception to his general argument that linguistic nationalism only became more important later in the nineteenth century. If the criteria for national identity and national boundaries are not

Kohn/Meinecke ↓ modernization/ social history still rely on these two

simply dismissed as ideologically superficial and instrumentalist in such studies, then the linguistic definition of nationality emerges epiphenomenally from the educated elite's modernizing efforts to create and dominate a standardized, monolingual realm of print culture. Sociologist Liah Greenfeld, though questioning the focus on modernization, adheres even more strongly to the older typology. For her, nations can either be civic or ethnic, individualist or collectivist, with German nationalism inherently illiberal and ethnically defined from its inception.[7]

Even one of the latest studies of German national identity from the cultural studies perspective, while rejecting the cultural-political dichotomy as an assumption, still arrives at much the same Franco-German, civic-ethnic distinction in its conclusions. Two still more recent works uphold both the essentially ethnic view of German national identity and the thesis of xenophobic continuity between early nationalists and National Socialists.[8] If the newer literature has not fully distanced itself from the framework and conclusions of the older idealist tradition, there is all the more reason to revisit some of the old questions about German nationalism through renewed attention to the realm of ideas. Consequently, such notions about German national identity in the first half of the nineteenth century as its exclusively ethnic focus, its intolerance for foreigners, and its relation to the *Sonderweg* thesis will all be put to the test in what follows.

The newer sociological and cultural theoretic approaches to the study of nationalism also help set the present work's research agenda in other respects. The "nation-building" studies that dominated the 1980s and early 1990s, for example, still acknowledge the gravity of nationality conflicts yet tend to view the disputes and the national movements behind them as mere byproducts, even if dangerously pathological ones, of the fundamental socioeconomic changes transforming modern European society.[9] Scholars taking this perspective on the study of nationhood emphasize the role of the middle-class intelligentsia in the construction of national identities as a part of the process of modernization, but attention often remains more focused on the concrete networks of "social communication" they controlled than on the ideas and symbols that filled them.[10] Considering the social and functional contexts in which the nationalist beliefs to be examined here were formed thus plays an important role in their interpretation, above all in looking at the implications for German national identity of the sociological phenomenon of the growing educated middle class and its claims to elite status.

On the cultural side, within the last few years the new wave of cultural historians have begun to document and interpret the symbolic social construction of German national myths, memories, and identities, as this turned upon the inclusion and exclusion of certain social groups on the basis of race, class, gender, and ethnicity. As such the drawing of imagined and social boundaries around various in-groups and out-groups in identity politics has claimed a central spot in recent work on nationalism. The fundamental relationship between the self and the (negatively portrayed) Other in the narrative construction of social identity, be it individual, group, or national, thus also hovers in the background here.[11] Yet rather than presuppose that theoretical framework as essential to national identity, the present study adopts certain historicist perspectives from the history of ideas in order to reconstruct the patterns of inclusion and exclusion in national narratives and institutions in its own way.

As this brief historiographical review should have made clear, plenty of room remains for examinations of German nationalist culture in the first half of the nineteenth century. In fact, such a study has become all the more necessary as a means of addressing neglected aspects of that complex phenomenon. The present investigation will take into account the insights of social and cultural historians into the means by which intellectuals created and publicized national movements and identities, but it will concentrate on exploring the origins, meanings, and consequences of the ideas of nationhood that pulsed through these networks of social communication. If the comparative malleability of national identities as "invented traditions," "imagined communities," or "collective memories" forms one of the most fruitful conclusions of recent scholarship on nationalism, then examining the cultural and intellectual contexts in which such national construction work took place becomes all the more important.

While taking cognizance of the insights of social and cultural history, the present investigation self-consciously pursues a distinct methodology, one that may prove useful in other studies of national movements and ideologies. Even as it takes advantage of interpretive possibilities opened up by various directions within the widespread "linguistic turn" that began in the 1960s, as well as by the socioeconomic model that experienced a dramatic take-off at about the same time, the historicist or hermeneutic approach employed here also owes much to the older history of ideas.[12]

In the specific interpretive strategies chosen as in its broad construal of contexts, this study selectively combines poststructuralist tendencies with those from the "Ideas in Context" exploration of political languages and ideologies associated with the work of Quentin Skinner. In general, the reader will find more emphasis on ideologically lower-profile background beliefs and deep-seated or even unconscious assumptions than in the Ideas in Context school of thought, while there is still more of the latter's stress on historicist reconstruction of ideational patterns, authorial intentionality, and the analysis of texts in the sense of linguistic records rather than of symbolic ritual or practices. Attention also focuses on specific, pragmatic political contexts to a greater degree than one typically sees among those influenced by poststructuralism. There is more stress on consensus and less on contestation than in either historiographical trend. Conscious contestation assumes less priority in a study that is primarily concerned to recover the operative underlying assumptions, the limits within which thinkers and politicians were able to conceive and construct their various versions of national identity, and thus to define that novel and nascent entity called the nation. As opposed to the discussion of political ideology in this same period, where boundaries and meanings were continually and self-consciously challenged, many of the strongest and most revealing aspects of national identity were rooted in precisely those areas where the intended "illocutionary force" or argumentative ramifications were much less powerful and even less conscious. For the same reason attention focuses less on single texts and authors than on the patterns of thought and contextual relationships that emerge more clearly from a wide-angle view transcending the nationalist or intellectual history canons.[13]

At the same time, however, the present study concentrates on explicit statements rather than on textual silences and ruptures, or what was not said. Its approach to "close reading" is literal but also sensitive to the importance of casual observations, tensions, and caveats, or even of beliefs only implied in the practical proposals being made. In pursuing the deeper and more distant connections that defined a "culture of nationhood," this study often goes well beyond the potential self-understanding of the contemporaries themselves. The historicist approach taken here, then, is also a kind of intertextuality, also a study of culture and mentality.

The present work also parallels cultural studies approaches without coinciding with them in its recourse to a more general culture concept from anthropology and intellectual history. "Culture" here is used in the broader sense of disparate and discrete sets of beliefs that still seem to interact and interlock in a particular historical system. It functions in some ways like a Foucauldian "episteme" or "discursive regime," in which underlying, structured, institutionally mediated knowledge about the way humans and the world work defines the parameters of the thinkable and helps delimit the inferences that may properly be drawn and the narratives that may be told by those who live and think inside that system. The present investigation, however, tries to avoid the sometimes restrictive rigidity and sharp discontinuities of epistemes, as well as the problematic conception of power relationships that go with the Foucauldian paradigm, opting instead for the looser, more flexible term "culture" to express this widest and deepest web of delimiting context behind interpretations of the world and its phenomena. It is thus to the search for any constraining common denominator beliefs about nationhood, beliefs that can come from seemingly quite distant or even unrelated areas of culture, that this work primarily addresses itself.

One scholar has remarked from the sociological perspective that broadening the study of nationalism to incorporate the "vague" ethnocentrism of the realm of culture and ideas would create an "impossibly large subject." Focusing the investigation on the deputies' speeches and writings from 1848 in tandem with their diverse yet richly relevant writings from the years preceding the revolution, however, reduces such a mound of material to more manageable proportions.[14] This move permits subjecting precisely those vaguer, more slippery aspects of nationalism to a rigorous scrutiny, without which it is impossible to understand fully the national politics of 1848, not to mention the content and attraction of national identity as a congeries of ideas and attitudes among educated Germans of the pre-1848 era.[15] At the same time this decision concentrates attention on precisely that influential social, political, and institutional network of people and ideas called the intelligentsia. The 1848–1849 German National Assembly, after all, provides a quite representative cross-section of the early nineteenth-century German nationalist intellectual elite.

This sense of the Assembly's representativeness emerges from almost any perspective one takes on the body (save gender, of course). It offers first a broad slice of educated political opinion—monarchist liberals, radical democrats, and even some reform-minded conservatives found their way to Frankfurt in May of 1848. While most deputies desired some sort of national unification, the spectrum from unitarists to federalists to reformist particularists was nearly continuous, stopping just short of those such as Bismarck or the Gerlachs who resolutely opposed any such strengthening of federal ties and would have no truck with the forces of Godless revolution. In terms of age and religious affiliation the Assembly also offers a broad range, even if it naturally does not reproduce the demographic distribution exactly. Protestants, Catholics, Jews, dissident German Catholics, and even atheists were all represented in Frankfurt. As for age and experience, at least three distinct generations sat in St. Paul's Church, including those who had already reached adulthood before Napoleon put a period to the Holy Roman Empire, those who had spent their formative years during the Napoleonic era and its national upheavals, and those younger members who had grown up in the subsequent age of restoration, agitation, and enthusiasm for foreign national movements such as the Polish and Greek. Geographically too the Assembly cast its net widely, drawing in deputies from the entire German Confederation and beyond. Included were such divergent locales as Austria and Prussia, northern states and southern states, small states and large states, states that had experienced French government and those that had not, those with constitutions and those without—not to mention provinces where the locals lived in close proximity to linguistically non-German peoples as against those in which encounters with other nationalities could only be infrequent, as with visitors, or theoretical, as through newspapers. In this way looking at the Frankfurt Parliament helps surmount one of the great difficulties encountered in studying German history throughout the nineteenth century, namely, the need to examine not just single states like Prussia or Baden but rather the whole range of experience in the various parts of the far-flung lands called Germany.

The Assembly deputies also offer a representative slice of educated Germany in another respect quite methodologically useful for the present attempt to reconstruct a German culture of nationhood, namely, through the quite varied subject matter on which the chamber's many significant authors had written in preceding decades. In addition to incorporating voices in the national movement beyond the oft-cited canonical figures, the broad selection of sources thus provided contributes to the contextualization of national identity by moving beyond the narrow range of nationalist programmatic works to explore a much wider array of texts where conceptions of nationhood could reveal other facets of themselves from less politically fraught perspectives. Deputies had, after all, invoked ideas of nationhood not just in nationalist or political tracts but also in fields as diverse as literature and the law, history and ethnology, religion and philosophy. By seeing how conceptions of nationhood functioned in such disparate intellectual and cultural contexts it is possible to get a deeper sense of their relationship to other crucial attitudes and beliefs in the broader surrounding culture. Deputies thereby touched on their understandings of nationality, but also on their self-understandings, as they attempted to construct not just a national identity but other group, cultural, and personal identities as well.

However representative the members of the National Assembly may have been, it is still true that not all the bright stars from Biedermeier-period Germany's cultural and political firmament gravitated to Frankfurt in 1848. Several figures crucial to understanding nationhood in particular as well as to providing orientation with respect to the more general ideas, attitudes, and philosophical systems delimiting Germany's intellectual horizons in this period have therefore been included to supplement the analysis. Kant and Fichte, Herder and Hegel, Niebuhr and Friedrich Schlegel, Alexander and Wilhelm von Humboldt, as well as such thinkers as the theoretician of the conservative Prussian *Kreuz-Zeitung* circle Friedrich Julius Stahl: all provide broad insights into the conceptual world of the early nineteenth-century educated elite while at the same time helping to map out the specific contours of its prevailing conceptions of nationhood.

With this nod to the intellectual forces filling the cultural ether in which Assembly delegates moved, the present study's basic range and intent have been fully set out. The work proceeds on the assumption that identifying deputies' specific conceptions of nationhood, as well as their implications for distinguishing among different peoples, drawing political boundaries, granting rights, and conducting foreign policy, contributes to understanding the early nineteenth-century German national movement and its associated brand of nationalism. This in turn will help explain the origins and course of the national conflicts that followed in the wake of the 1848 Revolution, itself driven in part by precisely that national movement, by precisely that nationalist mentality. The attempts to define the thing called Germany in both prerevolutionary nationalist theory and revolutionary nationalist practice, as well as the extent of the difference between them, ultimately have much to tell about the people, the politics, and the period.

Finally, a word should be said about the study's temporal bounds. For the intellectual and cultural background, this work extends to include not just the previous statements of the deputies themselves but also to incorporate the preceding mentor generation that had done so much to shape the cultural environment that shaped the Forty-Eighters in turn. The investigation of the revolution itself then follows the deliberations in Frankfurt from the preparatory Pre-Parliament in March of 1848 through the months-long wrangling over the final form of the constitution that came to a temporary end in April 1849 with the decision to offer a "Little German" imperial crown to the Prussian king Friedrich Wilhelm IV. After Friedrich Wilhelm had contemptuously spurned that crown as a "sausage sandwich," prepared by the Frankfurt butchers and bakers, the Assembly maintained its existence, but its star was clearly on the wane. Soon Austrian, Prussian, and other deputies began to decamp in an ever-swelling stream. Into the shadow world of the succeeding left-wing Rump Parliament and its moderate Little German counterparts in Gotha and Erfurt, or into the populist realm of the risings in support of the Frankfurt constitution in Saxony and southwest Germany, this study cannot follow. Conditions had changed so much, the imperatives to choose ideological sides in the struggle over alternative forms of national unity among the various popular and governmental options available in the spring of 1849 had become so strong, that the interpretive difficulties of accounting for shifting positions on nationality questions in the preceding Assembly debates pale in comparison. As the optimism and belief in progress that had been so essential a part of the liberal worldview wilted or even expired in the cold breath of revolutionary failure, the most extreme ideological deformations could occur, as evidenced by the subsequent rise of racialist theories in both France and Germany. A new world was coalescing, and a new history of it would have to be written.[16]

Having set out this study's parameters, historiographical background, methodology, and sources, all that remains is to sketch briefly its organization. Part One addresses the task of recovering important shared elements of underlying educated German ideas about nationhood. Part Two then turns to the problem of analyzing the complex nationality-related debates of the revolutionary era and determining how far the conceptions of nationhood sketched in Part One continued to shape the attitudes and the politics of the members of the national movement when the stakes grew that much higher during their moment of political power in 1848–1849.

Part One consists of two chapters that explore prerevolutionary beliefs and patterns of thought about nationhood. Chapter 1 analyzes the deceptively simple problem of the criteria by which contemporaries drew borders around peoples and nations, characteristics that included shared language, history, customs, religion, common consciousness, voluntary association, legal territorial limits, and racialist biological and hereditary features. Chapter 2 considers the responses of the future Frankfurt deputies to the key questions of how the nations thus defined should act, and how they should interact. It describes fundamental attitudes toward the world and history held by educated Germans of the period and highlights their consequences for both national identity and relations among nations. Taken together, these two chapters investigate the potential congruities between ideas of nationhood and other prevailing trends in the broader contextual culture, as for example the often observed but seldom explained resonances between nationalism and liberalism, historicism, and romanticism. Ultimately these chapters describe what can be termed a *Vormärz* culture of nationhood.

With the necessary intellectual and cultural background presented in the more synchronic Part One, the more diachronic Part Two goes on to grapple with the implications of this culture of nationhood for debates during the revolution. Chapters 3 and 4 consider the questions of political and cultural rights for German Jews (Chapter 3) and for the non-German-speaking minorities living within the borders of the projected German state (Chapter 4). Chapters 5 and 6 turn outward from these internal constitutional matters and deal with the Frankfurt deputies' attempts to define both the German nation's boundaries (Chapter 5) and its position among the other European nations (Chapter 6). The four chapters on the revolution ultimately present an exercise in "multiple contextualization" for the practice of the culture of nationhood.

Finally, the Conclusion offers both a concise restatement of the work's main themes as well as a few comparative observations on how the approach to understanding German nationalism taken here might affect the study of other nineteenth-century European nationalisms. Within this broader historical context the Conclusion depicts the intellectual and political dimensions of nationhood in the early nineteenth-century German national movement, a movement whose efforts at defining Germany in 1848 briefly brought about national unification, nationality rights, and national conflicts, the latter of which would ultimately drown both of the former in the same great revolutionary flood.

I | The *Vormärz* Culture of Nationhood

German national identity was not born at the end of the eighteenth century. Medieval nobles, Renaissance humanists, and Baroque literati had all at various times invoked some form of German identity that one might call national. Yet if problems of German self-definition and even a political "German Question" had existed before the late eighteenth century, they were certainly not couched, much less solved, in terms of those more modern constructions of nationhood that arose in the wake of the French Revolution.

In exploring the relationship between the Frankfurt parliamentarians and national identity, Part One thus concerns itself with roughly the half century before 1848. This period encompasses the political and cultural activity of the future delegates to the Frankfurt National Assembly as well as of those figures in the preceding generation who helped shape the deputies' cultural and intellectual milieu. In addition to profound social and economic mutability, this period was marked by such milestone events as the French occupation of Germany, the end of the Holy Roman Empire, the Wars of Liberation, the Karlsbad Decrees and the ensuing persecution of nationalist "demagogues," the 1830 Revolutions and pro-Polish agitation, as well as the increasing political strife of the decade immediately preceding the 1848 Revolution. This narrative framework provides a backdrop for Part One's more synchronic, thematic reconstruction of some of the future Frankfurt deputies' deepest and most enduring attitudes toward nationality.

In exploring the manifold resonances attached to nationhood in the minds of educated Germans during the first half of the nineteenth century, Chapters 1 and 2 tackle two distinct but interconnected aspects of pre-1848 German national identity. First, there was the question of who belongs to the nation, of the criteria by which a nation was defined and its

15

boundaries determined. This issue will be addressed in Chapter 1. Second, there was the question of how the collectivity so defined was supposed to act historically as one nation among many, of how the prevailing historical consciousness helped mold ideas about relations among nations and among the citizens who constitute them. Exploring the ramifications of this second facet of nationhood for the future delegates' ideas of nationality and national politics will form the principal object of investigation in Chapter 2.

The usual starting point for such an examination of German nationalist ideas remains the typological dichotomy between ethnocultural and civic-voluntarist brands of nationalism first set forth by Hans Kohn in the 1940s, as well as Friedrich Meinecke's related older distinction between the *Kulturnation* and *Staatsnation*. In such accounts German nationalists began to define their nation in terms of a common culture and language in an early phase of apolitical nationalism during the late eighteenth century, only to retain that ethnic definition after they had taken up demands for political self-determination as a nation-state in the wake of the French Revolution and Napoleonic occupation.[1] Yet as will become apparent, in formulating the nation-state ideal German nationalists desired above all to harmonize the discrepancies between the "culture-nation" and "state-nation" concepts that so disturbed them, and in the process they spun the cultural and political fibers of national identity inextricably into the ideological yarn of nationalism. This is true for their mentally drawn borders between peoples, for the groups they chose to include in the nations so delineated, and for the implications that such definitions of nationhood carried for political life both domestic and foreign. Typifying German nationalism as simply one or the other, cultural or civic, ultimately proves too restrictive. It was in fact precisely the reciprocity between what might seem at first glance to be purely cultural or political aspects of national existence that lent early nineteenth-century German conceptions of nationhood their intellectual flavor and ideological potential. It was also in this respect that liberal and nationalist ideologies disclosed the full intimacy of their mutually supportive relationship.

As a contextual framework for this wide-ranging portrayal of the future Assembly representatives' ideas of nationality, these two chapters attempt to uncover the ways in which liberal and nationalist beliefs sprouted from the common soil of the late eighteenth- and early nineteenth-century culture of *Bildung*. This culture of "self-formation" or "self-cultivation," of good Weimar vintage and neohumanist, neoclassical bouquet, with its

Jena offshoots in German romanticism and idealist philosophy, provided a formative educational influence for the large majority of the parliament's scholars, officials, and politicians.[2] The theory and practice of *Bildung* also helped set the parameters, conscious and unconscious, within which Germans of this milieu constructed not just their personal but also their national identities.

In the intellectual crucible of a Europe undergoing catastrophic change, Gymnasium- and university-educated Germans combined the self-assertive, individualist ethical and aesthetic imperative of the culture of *Bildung* together with its sense of longing for a higher organic unity to produce the compound ideal of an independent nation of free men. They thought of this nation as a collective individual, defined in space and with a will and distinct personality. It was an actor in its own right, and thus endowed with rights, honor, and the need for autonomy. The nation so portrayed strutted and fretted upon the world-historical stage, a stage upon which fallen mankind and the nations into which it was divided endured painful conflict in hopes of slow progress toward a better dispensation. Distinct interpretations of this national ideal flourished, but for the most part as variations on a theme. They were solo cadenzas within the larger symphony of ideas and attitudes that comprised an early nineteenth-century German culture of nationhood.

1 | Defining National Boundaries

*[handwritten marginal note: criteria by which edu. Germ. pre-1848 defined nationality + national bndries
• lang
• race
• customs
- laws
• religion
• hist. mem
- comm. cons.
all work tgthr]*

In pursuit of the structural principles underlying the German culture of nationhood, the present chapter attempts to set out the criteria by which educated Germans of the pre-1848 era defined nationality and national boundaries. Historians of the early German national movement have traditionally focused on language and race as the hallmarks of national identity, and these will receive due coverage here. At the same time, however, this study delves more deeply into the equally definitive role of customs, laws, religion, shared historical memories, and a general sense of communal consciousness. Examining these categories reveals several ways in which what might seem to be distinct political or cultural aspects of nationality actually interpenetrated one another, ultimately breaking down any attempt to typify German national identity as simply one or the other. Even without invoking a definition of politics whereby all things cultural are in any case political by virtue of necessarily being expressions of contested power relations in society, it is still possible to see how the varied criteria by which future deputies drew national boundaries and filled them with the constructions of national identity inextricably juxtaposed—yet did not wholly conflate—cultural and political realms of thought. It is a historical commonplace to remark on the difficulties of applying the so-called "nationality principle" of one nation/one state in the ethnic jumble of Central Europe, but there is still the need for a clearer understanding of what that nationality principle actually entailed, in conception and in application. The current chapter's focus on the varied boundary criteria for nationality will help fill in the conceptual contours of this less well-charted historiographical terrain.

Exploring these rather disparate but interconnected categories of national identity also bears consequences for understanding the theory and practice of prerevolutionary opposition politics. Nationalist and liberal ideologies were far from being inherently contradictory, or even merely associated by contingent circumstance, as historians have tended to argue in the past. On the contrary, not a few *Vormärz* liberal and nationalist demands at the level of local and national politics mutually reinforced one another. National identity combined cultural and political elements not just in the various criteria employed in drawing national boundaries but also in the creation of the sense of community that bound all those external markers of nationality into the spiritual whole that was the nation. Nationhood involved more than simply the cartographer's engraving of lines on a map or the ethnographer's systems of classification, but rather equally derived from a publicly mediated process thought by these men of the nationalist opposition to be most effective only within a liberal participatory political system. More crucially, when set within the representational realm of shared historical memories and a general notion of progressive *Bildung,* this politically forged patriotism perforated the potentially exclusionary boundaries of a strict ethnocultural form of national identity and led many in the Forty-Eighter generation to construe certain linguistically non-German populations as component parts of the German nation. In the German culture of nationhood, cultural and political elements of nationality had been bound together, yet this left the resultant nation-state ideal more open and inclusive than has often been thought for this period.

To start adding some flesh to this skeletal description of the boundary criteria prevalent within the culture of nationhood, a little preliminary lexicographic drudgery is in order. When educated Germans within the contextual culture of *Bildung* expressed their ideas about group identity, what vocabulary did they employ? And in particular, how did they distinguish between the portentous words *Volk* and *Nation?* This small excursus will help clear the way for what follows and will at least begin to suggest some of the reciprocity and overlap between cultural and political perspectives on the phenomenon of nationality.

In the "Nationalism" entry of a pathbreaking German historical encyclopedia, Reinhart Koselleck has presented the still-standard picture of the relationship between the two so-important words *Volk* and *Nation.* From a sample of five dictionaries spanning the semantically and conceptually crucial transition century between about 1750 and 1850, he identifies a trend toward the words' normalization, in which *Nation* applied to prepolitical groups united by cultural or ethnic affinity, while *Volk* referred to peoples organized politically into states. This situation neatly inverted the French and Anglo-American traditions, where "nation" came to carry more political freight than "people." In the same entry, however, Bernd Schönemann argues on the basis of a wide-ranging survey of the relevant philosophical literature that *Nation* and *Volk* were used nearly synony-mously during the nineteenth century. Even as the meanings attached to the concept of nationality varied greatly over that period by era and by so-cial group, both *Nation* and *Volk* at one time and another took on both ethnic and political meanings, without any trend toward standardization becoming apparent before the last decades of the nineteenth century.[1]

In general, Schönemann's view seems to reflect more clearly the situa-tion in early nineteenth-century Germany, where, at least among the fu-ture Assembly representatives and contextual figures examined in this study, usage of the various German equivalents for the richly connoted English word "people" displayed a large measure of mutual overlap. The left-wing earth scientist and political theorist Julius Fröbel, for instance, attempted just such an investigation of *Volk/Nation* word choice as Schönemann's in his twice-printed *System of Social Politics,* and he arrived at much the same result, namely, that German diction allowed no "definite conclusion" on the matter since both words could assume either mean-ing.[2] To take another example, in the influential liberal publicistic encyclo-pedia *Das Staats-Lexikon* the Badenese jurist, opposition politician, and future Frankfurt deputy Carl Welcker defined *Volk* to be a large group of men bound by common descent and communal living "in the natural sense," whereas "in the legal sense" *Volk* became a large group of men or-ganized into a state, in which common descent, though often present, was not necessary. Similarly, the editors referred readers seeking edification about the meaning of *Nation* or *Nationalität* to the entry "Volk, Volks-thümlichkeit, etc."[3] *Volk* and *Nation* thus each referred to both ethno-graphically and politically defined communities. Such ambivalent usage also affected the other principal term used to express ideas of nationality, namely, *Nationalität,* which as in English could refer either to ethno-graphic groups (particularly minorities) or to the condition of being a citi-zen of a certain state. Moreover, *Nationalität* often carried a significant third meaning and defined the state of mind associated with being part of such an ethnographic community or state.[4]

What all of this lexicographic detail suggests is that while early nine-teenth-century Germans certainly distinguished between ethnographic and political types of group identity, as we still do today, they by no means made such a sharp distinction. Instead, their notions of nationhood spun gyroscopically between these two poles, with civic and cultural connotations equally vivid in their minds when they conjured up the image of the nation—by whichever name. Trained rigorously in logic, these educated Germans could maintain such overlapping categories without fear of contradiction because the idea of the cultural nation immediately suggested political relations, while that of statehood just as surely pointed toward some measure of cultural unity as well. As the future deputy and constitution-drafter Friedrich Dahlmann put it in his influential *Politics* of 1835, it might be true that in primitive societies the people was more "*Volk* than state," but it was never true that a group could be a people without being a state as well.[5] The conceptual boundaries of cultural community and organized statehood flowed into one another.

Even if early nineteenth-century German political thinkers could remain comfortable with such overlapping, ambivalent diction regarding the problem of group identity, enough demons of unease still gnawed at their certainty that they felt compelled to make the boundaries between peoples seem somehow more natural, less arbitrary or artificial. This was particularly true during the Napoleonic era, when political boundaries fluctuated with the frequency, if not the regularity, of the tides. In the face of this man-made chaos, the modern science of physical geography began to take shape in the hands of such figures as Alexander von Humboldt and Carl Ritter, and "natural borders" began to seem more appealing than merely political ones.[6] As God had created the landscape, so had He created the nations of the world, and it seemed only reasonable to assume that regional and national differentiation would coincide, that the boundaries between peoples would be equally tangible, equally solid. The French revolutionaries had made the notion famous with their desire to round off France's borders in the Alps and along the Rhine and Scheldt, but even Ernst Moritz Arndt, greatest of the German publicists during the Wars of Liberation and a decided opponent of a French left bank of the Rhine, to the end of his life maintained a certain affinity with the idea of natural borders. Rivers, of course, would not serve the purpose, but seas and mountains did quite well, which left Germany the Swiss valleys and the beaches of the North Sea, Baltic, and Adriatic, while France abutted the Alps in Provence and the Dauphiné.[7] Other important figures such as the ancient historian Barthold Niebuhr and the philosopher Georg Wilhelm Hegel, arguing that waterways promoted communication whereas mountains hindered it, shared Arndt's preference for mountains over rivers as natural boundaries between peoples.[8] Perhaps surprisingly, given his general reputation as the most ethnically *völkisch* of *völkisch* agitators, even the venerable "Turnvater" Jahn sectioned Europe (exclusive of Russia) into nine large states separated by obvious geographical features such as the Alps and Carpathians.[9]

But despite a certain amount of support for the use of geographical landmarks in drawing national borders, many Germans of this period seemed to consider this procedure not much less arbitrary than the diplomatic machinations in Lunéville, Tilsit, or Vienna that were continually redrawing the map of Europe, and they sought instead to ground national boundaries in the categories of ethnography—particularly, of language. It was, after all, peoples who were being separated; therefore it was to qualities of the peoples themselves that one should look when attempting to carry out the divisions. In the *Staats-Lexikon* entry on "Natural Borders," for example, the democratic publicist and mayor of Speyer, Georg Friedrich Kolb, accepted that mountains, if not rivers, made acceptable boundaries, but he demonstrated the proposition by pointing out that mountains did indeed often separate peoples distinct in "mores, customs, habits, and language." He then went on to urge, "Let us leave the essentially *dead* boundaries, and search instead for the *living* ones grounded in the nationality of peoples. It is above all in the same *language* that the inner, most natural connection . . . makes itself known."[10] Language, not landmarks, made for the most natural of natural borders.

This view of language's important role in national differentiation was quite widespread, and it has, not without reason, tended to be the criterion most frequently singled out by historians of German nationalism. All of the famous names of the "nationalist awakening" at the time of the Wars of Liberation sang Hosannas to the German tongue. Who could forget Arndt's great marching song "The German's Fatherland," in which the sixth verse rings out that Germany's bounds extend "As far as the German language sounds," a sentiment echoed, interestingly enough, by Kolb in the *Staats-Lexikon* entry just above.[11] Fichte's famous *Speeches to the German Nation* of 1808 even raised German to the status of an "original language," fundamentally constitutive of the German people as such.[12]

In more general terms, the Germanist linguistic scholar Jacob Grimm stated definitively, "A people [Volk] is the embodiment of the men who speak the same language," and he too went on to assert that it was in languages, and not in rivers and mountains, that one should seek for borders.

Fröbel, by far less convinced of the nationality concept's claim to be the end-all and be-all of political life, still accepted that "it was in the separate languages that nationalities formed."[13] The seminal linguist Wilhelm von Humboldt deemed language "the breath, the soul of the nation itself," its development inextricably bound up with that of the nation which spoke it, and he argued that any effort to decipher a people's national character had to rely on knowledge of its language. "Without using it as an aid," he claimed, "every attempt to read national peculiarities would be in vain, for only in the language does the entire character manifest itself."[14] Language had firmly achieved a privileged status as guide to both national boundaries and national character in the early part of the nineteenth century.

Germans stood ready to acknowledge language's role in national differentiation for a number of very good reasons, ranging from the mundane to the epistemologically profound. Although Johann Herder, a central figure of classical Weimar and with Friedrich Schiller one of the fountainheads of nascent romanticism, is usually credited with initiating the trend, it is not as if language had not been a fundamental fact of ethnological thinking since biblical times, as in the Tower of Babel myth. It is, after all, one of the first things a traveler notices upon entering a foreign land. Moreover, Herder and most other philosophers had for millennia fixed on the gift of reason and particularly of speech as the essential human quality that set humankind apart from the beasts. If the truth revealed to original humanity had been fragmented and obscured by the Fall and other, subsequent human misdemeanors, it seemed only natural to expect a correlation between the lines of fracture in the human race leading to nations and those in the original human tongue leading to differentiated modes of speech. Henceforth any given people could possess but one perspective on divine truth, a point of view limited to one language, to one national existence. For Herder, speech and thought, nation and language, were intimately connected. A language's phonetics and grammar did not simply express the same thoughts in different ways but rather shaped those very thoughts into distinct national forms. Or as Fichte put it, "men are much more formed by language, than languages by men."[15] Nations in this view became unique, and that singularity both found expression in, and was produced by, national mother tongues.

As recent studies have emphasized, the centrality of language in national identity also owed much to more instrumental considerations. With the oppositional middle classes pursuing nationalism and socioeconomic modernization as interconnected programs, creating a literate, monolingual communicative realm became a crucial goal. Even more significant perhaps in explaining the role of German in the emerging national identity, the men of the national movement's educated middle-class elite thought its institutionalization as the language of high culture to be the strategic key to raising their social status against the dual threats of French cultural hegemony and aristocratic social domination. This sociological consideration was most keenly felt in the period from the eighteenth century to the end of the Napoleonic occupation, less so thereafter when the battle had already basically been won.[16]

A perhaps deeper facet of this new emphasis on the organic cohesion of national identity and native language, however, and the one that most clearly revealed the growing linguistically based theoretical divisions between nations, revolved around the epistemological issue of the relationship between thought, speech, and understanding. For ever since the days of Locke's *Essay concerning Human Understanding,* words had been considered basically arbitrary signs or sounds to express ideas. As such they came to serve the ends of the Enlightenment ideal of a universal reason, accessible to all humans by virtue of a shared fundamental human nature, and thus of a universal truth, fully translatable into any language "civilized" enough to have developed words to express abstract ideas. Even without resorting to the use of Latin or to the construction of speculative universal grammars, members of the Republic of Letters could create a body of knowledge comprehensible to the world-embracing cosmopolitan civilization through the important (European) vernaculars: French, English, German, Italian. One standard of reason and truth applied everywhere, and it provided the content for any language.[17]

Without going to the culturally relativist extremes sometimes claimed on their behalf, the groundbreaking thinkers of the broad historicist reaction to such Enlightenment rationalism in fact introduced an epistemological scheme radically different from the post-Lockean empiricist type, one in which all knowledge was at its very roots dialectical, mediated by linguistic exchange and discoverable only through hermeneutic means. Particularly after Kant, the individual mind was allotted an active role in the interpretation, even the creation of knowledge. The essential requirement for any communication or understanding between two entities in this dialectical process was that there be some hidden unity beyond the more visible differences. Where no such unity existed, no exchange of ideas or comprehension was possible. Moreover, at the same time that such an interpretive exchange became the necessary precondition for all knowledge, historicist thinkers emphasized that this unity could never be total, not so long as individuals remained distinct. Interlocutors were thus left locked in a permanently passionate yet unconsummated dialectical embrace, which in linguistic terms meant that no two languages, indeed no two individuals, would ever express or understand quite the same thought. Any communication between them would perforce be imperfect—not nonexistent, not even negligible, but simply somewhat obscured in translation. As Wilhelm von Humboldt formulated the idea, mutual understanding depended on commonality of experience and outlook, and thereby declined in a shallow gradient from closely connected to remote individuals, with the sharpest discontinuous jump occurring at the boundary between languages, that is, between nations and their associated distinct, syntactically based worldviews.[18] Since the fundamental assumption of a basic human unity in terms of both race and providential destiny still held true, however, often even more strongly than in Enlightenment thought, national divisions and linguistic barriers became neither fully impenetrable nor fully relative.[19] But in the gray area between the individual person and the human race, nations had suddenly been granted a much larger role in the development of knowledge and the unfolding of human history.

All of this attention to language in the sphere of national existence occurred within the context of the creation of the new sciences of comparative and historical linguistics by such figures as Friedrich Schlegel, Jacob Grimm, and Wilhelm von Humboldt. As already noted, after Herder differences in national language had come to imply syntactically divergent national thought-processes rather than just arbitrarily different words for the same concepts. These scholars accordingly sought to elucidate the historical and genealogical relationships among the world's languages on the basis of grammatical structures and morphological rules rather than the speculatively simplistic etymologies beloved of previous generations of philologists. The most well-known and portentous result of such investigations was the creation of an "Indo-Germanic" or "Aryan" family of languages that included Sanskrit, Persian, Latin, Greek, and the Romance and Germanic tongues.

For present purposes, however, the more important result was to fix ideas of transnational ethnic identities and affinities among the Germanic, Romance, and Slavic language families in the educated German consciousness. The notion of Teutons, Latins, Celts, and Slavs as distinct, coherent groups of peoples had of course been current for centuries, and it might seem reasonable to suppose that the definitive inclusion of Celtic and Slavic tongues into the larger Indo-European language family during the 1820s and 1830s would have made these different groups appear more closely related and less "foreign" in the grand scheme of things. Certainly Jacob Grimm himself recognized the Slavic languages as close relatives of the Teutonic. Yet he did not question the significance of Europe's division into these basic groups. Friedrich Schleiermacher for his part emphasized the potential communication difficulties between such larger linguistic groupings and ominously singled out the Slavic-Germanic opposition for his example. Even more strongly and explicitly, the liberal Tyrolean-born orientalist Jakob Fallmerayer rejected the idea that a general Indo-European affinity overrode "the characteristic hallmarks of the individual branches of this great class of humans." Such a view made the potential implications of his stormily received assertion that the New Greeks were of mixed Slavic-Albanian rather than Hellenic ancestry all the graver.[20] Just as the new organicist, historicist view of language had heightened perceptions of national divisions and their significance in human affairs, these changes also increased awareness of supranational identities. The anthropological space between the individual human and the human race had been filled not only by the concept of the nation but also by the idea of whole families of nations.

The contemporary discipline of philology, however, encompassed much more than just the field of comparative linguistics, and educated Germans similarly did not ascribe to language the role of sole agent or marker of national differentiation. They tended instead to join it with other, more broadly cultural characteristics. In brief invocations of nationhood's primary features, for example, language frequently appeared coupled with the words *Sitten* and *Gebräuche* (mores, or customs). Georg Kolb, who has already been encountered justifying the concept of natural borders on the grounds that they sometimes corresponded with ethnographic divisions in mores, customs, habits, and language, in turn supported the even stronger claim to language's status as the true natural boundary between peoples with the assertion, "So we find everywhere corresponding with this equality or difference in language, in the one case similarity, in the other divergence in mode of living, mores and customs, indeed in the peoples' entire being."[21]

This idea of language as simply one element within the larger national cultural matrix of course fit quite neatly into the general context of post-

Herderian and romantic ideas of the nation as an organic entity, in which all aspects of national life equally reflected or emanated from a core national character. What precisely these commentators might have meant when they pointed to this broader customary realm, however, often remained unclear. Herder himself had chosen to focus attention on folk poetry and folkways generally, while Wilhelm von Humboldt gave considerable attention to folk dances as well. Among future Frankfurt deputies of a more romantic bent, both Jacob Grimm and Ludwig Uhland shared Herder's faith in the value of *Volkspoesie* as the truest reflection of a people's interior life.[22] The eccentric early nationalist Friedrich Jahn felt passionately about folk dress and festivals, while the Young Hegelian aesthetician Friedrich Vischer mourned the loss of locally colorful dress across Europe as modern fashions homogenized previously strong national characteristics.[23] The legal historian Georg Waitz for his part pointed to the tenacity with which Germanic peoples clung to domestic architectural styles and units of land measurement, a tendency that still allowed the observant traveler to trace the boundaries of German settlement in the North and in the East much more surely than by the more changeable linguistic borders.[24] As proof of the continuing German nationality of German populations living outside the Confederation, the democrat Gustav von Struve added to language practically the entire cultural realm: mores, architecture, and family life, plus the arts, sciences, and literature.[25] But amidst this welter of cultural detail rose the central thought of the nation as an organic unity, its culture growing out of an underlying national character yet simultaneously shaping the national character of future generations in a reciprocal process of development.

For most delegates a focal point of this cultural relationship of mutuality between national customs and character lay in the realm of law, of national beliefs about politics, justice, and the ordering of common affairs. This should come as no great surprise. The Assembly, after all, contained a remarkably high proportion of representatives trained in the law at German universities and looking to Montesquieu as the healthiest product of a not very salubrious French Enlightenment tradition. By redressing Montesquieuan ideas of customary law in a new romantic, organicist fashion, the conservative founder of the school of historical law Friedrich Carl von Savigny had probably done more than anyone else to focus attention on this aspect of national life. Civil law, he thought, "is peculiar to the nation [Volk], just as are its language, mores, constitution." All together were a sort of unwilled, inextricably intertwined emanation from the underlying folk spirit or *Volksgeist*, come down through the generations in an unbroken but always-developing chain and maintained in the popular consciousness only by the continuous visible use of symbolic acts and forms.[26] Although more influential in the school of historical law's Germanist wing and with a more populist interpretation of the idea of "the people" as author of its laws, the liberal professor Georg Beseler still basically accepted Savigny's developmental scheme for the interconnected growth of national laws and culture. As Carl Mittermaier, leading Badenese legal scholar and future president of the 1848 Pre-Parliament, roundly informed the 1846 Germanist Conference, "Gentlemen, who will deny that nationality [Nationalität] expresses itself best and most purely in the nation's law?"[27] Immediately after Mittermaier's declamation the left-wing Badenese jurist Anton Christ spoke even more strongly of ideas of justice as the deepest expression of nationhood. "A body of law can be only a national law; law is nothing else than a nation's mores and customs," Christ fervently asserted, "and the law from this point of view is nothing else than the revelation of nationality, the embodiment of the life of the soul as it represents itself in a particular nation."[28] Surely no more deeply felt confession of the fundamental connection between a nation and its native laws may be imagined.

This point about the assumed deep, almost mystical relationship between a nation and the ordering of its social and political life cannot be stressed too strongly, for it spotlights one of the principal reasons why the idea of a purely cultural form of nationalism and national identity is bound to be misleading. Succinctly put, educated early nineteenth-century Germans' notions of culture ranged too widely and incorporated too much of what today might be considered purely political aspects of life. In the eyes of Beseler, Mittermaier, or Christ, if not of Savigny, even settling details of private or civil law opened the door to a great deal of political and legislative activity. When relations between genders, classes, and varied interest groups, not to mention more strictly constitutional questions from the sphere of public law such as the rights of citizens or the form of government, entered the arena, the manifold political implications of defining nations and theorizing national differences became glaringly apparent.

It might of course be objected that including legal and political matters in the German sense of nationhood along with Jahn's pseudo-Teutonic beard, clothes, and folkways undermines only the notion of a solely cultural, apolitical nationalism, not the idea of a dichotomous ethnic versus civic approach to drawing national boundaries. After all, if this more broadly defined national culture really was thought to emanate from a fundamental and sharply separated *Volksgeist* with a distinct national character, as Savigny, Beseler, or Christ would have it, then does that not imply that nationality truly was defined and delimited in the cultural realm, with the conception of culture merely widened to include forms of civil and public law as well? Politics would in this conception of nationhood simply be subsumed within the category of the cultural. Political boundaries between nations would imply cultural boundaries, and vice versa, as the so-called "nationality principle" (one nation/one state) has often been taken to mean. The Breslau historian Gustav Stenzel, for example, did indeed point to the special Germanic sense of liberty as the most significant difference between the national characters of Slavs and Germans.[29] Given that national forms of government and of civil law appeared to be so distinct, even hostile and mutually incompatible, such a view might even seem to militate against any plans to include different nationalities under one political system. At least it could have carried such an implication if Germans really saw nations as nothing but sharply differentiated ethnocultural entities—but that is precisely the point in question. If the national forms of legal systems were in part defined on some other basis that allowed for ethnically mixed polities, then the conclusion would not hold. In his book-length argument against foreign forms in German law, Christ still saw fit to include a telling footnote that allowed for the possibility of multinational government.[30]

If it seems odd for these Germans to have employed legal and constitutional forms in a taxonomy of national peculiarities, at least insofar as such Aristotelian or Montesquieuan categories as "monarchy" or "republic" could apply equally well to any number of varied national experiences, then it must seem even more surprising that they introduced another factor of equal importance into the analytical equation, namely, religion—and this in a place and time when almost all the nations they might wish to contrast had converted to Christianity, the universalizing religion, hundreds of years before! Yet if often overlooked, religion shared with both language and law a central place in contemporary conceptions of nationhood. As expressed so well by Friedrich Stahl, himself a Jewish convert to evangelical Lutheranism, when distinct national attitudes and behavior "are to be traced back to their common origin, this will be nowhere better sought than in the highest conceptions of it, in the consciousness of its relationship to the Divine."[31] The future deputy and conservative Catholic historian of the romantic Görres circle Ernst von Lasaulx followed his teacher Friedrich Schelling, who significantly had also inspired Stahl, in believing that national consciousness expressed itself externally in language but internally in a "common worldview, to be found preferentially in its religion." Hegel himself highlighted the centrality of religion in the *Volksgeist* and saw many other of its already-mentioned component parts, such as laws and constitutions and the arts and sciences, deriving from it as increasingly autonomous spin-offs in the course of humanity's historical progression to ever more philosophically sublime conceptions of its place in the cosmos.[32]

Moreover, for all these thinkers notions of the individual's relationship to God were parallel to his relations to social and political authority. Hence even under this new rubric the political and legal sphere preserved its crucial position in distinguishing among nations and stages of historical development. In the period under examination politics was still an ethical experience, indeed, in an unorthodox kind of way, a profoundly religious experience. Even if not all went to the lengths of Hegel or Johann Droysen in seeing the state as the highest earthly expression of morality, nearly everyone recognized that the state's purpose and that of all political life had to be the promotion of the individual's moral vocation in the interests of humanity.[33] Thus in the same way that consideration of the broader cultural realm of law and custom undermines the cultural-political typology of nationalisms, the introduction of religion into the national matrix fully explodes the conceptual barrier between these two types of experience.

In fact, religious or fused religious and political categories often figured determinatively in depictions of both national character and the role of nations in world history. Although Lasaulx's periodization of ancient and modern history traced religious outlooks through various stages of development within the same peoples, Hegel and many other important thinkers who similarly delineated the crucial eras of world history in essentially religious terms chose to associate each major shift with a particular people or family of peoples.[34] Typically, the Hebrews, Greeks, and Germanic tribes served as the fundamental turning points in such schemes of universal history. Much would be made of increasing trends toward individuality and political liberty, along with the greater degree of pure spirituality in conceptions of the Divine and of the inherent moral worth of the individual. In this context the Germanic peoples were always closely associated with the final transition to Christianity in the collapse of the Roman Empire and the rise of medieval and modern Europe. This might seem to mitigate the extent to which the religious criterion of boundary-marking could apply within the era of the Christian dispensation, particularly given the usual loose definition of "Germanic" to include the Latin-Romance peoples, yet the resourceful theorists of national difference took refuge in the internal divisions of Christianity. Struve, for example, argued for a correlation between Celtic, Slavic, and Germanic races and Roman Catholic, Greek Orthodox, and Protestant religion, respectively. The numbers of those who seized on a simple Romance-Catholic, Germanic-Protestant correspondence and ascribed to it its own world-historical importance were legion (though this did not stop the Tyrolean Catholic Fallmerayer from couching the Russo-German conflict in terms of one between the principal bastions of Orthodox and Catholic Christianity).[35] Religion offered early nineteenth-century Germans one more way in which even modern nations could be said to form not just the fundamental agents of history but also the basic subdivisions of humanity.

The degree to which not just national destinies but also national boundaries were seen to be intimately connected with religious forms showed itself nowhere more clearly than in scholarly efforts to determine genealogical and ethnographic relationships among the peoples of antiquity and prehistory. To uncover the real cultural and national relationships among the various populations of ancient Iberia, even Wilhelm von Humboldt's linguistic placename study ultimately had to resort to evidence of religious rites from the ancient geographers. The founder of modern geography Carl Ritter also relied on classical sources when he undertook a joint etymological and mythological exploration of the region between the Black Sea and India to support his thesis of ancient Asian migrations into Europe. The great classicist Karl Otfried Müller in *The Dorians* followed that tribe's migration and settlement pattern through traces of its characteristic cult of Apollo, while the Breslau classicist and future Frankfurt deputy Julius Ambrosch relied on cultic data to clarify ancient Rome's ethnographic diversity.[36] Of perhaps more immediate interest to the national movements of Central and Eastern Europe, Kaspar Zeuss, Grimm, Uhland, and to a lesser extent Niebuhr all made significant use of mythological data in their attempts to associate the ancient Scythians, Sarmatians, Dacians, Huns, and others with modern populations, chiefly Slavs, Germans, Celts, and Mongolian peoples. Religion was hardly the only criterion used in these esoteric investigations, but it was certainly important and sometimes clinching.[37]

Since the appallingly scanty source base loomed as the principal difficulty in all such efforts at ancient ethnography, researchers were forced to rely on the highly selective information provided by the classical geographers, which meant that as the ancients had deemed religion a close correlate of peoples and polities, the moderns had to reason on that basis as well if they were to get anywhere at all. Moreover, a similar argument holds true for many of the other criteria of national differentiation examined thus far. For in addition to origin myths and religious rites and customs, the Greeks and Romans also focused on domestic architecture and means of subsistence, social and political organization, laws, and such material goods as clothes and weapons in their descriptions of foreign peoples. They took language into account as well, but in distinguishing among non-Greeks it by no means predominated over the other, more broadly cultural and sociopolitical categories. In his famous description of the Scythians of the Volga steppes, Herodotus thus recounted among other matters their distinctive agricultural and burial practices, means of waging war, and language, while Tacitus retailed similar details about the cultural life of the Teutons, as well as discussing gender relations and the legal status of the free and unfree.[38] Perforce, such mixed cultural and political data also figured prominently in modern German analyses.

Beyond its mere interest as a fact of life for scholars at the time, this correspondence in criteria of nationhood between ancients and moderns raises the intriguing possibility that early nineteenth-century Germans of neohumanist educational background might have imbibed some of their fundamental conceptions of nationality from immersion in the classics. One scholar, for instance, has pointed to the ways in which certain ancient opinions came down nearly unchanged through the way stations of European humanism, as, for example, the classical division of peoples into indigenous, immigrant, and mixed populations. This analytical scheme had provided the impetus for Tacitus's depiction of the Germans as *indigenae,* a racially pure warrior people preserving its noble simplicity in the forbidding forests of the North, and figures like Arndt, Heinrich Luden, and Fichte at least partially accepted both this view of the Germans and this sense of the importance of linguistic or racial purity generally.[39] Of course modern Germans did not think like ancient Greeks and interpreted them in their own way. New conceptions of religion and of history in particular altered the intellectual environment in which Germans constructed national identity, which helps account for why they only partly accepted such notions of ethnic purity. Yet some of the mythemes, tropes, and categories with which they worked were probably taken from the ancient texts and reworked to suit new contexts. As young readers pored over their Homer, their Herodotus, their Tacitus, or their Caesar, they very likely absorbed some of the ancient attitudes toward ethnicity, political life, and the connections between them displayed so prominently there. And even if one prefers to assume that the broad cultural-political definition of nationhood described thus far was sui generis and somehow already in place in the modern German psyche, then it should at least be plain that familiarity with the classics provided considerable reinforcement of such ideas about what it meant to be a nation.[40]

Another area in which deep acquaintance with the classics at least confirmed early nineteenth-century Germans in their preexisting views of nationality and may actually have helped shape them is the historiographically controversial question of race. Greek ethnographers added to the more purely cultural or political characteristics of language, religion, customs, and constitution the physical or biological qualities of external appearance and community of descent. Herodotus and Tacitus took care to provide detailed descriptions of complexion, hair and eye color, and general body shape as part of their ethnological cataloging, and they even employed such data in their classificatory schemes to a significant degree. Again, the Germans followed suit. Niebuhr, Alexander von Humboldt, Zeuss, and others had to take positions on the matter in their attempts to settle the question of Scythian ethnographic affinity, with somatic qualities being decisive for Niebuhr.[41] Arndt's reception of Tacitean racial continuity has already been mentioned, and it is noteworthy that the radical democrat Struve could agree and argue that Tacitus's ethnic map of Europe in many ways still held good. Not only had the borders between the major ethnic groups remained fairly stable, but their respective national characters as revealed by the great annalist, Caesar, and others had also stayed much the same.[42] Thus at least some Germans allotted an important place to ideas of race and ethnic kinship in the hierarchy of criteria for nationhood, but the question remains, how important?

It is almost certainly significant in this regard that one of the principal attractions of the use of language in determining nationality and/or ethnographic affinity lay in the belief that it also served as the best guide to blood relationship. The family trees constructed by comparative philologists served neither as Linnaean-style systems of morphology-based classification nor as genealogical charts tracing the evolution of ever-changing languages without reference to the peoples who spoke them. Instead, they mapped out degrees of physical and cultural kinship, the two seeming naturally related. By this way of thinking, the recently discovered relationship among the various tongues of the Indo-European family represented not the diffusion of a language to other groups by whom it was subsequently modified but rather the dispersion of peoples from an ancestral homeland, during which peregrinations time, changed environment, and certain inner natural laws of development accounted for the eventual transformations. Scholars in this way combined linguistics with racialist beliefs to produce the fateful image of a race of Aryan conquerors storming across the steppes of Asia to take up residence in more hospitable European climes at the expense of the unfortunate autochthons. This idea revolutionized views of prehistory and made the chaotic destruction of the Roman Empire during the Migration Period seem the historical rule rather than the exception.[43]

Such ideas of an inherent connection between physical and linguistic descent were widespread. The organicist political theorist Karl Zachariä, for example, went so far in his advocacy of the language-as-pedigree idea as to state that there were no instances in which a people of one race spoke the language of another. And if Friedrich Schlegel, the brothers Humboldt, and Julius Fröbel all maintained a considerably greater degree of circumspection about such claims in light of the many known counterexamples and the general recognition of the transformative effects that political and ethnographic upheavals could have, they nonetheless still deemed language the indispensable tool for penetrating the mists of early history.[44] Moreover, this process of correlating linguistic and blood relationships also worked on a smaller scale among modern European groups. Fröbel and Struve, for instance, each elevated the Celtic, Germanic, and Slavic divisions to racial status.[45]

Yet before any real sense can be gleaned of the significance of such genealogical taxonomies to the men of the generation of 1848, the most important question remains to be addressed, namely, the degree to which they imagined that biological and physical aspects of nationality determined mental and cultural ones. What, as they would have expressed it, was the relationship between *physis* and *nous* in human existence? Were national differences ineradicable because biological, and thus resistant to educational or environmental alteration? How far and in what way did heredity determine the intellect itself or the products deriving from it? To what extent might such views have supported belief in natural inequality among nations and races? All of these questions have to be answered before the role of racialist thinking in early nineteenth-century German notions of nationality comes into sharper focus.

Exploring such issues involving the relationship between mind and body, nature and nurture, had become the order of the day for many during the late eighteenth and early nineteenth centuries, and not only in Germany. In France, for example, Pierre-Jean-Georges Cabanis and the Idéologues expanded the domain of physiology into ever more corners of the human psyche, while in both Vienna and Paris, and later in London and Edinburgh, the Austrian Franz Josef Gall and the French-born Johann Gaspar Spurzheim developed their new science of phrenology with its minute studies of character based on the relative shapes and sizes of cranial features. The Swiss Johann Caspar Lavater for his part systematized the art of physiognomy, or reading character from facial features alone, a pursuit that became the rage all over Europe from the 1780s and attracted varying support from Goethe, Schiller, Novalis, Wilhelm von Humboldt, and others. Among Forty-Eighters, Struve was an avid phrenological popularizer, while Arndt, Vischer, and Carl Vogt at least toyed with physiognomic studies.[46] And of course the entire Schelling-Hegel-Young Hegelian impulse in German philosophy pointed toward a monistic vision of the universe and of the mind-body relationship, typically in favor of spirit but later on tipping over into materialism with Feuerbach and Marx.

Although originally intended to facilitate interpretations of individual characters only, both phrenology and physiognomy were increasingly applied to national and racial characteristics as well. Even Spurzheim, cofounder of phrenology and an opponent of such an extension of its field of validity, could not help illustrating certain features with examples from national character traits, while Lavater wholeheartedly endorsed the idea of national physiognomies. In the hands of disciples such as Struve or the youthful Wilhelm von Humboldt, the focus on nationality or race often equaled or surpassed the attention to individuals. Struve even went so far as to claim that the explanation of racial differences afforded by phrenology served as one of the new science's strongest proofs.[47]

In terms of more general racialist views, vague belief in a physical or biological determinism certainly crept into discussions of the relative worth of human racial groups. Kant himself, though still emphasizing human perfectibility in the progress of the human race, did establish a racial classification system that turned on the inheritance of skin color yet that also held

implications for intellectual and cultural abilities. Thus the sage of Königsberg occasionally let fall doubts about whether Gypsies, Africans, or Native Americans would ever achieve a significant degree of industrious cultivation given the deficiencies of their inherited "inner endowments."[48]
Among future deputies Arndt posited an "indelible character" to human
races that would ensure the Hottentots never rivaled the English, while
Struve pointed to the example of the New World and stressed the primacy
of heredity over environment or education in the cultural superiority of
Caucasians over Native Americans and Africans there. Similarly, the liberal
orientalist Fallmerayer considered whites as opposed to the "colored"
races to be the natural movers and shakers of progressive world history,
and Vischer's Young Hegelian *Aesthetics* taught the aspiring critic that
only the white race was of truly aesthetic appearance, with all other races
partaking more fully of animal-like qualities. Most starkly of all, the political martyr and historian Georg Gervinus saw racial hierarchy as the frozen
result of an evolutionary process that had left "Negros" wholly incapable
of achieving civilization or higher culture through further educational development.[49]

For the most part, however, the figures dealt with here preferred to emphasize the role of human freedom over natural necessity, of *nous* over
physis. The natural scientist Fröbel advocated the triumph of positive human will and freedom over the negative determinism of internal and external nature through technology and education. Fröbel's publishing partner, the Young Hegelian Arnold Ruge, similarly thought that it was only
the national "Naturell" or *physis* that any longer stood against the movement of world history, yet he refused to give it any political weight as
against general human freedom.[50] Hegel also accepted the influence of
nature on humankind and its historical development, but in general he
thought that the realm of *Geist* or spirit was paramount. In this vein he expressed skepticism about both physiognomic and phrenological studies,
with voluntary deeds a much more reliable guide to character than frozen
facial or cranial features.[51] Schiller similarly thought one could read character more readily through mimetic features in volitional motion than
through wholly material predetermined stasis, a view echoed among future Frankfurt deputies by both the liberal Vischer and the Catholic conservative General Joseph von Radowitz.[52]

For many, this emphasis on free will as against biological determinism
carried over into their attitudes toward the question of human racial inequality. No one denied the inequality—they were not that relativist—but

neither did they feel they had to accept the situation as permanent or rooted in the blood. The Young Hegelian Wilhelm Jordan, for example, proudly welcomed the African race into the ranks of world-historical peoples as the result of their revolt, emancipation, and state-building efforts on the isle of Haiti. Haitian history proved, he said, "that all forms of the species man are equally capable of participating in the highest pleasures and working towards the highest achievements of our [human] race." In the *Staats-Lexikon* entry "Races of Man" Georg Kolb conceded the prevailing intellectual and cultural superiority of Caucasians, but he emphasized the role of environment in producing this inequality and predicted that a day would come when the other races could pursue "their very own process of development" without simply following the Europeans.[53] Finally, the earth scientist Fröbel applied the new idealist dialectical epistemology to argue that the fact of interracial communication and understanding necessarily entailed the presence of qualitatively if not yet quantitatively equal mental capacities. He later reiterated this point by quoting Alexander von Humboldt's quotation of his brother Wilhelm to the effect that the goal of the historical process was "to treat the entirety of humanity, without consideration of religion, nationality, or color, as one great, closely related tribe [Stamm], as one entity existing for the attainment of one goal, the free development of inner power."[54] The pejorative pessimism of Arndt and Gervinus aside, it must still be stressed that at this time sentiment lay strongly in favor of belief in a common humanity predicating the human race's psychic unity, a sense of *Humanität* that pointed straight toward a brilliant future of moral progress for all humankind.[55]

To sum up this account of early nineteenth-century racialist thinking, belief in the causal connection between mind and body, culture and biology, spread widely through educated circles, yet it was for the most part tempered there by a deep-seated faith in the power of free will and moral purpose over natural necessity. Even more, when the idea of descent entered into conceptions of race or nationhood, as it frequently did, it partook of a vaguely Lamarckian notion of heredity, in which acquired characteristics could themselves be handed down from parent to child. Lavater's musings on heredity in the *Physiognomical Fragments* showed this clearly, as did Struve's account in his *Handbook of Phrenology,* or even Vischer's vignette on the uniquely noble Greek and Italian posture, which was "in the race" but still had to be taught to the child—it was only the feeling that it had to be this way that remained "as instinct in the entire stock."[56] Such conceptions of heredity bore an important consequence for views of the relationship between biological descent and national culture, namely, that culture itself could be inherited. In other words, biology did not just help determine national culture but served as one more means for its transmission across generations. Therein lay the importance of race, for it implied genealogical descent, which in turn implied community of values and beliefs—by natural or educational endowment. At the same time that fascination with the interrelationship between nature and mind encouraged a more monolithic, predetermined view of culture, that relationship's mutuality led to a much less constraining or blood-oriented vision of race or nationhood. Culture had become rooted in the soil of nature with its element of natural laws, yet nature had thereby been transformed into the arena for humanity's ever-growing moral freedom. Or as Fröbel formulated the concept, while culture and custom joined with internal and external nature as aspects of negativity, this was a negativity destined to be overcome by humanity's positive freedom.[57] The world of consciousness had been buried in organicism, only to shoot forth from the ground more vigorous than before.

If one point about the beliefs of the Frankfurt liberals and democrats stands out above all others, it is their continued faith in the course of history as the advance of culture, of a progress envisioned as the transition from unreflectively organic institutions to ones infused with spiritual, moral, and intellectual self-consciousness. In terms of nationality, Friedrich Dahlmann set out this transition in the context of a shift from blood- to place-oriented patriotism as the firm foundation for political unity and the formation of states, while the post-Kantian philosopher Jakob Fries took one more step and set "spiritual unity" above geographical as the essential quality of nationality.[58]

In fact, all of the various criteria for nationhood explored thus far can usefully be brought together under this one rubric of common consciousness, or community of mind. Without that indispensable quality of self-awareness, members of the national opposition averred, none of the external characteristics of nationality had any coherent meaning or binding force. Unity had to be experienced; it had to be felt in the mind and the heart else it had no real existence. At least in this area the "national awakening" tradition of Arndt and Jahn still held sway. Just as a "mummy" is not a man, the author of the *Staats-Lexikon* entry on "Nation" or "Volk" declared, neither is "every group of men that has such things as descent, language, and customs in common a nation. It only becomes a nation when as opposed to other men they feel and recognize themselves as an entity and a self-contained totality." Or there was the democratic scientist Fröbel, who derived the equation "nationality equals national character plus national consciousness," that is, nationhood necessitated national distinctness combined with an awareness of it.[59]

Such views spanned the intellectual spectrum, for in addition to Fries, Jahn, and Fröbel, very nearly the entire post-Kantian German idealist tradition in philosophy espoused the primacy of the conscious mind. Hegel, for example, or following him Droysen, in part defined a nation's "Volksgeist" as consciousness, or "Bewusstsein," of its distinct customs, religion, and laws.[60] And even the school of historical law, though true to its Marburg romantic origins in highlighting the mysterious and unconscious workings of the *Volksgeist* as it unfolded in history, still firmly held that customs and laws were like language and had to be in continuous, consciously visible, and self-reflective use before they could be considered truly valid, truly national. The more liberal Germanist wing of the movement, so well represented in Frankfurt in 1848, took this notion even further in the direction of self-conscious publicity and self-government.[61] In the eyes of early nineteenth-century German nationalists, the nation had to follow the Delphic wisdom and know itself, else it was no nation at all.

By injecting this element of self-awareness into their notions of nationality, educated Germans once again demonstrated the compounding of cultural and political conceptions that defined the liberal nation. At least for the liberals and democrats, "common consciousness" in many ways meant simply "public opinion," and this had a great deal to do not just with how future deputies defined nationality intellectually but also with how they hoped to see it defined socially, politically, and institutionally. "Öffentliche Meinung" or "public opinion" with its concomitant idea of a free public sphere *(Öffentlichkeit)* formed the cornerstone of the liberal ideology, while at the same time it had come essentially to serve as a synonym for *Volksgeist* as well. The popular nationalist philosopher Fries, for example, called public opinion "the soul of the entire nation" and explained, "Spiritual national unity and personality, a national intellect, are only formed from the scattered lives of individuals through public opinion." Many other liberals of various stripes such as Droysen, Welcker, and Grimm basically agreed.[62] If nationality required a sense of being actively experienced, of common consciousness, then how else could the consciousness-raising necessary to achieve that state come about except through the medium of public opinion? Nationalists at the time saw as clearly as modern students of nationalism could wish that constructing or cementing a feeling of nationality and of patriotic belonging depended crucially on being able to inculcate such ideas and visceral emotions in the public at large, through speeches, meetings, monuments, festivals, organizations, scholarship, and education from primary through university levels. Nationhood, however natural or cultural it might be, was still in essence a public, a political experience.

Uniting nationality and politics in this way allowed members of the nationalist opposition to emphasize the mutually reinforcing and interlocking quality of their liberalism and nationalism, of their twin calls for unity and liberty. Three of their most cherished demands—the creation of a free public sphere, of an oral, public court system (often with some form of jury), and of self-governing institutions at all levels of society—together aimed at realizing the ideal of the strong, free citizen in a free society and a strong national community, with each reciprocally strengthening the other. In addition to allowing enlightened public opinion to dictate policy, free speech, a free press, and a broader and more public forum for political and legal participation would fuse individual or group opinions into a general, or national, will.[63] Liberal nationalists similarly hoped that local self-government and a lively associational life would serve as "nurseries for character" and "schools for the strong, practical citizen." These institutions would provide the necessary intermediate stages for formulating public opinion and would promote the development of forceful, independent citizens capable of participating in such debate and pursuing their own individual *Bildung*. At the same time, these forms of local involvement would also foster a sense of connection with the commonweal and with the nation as a whole. As recent scholarship has emphasized, national and local or regional identities were far from being mutually exclusive, often tending rather to reinforce one another in the process of construction. Local patriotism, nationalists hoped, would ultimately nourish national patriotism, while the free public sphere would allow such sentiments to take shape in meaningful forms, all the more so as it offered would-be national revivalists the means to teach readers and listeners to recognize all the characteristics they shared with their fellow citizens. Conversely, without these institutions the nation would be neither truly free nor truly a nation. It would lack the means of creating the community of mind that alone could instill a feeling of nationality or of patriotic commitment to the nation.[64]

Consequently, for liberal nationalists the desire to form a nation helped motivate and legitimate liberal political demands. It also transformed the patriotic commandment to defend one's fatherland into the necessity to defend its free institutions as well, for these had suddenly become ideologically charged as an integral part of the nation itself and of its cultural-political heritage. In the liberal and democratic view, being a nation meant being free, and being free entailed being a nation. Many contemporaries and later historians have pointed to the twin goals of *Einheit* and *Freiheit*, or unity and liberty, as being mutually contradictory or at least in tension. This liberal nationalist dichotomy has even been seen as the fundamental weakness in the German liberal program, above all in Bismarck's time but earlier as well. Potential tensions there certainly were, yet among the Forty-Eighters unity and liberty were much more often seen as mutually reinforcing.

German liberals, then, devoutly believed in the value of an active, independent citizenry participating in a vibrant political culture as the only secure foundation for a free, strong nation both domestically and externally. This tendency draws them more closely into the context of an "ancient republicanism" providing the intellectual underpinnings for both the Anglo-American and Jacobin political traditions. Historians have often noted how such Jacobin values swept across Europe on Napoleon's imperial coattails and influenced the anti-Napoleonic national awakenings in occupied lands such as Germany and Italy. Without seeing any particular contradiction, however, they have gone on to depict the liberal, ancient republican ideology as singularly inoperative in the context of the ostensibly ethnic nationalism of Central and Eastern Europe. In Western Europe too, for that matter, nineteenth-century liberalism has typically been seen more as a reaction against the civic humanist model in favor of a Lockean political and economic doctrine that stressed natural rights and the individualist pursuit of self-interest as the best basis for a dynamically progressive society. Yet historians have depicted the situation in the German lands in even bleaker hues, with neither the ancient republican nor the rights-based political traditions figuring strongly there. In Central Europe liberalism has seemed to have formed but a thin mist upon the nationalist waters, soon dissipating to leave behind nothing but an illiberal, duty-based, authoritarian, militarist ethnocultural nationalism. And by the later nineteenth century an ideology and a political system fairly well fitting that description had found a warm reception from large segments of the German population.

Yet since numerous other intervening factors could explain the transition, this fact of a shift actually says very little about the ideological relationships prevailing within the general milieu of liberal and nationalist ideas and ideologues before 1848. As this chapter should have shown already, Germans conceived of nationhood in both culturally and politically charged terms—indeed, their ideas of culture and politics, and of ethnicity and community, were by no means neatly separable, neither by them nor by historians. This circumstance helped prop the door open for a deep, mutually supportive cross-fertilization of liberal and nationalist ideas, even in the context of a sense of nationality allegedly more "ethnic" than that proposed as the standard in Britain or France. As should come as no surprise for a political elite breeched and matriculated in classical literature and history, a modified ancient republican ideology analogous to that described elsewhere survived and even thrived in Germany.[65] Liberalism and nationalism were not just strange political bedfellows in the first half of the nineteenth century but were instead intimately connected through concurrent development within the same places, times, and minds. In the view of most members of the national opposition, nationhood required liberty, rights, broad participation, a common mind and will, if it was to have any real meaning, any real existence, at all.

This interaction between liberal and nationalist ideals bore important consequences not just for the nation's internal political structuring but also for the drawing of its national borders. Situating definitions of nationality in the realm of a common consciousness supported by the free exchange of ideas, broad political participation, and locally inspired national patriotism opened up a new range of criteria for nationhood and national cohesion. Significantly, such a move allowed for the inclusion of populations within the German nation who by some other, purely external criteria might not qualify as German. This follows from the fact that a sense of community, a feeling and memory of long-standing political unity and struggles for liberty, is supposed to have comprised the mortar binding the national identities of civic-voluntarist nations, in other words, of those whose criteria for national membership ostensibly did not include language or descent. Three Austrians of the *Vormärz* liberal opposition, for example, the radical Franz Schuselka, the moderate Baron Viktor von Andrian-Werburg, and the reform conservative Count Friedrich Deym, each reckoned that the best chance to keep the Austrian monarchy together and of use to the German nation involved granting rights of local and provincial self-government on a liberal basis. This act of statecraft was designed to satisfy the non-German-speaking, chiefly Slavic nationalities' desires for civil and political equality while simultaneously laying the foundations for a newer, stronger Austrian national consciousness. Local patriotism, Andrian, Schuselka, and Deym thought, would still breed the national variety, even when certain cultural differences might have suggested otherwise.[66]

As an added inducement for the other Austrian nationalities to arrive at a new appreciation of Austrian nationhood, Schuselka highlighted the benefits of being part of a great power. Interestingly, many other hopeful observers in Germany believed the creation of a strong, liberal German state could raise consciousness of broader German or even Germanic national affinities and convince "German" areas outside the Confederation to return to the Reich. In the so-called "magnet theory" of German nationalism, provinces such as Alsace or states such as the Netherlands, Belgium, and Switzerland might find the economic and political advantages of close ties with such a large and powerful Germany so attractive that they would elect to return to the "mother" country. Such observers did often recognize that these groups would be reluctant to join an illiberal Germany at the expense of their constitutional privileges in the liberal Brussels, Hague, or Paris monarchies (or the Swiss cantons), that is, that political self-determination and patriotism also played a great role in the process of national identity.[67] Yet even here, although the motivation for such hopes on the German side partly involved ethnic and linguistic criteria for nationhood, many such optimistic pundits would have expected the reunions to include the French- or Italian-speaking districts as well. If self-identification were to be the ultimate criterion for joining the German nation, then its definition would have to be expanded to admit peoples considered non-German by other benchmarks.

Of course, the ultimate justification behind both the Austrian and transGerman plans rested on a sense of tradition, of history—in part the simple fact of current or previous possession, but equally the consciousness of historical community resting upon centuries of political association within the Holy Roman Empire. As recent scholars have stressed, the construction of what has variously been analyzed as a "national historical narrative," a "national mythology," or a "national memory" made up a crucial part of the nation-building enterprise. The role of such constructed national pasts and of historical consciousness generally will be more fully explored in the following chapter; here it is sufficient to note their implications for the drawing of national boundaries.[68] Crucially in this context, the formulation of such national pasts offered yet another means of going beyond a bare ethnocultural identity. It offered a way to reconcile mythicized ethnic markers with memories of long-standing multinational association and to facilitate the inclusion of non-German-speaking groups within the German nation. Emphasis on a purely historical and political vision of nationhood has typically been seen as the province either of the western civic-voluntarist nation-states or of the reactionary governments of the eastern multinational empires, yet similar thinking clearly appealed to liberal and democratic nationalists as well. Historians never fail to point to medievalizing trends in German cultural and political life, hearkening back as they do either to the twelfth- or fifteenth-century splendor of the Holy Roman Empire of the German Nation, yet they have for the most part treated this as simple glorification of that "German Nation's" past. Otto Dann, however, has quite usefully pointed out that such reveling in imperial prestige also entailed the predisposition to multinational rule.[69] German nationalism grew up in a place and time in which ethnographic and political borders did not coincide; the historical consciousness of its proponents to a great extent moved in spaces and times in which that was equally true.

Where, then, does this leave the question of the applicability of the so-called "nationality principle" in the realm of border-drawing? Given the mix of cultural, political, and historical components of nationhood whirling in the minds of future deputies when they turned their thoughts in this direction, the probability that narrowly cultural or linguistic criteria for the fixing of national boundaries would prevail must be accounted fairly low—all the more so as these men were realistic enough to recognize the impossibility of doing so cleanly amidst the ethnographic welter of Central and Eastern Europe. Even the Württemberger Paul Pfizer, who based his proposal for a Prussian-led "Little German" empire on the proposition that under conditions of increasing liberalization multinational states would very likely fragment along nationality lines, retained a loophole in his invocation of the nationality principle. If the slightest cultural or political inequality of treatment was enough to justify secession, Pfizer maintained, when those unequal conditions had not been met separation was not legitimate. Struve, whose strict application of the nationality principle included proposals for population exchanges to smooth out ethnographic irregularities, remained the rarity in this period, and even he seemed to expect that provinces such as Bohemia and Moravia would remain with Germany in future.[70] Similarly, though the Arndtian dream of bringing together the whole of the German linguistic community under one national roof enjoyed a certain vague and sloganistic popularity, it never formed the basis of anyone's serious thinking about German national borders. And even if it had, such an all-encompassing Germany would have included millions upon millions of non-German-speakers if it were not to give up all semblance of territorial integrity. While it was not certain where precisely the boundaries of the new state might be placed in 1848, the open-endedness of the *Vormärz* culture of nationhood in these matters made it unlikely that the Frankfurt deputies would go to either extreme of refusing to incorporate non-Germans or of demanding the incorporation of far-flung Germans into the new German national state.

Iterations of the "nationality principle" would play a part in the determination of Germany's borders in 1848, but the nationality principle so invoked would not be restricted to linguistic criteria for nationality of the sort seen in 1919. Before 1848, educated German conceptions of nationhood encompassed more than just language, more even than culture in a broad sense. The Kohnian dichotomy between cultural and political definitions of nationhood and types of nationalism fails to do justice to the complexity of contemporary thinking about problems of national belonging and national allegiance. Language did claim a place within the *Vormärz* culture of nationhood as an important criterion for establishing boundaries between nations, not only because it was the most obvious ethnographic difference between peoples but also because the new historicist dialectical epistemology helped raise ideological barriers to mutual comprehension between individuals and nations. Yet language did not hold this position as boundary marker by itself—mores, customs, and folkways, laws and constitutional predilections, religion, shared historical memories, and consciousness of community all filled out the content of the political culture of nationhood. Race and biological descent also joined these elements, but in this period they were by no means necessarily the deterministic factors they would later become. Race constituted but one more element of the contemporary culture-nature fusion and was subject to being overridden by the power of free will that in the German culture of *Bildung* was so fundamental to the conception of the moral vocation of individuals, nations, and humanity as a whole.

All of these components of the nationality concept comprised a culture of nationhood, one necessarily political because these components only achieved active meaning and utility within the context of a liberal participatory process. In envisioning a mutually reinforcing relationship between the liberty and the national identity of the citizen-patriots who made up the nation, Germans of the culture of *Bildung* interwove the strands of liberal and nationalist ideology as they did those of the cultural and political aspects of nationality. Nationhood thus became not just a dead conglomeration of objective criteria but a living one infused with subjective elements as well, a circumstance that presents yet another transversal of the standard typology. In this ideological environment non-German groups who by certain criteria were considered nations in their own right could find a place within the educated midcentury German's conception of the German nation. Whatever the practical difficulties attendant upon such an endeavor, the construction of a unified but linguistically multinational German national state would have violated neither the internal logic of national boundaries within the *Vormärz* culture of nationhood nor the various expressions of national identity deriving from it.

2 | The Nation as Historical Actor

The previous chapter disclosed the fundamental bonding of cultural and political elements in conceptions of national boundaries and national identity within the *Vormärz* culture of nationhood. Not least among the important components of this compound national identity was a sense of shared historical memory. Through engaging references to a medieval past when multinational polities were commonplace but colorful, efforts to establish a "national memory" served as potential rallying points for instilling a patriotic common consciousness that might transcend possibly divisive cultural fault-lines in an era of emergent secessionist nationalism. As the present chapter reveals, however, history as it related to nationhood was more than just the memory of shared experiences, more than just local color in romantic art and literature, more even than a presentist tool for ideologues from across the political spectrum. The historical consciousness of the men of the Forty-Eighter generation bore much more far-reaching ramifications for their conceptions of nationality, ramifications that made up the second key structural component of the German culture of nationhood in the first half of the nineteenth century.

For these educated Germans history formed a realm of progress through conflict, of constantly shifting relationships that offered both the threat of dissolution and the opportunity for advance. History was anything but static. As the liberal ideal of *Bildung* led future deputies to think of social and political relations as necessarily confrontational, that same notion expressed itself in the historicist tendency to conceive of history as an equally dynamic process. As post-Kantian dialectical epistemology seemed to raise the linguistic and mental barriers between nations ever higher, idealist and romantic historicists decreed that there could be no progress without conflict, a conflict among ideas and individuals and, crucially here, among nations. Similarly, just as the liberal view of society led

48

to an insistence on self-assertion and growth through a sense of personal honor, rights, and autonomy, the historicist vision of history facilitated the translocation of such ideas to the realm of nations as collective persons, in which national development and self-assertion followed from national honor, rights, and independence. And just as the dialectical world of public opinion and participatory patriotism provided the context for a symbiotic relationship between liberalism and nationalism in the construction of national boundaries and identities, the confrontational arena of international relations offered another setting for reciprocity between these ideologies—through the ideal of the patriotic citizen as the pulsing heart of both the nation's free institutions and its self-assertive strength. Only through the honor-bound liberty of its internal life could a nation muster the moral force needed to exert itself as an actor on the world-historical stage, and only through self-confident and honorable striving in that vale of conflict could a nation foster its proudly patriotic citizenry. In a world where nothing was stable, nationhood could not be a matter of boundaries alone. In the midcentury German culture of nationhood, nationality necessarily meant the means of defending those boundaries as well.

Even more than the one preceding, the current chapter highlights the implications of using the culture concept in analyzing such attitudes toward nationality. In the previous chapter it became clear how widely disparate elements of the broader contextual culture were reworked and rewoven into their new positions within the culture of nationhood. This aspect of the construction of national identity could be seen in the role of such malleable conceptions as race and religion, or even at the more esoteric cultural level of epistemology. Prior traditions, assumptions, and debates within these distinct but related cultural fields provided materials for the development of national identity but also set parameters for it. Without minimizing the capacity of the human mind for self-interested rationalization or simply for harboring a mass of ill-examined inconsistencies, it remains nonetheless true that the deeply-held tropes from these other cultural contexts could not be altered completely or at will to fit the new national identities, even on those not necessarily so frequent occasions when contemporary thinkers were aware of all the connective influences that might need reshaping in that project. At the same time, the ongoing cultural construction work in such a fundamental and far-reaching area as national identity obviously sent transformative vibrations in the other cultural direction as well. Such considerations of the wide and deep interplay between the contextual culture and the culture of nationhood assume par-

[handwritten margin note: Identities brought to tgnr to form nat.]

ticular prominence in the present chapter, as it examines how strongly felt beliefs about individual, political, and historical processes and identities were brought to bear to make sense of a world increasingly defined in terms of nationality.

Without focusing on such deeper cultural implications of nineteenth-century views of history and nationhood, recent scholarship on German nationalism has paid a good deal of attention to the dimension of historical consciousness. In particular it has been concerned to theorize efforts to construct a national past that could support the growth of national identity. Studies investigating this aspect of national consciousness have variously invoked notions of national narratives, national mythology, or national memory. From whichever theoretical perspective, it is immediately clear that by 1848 certain powerful tropes had come to occupy central positions across a broad range of such synthesized national pasts, and that these ideas deeply colored the way contemporaries thought about Germany and its role on the world-historical stage. Yet however common the urge to create, or at least to enjoy, a clearly defined national past and collective memory, it would not do to underestimate the multiplicity of such potential identities and the highly contested nature of such nationality construction projects. This was especially true in a Central Europe scored by diversity along geographical, religious, political, and not least personal lines. Except in very broad outlines, the period before 1848 did not see the emergence of any single commonly accepted historical "master narrative" or "national mythology." Moreover, efforts to create such narratives were always subject to strong constraints deriving from the cultural contexts in which they were made, and it is rather to this overarching culture and the historical consciousness within it that one must preferentially look to explain the structural similarities observed.

[handwritten margin note: can't create nat. ID w/ alienating (people who don't assoc w/ nat. history) — not attempted pre-1848]

The role of the common "golden age" trope illustrates both points about the sources and limits of agreement across the range of proposed German national pasts. On the one hand, the widespread adoption of a golden age/collapse/rebirth plot sequence represents a fairly clear case where the national historical narrative conformed to a template deep-set within the historical consciousness of educated Germans in the first half of the nineteenth century. The pattern derives from a secularized salvation story, one often applied not just to German but to European and world history as well. Just as the Edenic period came to an abrupt end in the Fall, to be followed by a journey through the vale of tears to the millennium, secular history could be provided with analogous milestone events and inspiring moral overtones. In the case of the German national past a golden age of Germanic power or virtue was supposed to have given way to a humiliating period of national decline, only to be followed by a slow, painful climb back to strength in an era of "national awakening" that would culminate in national unification.

Past the basic pattern of golden age, collapse, and rebirth, however, the similarities break down quickly. Previous scholars have recognized some of these distinctions, but they have typically reduced them to those between two competing camps, the liberal or *Burschenschaft* nationalists and the romantic conservatives (sometimes also deemed nationalist). The typically Protestant or unorthodox liberals, such studies conclude, held up the Teutonic *Vorzeit* of Tacitean noble simplicity as the Arcadian age, its apotheosis the battles by Arminius and his successors that preserved Germanic independence from a corrupt Roman Empire and ultimately led to its destruction. This glorious period was followed only too closely by one of decline as the previously pure world of Teutonic freedoms was itself corrupted in the encounter with Rome, emerging from it saddled with kings, Catholicism, and feudalism. The romantic conservatives, of course, above all the Catholics among them, valued the hierarchical Middle Ages and Church much more highly, lauding the glories of the Holy Roman Empire in the days of its European preeminence. In both schemes the Thirty Years' War and the Napoleonic occupation vied for the position of nadir in the historical narrative, with the succeeding age as one of potential renewal, in a liberal or restorationist direction according to the political preferences of the narrator.[1]

While the above dichotomy serves as a useful guide to the contested landscape of the German national past, the diversity of competing narratives actually cut across these lines too, with geographic and even personal differences joining those of politics and religion in shaping the historical selection process. This finer fragmentation can be most easily seen in examining the casting of protagonists for the national drama, but it also emerges in the choice of golden ages. As for the latter, liberal nationalists were neither so universally enamored of Teutonic prehistory nor so disenchanted with the medieval period as dichotomous studies tend to assume. Most certainly paid the obligatory homage to their freedom-loving Teutonic forbears, Heinrich Luden, Ernst Moritz Arndt, Jakob Venedey, Johann Droysen, and Carl Welcker being but some of those from across the political and geographical spectrum who did so. The liberal activist and historian J. G. A. Wirth, however, chose to highlight the brutal "shadow-side" of the *Vorzeit*, with the freedom-trampling Teutonic nobility blackening the noble Teutonic character.[2]

More significantly, even when praised the Teutonic era did not typically claim sole status as golden age. While Droysen and Luden followed the ostensibly standard pattern of seeing exposure to the Christian-Roman world as the onset of medieval decline, many other commentators followed a tendency even more deeply fixed in the educated German historical consciousness. As noted in the previous chapter, a classic historical trope in this era was to equate the special German national mission with its progressive fusion of Roman, Christian, and Germanic elements to create the basis of the world-changing Western European civilization. It should therefore come as no surprise to find Venedey and Welcker among the many depicting just such a transition, and to find them and others selecting alternative golden ages from the rich tapestry of medieval history.[3]

Here the diversity among national narratives again comes to the fore. Many narrators turned to the summit of German political strength in the high medieval Holy Roman Empire for their golden age, a move that at least had the virtue of providing a clearer symbol of federative national unity and power than did the division-riven Teutonic *Vorzeit*. For a national movement striving for a greater degree of national unity and power in the present this was only reasonable. Yet even here the choice was wide, with some opting to place the peak among the Saxon, others the Frankish, others the Hohenstaufen dynasties.[4] The democrat Wirth for his part put the pinnacle of German greatness in the period of the Frankish and Swabian kaisers, yet he was also among those who drew attention away from the emperors and emphasized the role of the German cities with their freer constitutions and active Burgher class.[5] Although one point of near-consensus was the empire's declining strength after the death of Frederick II, concentration on the imperial cities or the Hansa allowed even the late Middle Ages a share in Germanic glory. Compared to the Teutonic era, the Middle Ages generally offered a more civilized and centralized German culture and polity for nationalist sensibilities, but depending on political or even personal preferences, the specific golden age selected for normative symbolic use could still vary significantly.[6]

If the wide choice of potential golden ages almost inevitably led to disagreement, the much broader panoply of historical and mythic heroes from which to select led to even greater disparity. Some commentators lauded Charlemagne for his services to scholarship and to Germanic language and law, but more tended to critique or even vilify him for his war against Saxon freedoms or his ambition to construct an unnaturally large empire. Barbarossa, though stirring, had not yet awakened as a clear symbol of German unity, even in the age of Heine. Some portrayers of the national past indeed praised him and other Hohenstaufen rulers, but just as many remained cool in light of the Italian campaigns often taken to have weakened Germany or of the Hohenstaufen tendency to attack free city constitutions wherever they might be found, in Lombardy or at home.[7] For more recent times, geographic, dynastic, and religious considerations clearly restricted the potential appeal of figures such as Frederick the Great, Maria Theresa, or her son Joseph II, but political and nationality-related issues did as well. Frederick, for example, might be a symbol of renewed German military might to non-Austrians, but his predilection for French culture and mechanistic statecraft thinned the ranks of his admirers among the Forty-Eighters.[8] Finally, while it might seem obvious that the heroes of the "national awakening" and the supposedly "national" struggle against Napoleon would be the most universally celebrated figures among the men of the national movement (as they were), selection proved politically, socially, and geographically disputatious even there: Stein or Stadion, Yorck or Hofer, Jahn or Queen Luise, Blücher or the Archduke Charles. Agreeing on the cast of characters in the national historical epic was no easy proposition.

The case for national hero might seem stronger for the more hazily distant figure of Arminius, or Hermann. The playwrights Kleist and Grabbe certainly dramatized his exploits, while Arndt treated him as an almost Christ-like redeemer. For Paul Pfizer, Arminius's rallying of certain Teutonic tribes at least proved that early Germans did not completely lack a "spirit of unity." The Catholic publicist and historian Georg Phillips for his part accepted Arminius as a potential symbol of national unity but tried to deflect the figure's obvious anti-Roman, anti-Catholic appeal. Yet opinion divided on more than just religious lines. The radical future deputy Moritz Hartmann of Bohemia, in a poem otherwise pouring scorn upon the weak-kneed German propensity for memorializing dead heroes, made an exception in the case of Arminius and his Teutoburger monument, insofar as they might inspire Germans to take a more active (read violent) role in political affairs. But the democratic martyr Wirth emphasized in his *History of the Germans* that Arminius's battle was only for independence, not for freedom, and Arndt himself thought that Arminius was lucky in the people over whom he ruled, since Teutonic love of liberty could check his overweening ambitions for foreign conquest and strong rule.[9]

Since not even Arndt considered Arminius's faction-mongering post-

Teutoburger career particularly inspiring as a symbol of German unity, the fate of "Hermann" as mythic hero only serves to underline a basic truth about *Vormärz* nationalism—no one hero or set of heroes could supply the symbolic unity necessary to transcend German diversity. Ultimately only the German people as a whole could be the protagonist of its own history, and a vacillating one at that, often forgetful of its own greatness and destiny. It was thus a noncoincidence of deep significance that the larger-than-life female figure of Germania, Athena-like genius of the German nation, would be chosen to be its symbolic representative at the Frankfurt National Assembly in 1848. Germania, suitably decked with the trappings of Holy Roman imperial glory and drawn from the crucially excluded category "women," was the only figure who could symbolically bring together the national past and the national present.[10]

The midcentury vision of history, then, was in one sense presentist and static, comprised of historical events and figures scattered on an open field from which nationalist or government publicists could reap a fruitful if diverse harvest of images selected to promote a healthy sense of rooted national identity in their readership. At the same time, however, a decidedly dynamic philosophy of history overlay their understanding of these events and helped limit the extent and direction of their gleanings. For direction there was. However much freedom of invention the would-be historian or myth-maker laureates might have, their imaginations were still ultimately constrained by the cultural contexts in which they operated. Certain deep-seated beliefs from the culture of nationhood, and even more broadly from the underlying culture of *Bildung*, set loose boundaries to the cultural space in which contemporaries were free to construct their narratives and assemble their collective memories. These cultural parameters in turn helped shape future deputies' broader conceptions of nationhood and their attitudes toward relations among nations.

Educated midcentury Germans drew two fundamental lessons from their readings of the past—history meant change, and it meant conflict. Theirs was a Heraclitean view of existence, in which all was motion and struggle, yet with the hope of redemptive unity arising from such disparate opposing forces. This faith in ultimate harmony derived partly from the romantic and historicist epistemological trope of reconciling diversity and unity, but it was nourished above all by a sometimes secularized Judaeo-Christian theodicy that gave all the chaos and misery its meaning within a world-shaping mission. History from this philosophical perspective became a process, an unfolding. Liberal notions of progress have already been touched on in connection with their vision of a *Humanität* spanning races and languages and pointing toward a better future as humans fulfilled their moral vocation. But such progress worked above all in the context of liberal belief in the all-determining power of publicity and freedom of opinion to serve as the engine of nations and of the civilizing process generally. This progress gave the course of history its direction, its goal, indeed the very idea of a "course of history" leading to some dimly envisioned but better future condition of humanity.

And this progress only came about through conflict—among rival opinions in the public sphere, among merchants and manufacturers in the marketplace, among nations on the plains and oceans of the world. As the organicist political theorist Karl Zachariä asserted, nature created "struggle and movement," and "precisely this struggle is the principal source of all culture and civilization."[11] The great dramatist and philosopher Friedrich Schiller in his seminal *Letters on the Aesthetic Education of Mankind* made clear the connection between personal and historical *Bildung* and pointed to the miserable alienation of the modern individual as the unfortunate point of departure for progress, in which humanity seemed to know no other way to advance than to destroy the "totality" of the individual character by setting its single powers at odds with one another. Yet this dilemma posed the problem whose solution Schiller believed would usher in the age of freedom and wholeness, when change and eternity, Being and Becoming would finally find their equipoise.[12] Hegel, and indeed most of those in the German idealist tradition, posited an extreme dialectical view of historical change, through which human autonomy and completeness would emerge from alienated society in the moral realm of the state, at the end of a historical process pitting Idea against Idea, people against people. Across all these different perspectives there was a sense that collision and conflict were necessary preconditions for the development of persons and nations alike.

This conflictual view of the nature of historical change and progress was intimately connected to the new hermeneutic understanding of the world and knowledge within the culture of *Bildung*, in which any exchange or comprehension between two minds posited an underlying similarity that lay in uneasy tension with the ineradicable differences between them. Without the similarity, the continuity between the interlocutors, there could be no understanding, while the differences ensured that such meaningful exchange would always be discontinuous, jolting, and incomplete—

but all the more meaningful through the provocation of difference. Equally with the process of history, any development required an underlying continuity, but for there to be any forward motion radical difference had to be present as well. Nearly the entire idealist school of thought in history followed Wilhelm von Humboldt and the philosophers in the new dialectical epistemology and drew from it a dialectical sense of historical change. Such historians saw history as a succession of collisions among discrete, individualized Ideas or the diverse nations who represented them as they struggled to direct historical events. These battling particulate elements of the historical process found their reconciliation, their adherence to a distinct course of history, only through the harmonic dispensation of a divine or universal plan. This plan in turn could only be divined through the historical or "genetic" method of interpretation, in which truly understanding a historical event or even a present-day phenomenon required a knowledge of its origins and historical trajectory. Most significantly in the present context, the new historicist methodology was applied first and foremost to the history of nations as the elementary structural units of humanity and history. Humboldt, Hegel, Boeckh, and Ranke may have instigated such historicist tendencies in their own distinct ways, but the scheme was more than widespread.[13] This circumstance left the dialectically progressivist historical consciousness at the center of the culture of nationhood.[14]

This vision of history as conflictual process held sway just as strongly among future Frankfurt deputies as among the intellectual luminaries above. Love and hate formed the polar motive forces in world history for the historian Arndt, while the phrenologist Gustav von Struve emphasized the necessity for both individuals and nations to possess the human "destructive drive" in a world where "creation and annihilation, beginnings and endings walk everywhere hand in hand," and where "the necessary, unavoidable preparation for all creation is destruction." The post-Kantian political theorist Paul Pfizer echoed both Schiller and Struve in his contention that the "vocation of man" was the "visible development of all powers in all-round activity," and that this process of *Bildung* entailed a continual conflict involving even physical force, just as in irrational nature "light and darkness, production and destruction wrestle in constant struggle."[15] Prominent idealist historian Johann Droysen envisioned the world as a "creation without Sabbath," as a never-ending battle in which "the right of victory is the victory of a higher notion of right," while his more youthful Hegel-influenced colleague Wilhelm Jordan already enunciated the tragic, remorseless doctrine of world-historical progress through a centuries-long, pain-filled "process of fermentation" that would help make him famous in the context of his speech on Poland in the summer of 1848.[16] In all of these conceptions of historical teleology and conflict, the old Enlightenment image of progress as the struggle between the forces of light and darkness in the sphere of public opinion had been replaced by a sense of the civilizing process no less sure but considerably more historically complex and morally ambiguous.

With Droysen and even more with Jordan, the sort of runaway historicism hastening toward an amorally relativist "night in which all cows are black," often decried in Hegelian historical philosophy by later commentators, first appeared on the public stage of the German historical drama. Such an attitude sprouted from the union of Heraclitean and teleological historical understandings. From this perspective history offered the prospect of a long, hard road strewn with the bodies of those fallen in the name of progressive striving. Most deputies at St. Paul's Church had not traveled so far down that historicist path as Droysen or Jordan, but they had generally accepted the lot of fallen humanity in a fractured world, a world of instability and conflict illuminated at once by the covenanted rainbow of progress and the fiery sword o'er Eden. Without recognition of the extent to which future deputies shared this deep-seated belief in flux and opposition as the driving pistons of history, neither their ideas of nationhood before the revolution nor their national politics during it can be fully understood.

One of the most important effects of this processual view of history follows from the simple observation that if everything historical lies in a state of flux, then so too must national borders. From the Dorians, Celts, and Scythians, to the Huns, Teutons, and Slavs who assailed the later Eastern and Western Roman Empires, classical sources told of the chain reactions of tribal migrations and barbarian conquests that more than anything else seemed to have shaped the face of history and the map of Europe in the ancient world. With such a knowledge of history, midcentury Germans accepted that boundaries between states and peoples were anything but stable. They even contributed their own canto to this historical epic with their reconstruction of the conquering Indo-European diaspora. Moreover, all of this migration and mixing of peoples led not just to a shifting of borders or a replacement of one people by another but also seemed frequently to have stimulated cultural mixing. As noted above, most contemporaries saw the fruitful Migration Era compound of Roman imperial, Christian universalizing, and Germanic libertarian traditions as the catalyst of the progressive transition to medieval and modern European civilization. Herder, Hegel, and Friedrich Schlegel all highlighted this process in their respective philosophies of history, while among future Assembly deputies Welcker, Sylvester Jordan, and the democratic publicist Jakob Venedey each imputed considerable explanatory weight to it as well. This genealogical, cultural, and political miscibility worked both ways, often turning the Romance peoples into honorary members of the category "nations of Germanic extraction," while also being seen as operative within Germany itself.[17]

Thus even the popular mythic trope of the Germans as a pure, indigenous people collided with the still more fundamental belief in the German cosmopolitan national mission to bring *Bildung* to the world through assimilating, reworking, and disseminating its diverse cultural heritage. Despite Arndt's ideas of ethnic purity and Fichte's notion of an "original [German] language," most contemporaries showed full awareness of the extent to which large swaths of the trackless forests once denominated "Germania" by Tacitus had been settled by Slavic peoples. Fichte himself pointed out that the Slavs had controlled Germany to the Elbe, a fact known to any reader of Gustav Stenzel, Friedrich von Raumer, Friedrich Dahlmann, or Georg Phillips, to name some of the popular medieval historians who later graced Paulskirche benches.[18] The ethnographic cartographer and future Frankfurt delegate Karl Bernhardi even called for a communal effort to discover and catalog as many residual Slavic names, words, and customs in Germany as possible.[19]

It is worth noting in this context that contemporary commentators did not react so negatively to the idea of mutual cultural influence as one might expect from the organicist-exclusive xenophobia usually portrayed in the literature and based largely on Jahn, Arndt, or the "devourer of the French" Wolfgang Menzel. The organicist innovator Herder, for instance, cited the example of the Normans and the English to acknowledge the benefits of occasional intercultural "graftings," while Jacob Grimm used his position as president of the 1846 Germanist Conference to argue, if not for an end to linguistic and legal purification efforts, then at least for more modest limits to them.[20] Nor is this an instance where the ostensible split between chauvinistic liberal nationalists and romantic Christian conservatives explains differences in opinion, for once again liberals prove to have been much less infected with anticlerical, antimedieval xenophobia than often thought. Organicist thinking did not lead to the rejection of all foreign elements but rather to an ideal of growth and development in continual interaction with the cultural environment. Thus Georg Waitz, one of those who did stress original Teutonic purity and virtue, still considered that the absorption of foreign ideas and customs presented no threat so long as they were fully integrated and "made one's own" in the transformative process of adoption. Indeed, for Waitz and for others, what made Germans such a potent cultural force was precisely their knack for incorporating the experiences of other peoples. Most Germans of this period had at least a resigned acceptance of their mixed linguistic, legal, cultural, and genealogical heritage—more than a few deemed it Germans' greatest virtue.[21]

For present purposes, however, the most important aspect of these shifting borders and cultural collisions focused attention on the plains and mountains of Eastern Europe, where medieval settlement patterns were reread in terms of modern nationality. During the so-called "eastern colonization" period, German political and cultural conquests supposedly rolled back previous Slavic gains east of the Elbe and on into Poland, the Baltic, and the Danube basin. The Catholic conservative historian Phillips saw this process partly as the reactivation of an original Germanic population that had never fully succumbed culturally to Slavic rule, thus preserving a Fichtean or Arndtian kind of folk continuity (but not purity). More typical, however, were Stenzel's sketches, which put the emphasis on the forceful and/or voluntary germanization of the resident Slavic populations. Customs, laws, social institutions, even language and blood became ever more Germanic with the incursion of both a German military caste and agricultural or mercantile settlers.[22]

Such historians quite openly couched this process in terms of the advance of a superior Germanic civilization at the expense of Slavic cultures none too highly thought of. Although folklorists such as Grimm, Uhland, and Count Auersperg followed romantic literary cosmopolitanism to the extent of admiring the richness of Slavic folk poetry and ballads, Herder's encomium on the Slavs for the most part found little echo in Germany. The orientalist Jakob Fallmerayer, as part of his campaign to prevent Germans from underestimating the Russian menace, did insist that Slavs too belonged among the culturally productive peoples of the world, yet he reserved judgment on the question of whether this family of nations would prove itself to be as capable of progress as the ancient Hellenes or modern Germans.[23] For the less nuanced majority of commentators, Slavic peoples lacked among other important qualities a true state-building capacity or appreciation of individual liberty, as evidenced by the unhappy examples of Poland and Russia respectively. Nor did they possess the requisite know-how or desire to engage in the progressive city-based economy and society characteristic of Western Europe's broadly Germanic populations. Even German agriculture sprouted more productively in the East than did the Slavic. Whatever civilization of the modern Western European variety there was to be found in Eastern Europe, German pundits averred, derived from Germanic influence or settlement.[24] This point of view tended to equate the late-medieval advance of German *Bildung* in the East with the general progress of humanity, a no doubt immensely satisfying but no less fateful belief for early nineteenth-century Germans to harbor.

Such a belief loomed all the more satisfying and fateful in that contemporaries saw this ephemeral quality to national and cultural borders as a characteristic not simply of ancient and medieval times but also of the modern period. If history was a process, it was a process not yet completed.[25] Despite Dahlmann's assertion that in the course of time "national migrations cease" and give way to place-based patriotism, many thought that time rather late in arriving, particularly in the Slavic East. To the west the tragic fate of the seemingly doomed Celtic peoples shone like the writing on the palace wall, while the Württemberg liberal Pfizer capped his call for eastern as opposed to overseas colonization by declaring that the thousand-year struggle between Germans and Slavs had not yet been fought to its conclusion; the "Völkerwanderung" or "migration of peoples" was not yet complete.[26] In Austria the moderate liberal Baron Andrian thought that Germans would lead in *Bildung* in the Habsburg monarchy for some time to come, and the more radical Franz Schuselka predicted that peaceful germanization there would continue apace. The East Prussian Wilhelm Jordan for his part singled out Prussia as the strong force behind the ongoing advance of German *Bildung* and of a general progressive education for freedom and citizenship, in this case in Poland.[27]

Although the process seemed to give German imaginations more room to catch fire amid the wide expanses of Eastern Europe, numerous hopeful pundits thought they observed similar historical trends in the Northwest and prognosticated a glorious future for peaceful German cultural conquests in the Low Countries, Schleswig, even Denmark itself. Arndt, Grimm, the Jewish Bohemian opposition publicist Ignaz Kuranda, and the Listian Prussian liberal Gustav Hoefken were but a few of the many who took an interest in the Flemish movement in Belgium, while Dahlmann and fellow historian Andreas Michelsen adduced northward-creeping German language and high culture as part of their arguments at the 1846 Germanist Conference in favor of retaining the Schleswig-Holstein union and its connection with the German Confederation.[28] Pan-German thinking in the *Vormärz* thus involved not just the reacquisition of old Holy Roman imperial territories through the attraction of a newly powerful German state, as seen in the previous chapter, but also their partial germanization in face of an ostensibly superior and more progressive German culture. Such germanization might not rob the natives of their national identities, but fuller assimilation remained a distinct possibility.

Either happenstance, of course, was exactly what Danish or Czech nationalists wanted to avoid with their own cultural revival and national consciousness-raising activities. This left them treading a fine line between absorbing general progressive European (and thereby German) culture and trying to modernize their own languages and cultural apparatus to support the burdens of modernity without losing their own distinct identities in the process. Precisely this "tormenting dilemma" gave Germans their confidence.[29] Conflictual, progress-oriented history inherently had a direction, and that arrow seemed to them to point straight from earlier germanizing and modernizing successes to a future golden with tributary gains for the German cultural watershed.

Contemporaries generally recognized that the days of marauding hordes sweeping across Europe had passed, and that any transformations of national boundaries would more likely occur through the agency of such classic liberal means as intellectual and economic competition among nations. Yet some of the aura of natural necessity, inevitability, and even desirability still clung to their image of violent national conflict and warfare. In the tradition of Hugo Grotius, early nineteenth-century Germans still saw nations as individual entities endowed with personality and will in their own right. As such they roamed the world and history in a state of nature bridled only by the feeble reins of diplomatic intrigue and the law of nations, neither under the complete control of the force of public opinion that alone might ensure equilibrium and peace. Unlike single individuals, these collective entities had never taken refuge in a social contract in order to achieve the legal security provided by an overarching representative government. In such a situation peace could not be counted on, and the potential for war had to be met with internal hardihood. Herein lay part of the strong connection between domestic liberal politics and national might abroad. For as political conflicts within the public sphere helped mold the patriotic citizen willing to take up arms and defend the fatherland in good ancient republican fashion, the need to prepare the sinews of war and occasionally to flex them helped temper the politically active moral fiber of citizens and nation in return. War and conflict, though still to be avoided when possible, were never to be shunned entirely or out of weakness, for they brought benefits as well as costs. Although Hegel expressed the sentiment more strongly and with more uncompromising philosophical rigor, others also feared the effects of too much luxurious and perhaps decadent peace on the moral as well as physical force to be mustered among the citizenry.[30] Such ideas of the productive potential of war and armed preparedness by citizen militias resonated all the more forcefully in conjunction with a belief in the inseparability, indeed inescapability, of conjoined creation and destruction in nature, conjoined conflict and progress in history.

Many, while bowing to the consoling faith that harmony and order would surely emerge from conflict and chaos, would still have preferred to smooth the path of true progress and hasten its peaceful consummation. Yet even they felt compelled to recognize the unfortunate likelihood of national conflict and to think and plan with that probability in mind. Any liberal desires for national greatness and power have to be seen not just as attempts to inflate national pride but also as efforts to ensure national survival in a world where liberty demanded vigilance. The Austrian radical Schuselka, for example, supported his claims that all of Austria must remain in close association with the rest of Germany by asserting that in this current age nonworld powers were surely doomed. The Badenese democrat Struve for his part posited an almost autarkic territorial ideal for the modern state, in which size, strength, and resources crucially served nations in the strenuous activity of keeping pace in the "developmental world-struggle."[31] And Georg Gottfried Gervinus, Struve, and Arndt were but a few of the many liberals and oppositionists who followed Friedrich List in striving for a German economic and political world-power status anchored by the free-floating strength of a large German fleet. From this general desire to form an economically and militarily defensible power in the center of Europe flowed much of the liberal tendency to deem worthy of the status of nationhood only those countries of sufficient size, population, and resources to be able to support that position.[32] It was in this context of a widespread and deep concern for Germany's future national stability within the ever-turbulent currents of history that all of the interconnections between liberalism and nationalism, and internal and external strength, unity, and liberty, ultimately fused together into one great ideological mass.

It might seem strange for a generation of liberals and nationalists, who clung to faith in progress with optimistic ardor, to expend so much mental anguish on establishing national strength when German culture appeared to them to be in the vanguard of humanity's general advance, but to some extent at least they did. One answer to this dilemma follows simply from recognition of the degree to which this age of classic liberalism was an era of Smilesian self-help. Sitting back in relaxed anticipation of the golden apples to fall into one's hand from the Hesperidean tree of progress would never get anything truly worthy accomplished—such accomplishment could stem only from the fruits of one's own labors. Moreover, nothing that was not earned through hard work and struggle was of any real or any moral value anyway. Character and moral fiber had to be strengthened in the hard stoic school of experience, a belief already noted in connection with the ancient republican emphasis on the beneficial effects of militias and wars on citizens and states alike. In national terms autonomy had to be striven for, partly through a chain of self-assertive, self-governing political activity from the local to national levels. The doctrine of self-help at either the individual or national levels eminently suited a people and a time in which progress was seen as limping from a historical battleground. This remains all the truer against the general backdrop of the neoclassical, neohumanist culture of self-formation or *Bildung* with its activist, individualist ideal and its belief in struggle, so characteristic and formative of the generations under examination here.[33]

But just as fundamental as the self-help, self-formation ethic in explaining the contemporary sense of uncertainty that sometimes grayed an otherwise roseate vision of Germany's dawning future is the fact that for these Germans of the educated elite, progress by no means proceeded with unswerving Condorcean linearity. Immersed in the classics as they were, early nineteenth-century Germans had by no means fully shaken off ancient Polybian and Platonic schemes of cyclical history. Time's arrow consequently resembled more the graph of an ever-looping, upward-tending cycloid than that of a straight line. Though the march of progress would continue unabated, many an individual nation might pass through each of the ages of man, from youth through maturity to senility, along its path. Schiller employed floral imagery to express the idea and likened single states to annuals, Enlightenment itself to a slow-growing perennial plant requiring much long, nurturing care, while for Hegel the World Spirit crept mollusk-like from nation to nation, leaving but dead, empty shells in its wake.[34] Similarly, Pfizer and his future Frankfurt colleague the Freiburg professor Franz Buss admonished that history was not continuous progress, that individual peoples matured and decayed within the general forward trend. Welcker and Struve each constructed elaborate historical theories upon this cyclical-linear fusion, with Welcker tellingly warning that only constant upward striving could stave off the onset of senility in a mature Western European civilization of no-longer-young Germanic heritage.[35] Even the left-wing Heidelberg historian and future deputy Karl Hagen, who explicitly argued that the ancient rise-and-fall cycles of history had been nullified in modern times by the development of a cooperative European civilization among western nations, still could not guarantee a permanently ascending future for any given nation. And on the other end of the scale, while the conservative Catholic classicist Ernst von Lasaulx is usually held up as the most prominent precursor of a Spenglerian cyclical-declinist theory of history, he still maintained a messianic faith in the divine human destiny to come. Yet the Germans might well not be the chosen ones to bring about the millennium. Another more youthful people might step in to fill the void.[36]

German fears that they might serve as mere grist for history's progressive mill surfaced most frequently and sharply amid general expectations of a conflict between "Germandom" and "Slavdom" (Russia above all), a confrontation Germans thought could not and should not be avoided but that carried no guarantee of a happy result. Because national antipathies were often thought to be natural, almost racial qualities, the showdown could not be avoided, and because autocratic Russia seemed to stand in the way of liberal progress, it should not be.[37] Some Germans possessed enough bravado not to worry overmuch about the outcome. Arndt, for instance, agreed with Fallmerayer that the Russians were by no means contemptible foes, but he did not share Fallmerayer's deeper concerns and expressed his firm conviction that as Germans had been their teachers and masters for a hundred and fifty years, "if at some point supremacy between them and us must be fought for with the sword, then with God we will still be their masters."[38] Karl Hagen and Arnold Ruge, though still generally confident, worried that the Pan-Slav movement's appeal to the spirit of "Nationalität" might provide the Russians with the moral force necessary to compensate for the merely physical force available to their despotic government.[39] More dramatically, Pfizer held out the possibility of Germany's "annihilation" at the hands of the Slavic "national enemy," terms showing how such commentators' language regarding the coming conflict sometimes verged on the chiliastic, not to say hysterical. The Austrian exile Schuselka thought Eastern and Southeastern Europe were soon to become "the scene of events of world-wide importance" and urged Germans to prepare for a coming "world struggle" and "historical catastrophe."[40] Even if the Russophobe vision of an apocalyptic struggle between East and West, Russia and Germany, had not yet reached the pitch it would attain during the strained period of the revolution itself, the first piercing notes had already begun to sound with increasing frequency in the years immediately preceding.[41]

In such a world of continuous struggle and potentially disastrous instability the contemporary German hypersensitivity to questions of cultural, political, and military strength, self-reliance, and preparedness begin to seem quite fitting. Yet the haunting shades of Heraclitus and St. John joined hands with those of Grotius, Burke, Kant, Schiller, Adam Müller, and a host of others in contributing to the vehement demands for German cultural and political autonomy. Both through the natural law tradition and through romantic organicism, the act of conceiving of nations as corporate individuals was pregnant with implications for how midcentury Germans thought nations should act if they were to survive in a world populated by other similarly defined entities. This tendency to predicate ideas of national and international politics upon the "moral personality" of nations worked all the more forcefully in the context of the contemporary culture of *Bildung* with its strongly characterized emphasis on self-assertive individualism, autonomy, and moral vocation. Within this complex field of intellectual forces, in which ideas of individuality and community thrummed in constant tension, seeking resolution and release in the harmonization of personal and communal end purposes, notions of personhood and self-assertion at the individual level were all too easily transposed to the national. Nations acquired the status and characteristics of distinct moral personalities, and with them the rights and honor that citizens demanded for themselves. From the perspective of the nation as collective individual, the arena of national conflict and competition took on a whole new dimension.

Romantics have long been credited with thinking of nations as living organisms, but less well appreciated in recent decades is the extent to which those outside the romantic mainstream were able to mesh such concep-

organicist

tions with older natural law traditions of "moral personality" and to endow nations with a national will, a national personality, and a national individuality.[42] Even if it did not assume the same depth and shape as in romantic thought, this organicist thinking, derived partly from Burke but also from Herder and other indigenous figures, spread quite widely through the German cultural community. A liberal such as Dahlmann, with his notion of the state as a "spiritual and bodily whole," sounded much like the romantic Adam Müller with his idea of the state as "the inner connection of all physical and spiritual riches, of a nation's entire internal and external life into a great, energetic, infinitely vibrant and living whole."[43] Even legal theorist Heinrich Ahrens, though operating much more fully within the bounds of the natural law tradition, can still be considered part of the organicist thrust in post-Schelling idealist philosophy, in which the state appeared as a living personality or entity through its "ethical unity" or "ideal will." Conrad Cucumus, yet more faithful to the idea of the social contract as the foundation of law and states, still argued that only the rational constitution itself lent a state the desired organic as opposed to merely mechanistic unity.[44]

Members of the romanticizing school of historical law often tried to combat the perceived mechanistic and republican implications of the natural law doctrine of the state's legal and moral personality. But they were still perfectly at home thinking of nations and states as individuals, and it is surely significant that at least some of that movement's Germanist elements in some ways fused romantic and idealist notions of state individuality and personhood. In an 1837 review, for example, future constitution-drafter Eduard Albrecht provided the impetus for the later-dominant view of the state as an organic and juridical personality, while his colleague Georg Beseler remarked of two other forms of collective personality, "the association and the corporation are just as little a fiction as the state itself is; in the collectivity so organized there resides an organic life, a personality, whose meaning one entirely misunderstands if one simply construes it in contrast to that of an individual man."[45] The collective personality was not the same as the individual type, but it had its own similar existence. In the minds of a broad spectrum of contemporary Germans, ideas of individuality and nationality hovered in close but uneasy association.

Ideas of personhood and nationhood may not have formed exact analogs in early nineteenth-century German political thought, but enough points of contact and mutual influence remained that it becomes necessary to understand notions of individual rights and honor more fully before one can appreciate how these legal and moral constructs functioned in the culture of nationhood. To begin with, the individual human possessed an absolute centrality and worth as the concrete manifestation of the highest universal ordering principle, either reason, divine reason, morality, or Godhead depending on the degree of religious conviction in a given thinker's spiritual makeup. The individual so described was endowed with the moral vocation to make free and independent judgments and to act accordingly, with the sum total of such autonomous decisions merging in the course of time to fulfill the progressive moral promise of the human race's overarching vocation.

Crucial here was the insistence on personal autonomy as recognition of the infinitely human values of reason and morality. This insistence formed the basis of the entire liberal-democratic program of individual rights and liberties. The right to life, to property, and to freedom of action so long as it did not infringe on that same freedom in others all followed as essential to the doctrine of legal and moral personality and autonomy. Although nearly always overlooked in accounts of liberal political and social theory, the right to externally recognized honor also figured centrally there. So crucial was this notion of honor as a right that at times it was almost identical to the notion of "right" itself. The necessity of fulfilling one's individual moral calling if humanity were to achieve its own set the requirement that one be able to decide and to act on one's own volition and without unnecessary hindrance from other wills or from external authority. And since liberals fervently believed progress would come, that the human vocation would be fulfilled, that God had not granted humans the qualities of reason and morality only to see them go unused and their dictates unrealized, they took heart that the essential human liberties, rights, and respect would eventually emerge into the halcyon glow of the rule of law or, as they called it, the *Rechtsstaat*.[46]

Although many in the natural law tradition set out the above scheme in more or less its full complexity, with stronger or weaker emphasis on the necessity of juridically recognized honor, the influential liberal legal and political theorists Paul Pfizer and Carl Welcker did so most expansively. Pfizer's 1842 *Thoughts on Law, State, and Church,* for instance, provided perhaps this legal theory's completest single statement. Pfizer argued there that although one could define several distinct rights, including life, liberty, property, and honor, there was really only one human right: "the objective validity or external respect and recognition of his inner spiritual, as of his external physical free-acting will." The claim to such validity, he

Pfizer: human right
= {HONOR}

Welcker: Diminution
of honor ⟶
infringe on rights

continued, attached to "all those beings, but only to those, who have a moral vocation and must fulfill it—because whoever *should,* must also be able to *do,* for should and cannot is a contradiction." Prominent here were both the centrality of the individual human moral vocation and the absolute necessity for its social and political recognition if it were ever to be realized. And as Pfizer made clear at a later point, recognition of the individual's rational-moral capacity basically served as the definition of honor—any questioning of that honor questioned one's essentially human status, and hence represented a deprivation of rights and the ability to act freely.[47] In important respects honor was the fundamental human right.

Welcker stated the central role of honor even more emphatically: "For since all right rests upon self- and reciprocal respect for the moral, juridical personalities, the possibility of all other rights depends upon that of juridical honor." In Welcker's view any diminution of honor was an infringement on rights, and vice versa, as he remarked in arguing the necessity for citizen honor in resisting despotic rule: "to the extent that honor is legally annihilated, the law and its sacredness must also cease. And equally, every intentional, illegal contempt for or injury of a person's rights, as the indispensable consequence of recognition and respect for his personal dignity, must also be an injury to his honor."[48] For Welcker as for Pfizer, the individual personality required recognized respect and rights-based autonomy in order to perform its allotted role in the moral development of mankind.

Although Pfizer and Welcker formulated the scheme more completely and with more attention to the word and concept "honor" than most other future Frankfurt representatives, enough of the Assembly's other political and legal theorists operated with similar ideas to establish it as a widespread trend.[49] Without using the term honor, the moderate natural law professor Cucumus opened his textbook on Bavarian public law with a concise statement of the dependence of a realizable moral vocation on its political recognition, while the more liberal Ahrens, one of the foremost exponents of the natural law tradition in the 1840s, defined a "right of personality" that provided for the recognition, maintenance, and development of personality in all its many facets, including the right to respect of one's "*dignity* and *honor*" as a rational and moral creature.[50] Ahrens also put great stress on the necessity for autonomous decision-making if there were to be any true progress, a point of view shared by virtually any liberal deserving of the name. This included the disciple of the school of historical law Georg Beseler, who favored "people's law" over "jurist's law" precisely because he rejected the paternalist view of government as a sort of guardianship for its subjects. Beseler even echoed Pfizer, Welcker, and Ahrens in declaring that "the feeling of honor and liberty . . . will only be preserved and nourished through an autonomous rights status in public life."[51]

Given that most historical law practitioners purposely avoided the sort of sweeping theoretical and programmatic statements found in the rationalist natural law tradition, Beseler's observation becomes all the more precious as an indication that such views of essential human rights and honor penetrated the educated German milieu quite deeply, even beyond the natural law jurists. In this context too the formative educational role of the culture of *Bildung* for observers from across the cultural and political spectrum has probably been underestimated. The conceptual framework of the culture of *Bildung,* with its individualist ethic of autonomous development through social recognition and intersubjective exchange, clearly also played a large part in shaping the educated German culture of nationhood in the same period. In this case deep commitment to the values of personal *Bildung* and honor upheld aspects of an older tradition of rights-based liberalism even among those in whom one would not expect to find it. Such commitment also held implications for conceptions of nationhood.[52]

Before applying this discussion of individual autonomy and honor to the national level, it has first to be examined in the context of the ongoing controversy surrounding conceptions of honor and the place of duels in nineteenth-century German society. The standard picture pits the late eighteenth-century bourgeoisie against the nobility, with the middle-class literati attempting to eradicate or tame the feudal anachronism of aristocratic corporate honor and dueling by democratizing and internalizing it. Such figures as Wolff, Lessing, Schiller, and Kant, the story goes, redefined honor to mean not prestige, reputation, and external recognition of moral worth but rather self-recognition of one's own moral value—aristocratic honor became bourgeois virtue. A recent upsurge of interest in honor and dueling during the Wilhelmine period has focused on the alleged moral collapse and "feudalization" of middle-class Germans in the face of successful Bismarckian unification, a shift that led the bourgeoisie to abandon their efforts to stamp out corporate honor and instead adopt much of the old code in order to establish themselves as "men of honor" or *satisfaktionsfähig* in the eyes of elites and fellow citizens. One such study by Ute Frevert, however, has suggested that the standard portrayal has been overdrawn, and that in fact the mingling of middle- and upper-class notions of honor and of the moral value of dueling began much earlier, certainly by the early part of the nineteenth century.[53] Settling the question is obviously important in the present investigation, for it matters a great deal what exactly someone meant by individual honor when he invoked the ideal of national honor. Did the predominantly bourgeois liberals of the National Assembly feel the need only for the internal, shopkeeper's honor of virtue and good faith, or did they require external recognition of their rights, autonomy, and infinite moral worth to the extent that they were ready to step to the line and defend their claims with blood whenever and wherever someone seemed to have impugned that state of personhood?

A survey of delegates' pre-1848 writings suggests that Frevert remains truer to the nuances of the debate, and that in fact many liberals and democrats believed it was unworthy and indeed unmanly not to be ready to defend one's rights and honor. In some respects, of course, the older picture still holds good—the opposition certainly wanted to demolish established notions of corporate honor, and in particular the exclusivity and inequality of institutionalized military and caste honor. Relatively conservative thinkers such as Stahl, Hegel, and the future deputy General Joseph von Radowitz (the latter not unnaturally) could defend some version of estates-based honor, but most of the figures examined here rejected it. Rather than eradicate or utterly redefine the idea of honor and duels, however, they typically preferred to extend its sphere of applicability to the politically active classes, that is, to those believed to be economically and morally independent already and hence of equal worth to the old elites.[54]

It has often been noted, for example, that as part of their plans to reform university life the post-1815 nationalist student fraternities hoped to do away with the repugnant institution of student saber duels. Actually, though, only a minority in the movement wanted to end duels as such. What Arndt, Jahn, and the *Burschenschafter* really hoped to do was to regulate duels in such a way that only true affairs of honor, insult, and injury resulted in armed conflict.[55] As part of his emphasis on the connection between rights and honor, Welcker put in a strong plea for duels as a means to stave off materialism and despotism by stiffening a manly, courageous sense of personal honor, an honor that was neither purely internal nor external but rather a combination. Moreover, Welcker thought that heightening the level of public honor would help cement a sense of liberty and patriotism, hence his contention that "Concern for the preservation and promotion of honor and of a sense of honor . . . is perhaps the most important task of all politics today."[56] For a generation of politicians, publicists, officials, and scholars socialized to a large extent within the universities, student fraternities, and elite-filled government bureaucracies, it should really come as no surprise to discover how large a measure of intoxicating older ideas of honor they had imbibed, an attitude all the easier to adopt in light of the Roman, German, and natural law traditions, which themselves placed such emphasis on juridical personal honor as the key to rights and freedom. And less easy to demonstrate but perhaps most important, the idea of personal honor and its concomitant moral autonomy seemed to promise powerful props to establishing that Schillerian "totality of character" so central to the individualist culture of self-formation.[57] Although many liberals abhorred duels, and some repudiated the cult of honor that justified them, most remained strongly committed to an honor of inner self-worth that commanded and demanded external respect.

From this more nuanced image of the place of personhood and personal honor within educated early nineteenth-century German views of the world flow important consequences for the even less well-explored concept of national honor. Very little has been written about it, and with the exception of Geoffrey Best's fine lecture series what little there is has been somewhat cursory. Best quite justifiably emphasizes the contribution made to the idea of national honor by the military caste, whose notions of personal honor and dynastic service were basically democratized and transferred to the nation itself as the bearer of honor. Such a move could lead, as in the Jacobin case, to a focus on honor as glory and conquest, suitably transformed into a national liberating or civilizing mission.[58] This notion of national honor as prestige, adopted and adapted from either the dynastic concern with "reputation" or the aristocratic-military thirst for glory, has exhausted historiographical interest in the subject. Enough to know that national honor was often employed in bellicose outbursts to justify warfare against one's neighbors, that it was inherently "bad"—little else has seemed needed to be said.[59]

Yet as set out above, honor meant much more to these thinkers and politicians than either glory or virtue, and since the concepts of honor and autonomy assumed such a central position within liberal political theory and culture, they must have resonated a great deal more powerfully and complexly with ideas of nationality than older portrayals allow. Across wide bands of political and legal opinion, after all, the very theory of public law, the law of states and nations, rested fundamentally on deep analogies between nations and individuals. Much of this intertwining has already been touched on in other contexts: the nation as collective moral and juridical personality, with its own moral vocation mediating between those of individuals and that of humanity as a whole, and with its own rights and duties, its need for liberty, autonomy, and honor. Though not all theorists established all the connections between the individual and national levels of personhood, and though some such as Beseler or Stahl attempted to limit the extent of such analogical thinking, enough firm statements remain to demonstrate that such thought processes did go on and did have far-reaching ramifications. Hegel, for example, spelled out the rights-honor connection when he deemed recognition of a state by others the "first, absolute right," and he believed that "autonomy" or "external sovereignty" took pride of place as "a nation's first freedom and highest honor." The anti-Hegelian *Burschenschaft* philosopher Jakob Fries similarly highlighted the political link between honor and rights and showed even more clearly than Hegel how such thinking worked at both the individual and national levels. Having just defended the institution of the duel as helping to establish the ideal of personal autonomy and equality in society, he went on to add that the same reasoning applied in the realm of nations. "Preaching peace to others helps no one," Fries declaimed, "but to be faithful to one's own honor, and where necessary to render opposition unto death against any overbold attacker, will elevate our own power even through bloody wounds and will soon allow us to live in the inner tranquillity of our own rights."[60] The connection between rights and honor was not just a chance linguistic juxtaposition but rather revealed deep-seated beliefs about the harsh realities of existence, for individuals and for nations.

Future Assembly delegates too seem generally to have acknowledged the stark necessity of honorably defending the rights of the nation as a collective person. Pfizer flourished the banner of national honor in its sense of prestige by joining it with "greatness and power," but he also stressed that it involved the "recognition of national personality" and asked the probing rhetorical question, "So long as honor, the prerequisite of all rights, is lacking, can the German nation thusly elevate itself to the peak of its spiritual and moral vocation?" The mixture of bourgeois and aristocratic notions of honor emerges clearly here, as does the role of the connection between rights and honor at the level of persons and of nations (conceived as collective persons) within the culture of *Bildung* and the culture of nationhood.

Welcker for his part spelled out the implications of the link between rights and honor for the politics of nationhood even more forcefully when he opined that wars for honor were just, certainly more so than wars fought over material concerns. "But if a people and its government allow their honor to be injured and themselves to be insulted without penalty, if they allow their respect and position of dignity to be stolen from them," Welcker argued, "then soon, despised at home and abroad, they will have lost the strongest protection and the noblest force for worthy steadfastness and courageous defense."[61] In a modification of ancient republican thinking, Pfizer and Welcker had each remarked elsewhere on the reciprocal relationship between personal and national honor, with personal honor supporting patriotic strength and courageous willingness to defend the fatherland, while the latter's well-deserved position of dignity among its fellow nations inspired both public and private honor. Georg Beseler once again illustrates the potential spread of such attitudes, coming as he did from northern Germany and from the Savignian school of historical law rather than from the more natural-law based form of liberalism in southwest Germany. For Beseler also stressed the reciprocal need for personal and national honor, as when he complained of how Germany's paternalist governments and political fragmentation had ensured that "the otherwise so noble and proud German nation loses immeasurably from its firm posture and self-confidence and could almost become a laughing stock abroad."[62] Germany's fragmentation had inhibited its ability to assert itself internationally or achieve a proud national identity (hence the need for national unification), while the paternalistic dynastic governments had prevented the growth of strong autonomous citizens in a dialectical public sphere (hence the need for liberal reform).

Thus did early nineteenth-century Germans ultimately translate their interwoven ideals of personal autonomy, liberty, self-reliance, justice, and honor from the individual to the national, and from the domestic to the international planes. They were consequently bound to approach matters of national rights, honor, and self-assertion with a certain swaggering oversensitivity, all the more so since both as predominantly middle-class arrivistes and as members of a nation with a similarly new and shaky claim to equal status they were only too aware of the gap between their assertions and their probable reception among the older, established classes and nation-states.[63] Though not without some savor of thirst for glory, the contribution of national honor to national conflict owed more to a deep-seated belief in the necessity for defending autonomous rights and personhood in a confrontationally historicist world where these qualities seemed ever-threatened, even to the point of extinction. The reciprocal interrelationships among honor, rights, and autonomy within the liberal and nationalist ideologies were at once theoretically central and rife with implications for political practice, a fact that makes it all the stranger that these connections have never been emphasized or even really pointed out until now.

In all of the preceding discussion theoretical constructs of collective personality have been applied more or less indiscriminately to both the terms "nation" and "state," and of course a reasonable objection to this procedure would be to note that these are hardly the same things.[64] How could a German nation represented only by the Confederation, which was merely an association of sovereign states and not truly sovereign in its own right, qualify for the rights, autonomy, and honor assigned to juridical personalities and corporations in legal theory? In the context of a cultural-political typology of nations and nationalisms such a move would be all the more questionable, yet insofar as one of the main threads running through this survey has been a critique of this typology, placing the issue in that context actually holds the key to explaining why the question never would have seemed problematic in mid-nineteenth-century Germany. Even Hans Kohn remarks on the fact that the romantics did not distinguish clearly or consistently between state and nation, and given the contention set forth here that notions of race, culture, and politics, and of genealogical, cultural, and political borders overlapped in many respects, one can only agree with Kohn's observation.[65] Moreover, with the possible exceptions of Austria, Prussia, and Bavaria, and with all due regard for the strength of *Vormärz* liberals' particularist loyalties, none of the German sovereign states bore the same emotional and rhetorical weight as did the German nation as a whole. Even without a state the "deutsche Nation" had honor, and it had rights, as the examples discussed above attest.

But most critically of all, the vast majority of future delegates felt intensely the residual discrepancy between nation and state, with the consequent inability to settle the legal and moral qualities of the latter upon the former. They felt it so deeply that it more than any other single reason explains why they demanded that the German nation unite and acquire sovereign statehood. Other goals of a modernizing nationalism might be accomplished by other means, but if reading clubs and customs unions could raise national consciousness and bolster the nation's economic position, neither could redress the lack of German sovereignty and prestige. National honor did not simply mean glory and reputation to these men, yet neither could a purely internal pride in their nation's virtues and achievements ever replace the external recognition and respect they thought due it. They openly desired power and a strong, worthy position among the nations of the world, yet they longed for it not just as a means of personal and national gratification but also as a way to ensure that Germany's voice would be heard, that it would have the nation-state status that alone allowed a proper self-assertion of its national rights, rights expressed very often in the language of honor. If the German nation could not make good its claims to statehood and recognition by foreign powers, then not only would it remain at the mercy of foreign and dynastic diplomacy, but it would also in essence receive a slap in the face, a denial of its collective personhood with the concomitant denial of its moral status and vocation. The nation would thereby lose the mutually reinforcing benefits of citizen and national honor, of strong liberal institutions and a strong international presence. In the eyes of many nationally minded midcentury Germans, failure to assert one's claim to full nation-state rank entailed the destruction of all hopes of gradual, conflictual historical progress stimulated by the culture of self-formation in which they matured.[66]

As participants in the culture of nationhood and national honor, nearly all who found their way to Frankfurt in 1848 shared the firm conviction that they must officially make a state of a German nation already culturally and politically bound in their minds. As Arndt observed, there might be some cultural advantages to political fragmentation, but the "first commandment" of national existence was to defend oneself and to fend off insult, hence the need for unity, above all in military matters. The feelings of an economic liberal such as Friedrich von Raumer, who placed so much importance on the German Customs Union and the trade treaties resulting from it because Germany finally appeared there as a recognized "great power in the commercial world," also have to be seen in this context of national rights and national honor, and not just of national interests.[67] And bringing the economic and military aspects of the issue together, perhaps no one expressed the German feeling of dishonorable impotence more strongly than the Swabian-bred Hamburg historian Christian Wurm in his lecture at the 1847 Germanist Conference in Lübeck, "The National Element in the History of the German Hansa." There, amid the former glory of the great Hanseatic town, Wurm brought the historical trope of national degradation into the present and declared, "I believe that every German must feel it as a humiliation without example in history that such a great nation does not know how to make good its claims to unity abroad, that the puniest state can subject it to any insult, and it has no weapons with which to meet it."[68] In this period and among these men, notions of national honor and of nationhood were so closely intertwined as to be inextricable.

Having expended most of the chapter in setting out the intellectual context to conceptions of nationality and of national conflicts, autonomy, and honor within the framework of dialectical historicism, the question still remains of what all this implied for the political choices to be made during the 1848 Revolution itself. How much, for instance, did ideas of national honor and of natural national antipathies resonate within the delegates' conflictual progressivist historical consciousness to predetermine the many nationality struggles that erupted during the revolution? Enough has certainly already been said to make it plain why deputies expected national conflicts, were ready to meet them with belligerent words and force, and even to welcome them to some extent. Their understanding of history taught them that conflict was both inevitable and necessary. Their belief in the significance of national and cultural differences included the notion that certain national groups were basically destined, by natural or by political constitution, to fight one another for cultural and political hegemony, an idea that played out particularly strongly in the context of Slavic-Germanic ethnographic antipathies and of Russo-German, autocracy-democracy dichotomies. And, finally, their conception of the law of nations, in which nations as collective individuals asserted their national rights and honor within the loose framework of an international system little different from a Hobbesian state of nature, further heightened the likelihood of the sort of nationality conflicts witnessed in 1848.

At the same time, however, prerevolutionary ideals of international liberal and democratic fraternity against the dynastic threat and in the interests of the general progress of humanity, ideals that provided the basis for faith in a "Springtime of the Peoples" in March of 1848, cannot be dismissed as wholly lacking, certainly not among the democrats nor even among the moderates. With their plans for a European "Congress of Nations," radicals such as Ruge, Struve, and Julius Fröbel certainly reached farther toward a Kantian "eternal peace" than most, but liberals such as Droysen and Sylvester Jordan also believed in the potential for a Mazzinian or Herderian harmony among nations and national interests once they were reorganized along nationality lines and liberated from destabilizing dynastic diplomacy.[69] Even Pfizer, convinced of the inevitability and desirability of national conflict and resistant to the idea of a world government, still held out hope for eventual peace through the agency of his prophesied "world church." The liberal theorist Ahrens, with his romantic conviction that diversity drives development and that each people has its own innately valuable individual personality and calling, predicted a coming era of a "universal balance of power" in which all nations would strive in their own unique ways to achieve a common end.[70] The key to most such thinking lay in the simple fact that the moral vocation of nations as of individuals served ultimately to advance the moral vocation of humankind, that in fact they received their true moral worth only through the larger, more general end purpose of the universal or divine plan.[71] Although more than enough intellectual fire lay banked to ignite a revolutionary conflagration, the *Humanität* ideal of Herder, Schiller, and the Humboldts certainly lived on in the minds of most educated Germans of the generation of 1848.

But these are questions best followed up in the course of tracing the continuities and transformations of prerevolutionary theories amid the practice of the revolution itself. The goal of this chapter and the one preceding chiefly involved reconstructing a portrait of mid-nineteenth-century German beliefs about what it meant to be a nation from the multiply related perspectives of ideas of language, culture, race, liberal politics, legal theory, historical consciousness, and honor. Two contentions stand out for their centrality and explanatory power. First, as shown in the previous chapter, the now-traditional ethnic versus civic typology of nationalism is inappropriate when applied to the German case in this time period. Even for the Arndts and Jahns of the "national awakening" era who usually draw all the historiographical attention, but above all for the dozens of other early nationalists examined here, cultural and political boundaries overlapped and nearly melded under the rubric of common consciousness. Simultaneously, ideas of ostensibly cultural nationhood inherently intermingled with and helped shape liberal political theories, which in turn helped mold the definitions of nationality. In liberal and nationalist doctrine the ancient republican political process buttressed both the common consciousness of national identity and the patriotic citizen strength that upheld a nation's internal liberties and external autonomy. In the conflict-ridden if progressive world that future deputies saw through dialectically historicist lenses, national identity and national honor were equally fundamental aspects of nationality.

The second important contention set forth in these two chapters, that from which nearly all the other significant points directly or indirectly follow, highlights the influence of a common set of ideas provided by the general educational background of a neohumanist, classicizing culture of self-formation, a culture and an influence that helped define an early nineteenth-century German culture of nationhood. It was a "culture of nationhood" rather than simply a nationalist ideology in part because nationality as a concept was becoming such a fundamental category of thought (even unconsciously so) in German intellectual life of this period. As such, the facets of nationhood discussed above impinged crucially on almost all other components of the broader culture in which the concept of the nation lay embedded, from art and literature to economics and science.

At the same time, the various prevalent conceptions of nationhood cannot be fully grasped without comprehending those elements of the broader contextual culture that shaped them in turn, above all the culture of *Bildung.* Against this background German romanticism, idealism, and liberalism appear much less disparate than normally depicted, each being rooted in the thought of Schiller, Herder, Wilhelm von Humboldt, and other icons of the Weimar-Jena classical period. Such a culture of nationhood consequently could and did spread quite widely in the intellectual and educational milieu of the generation of 1848. Belief in the importance of individuality and autonomy, of diversity in tension with unity, of history as the development of opposing forces toward a more harmonious reconciliation of such conflict: all received a special imprint and force within this context. Even the multivalent cultural, political, religious, and racial conceptions of nationhood examined in the previous chapter owed more than a little to early and continuing exposure to classical sources, as did the fundamental notions of historical flux and the transience of nations. That this culture of nationhood was not monolithic, and that it was defined principally at this deeper structural level rather than at the more self-reflective surface level of ideology, emerges most clearly in the context of attempts to construct a national past, where despite certain basic patterns the lasting impression remains one of competitive diversity in contemporary visions of the German nation. Individualist and neoclassicist, historicist and dialectical, within the deep-seated parameters of the German culture of nationhood culture and polity combined to form the always-striving whole that was the nation.

II | Nationhood and Revolution in Germany, 1848–1849

"The first shot fell in the mountains," wrote the radical poet Ferdinand Freiligrath, referring to the Swiss origins of the continent-wide revolutionary unrest in the winter and spring of 1848. Although sparked from abroad and with distinct local causes and concerns beneath each of the various revolutionary eruptions across Central Europe, it remains the case that the 1848 Revolution in Germany was just that—a German revolution. Each of the separate movements in Baden, Hesse, Prussia, Austria, and elsewhere shared goals with the others, goals set forth in the so-called "March demands." At the state level this reformist agenda included such items as juries, a free press, and citizen militias. Yet as the discussion in Part One has shown, the leaders of the various opposition movements also shared some crucial assumptions about nationhood generally and Germanness in particular. Not surprisingly then, all the revolutionary outbreaks also witnessed demands for a national parliament that would see to the institution of a truly national government to replace the seemingly decrepit apparatus of the German Confederation. With this common background, and with its ability to draw on the institutional network of the "organized nationalist movement" that had become increasingly dense and popular in the course of the 1840s, it did not take long for the national movement to mobilize. Already by March 5, a group of opposition notables had gathered at Heidelberg to call for just such a constitutional convention.[1]

Deciding to construct a national state and actually doing so, however, were entirely different matters. If there had been a significant degree of contestation over the construction of national identity within the common culture of nationhood before 1848, the balance shifted much more forcefully toward contentiousness during the revolution itself. Hard choices had to be made about which potentialities latent within that culture of nationhood were to be realized as the political stakes grew clearer and higher for those with differing visions of the national future. Examining how the cultural parameters of nationhood described in Part One continued to shape thinking as they were implemented during the revolution will form the basis of discussion here in Part Two. Attention will also be paid to the question of how far those conceptual boundaries were themselves challenged in the course of the revolution. Yet as will become clear in the chapters that follow, to a surprising degree deputies did remain within those bounds and express common attitudes toward the experience of nationhood. The signs of later divisions, though present, were fainter than expected.

In addition to contestation among those assembled in Frankfurt, the architects of national unity encountered even greater obstacles when they confronted their problematic relationships with other national groups both inside and outside the various proposed borders of the new Germany. Already by April nationality conflicts had realized the potential for violence to three of the four points of the compass. The Prussian army was engaged in suppressing armed Polish units in the Prussian Grand Duchy of Poznania after violence had broken out between that province's German and Polish inhabitants, while to the north Prussia had intervened to defend the German-led Provisional Government in the Danish Duchy of Schleswig against the forces of the Danish king. Similarly, the revolution in northern Italy had become a war of liberation against the Austrian overlords, and while in the federal parts of the Habsburg Empire civil war had thus far been avoided, relations between Germans and Czechs in Prague had noticeably deteriorated from the spirit of fraternity that initially greeted the fall of Metternich. This political context of ongoing nationality conflict and attempts at conflict resolution must always be kept in mind in exploring the various nationality-related Assembly debates of 1848.

The four chapters of Part Two carry out a thematic analysis of these nationality-related debates, with the German culture of nationhood set out in Part One as their basic point of reference. Chapters 3 and 4 each focus on efforts to define Germany in what might be called the domestic realm, where deputies confronted problems relating to groups within the proposed borders who were at least potentially distinct from their Christian, German-speaking counterparts. Chapter 3 deals with the question of civil and political rights for the German Jewish minority, a group that was not self-evidently a purely religious entity. The chapter delves once again into the prerevolutionary era to probe future deputies' attitudes toward this issue before moving on to analyze the discussions in Frankfurt that led to the near-unanimous grant of full civic and political equality to German Jews. Chapter 4 in turn considers the equally well-supported extension of equal rights to non-German-speaking populations, but it also deals with the distinct question of linguistic and cultural rights of autonomy for these same groups. Taken together, these two chapters show that the fusion of cultural and political conceptions of nationhood, in tandem with the equally fundamental belief in progressive dialectical historical change, continued to guide deputies' thinking during the revolution itself and ensured a more inclusive German national identity, one still open to those who in certain respects were different or potentially foreign. At the same time, though, these chapters unveil the dangerous expectations of partial cultural assimilation that went along with the emphasis on the conflictual nature of historical change and the mixed political-cultural basis of national identity in the culture of nationhood.

Chapters 5 and 6 then move from such internal constitutional matters to consider the ways in which the Frankfurt parliamentarians attempted to define their nation externally. Chapter 5 confronts the very basic but ultimately insoluble question of where to draw the new Germany's boundaries. In particular it examines the extensive discussion surrounding three of the most vexing border disputes, that in the mixed Danish-German Duchy of Schleswig, that concerning the mixed Polish-German Grand Duchy of Poznania, and finally that dealing with the central question of the whole revolution: would all, part, or none of the Habsburg monarchy unite with the new German national state? The political alliances and the political stakes involved in these debates provoked a great deal of heat and a multiplicity of proposed borders, but even in this case the parameters of the prerevolutionary German culture of nationhood suffered surprisingly little derangement amid the contending political, religious, and regional factions. Chapter 6 then addresses the issue of how deputies thought the German nation thus defined should interact with other peoples. The discourse of national honor and autonomy, as well as the acute and aggressive fears of almost inevitable violence, feature prominently here, as does the associated tendency to think in terms of larger transnational ethnic groupings that themselves seemed almost destined to catastrophic collision as history took its relentless course. Particularly in these chapters, it becomes apparent how some of the very elements of the culture of nationhood that

made for a more open, liberal, and tolerant national identity could also un-
fold a more aggressive or even hysterical side. For the latter tendencies to
gain the upper hand and result in exclusionary nationalist ideologies and
policies of forced germanization, however, the deepest assumptions of the
contextual culture of nationhood had to change. Only in the later part of
the nineteenth century, therefore, would they slowly yield to newer forms
and conceptions of radical mass nationalism and *völkisch* national identity.

3 | The German Nation and the German Jews

Products of the *Vormärz* culture of nationhood described in Part One, the politicians, publicists, and scholars of the Frankfurt Parliament in the spring of 1848 took up the many nationality-related issues that had to be settled before they could complete their task of constructing a German national state. The debates to be examined in the present chapter, those surrounding the legal and political status of German Jews within the new nation, form a particularly appropriate point of entry into the broader investigation of the Assembly's handling of such matters, for with the Jews delegates confronted a population seeming to hover between the status of religious group and nationality.

The literature on both anti-Semitism and German liberalism reflects this sense of uncertainty. An older view presented the German liberals of this period as doctrinaire proponents of rights-based natural-law religious freedom, in which German Jews were as deserving of equality before the law as anyone else. More recent works by authors such as Paul Rose and Reinhard Rürup, on the other hand, have pointed to liberal and democratic ambivalence in applying such principles to a people considered somehow dangerously foreign. In these revisionist studies what contemporaries termed the "Jewish Question" appears as a matter of nationality-related, even protoracialist views of Jewish national character, and not simply as one of religious difference. Sharing the prevailing anti-Jewish religious and socioeconomic stereotypes, even doctrinaire liberals such as Carl von Rotteck could oppose emancipation at least until Jews had first shed their undesirable character traits. Even when liberals did accept the necessity of establishing legal and political equality between Jewish and Christian Germans, they allegedly did so only from a desire to accelerate the assimilation, partial or total, of the foreign element. In either case a negative image of Jews motivated the process, and in these studies that is what counts.[1]

Most such revisionist studies of opinions on Jewish emancipation focus on the general roots of anti-Semitic thinking, as represented either by a few indubitably anti-Semitic voices or by a fairly narrow selection of liberals. The present investigation of a geographically and politically broad sample of prominent *Vormärz* oppositionists in many ways provides the first wide-ranging treatment of liberal views on the Jewish Question.[2] This research has produced four main findings. First, the Frankfurt deputies applied their conceptually mixed ideas of nationality to define the German nation in an open and tolerant fashion that left German Jews an integral part of that nation. As members of a constitutionally recognized religious denomination, German Jews were unconditionally entitled to all the rights of the German citizen, an attitude reflected in the near-unanimous Assembly debates and votes establishing full civic and political equality in August 1848.

Nevertheless, investigation of the future deputies' prerevolutionary utterances reveals the significant presence of nearly all elements of the anti-Jewish stereotype highlighted in revisionist scholarship, particularly among religious conservatives but also among liberals who supported emancipation in Frankfurt. A close reading of the Assembly proceedings also discloses perceptible echoes of such pejorative views, and not only in the shrill jeremiad of the lone-wolf anti-Semite Moritz Mohl. This second main finding lends some weight to the arguments of historians such as Rürup and Rose who treat liberal desires for assimilation of the foreign Jewish element as the root of their support for emancipation, with the latter merely the means for the former.

Third, then, in keeping with their faith in history as a dialectically progressive process, deputies did harbor expectations of Jewish assimilation. They did not, however, typically view this assimilation as radical. Jewish religion and identity would remain intact so long as their integrity could be maintained within the liberal but culturally normed German public sphere, a notion of acculturation—to distinguish it from full assimilation—not so different from that of the reformist German-Jewish Haskala movement.[3] Moreover, against the revisionist view it must be stressed that assimilation in the sense of shedding bad character traits no longer appeared as a precondition for emancipation in constitutional doctrine or political rhetoric, whatever silent hopes deputies might have had. The Forty-Eighters can even be seen as doctrinaire liberals on this point, so long as it is understood what that doctrine truly prescribed.

One way to resolve this seeming contradiction between liberal ambivalence and emancipatory tolerance toward German Jews is to take into account the element of time (the fourth main conclusion). During the 1830s and 1840s, members of the nationalist opposition increasingly opted for doctrinaire solutions to the Jewish Question as a religious issue, and they grew ever less receptive to anti-Jewish rhetoric, even when invoked in the cause of emancipation. From this perspective the Frankfurt National Assembly of 1848 appears as the culmination of a trend, with Jewish civil equality accepted as a matter of course and anti-Jewish rhetoric shunned there as inappropriate in parliamentary discourse. As a result of the mixing of cultural and political ideas of nationality in mid-nineteenth-century German thought, liberal nationalists did not have to insist on either total exclusion or total absorption of a culturally distinct population in order to achieve a comfortable and workable degree of national and political unity. German Christians and German Jews could still be Germans together.

Historians of early nineteenth-century anti-Semitism have rightly pointed to the significance and extent of anti-Jewish ideas both old and new at that period, ideas that made such a transreligious fraternal ideal of nationality seem only too problematic to many Germans at the time. They emphasize, for example, the persistence of older religious motives for anti-Jewish feelings in an ostensibly more secular age. Many elements of the modern anti-Jewish worldview were in fact holdovers from the Christian anti-Judaic stereotype of the sort rendered canonical by the late seventeenth-century scholar Johann Christian Eisenmenger in his tendentious sourcebook for later defamers of Jews and Judaism, *Judaism Revealed*. That the Talmud constrained Jews to cheat and injure Christians through usury; that Jews were either incapable of taking up noncommercial occupations or unwilling to; that belief in a Messiah who would lead Jews back to rule in Zion prevented them from feeling patriotic attachment to their countries of residence: all these stock derogations could be found in the late medieval Christian tradition of anti-Judaism. Moreover, these archaic notions merged easily into newer organicist and nationalist formulations of the anti-Judaic stereotype in terms of a difference in culture- and descent-based nationality.[4] The post-Kantian nationalist philosopher Jakob Fries, the Berlin historian Friedrich Rühs, the rabid and indubitably racist anti-Semite Hardtwig von Hundt-Radowsky, the Young Hegelian radical Bruno Bauer, and even the doctrinaire liberal Carl von Rotteck, the convert communist Karl Marx, and the sage of Königsberg Immanuel Kant are but some of the most-cited and most famous figures invoked to illustrate the prevalence and invidiousness of most or all of the above elements of anti-Jewish prejudice across a variety of ideological and political perspectives in Germany at this time.

Given this prevalence of anti-Jewish attitudes, revisionist historians also have to be taken seriously when they reject the automatic assumption sometimes made that the western Enlightenment tradition of natural law liberalism must have applied to the Jews. Instead, the Enlightenment rationalist critique of religion, with its anticlerical and antihierarchical tendencies, bore down at least as hard on Judaism as on Christianity and served to perpetuate negative Jewish stereotypes into a new era and into progressive as well as conservative circles.[5] Similarly, the Rousseauian idea of a civil religion binding upon all members of a political community was easily transmuted into pressure for the eradication of Judaism as a divisive element in society, and the more general ideal of cultural and political unity inherent in the Enlightenment concept of "the people" or "the one and indivisible nation" militated against a pluralist tolerance for Jewish difference. In these contexts one could call for the exclusion of the dangerously different Jews from the body politic or one could call for their complete digestion within it. At any rate, according to this view Jews and Judaism were often eyed with the suspicion of immemorial prejudice and were welcomed into the modern German nation upon highly restrictive conditions if at all. Even the originator of the whole program of Jewish emancipation, Christian Wilhelm von Dohm, phrased his proposal for the "civic improvement of the Jews" in such a way as to imply the necessity of bettering not merely the Jews' legal status but their "character" as well.[6]

Yet however true it is that such views spread quite widely within the early nineteenth-century German intellectual community, it is surely significant that, Ernst Moritz Arndt, Turnvater Jahn, and Gabriel Riesser aside, very few Assembly delegates receive coverage in the general literature on anti-Semitism and emancipation. This fact leads to the first important point regarding the national opposition and the Jewish Question, namely, that future Frankfurt representatives participated very little in the pamphleteering war surrounding the *Vormärz* Jewish Question. Many of them certainly staked out positions on the issue, but for the most part they did so in the various provincial diets or in footnotes and digressions within publications devoted to broader subjects. Some future deputies did feel deeply about the matter, going so far as to help organize petitions and parliamentary campaigns, or simply to speak with conviction, even vehemence, when called on to defend their views. For most, however, the Jewish Question did not lie at the center of their concerns. Arguments to the effect that German Jews somehow served as the mythic mirroring "Other" against which German national identity was negatively defined can at best be true for a limited number of anti-Jewish activists, patently much more sensitive to the presence of a "foreign" Jewish element in the German nation than were most of the individuals investigated here.[7] The prerevolutionary opinions of future deputies on the relationship of German Jews to the rest of the German nation can be highly instructive for interpreting educated Germans' general ideas of nationality, but they served more as a weather vane for shifting intellectual winds than as the magnetic north by which nationalists oriented themselves.

With this proviso, let it be stated clearly at the outset that most of the anti-Jewish images and arguments set out above can indeed be found among the future Frankfurt deputies, not just among the few conservatives but among a geographically broad spectrum of liberals and democrats as well. Rotteck was not the only Badenese liberal who opposed freedom and equality for a Jewish community perceived as morally degraded and even harmful. In the so-called Baden Reform Diet of 1831, for example, Rotteck's editorial partner on the *Staats-Lexikon,* Carl Welcker, invoked images of a Jewish theocratic state, of Jewish usury among the Badenese peasants, and of Jewish contempt for Christians as reasons to oppose emancipation, while the more radical Johann von Itzstein informed the Diet that for the Jews, "Money and trade are their idols."[8] In Electoral Hesse Sylvester Jordan applied his doctrinaire liberalism to the issue of religious freedom and spearheaded the charge there for the most thoroughgoing emancipatory legislation of any German state, yet he accepted the notion of Talmudic immorality and believed that emancipation would have beneficial effects in ameliorating such defects in Judaism. From similar liberal premises the moderate Bavarian Conrad Cucumus provided an even sharper indictment of Judaic iniquities, concluding that emancipation could only be piecemeal, on a case-by-case basis in which individual Jews would receive equal citizenship when they showed themselves to have absorbed enough of the more modern and morally uplifting attitudes of the surrounding citizenry.[9]

In Hanover and Prussia Friedrich Dahlmann adumbrated the anti-Jewish stereotype in classroom lectures and in his influential *Politics* of 1835. In keeping with his opposition to French-style natural law liberalism, Dahlmann deployed his derogatory image of Jews in an attempt to settle the emancipation issue in a gradualist quid pro quo arrangement, as a "question of state" rather than of "humanity."[10] The Prussian Young Hegelian social and religious critic Arnold Ruge called Jews "maggots in the cheese of Christianity," while his Württemberg counterpart Friedrich Vischer embraced Hegel's negative depiction of the ancient Hebrews and went even further by associating certain undesirable Semitic character traits with their allegedly distinctive physiognomies.[11]

For his part the Young Austrian poet Count Anton Auersperg invoked the image of Ahasuerus, the eternally, tearlessly wandering Jew, to suggest the enduring nature of Jewish separateness, difference, and hostility. His poem "Five Easters" not surprisingly also put the Jewish-Christian "millennia-sworn war" into its original religious context of deicide, while he and fellow Austrians Franz Schuselka and Karl Möring followed Itzstein and Cucumus in alluding to Jewish Mammon worship.[12] Of such allegations of Jewish avarice, however, the deepest-cutting because most sharply drawn occurred in Heinrich Laube's Young German novel *The Warriors*, with its portrait of the "hawk-nosed" Polish Jew Manasse, a miser whose human sympathies could only be elevated above gold by concern for his own flesh and blood—about anyone else Manasse cared nothing. In a polemic against Giacomo Meyerbeer in 1847, Laube again struck the Jewish greed chord, but he also located the site of Jewish difference in the national or even racial realm when he termed Jews "an oriental nation totally different from us, as they were two thousand years ago."[13] Against such an evidential backdrop, it would be impossible to deny the currency of anti-Jewish stereotypes among midcentury German liberals. The above examples illustrate not only the broad political and geographical dispersion of anti-Jewish discourse but also the diversity of images and arguments attached to it.

The examples above also begin to suggest the range of opinion on the question of Jewish emancipation itself. Emphasis on Jewish foreignness in the socioeconomic, religious, or physical realms by such figures as Cucumus, Dahlmann, Auersperg, and Laube also carried with it intimations of injurious hostility to the host Christian populations, yet these concerns allowed the widest range of solutions. Welcker, Itzstein, and the Badenese opposition at least temporarily opposed emancipation, while for Dahlmann and Cucumus it could only be very gradual, and for Laube, Schuselka, and Sylvester Jordan it had to be as immediate and full as possible. The common denominator, of course, was that Jews were expected to change their characters and become more morally benign by becoming more like Western Europeans.[14]

Both the assumptions of Jewish transmutability and of Jewish bad character can be traced back to Dohm's initial setting of the terms of debate on the Jewish Question in the 1780s, as can the view that it was the Christians who were responsible for the problem in the first place. In the same way, and despite the range of opinion on emancipation, most members of the *Vormärz* national opposition generally agreed with Dohm about the efficacy of some form of emancipation in bringing the desired changes about.[15] The medieval historians Friedrich von Raumer and Gustav Stenzel, Sylvester Jordan, even Auersperg and Laube: all pointed to previous repressive and dishonoring Christian attitudes toward the Jews as the root of Jewish commercial obsession and of their general lack of virtuous probity and humanitarianism. Changes in the Christian ecumene could thus produce changes in the Jewish community. Although some such as Laube may have referred to the disappointing lack of improvement in the Jews over the past two thousand years, neither he nor very many other Frankfurt liberals drew the conclusion that this situation was frozen for all time in a petrified Jewish people. These men were, after all, imbued with a Heraclitean sense of history as the dynamic seat of progress through the resolution of conflictual diversity into harmonious if multiplicitous unity. Hence even those with a strong belief in the magnitude of the problem of Jewish integration into German national life did not despair at its accomplishment. Liberals like the 1848 Hanoverian March Minister Johann Stüve, who cited Tacitus to drive home the point of enduring Jewish incorrigibility, never dominated the oppositional political landscape. Those such as Rotteck and the Badenese who opposed emancipation still made it clear that Jewish acculturation, and thereby Jewish equality, would come in time.[16]

Moreover, this admission from opponents of emancipation in Baden was not simply a weak attempt to salve their liberal consciences at a perceived inconsistency between their adherence to human rights doctrine and their refusal to apply it fully in the Jewish case. Revisionists obviously have good grounds for rejecting the presupposition that rights-based liberalism and religious freedom automatically entailed the granting of equal legal status to German Jews, but the further assumption that liberals must have been inconsistent regarding Jews alone rests on a slightly mistaken notion of German natural law teachings on the matter of free conscience in this period. Religious freedom, even in its most general theoretical formulations, almost never came without conditions—in fact, it came with two. First, and more significantly in limiting Jewish equality, liberals insisted in genuine ancient republican fashion that rights entailed duties. The price of freedom was defense of the polity and its institutions, hence each citizen had to fulfill certain obligations: to pay taxes, to serve in the militia, to involve himself in the political debates of the day. Moreover, to enjoy equality before the law, these burdens had to be borne equally. In terms of religious freedom this all meant that those confessing a religion whose commandments prevented the free and full fulfillment of political duties forfeited the claim to full and equal rights. Paul Pfizer, for example, followed this chain of reasoning to justify the exclusion of Jews from public office, while from a more historicist legal perspective Dahlmann still invoked the correlation between equal rights and equal duties to support his idea of a gradual quid pro quo form of emancipation, in which one could ensure that Jews did not enjoy the benefits of citizenship without also shouldering its burdens. This was just one instance of the general liberal argument for the normative exclusion of certain groups from the rights of full participation, an argument typically applied more rigorously in the case of women and the lower classes than in that of Judaism.[17]

Even more widespread in the contemporary literature on legal and political theory than the insistence on equal rights and equal duties was the Lockean requirement that a religion not involve anything detrimental to the continued existence of the state. In Sylvester Jordan's formulation this second condition meant that for any religion incorporating such subversive elements not even public worship (much less full civic equality) could be tolerated but only its private form. This may sound like such a profound restriction on religious freedom as to render the term meaningless, but such was hardly the case, for Jordan then turned the point around to argue that any religion tolerated to the extent of having its claim to public worship recognized had to be granted equal status with all other religions existing in the state. Moreover, Jordan and others who opened religion's doctrinal realm to juridical and etatist claims restricted the state's involvement to matters affecting the rule of law, typically intending only to keep at bay the specter of the old Münster Anabaptists, a Reformation sect that had preached commonality of women and property. Denial of monotheism could also enter in as justification for branding a religion dangerous, but none of these provisions, of course, hindered the inclusion of Judaism as an equal partner in the modern liberal state.[18]

Still, just such normative stipulations attached to the granting of religious freedom and equality made it easier for liberals to justify the as-similatory drive associated with Dohm-style educative emancipation within their legal theory. If Jews were found wanting in their level of polit-ical culture, then perhaps they could be raised to a higher level that would allow them to participate fully in the life of the nation. The question natu-rally arises in this context of just how much change Jews were expected to undergo before they would be considered equals in this social contract. Laube, for instance, has sometimes been depicted as demanding the eradi-cation of Judaism and Jewish identity, and certain it is that he put the Jew-ish Question in extreme terms in his attack on Meyerbeer of 1847. Ar-guing for the "most radical possible" emancipation, Laube posed the dilemma, "Either we must be barbarians and drive out the Jews to the last man, or we must incorporate them into us." Similarly in his earlier novel *The Warriors,* Laube's mouthpiece Valerius informed his Jewish friend Joel that emancipation would require a sort of death of Judaism. Yet Valerius equated the emancipation of Judaism with its enlightened rational reform through abandoning the "letter of tradition," while in 1847 Laube essen-tially called for giving up Mammonism and obsessive commercial competi-tiveness. He even supplied two examples of what it meant to be a "nation-alized" German Jew: Berthold Auerbach and future Frankfurt deputy Gabriel Riesser. Auerbach maintained his Jewish identity but showed an understanding of Swabian rural life unmatched in German literature, while Riesser served as the most active defender of the Jewish claim to un-conditional equal rights. Although Laube stood near the extreme end of the liberal assimilatory spectrum, even he did not demand or expect the total erasure of Jewish religion or cultural identity.[19]

It is important to realize that for the men of the national opposition, as-similation was not a static ideal but formed part of a dynamic historical process. Assimilation became part of the historical dialectic toward prog-ress in the public sphere, in which broad-based political participation and the enjoyment of rights and freedoms rooted in the citizen's self-respect and honor engendered both national patriotism and the formation of an enlightened public opinion. As Sylvester Jordan expressed the idea, Jews were certainly capable of "improvement," yet "*true* improvement is con-ditional upon *self-respect,* and the latter upon the *legally secured enjoyment of all human rights.*" He went on to argue "that the moral and intellectual cultivation of the Jews everywhere keeps pace with the civil and political treatment they encounter."[20] Most liberals very likely did hope for in-creased Jewish-Christian interaction and integration at both the social and spiritual levels, yet this was to come about not through legal restrictions but through moral force and intellectual persuasion within the free play of the public sphere. Consequently, assimilation would only take place at the level of high culture and the establishment of a common patriotic consciousness of national identity. It would not encompass the entire realm of cultural experience and group or individual identity. Demands sometimes heard even in liberal circles for the end of circumcision or dietary laws, or for the shifting of the Jewish Sabbath to Sunday, do not seem to have been prevalent among those who found their way to Frankfurt in 1848.

Instead, so long as Jews developed enlightened humanitarian sympathies beyond the narrow confines of their own social group, and so long as participation in German print culture and political life ensured that they would apply those sympathies to their fellow citizens and be ready to obey all laws and fulfill all citizen duties shoulder-to-shoulder with other Germans, no further assimilatory demands could reasonably be made of the German Jew. Certainly only a few liberals envisioned the loss of Judaic religion as part of the civil and political integration of formerly separate Jewish communities. However much some might have longed for conversion as part of the fulfillment of Christian revelation, it did not play a role in their political thinking. Among liberals, after all, the only aspect of religious freedom truly recognized universally and unconditionally was pure internal freedom of conscience—the sphere of law never reached into the citizen's head.[21]

The only notable disagreement on this point among future Assembly deputies arose among the Christian, especially Catholic, religious conservatives, who felt that the only way for a Jew to become worthy of equal political and civil rights with Christians was for him to confess his error and accept baptism. Yet significantly, given the historiographical association of new types of anti-Semitism with the anticlerical left, such religiously conservative commentators also employed newer forms of anti-Judaism alongside such older conceptions. They too stressed the intimate connection between Jewish religion and Jewish nationality, with Jews indeed figuring almost as the archetypal nation in their long-maintained purity of national descent and culture. The extent of Jewish financial power as well as their conspiratorial desire and capacity to injure their naive Christian hosts could also attain near-mythic proportions. The religious conservatives' desire to see political legitimacy continue to be based on religion rather than secular concerns, as seen in the ideal of the "Christian state," also played an important role in their assessments of the Jewish Question. This fact helps explain why they were often more willing to listen to arguments for equal rights in the sphere of civil rather than constitutional law. But most important, their strong antipathy to the Judaic religion-nationality ultimately nurtured not just opposition to emancipation but also a pronounced skepticism about the prospects for either eventual assimilation or conversion among a people seen as almost incapable of change.[22]

Such views found adherents in important sectors of religious conservative opinion, above all among militant Catholics. This emphasis on the visibility of anti-Jewish sentiments among Catholics again runs counter to current opinion, which highlights the role of disaffected Protestants in the dissemination of these attitudes. Yet at least among the figures examined here, Catholics seem to have taken the leading part. The Freiburg professor Franz Buss tried to stem the emancipatory tide in Baden in the later 1840s, as did the rector of Giessen, Justus von Linde, in Hesse. In Bavaria elements of the romantic Görres Circle, including the future deputies Ignaz von Döllinger, Georg Phillips, and Ernst von Lasaulx, expressed belief in the religious and national roots of Jewish iniquity and enmity, as did the ideologically related ultramontane church historian Johann Sepp.[23] In Prussia both the Silesian magnate Prince Felix von Lichnowsky and the national-minded reform conservative General Joseph von Radowitz, confidant of King Friedrich Wilhelm IV despite his Catholicism, also opposed emancipation on these grounds. In a speech prepared for the 1847 Prussian United Diet, Radowitz deployed a whole battery of such arguments against Jewish emancipation, including the connection between Jewish religion and nationality, the ideal of the Christian state, and historically based doubts about whether Judaism could ever dissolve in civil society.[24] Across Catholic Germany of the *Vormärz*, then, some of the more militant conservative voices not only opposed emancipation but also interlarded more modern, secular anti-Jewish rhetoric with the older religious forms.

Among Protestants the evangelical Ernst Moritz Arndt also thought that German Jews could only become part of the German nation through an assimilatory process ending in conversion. Although opposed to emancipation, Arndt did interestingly echo Dohm's ideas to the extent that he insisted on "humane" treatment for Germany's Jewish population, a posture that would only accelerate the melding.[25] While often skeptical, for the most part not even the Christian conservatives among the future Assembly delegates denied individual Jews the right or the capacity to join the German nation. Yet by insisting they could not do so as confessing Jews they demanded the highest assimilatory price of all.

As the preceding discussion of delegates' ideas in the prerevolutionary period should have shown, the liberals and democrats of the national opposition did maintain a certain ambivalence regarding the position of German Jews, but this attitude did not involve quite such a slap at liberal theory and values or quite such a strong demand for the end of Jewish difference as has sometimes been argued. An anti-Jewish stereotype stood firmly planted in the early nineteenth-century German liberal worldview; hence if Jacob Katz is correct in singling out its continuity from Eisenmenger to the Richard Wagners and Wilhelm Marrs of the later nineteenth century as the key link between the older and modern anti-Semitic traditions, then perhaps enough has already been said to implicate the early nineteenth-century German liberal movement as a crucial vector of this ultimately fateful image across the emancipatory era.[26] But if liberals can never be wholly exonerated for their role in perpetuating a jaundiced view of Jewish social conditions and a nonpluralist notion of emancipatory freedom, it remains nonetheless true that they formed the only influential group to press for an end to exclusionary and repressive treatment of Jews. In growing numbers and with increasing vehemence, the members of the national opposition took up rhetorical cudgels in defense of Jewish political and civic equal rights and of Jewish character in face of the prevailing defamation. By the early 1840s at the latest, anti-Jewish images and arguments met with an ever chillier reception and were eventually driven almost entirely from the realm of polite political discourse.[27]

This trend first leaps to the eye at the state level of proposals for progressive Jewish legislation. In Electoral Hesse (1833), the Grand Duchy of Hesse (1846), the Prussian Rhineland (1843, 1845), Baden (from 1846), and the entire Kingdom of Prussia (1847), diets petitioned for or passed far-reaching if not always total emancipatory measures, while in the Free City of Hamburg at least the use of anti-Jewish rhetoric was "no longer fashionable," its typically déclassé propagators absent from higher-profile political gatherings.[28]

The growing support for unconditional emancipation in the 1830s and 1840s is also apparent among future Assembly deputies, many of whom played leading roles in the movements for Jewish equality in their home states. Sylvester Jordan carried the banner for Jewish emancipation in the Diet of Electoral Hesse during the constitutional conflict of 1831–1833, while in the Grand Duchy of Hesse the left-liberal lawyer Theodor Reh, who had already argued for equality in citizenship law in 1834, introduced the motion to nullify "all special ordinances against the Jews" into the newly elected liberal diet in 1847.[29] In Hamburg none other than Gabriel Riesser battled for Jewish rights, and among his allies figured the national-ist historian Christian Wurm. The exiled Austrian radical Franz Schuselka sounded the call for full emancipation as part of his attack on the Met-ternichian system, while the prominent Jewish editor Ignaz Kuranda and the Jewish-descended poet Moritz Hartmann helped reinforce emancipa-tionist views among the 1840s Austrian opposition. In Baden the future delegates marching toward emancipation were legion, including by the 1846–1848 Diet: Welcker, Itzstein, Carl Mittermaier, the liberal publish-ing partners Karl Mathy and Friedrich Bassermann, the Protestant pastor Karl Zittel, the liberal Catholic Dean Vinzenz Kuenzer, and the radicals Friedrich Hecker, Lorenz Brentano, Anton Christ, Christian Kapp, and Karl Metz.[30] Prussia similarly offered a wealth of recruits to the cause. By the time of his 1846 volume on Prussia, the Königsberg political geogra-pher Friedrich Schubert openly called for the extension of citizenship and full equality to all Jews in the kingdom, while at the 1847 United Diet the aristocratic Westphalian opposition leader Georg von Vincke gave a biting critique of Friedrich Wilhelm's proposed Jewish legislation. In the Rhine-land the liberal Mennonite Hermann von Beckerath led the charge for Jewish civic and political equality in both 1843 and 1845, while he and the Catholic Gustav Mevissen joined Vincke among the most important speakers on this issue in Berlin in 1847.[31] During the 1830s and especially the 1840s, the future Assembly delegates coming forward to combat the exclusion of German Jews from the life of the nation formed an ever-growing liberal phalanx.

This process involved not just a growth in numbers but also a change in tone and rhetoric. The Jewish Question increasingly became a Christian Question. The problem seemed now to lie not so much with a Judaism needing a reform achievable only through legislative action but rather more with an illiberal, retrograde government policy intent on keeping Jews separate from those who should be their fellow citizens. Talk of as-similation hardly vanished entirely, but it lost its front-and-center position. Human rights, equality before the law, freedom of conscience, fraternity:

these concepts and phrases now dominated pro-emancipation discourse, while anti-Jewish utterances concentrated in the speeches of the ever-smaller groups of conservative or lower middle-class opponents.

Within the logic of the liberal doctrine of human rights, such de-emphasis of assimilatory arguments and anti-Jewish stereotyping went hand in hand with increasing support for unconditional emancipation. As shown above, the limiting conditions of rights theory implied that if a religious or social group were shown to be able to fulfill all civic duties and to harbor no teaching or impulse harmful to the state, then any restrictions of that group's full civic and political equality were nugatory. The question of Jewish emancipation thus suddenly boiled down to the pragmatic debate of whether Jews were so capable and whether Judaism did include socially, morally, or politically detrimental elements. Opponents could consult their copies of Eisenmenger and maintain that it did, that since Jews and Judaism could never comport with the moral values behind the legislation and institutions of a Christian state, emancipation was illegitimate. Hermann von Beckerath's famous speech at the 1843 Rhenish Diet, on the other hand, perfectly exemplified the transformed emancipatory rhetoric. Beckerath conceded at the outset that the state did possess the right to demand that a religion contain nothing "contradictory to the conditions of its [the state's] existence," but he then went on to unleash a whole arsenal of arguments demonstrating that Judaism did not involve any such subversive elements and refuting anyone who said it did. He pointed out that Judaism and Christianity shared the same roots and the same moral and political values. He read excerpts from a Jewish textbook to show that Eisenmenger-like Talmudic criticisms rested upon mistaken assumptions about rabbinical exegetical methods, and that Jewish youths were taught the same respect for state authority, patriotic duties, and their fellow citizens as were Christians. He cited the examples of France, Belgium, the Netherlands, and Britain to show that when given the chance Jews did in fact become model citizens. And he ended by couching the whole in terms of the liberal ideal of self-cultivating *Bildung*, of freedom and a moral vocation for humanity. "Let us not hard-heartedly disown one whom God let be born our brother," Beckerath movingly intoned, "let us give him room to develop unhindered every talent, every power the Creator lent him, for the salvation of humanity!" Only a positive image of Jewish life and capabilities emerged here, and in the strongest fashion.[32]

By no means, however, did all future delegates wean themselves away from anti-Jewish stereotypes in this period of advancing emancipation.

Despite Beckerath's positive approach, at the Prussian United Diet Vincke still disavowed any particular sympathy for Jews as motivation for granting them rights, citing the qualities of greed, obsequiousness, and cowardice against them. Beckerath's fellow Rhenish crusader for emancipation, Mevissen, held up the specter of the corrosive effects of Jewish hostility and cultural despair in literature and finance, a problem set to grow worse if the unjust oppression that caused it was not rectified, and he also looked forward to the dissolution of a separate Jewish "nationality" when that occurred.[33] And despite Brentano's claim that the "battle for religious freedom" was also a "battle against prejudices," some of his fellow Badenese representatives still felt uneasy with Jewish financial dealings. The liberal Mathy argued for rural credit institutions with the assurance that he voted as eagerly for "freedom from the Jews" as for "freedom for the Jews," while the radicals Friedrich Hecker and Karl Metz both hoped that granting legal equality would encourage Jews to turn away from trade and usury.[34]

Such ongoing anti-Jewish thinking among future deputies raises the further question of whether the general transition actually represented changes of opinion on the part of individual liberals. Since Hecker, for instance, had opposed emancipation well into the 1840s, his remarks on Jewish usury in 1848 suggest that he changed his mind not so much about the Jews themselves as about the efficacy of full citizenship status in ameliorating Jewish delinquencies. His fellow Badenese Welcker, on the other hand, presents one of the few cases where an individual can clearly be seen to change his views, for already by the 1833 Diet he had broken with his close colleague Rotteck on this issue and had begun to defend emancipation on human rights lines.[35] Such examples, however, are rare. Most future delegates simply came onto the political scene with their moderately assimilationist, mostly rights-based emancipation ideas already in place. Given the historical selection process by which men likely to be elected to the National Assembly in 1848 were very often only coming into such political prominence as to leave records on this issue in the course of the 1830s and the 1840s, that is, at a time when the general transition of opinions on Jewish emancipation was already in full swing, no other situation could reasonably be expected. The most probable explanation for the general shift would seem to involve a changing of the oppositional political guard, as new recruits were drawn in and as formerly junior men began to fill senior leadership roles; the evidence, however, really allows no firm conclusion. At the very least, such a turnover in personnel facilitated the increasing popularity of the purer rights-based emancipation, all the more so as those who were fully schooled in the post-Humboldtian culture of *Bildung* began to reach political maturity.[36]

Yet many other, external, factors could have been at work to bring into play the inclusionary, assimilatory implications of the liberal culture of nationhood and its dialectical, dynamic view of history. One scholar, for example, has argued that the upsurge of French-style liberalism in western Germany following the impressive success of the 1830 July Revolution gave impetus to the cause of Jewish emancipation in Hesse-Darmstadt through the recognition that equality before the law had to apply to all.[37] In an interesting analysis of the situation in Baden, another historian has suggested that the liberals' decision to apply their ideals of religious freedom to Jews emerged only in the context of their counterattack against the forces of a rising organized Catholic conservatism after the 1837 Cologne mixed-marriage conflict and especially after the latter's onslaught against the fledgling liberal German-Catholic movement in 1845–1846. This account may well tell the true story in Baden, and while its emphasis on the defense of Christian dissent does not always fit the timing of the transition elsewhere nearly so well, the desire to let off a few salvos against the "Christian state" concept of both the conservative Protestant Prussian government and its conservative Catholic opponents very likely played a role in encouraging the liberal decoupling of church and state, citizenship and confession.[38] In Cologne and the Prussian Rhineland the shift was facilitated not just by a turnover in personnel at the top of the Rhenish liberal movement but also by a new economic and intellectual climate, one more optimistic and open to dynamic change and the recognition of new social realities. As regards the situation of the Jews, this meant that liberals acknowledged the existence and just claim to full citizenship of a rapidly growing middle-class Jewish community, acculturated in part through acceptance of the ideas of the Enlightenment Haskala movement for the reform of Judaism.[39]

This sense of dynamic openness may also have applied elsewhere in Germany during the 1840s, as Jewish emancipation became coupled with an increasingly far-reaching package of liberal reforms. In southwestern Germany emancipation had always aroused sharper opposition at the local level where concrete local interests were more directly affected. Given that the liberal movement of the 1830s and especially the 1840s was increasingly national rather than particularist, differences of scale and perspective meant that including German Jews on an equal basis in the life of the German nation loomed much less threatening than would the same measure at the state or municipal level. Moreover, the prerevolutionary 1840s had witnessed the rise of an almost chiliastic expectation of and desire for radical reform, be it political or social revolution or a cataclysmic European war for national freedom against the forces of the Russian czar. Against the backdrop of such sweeping changes, neither perceptions of Jewish difference nor grants of Jewish equality could inspire the kind of fear they had in the period after 1815, an era of retrenchment, so longed for yet so seemingly fragile after the quarter century of transformative conflict just preceding.

When the March Revolution of 1848 propelled the liberal nationalists to the fore, the shift in the terms of debate on the Jewish Question was carried nearly to its logical conclusion by presenting it simply as a deduction from the fundamental premises of human rights, religious freedom, and equality before the law. The liberals no longer had to tailor their rhetoric to suit the sensitive notions of conservative governments, opposing majority parliamentarians, or hometown parochial interests. Instead, they could start with a clean slate and construct arguments from principle on the basis of political theory. Hence in the April constitutional draft of the Committee of Seventeen, penned principally by Dahlmann and his fellow exile from Göttingen Eduard Albrecht, the Jewish Question did not even receive specific mention. The bald statement that religious confession would be no bar to full citizen rights served to cover all eventualities.[40]

The Constitutional Committee of the successor National Assembly, in which Dahlmann was again prominent, chose to ignore the draft of the Seventeen in favor of its own declaration of Basic Rights, yet it ended by taking much the same approach. The Germanist legal historian Georg Waitz pointed out early on that the general statement of "equality before the law" for all Germans entailed the emancipation of the Jews, and no one saw fit to contradict him. As a matter of course, if the Constitutional Committee had its way Jewish emancipation would pass into law surely if without fanfare. The Jewish case received no explicit statement; the general rule of separating religion from citizenship applied impartially to all. Reminiscent of an argument used by Rotteck to oppose emancipation in Baden in the 1830s, Waitz acknowledged that it would not receive a warm welcome in all parts of Germany, but unlike Rotteck, the men of 1848 refused to cater to a benighted segment of public opinion that stood in the way of enlightened rational principle.

Other echoes of past anti-Jewish and antiemancipation arguments were also heard in the Constitutional Committee's brief discussion of the Jewish Question, and with the same pro-emancipation result. Urging caution, the politically moderate but religiously conservative Brunswick Lutheran church historian Karl Jürgens saw the matter partly in terms of a difference in nationality rather than religion. He too was for emancipation "in principle," yet he felt it was not "so much the opposition of confession, but rather of nationality" that stood in the way of immediate emancipation and that nurtured deeply rooted "antipathies" in the people at large. The liberal Austrian jurist Gustav Schreiner similarly came out for emancipation "in principle" while still invoking an older tradition of economic fears of Jewish equality, fears that at least in some Austrian territories reflected not merely "prejudices" but also "real conditions." But despite a certain lack of enthusiasm on the part of some committee members, the measure passed with little debate as simply a self-explanatory matter of rights, with reference neither to assimilation nor to Jewish iniquities. The only other time the Jewish Question was broached in committee, for instance, the leftist Gottlieb Schüler urged that the rules barring Jews from many trades be nullified in order that freedom of occupation truly come to fruition. He did this not because he felt that Jews stood somehow culpable and in need of special persuasion to undertake noncommercial professions, but because such restrictions caused "infinite harm to the moral force of men as well as to the material forces of the nation." Liberal ambivalence had not faded entirely, but during the previous two decades it had shifted decidedly against the anti-Jewish and in favor of the rights-based emancipatory sides of the equation. Both of these tendencies would be clearly illustrated in the parliamentary debates that followed.[41]

In his infamous speech of August 1848 in favor of restricting Jewish civil rights, the unaffiliated leftist Moritz Mohl clarioned charges of both usury and separate nationality against German Jews, thus amplifying those fainter echoes of the old anti-Jewish stereotype let fall by Jürgens and Schreiner in the Constitutional Committee.[42] "As a result of their descent," Mohl declared, "the Israelites do not belong to the German nation, no one will dispute that, and they cannot ever fully and perfectly belong to it." He clarified his remarks to the effect that it was the Judaic religion that kept Jews a separate nationality by hindering "familial mixing," and his peroration culminated in the arresting and disturbing image of the Jewish population of Germany "forever swimming upon the water of the German nationality like a drop of oil." Such an incipiently racialist perspective on the Jewish Question might be the most portentous aspect of Mohl's speech, but at the time his invective against "Jew-usurers" and "peddler Jews" who were leeching German peasants white proved more rife with pragmatic consequences for his legislative motion. For Mohl did not deny political rights to German Jews, and he expressly welcomed the presence of Jewish representatives at the National Assembly. The alleged Jewish inability to join the German nation apparently did not affect their political status as citizens. Since Mohl believed emancipation would only make the problem of Jewish petty trading and broking even worse, however, he broke with liberal principle and proposed tutelary exceptional laws that would forbid such practices and encourage Jewish youths to take up more honorable trades. Mohl tied the nationality, religious, and economic strands of his argument together by urging the view that more than anything else the Jewish refusal to identify and "meld" with those they lived among, an obstinacy occasioned by their religion, promoted their financial depredations among the rural lower classes. In all these respects Mohl's discourse provides a compendium of *Vormärz* anti-Jewish rhetoric.[43]

Mohl's speech has sometimes been taken to express more widespread views; others have seen it as an isolated outburst. Certainly the hisses and catcalls with which delegates greeted each stage of Mohl's argument, and the cheers and applause with which they received Riesser's defense of Jewish character and Jewish rights, proved illustrative of the Assembly's overall attitude to the Jewish Question. The fact that a few weeks later the delegates elected Riesser vice president of the Assembly also undoubtedly said something to the point. It is worth noting that in his rambling speech in favor of separation of church and state, the convert Catholic historian August Friedrich Gfrörer of Freiburg touched on the "Jewish influence and shady financial dealings" of the princely courts in Germany before the Thirty Years' War, while the liberal Prussian administrator Gustav von Saltzwedell supported his claims for church independence from state oversight by contrasting theocratic Judaism and Islam with Christianity, the "religion of personal freedom."[44] But such harking back to views that could have been heard more often in the early *Vormärz* proved rare and inconsequential. The only real reference to the old assimilatory ideal of a change in Jewish character to follow upon emancipation came from the relatively obscure Württemberg Catholic priest Georg Kauzer, who recalled the debates when opponents of emancipation had cried, "Let the Jews change, then we'll emancipate them," while supporters had responded, "Let us emancipate them, then they'll change." Kauzer himself supported the latter stance here, but significantly he also believed in religious equality as simple "justice and freedom."[45] Anti-Jewish references had by no means disappeared, but at Frankfurt in 1848 as opposed to earlier venues they had to be sought amid the rhetoric with a sieve rather than a shovel.

The other issue where the themes of Jewish separateness or nationality could be discerned was that of civil marriage. This point of reference had been implicit in Moritz Mohl's admonitory blast at Jewish unwillingness to enter into familial ties with gentiles, a religiously grounded refusal that resulted in national distinctness. Some liberals, however, thought the problem of Jewish particularism lay more on the Christian side and sought to remove the laws forbidding Jewish-Christian intermarriage or requiring that the children of such mixed unions be raised as Christians. From the Jewish perspective Riesser urged such a legislative change as an effective means to end the old "tribal separation" between the two religious groups, while from the Christian side Carl Mittermaier successfully pushed through an amendment to the original Constitutional Committee formulation of the civil marriage clause to include the statement that "difference of religion is no obstacle to civil marriage." He hoped that thereby "the partitions between the confessions would finally fall everywhere," the "confessions" here referring to Judaism and Christianity.[46]

Although Riesser and Mittermaier did not do so, such religious differences could be conceived in national terms. Riesser's left-liberal Bavarian colleague Marquand Barth, for instance, cited as an example of the sort of exceptional laws that would have to be repealed the "withdrawal of connubium, through which the national difference of the Jews was so to speak perpetuated."[47] Such statements might lend credence to the idea that German liberals still hoped for nothing less than the biological dissolution of Judaism within the body of the German nation, yet given this period's relatively loose, overlapping concepts of race and culture such a conclusion would be overdrawn. Greater frequency and intimacy of interaction between Christians and Jews did not necessarily entail the complete fusion of the two or the end of Judaism, particularly given the provision for children of mixed marriages. Some deputies may have wanted precisely such a peaceful solution to the perplexing problem of Jewish difference, yet even for them the devoutly wished consummation would only come about through the liberal free play of dialectical historical processes, not through legal or physical restrictions. No one posited such a fusion as the entry fee to civic and political equality. German Jews would be given every chance to resist dissolution and to maintain their distinct identity, so long as they now did so as a component part of a liberal German nation.[48]

If Jürgens, Mohl, and to some extent Barth were all ready to see the Jewish-German distinction in national terms, such a view was also powerfully contradicted by other deputies. The moderately liberal but religiously conservative Catholic rector of Giessen Justus von Linde, for instance, denied on territorial grounds that German Jews made up a separate nationality, while Riesser rebutted Moritz Mohl's nationality-based claims for legal inequality with the stingingly apt rejoinder that by setting up a situation in which the only way to end the national separation would be to end that of religion, Mohl managed "to make a lie out of nationality [Volksthum] and religion with one blow."[49] Riesser also tellingly buttressed his demand for full Jewish legal equality with the observation that, insofar as the Assembly had already given similar assurances to non-German-speaking nationalities, it would indeed be strange to refuse the same protections to a "class" of citizens who did speak German and did not think of themselves as a separate nationality at all.[50] Assembly delegates still recognized a certain social distance between Jews and other Germans, a distance many hoped to see lessened in the coming era of the free society. But by and large they saw this distance as rooted not essentially in descent but rather in custom and above all in religious belief, as attested by the Jewish Question's very locus in the section of the constitution devoted to relations between church and state.

Some revisionist scholars, still skeptical of the Forty-Eighters' commitment to Jewish equality, have argued that ambivalent liberals in Frankfurt were simply driven to emancipation by the force of revolutionary public opinion. Certainly the appeal to public opinion formed a common motif in pro-emancipation speeches. Riesser asked rhetorically whether public opinion did not rather oppose than favor the reinstatement of exceptional laws against the Jews, to which "several voices" responded "For five years!" In his capacity as rapporteur for the draft of the Basic Rights, Georg Beseler similarly brushed aside Moritz Mohl's proposal for Jewish legal inequality with the remark that the matter had already been decided in "Germany's public opinion."[51]

On the other hand, Assembly deputies were fully aware of the riotous acts of popular violence perpetrated against Jews in many parts of the German Confederation during the revolution and opposed them categorically.[52] Waitz's and Schreiner's recognition in the Constitutional Committee of the fact that Jewish equality would not meet with wholehearted approval everywhere in Germany has already been noted, and Georg Kauzer, for one, similarly thought that popular "prejudice" might protest the "opening of the ghettos." Yet Kauzer also believed that this popular prejudice would eventually adapt and accept emancipation, a view that illustrates the liberal self-image as leaders and educators of popular opinion rather than simply its mouthpieces or slaves.[53] The solution to this dilemma of whether the Assembly followed or shaped public opinion, of course, lay partly in the fact that divergent views on this question could be heard all over Germany. But even more central was the peculiarly plastic liberal understanding of the concept "public opinion," as something that must be just, rational, and in line with the ideology created and represented by the liberals themselves. In short, it had to be enlightened—that was the only mandate liberals felt they had a right to represent. If liberals did follow the dictates of such an enlightened public opinion, they obeyed a creature of their own making that resided principally in their own imaginations. If this force drove them to Jewish emancipation, then they drove themselves.

But whatever drove the national opposition to emancipate in 1848, the fact remains that delegates at the national level placed on the scales an unconditional equality that followed directly from their constitutional theory and the underlying culture of *Bildung* and culture of nationhood. This commitment far outweighed any residual liberal ambivalence, assimilatory demands, or anti-Jewish images. The liberal Danzig Catholic Johann Osterrath took this theory's freedom of conscience even further and argued that full religious freedom required the recognition that "another person wants *something different* than I do, and . . . I honor this difference in recognition of that other's independence."[54] Such a fully pluralist vision of society and individual autonomy was exceptional in the nineteenth century, but neither was it as far detached from liberal views as often thought.

For distinct reasons of their own, both the leftists and the conservative Catholics pushed for a radical statement of religious freedom based on a total or near-total separation of church and state, the left hoping thereby to secure the rights of unbelief and unlimited sectarianism as a blow against powerful church establishments, while the Catholics thought to win independence from government interference for the Catholic Church. Everywhere else on the political and geographical spectrum, delegates paid homage to the previously sketched theory of a freedom of confession limited only by the necessity that the religious groups so freed not radically endanger the existence of the state. The proposed amendments to the clauses on church-state relations by both Jürgens and the eccentric conservative Prussian jurist Maximillian Grävell, for instance, each gave the state the right to determine whether a given religion forfeited its right to equality or even toleration through an incompatible "worldview." The version of the confessional equality paragraph proposed by the party of Riesser, Barth, and Christian Wurm shared with the Constitutional Committee draft the statement that "religious confession may not injure citizen duties," even as it added a clause forbidding exceptional laws tied to religious affiliation.[55] Although both the Lutheran Jürgens and the Catholic Lasaulx bemoaned the lack of reference to Christianity and the Christian state ideal in the constitutional draft, each also explicitly recognized Judaism as an established religion entitled to full equality under the law. At least in 1848, religious conservatives of their ilk worried much more about creeping religious indifferentism and racing radical atheism than they did about patently God-fearing Judaism. With the exception of Moritz Mohl, no one intended to invoke the restrictive loophole in liberal rights theory against the Jews.[56] Freedom of conscience and legal equality for believers of all religions, including Judaism, followed simply and surely from liberal political theory.

While some liberals could be charged with lack of enthusiasm in their promotion of Jewish emancipation, it must still be emphasized that many others proved quite serious about seeing the principle of religious freedom carried out in favor of their Jewish fellow citizens in concrete terms that would affect their daily lives. Barth, for example, in supporting his and Riesser's "no exceptional laws" amendment, explicitly broached the problem of ensuring that the basic constitutional statement would really equalize Jewish legal status at all political and judicial levels. He feared that anti-Jewish lower court officials might seize the chance to apply the exceptional laws still on the books against Jews in areas such as marriage, contracts, and testamentary oaths. The Austrian radical Franz Schuselka similarly introduced a motion to ensure that refractory local communities would not deny citizenship and settlement rights to Jews, while Osterrath and Linde also made suggestions about how to transform the theoretical statement of freedom and equality into enduring reality.[57] In the end the Assembly decided not to include the specific provision against exceptional laws, but it did so only upon Georg Beseler's assurance that "If we give the Jews equal rights with the other religious associations, the exceptional laws thus necessarily fall away."[58] From Linde and the Catholics, to Beseler and the liberals, to Schuselka and the democrats, emancipation at once principled and practical was the order of the day.

Yet if enough has been said here to make further inquiry into the sincerity of liberal and democratic support for emancipation otiose, the same cannot be said for the religious, particularly Catholic, conservatives, who had opposed the measure with a welter of anti-Jewish arguments in the years before the revolution and who may have simply tacked in an ill wind rather than sailed wholeheartedly with the prevailing current in 1848. The arguments of the Catholic parliamentary faction for the independence of the church from state oversight, after all, presupposed a certain measure of religious equality to ensure that governments not be able to put pressure on Catholics through restrictions of their rights. The future cofounder of the Center Party August Reichensperger spoke in favor of the "principle of the equality of all citizens," and consequently against exceptional or "special laws" as restrictive of precisely that full citizen status, a view seconded immediately thereafter by Linde.[59] For these men the presumption of sincerity seems safe enough. Linde, after all, had made little use of anti-Jewish stereotypes in his previous publicistic opposition to Jewish emancipation, preferring instead to construct technical legal arguments based on the 1815 Federal Constitution to stiffen the case against Jewish equality but even more against recognition of the renegade German-Catholic movement. Now that the Federal Constitution no longer had force of law or determined the basic legal principles upon which the new nation was to be constructed, Linde simply turned those legal technicalities to work for the Jews rather than against them.[60]

Yet for all that some among the Catholic interest group at the National Assembly defended religious liberty and equality from conviction, many others simply swallowed the inevitable as part of the revolution's bitter medicine and attempted to turn the tables on the often anticlerical supporters of church-state separation by using that principle to free the Roman Catholic Church from unwanted government supervision. The ultramontane church historian Dr. Sepp, for example, claimed that he at least worried more about contemporary irreligiosity than about any of the established confessions, all of which, Christian and Jewish alike, were threatened by the ideas of radical atheists. In this context Sepp defended Christianity as the "religion of freedom," the first to teach the virtues of equality and fraternity. But later in his long speech Sepp revealed the tactical maneuvering behind his support for such equality when he argued that

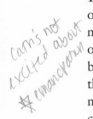
Cam's not excited about # emancipation

now that the "unbaptized" could become state officials, it would be mere presumption to demand of the Church that it let its prebendaries and theological professors be appointed by such as these.[61] General von Radowitz stated the strategic nature of such deployment of the political language of religious freedom quite openly. In declaring the "equal rights of all religions," he maintained, the new state had "thrown off its Christian character . . . Whether one rejoices or mourns at this does not matter—it is a fact." And from recognition of this fact of the revolution, Radowitz and very likely many other conservative Catholics went on to demand the independence of church from state as the best of a bad business.[62] That Radowitz had overcome his strong dislike of Jewish emancipation and abandoned his support for the Christian state concept of a year earlier in the Prussian United Diet does not seem very probable, and he presumably welcomed the efforts of King Friedrich Wilhelm and his ideological helpmeet Friedrich Stahl to restrict the emancipatory clause of the royally proclaimed Prussian constitution of December 1848 in such a way that Jews did not actually receive full citizenship and equality.

For Sepp no doubt at all of his unrepentant anti-Judaism need remain. Sepp had given emancipation only the most backhanded of support in a pamphlet for the voters of Upper Bavaria in 1848, and the very next year he stepped forward in the Bavarian Diet as one of the most rabid opponents of King Maximillian's proposed Jewish emancipation bill. In fact, the protoracist argumentation he expounded there made Moritz Mohl's rhetoric seem tame and tolerant in comparison, for in addition to opposing even the political equality of Bavarian Jews Sepp made use of some of the most repugnant anti-Jewish imagery to be found anywhere in nineteenth-century Germany. Emancipation did not take place between "Christians and Jews," he informed the Diet, but between "Germans and Hebrews," and he continued his foray into the biological realm of anti-Jewish arguments with references to the Jews as parasites. This itself was nothing new in the annals of anti-Jewish invective, but when he likened Jewry to "a foreign organism, a tumor that has settled into the body of the state and sucks the blood and marrow from it . . . It lies in our body like a tapeworm we cannot get rid of," Sepp dredged disturbingly repulsive depths unknown to even the most ambivalent supporters of emancipation.[63]

At least in the case of men such as Sepp, Radowitz, and of course Moritz Mohl, the discussion above should have made it abundantly clear that the 1848–1849 Frankfurt National Assembly could never have claimed to be unanimously and sincerely pro-emancipation, much less philo-Semitic. But despite the traces of *Vormärz* liberal anti-Jewish stereotypes lingering in the utterances of Jürgens, Schreiner, or Saltzwedell, the evidence presented here should also have demonstrated even more solidly this chapter's other primary contention, namely, that the liberal and democratic national movement had undergone a certain purifying process in the course of the 1830s and 1840s that left its leading adherents emancipators from principle by the time of the revolution. They may not always have been the most enthusiastic proponents of emancipation—for most the issue was simply not that central. But partly for that very reason, they had also become much less prone to demand unacceptable degrees of assimilation, still less the total eradication of Jewish identity, from persons generally thought of already as just fellow Germans of another religious conviction. Those imbued with the *Vormärz* culture of nationhood much more typically contented themselves with striving to involve all potential citizens in the higher cultural and political realm of the German public sphere than they did with endeavoring to remove all traces of foreignness in the German public body through an excess of xenophobic zeal. It is always important to keep in mind the context of debates within Germany's Jewish communities, in which many traditionalist Jewish leaders had opposed the sort of emancipation pushed for by liberals like Riesser and his Christian colleagues, precisely because they foresaw the kind of assimilatory pressures that Jewish identity would be subject to within that culturally normed public sphere. Yet by 1848 itself, even these opponents of emancipation had typically come around to accepting both Jewish civic equality and the challenges it presented for the maintenance of Jewish identity in a changing world. Leaders of Reform, Neo-Orthodox, and traditionalist communities alike seemed confident of their ability to resist unacceptable degrees of acculturation or even assimilation in the new liberal regime. Thus the Frankfurt constitution may well have presented a mutually satisfactory framework for coexistence in a German nation-state.[64]

If continuing to share even a part of the prevalent anti-Jewish stereotypes be enough to establish a person or group as an accessory in the rise of the post-1870s anti-Semitic movements, then German liberals and democrats must share part of the blame. Yet it would be going too far to condemn them for not trying to combat such prejudices, for they did try. If it is unlikely that liberals had shed all their sometimes negative views of Jewish religion, culture, and social conditions, the fact remains that by the 1840s they had almost wholly ceased to employ such rhetoric and had begun to exert powerful moral pressure against any who did. And it would be stepping well past the evidential fulcrum to suggest of the Assembly delegates that "nothing was further from their minds than the recognition of rights of minority groups or communities whether ethnic or religious."[65] Few Assembly deputies believed that expunging all particularist cultural identities in the nation's population constituted the best approach to the all-important problem of ensuring a united, engaged, and patriotic populace sharing certain essential values and goals. As will be seen in the next chapter, such thinking carried over into their views about the non-German-speaking nationalities as well. For both religious and nationality groups the road to progress had to be paved with liberal guarantees of rights and with confidence in the dialectical establishment of harmony through the historical process. If the early nineteenth-century German culture of nationhood hardly presented even a façade of postmodern pluralism, it still roofed a national mansion having many rooms.

YAY LIBERALS!

4 | Citizenship and Nationality Rights: The Paradox of the Non-German German

Jewish civic and political equality had passed the Assembly with comparatively little opposition, its provisions taken as given, deducible from the culture of nationhood's basic liberal ideal of *Bildung* and its concomitant, equal treatment under the law. In the same way almost none of the delegates ever questioned the assumption that those who could be deemed non-German by at least some, typically linguistic, criteria would still be entitled to the same full rights as all other citizens of the new German national state: nationality was to be a "political concept." Any Poles, Italians, Danes, or other non-German-speakers living within Germany's borders would enjoy the same legal protections under the constitution, and they would be able to exercise the same rights of political participation.

When the German parliamentarians addressed this question of equal rights for individual non-Germans, however, they nearly always coupled it with the very different issue of whether the other nationalities, as collectivities, would receive special protections for their separate linguistic and cultural identities, and whether they would be granted the privilege of some political autonomy at the level of local government and administration. These latter notions of group nationality rights provoked considerably more debate. Both from a desire to propitiate the disgruntled and distrustful Slavic populations of Austria, and from a basic sense of natural justice, deputies almost universally opposed the idea of forced germanization or even of discrimination against other languages and nationalities. Yet on the question of precisely how far the "nationality" of these other populations could be accorded separate and autonomous status without undermining the German national state's essential unity, opinion ranged more widely. As had been the case in their thinking about the Jewish Question, without demanding the complete absorption of culturally distinct elements within the German body politic, many delegates still re-

110

vealed intransgressible limits to their tolerance for multinational coexistence, multinational nationality. Nationality was still a cultural concept as well.

still prejudices

Neither the determination of citizenship qualifications nor the granting of nationality rights has received much historiographical attention, yet examining each issue in the context of the 1848 Frankfurt debates clearly exposes both the melding of cultural and political components of nationhood and the precariousness of attempts to separate them by contemporaries or by later observers. Where previous historians have mentioned the matter of non-German political and cultural rights guarantees at all, they have typically remarked on the policy as one of simple toleration. Some authors accept this toleration as genuine; others see it as but a self-serving tool to facilitate German territorial aggrandizement. While tolerant inclusivity both principled and pragmatic was certainly present, however, close reading of the Assembly's debates and legislative measures also discloses heretofore unnoticed restrictions in the concept and extent of nationality rights. The fact that equality in citizenship rights was never doubted, while rights of cultural and political autonomy proved problematic, cuts across the general category "toleration" (in either guise) and points to deeper-seated attitudes within the culture of nationhood. Tolerance for cultural diversity in the German polity remained ingrained in the deputies' mixed ideas of nationality, but it could only stretch so far. With even the best of good intentions, the paradox of the "non-German German" would have presented deputies with a nearly insoluble dilemma requiring far-reaching compromise. With something less than perfect good will, the knotty problem became intractable indeed.

cult = auto = bigger issue than atik rights.

From the revolution's earliest stages, the thorny semantic tangle of the "non-German German" demanded the clearest statements of intent. The idea that the Slavic peoples of the Austrian Empire's federal territories should participate fully and equally in the politics of the new German state was almost never questioned, yet its first revolutionary adumbration occurred at the Pre-Parliament when Anton Wiesner of Vienna, one of only two Austrians at the gathering, felt compelled to admonish the other delegates for having forgotten "the millions of Slavs who are our brothers." In particular he objected to the use of the phrase "jeder Deutsche" or "every German" in the election regulations, proposing instead the nationally neutral alternative formulation "jeder Staatsangehörige" or "every citizen." With the latter wording it would be obvious to the various linguisti-

vs.

cally non-German inhabitants of the old federal territories that they too, and not just German-speakers, were included in these provisions. Wiesner's proposal was accepted immediately without the formality of a vote, a move that shows all the more clearly how little doubt existed that the Slavic and other nationalities were meant to participate fully in the construction of a new nation, meant in part to be their own nation as well.[1]

Throughout the revolution the German nation-builders sincerely believed that if other national groups were to be incorporated in the new state's territory, they had the right to be represented in its political structure as well. The only debate was about whether it was ultimately more troublesome than helpful to declare this principle publicly in order to alleviate any residual mistrust on the part of Slavic or Italian populations. As in the Jewish case the issue simply involved the reciprocity of rights and duties. To make the public sphere work in liberal ideology, in order for it to produce the requisite degree of patriotic unity, all rational, independent (male) members of society had to participate, and so long as they stood ready to fulfill all their citizen obligations, they were entitled to all their citizen rights. Since no one seems to have argued that maintaining a mother tongue other than German would interfere with the equal performance of these duties, none questioned the egalitarian allocation of rights either. There was plenty of debate about the socioeconomic criteria for full citizen rights but none about the ethnographic. At this point in the evolution of the liberal culture of *Bildung*, belief in equality, in the vocation of each individual human being as a vital part of the vocation of the nation and of humanity as a whole, retained its central position in the pantheon of liberal principles. Some nationalities might be able to contribute more to the progress of the race than others, yet under the proper conditions of equality and the rule of law, each citizen of any nationality could do so in his own way.

Delegates continued to uphold the independence of citizenship rights from cultural nationality or language throughout the revolution, as debates through the final passage of the constitution in 1849 make clear. After the Pre-Parliament's comforting decision, both the Committee of Fifty's proclamation of April 1848 and that of the Assembly in May coupled their more famed guarantees of cultural rights for non-German-speaking groups to statements assuring them of their entitlement to the full rights of citizen participation. The Austrian Titus Mareck, instigator of the Assembly nationality protection measure, stated explicitly, "all citizens of a state united with Germany but who do not belong to the German people [Volksstamme] are due all rights of German citizens," and Friedrich Dahlmann included an analogous clause in his reformulation of the resolution for the Constitutional Committee.[2]

Even among the Fifty in April there had been some argument about whether the Committee might borrow more trouble than it settled to proclaim the citizenship guarantee openly rather than leaving it unstated. It was thus surely significant that the Constitutional Committee's June draft of the Basic Rights altered Dahlmann's official version of the Mareck proclamation by striking the citizenship clause and leaving only those concerned with the use of other languages in administration, courts, schools, and churches. This emendation in no way indicated slackened support for participatory citizen rights as opposed to linguistic protections, yet Committee members now showed themselves reluctant even to broach in the constitution the possibility that citizenship and nationality might be divergent concepts. In the wake of the June bloodbath in Prague and of the subsequent enervating wrangling over the Law for the Provisional Central Power in the Assembly, the writers of the constitution strove even more zealously than before to cement Germany's political unity and strength. Constitutionally acknowledging the political as opposed to simply cultural existence of other national groups within Germany through an open statement of their rights of citizenship seems to have struck some parliamentarians as potentially problematic in this regard.

These modifications to the Dahlmann-Mareck proclamation foreshadowed the course of the next important Assembly debate on the constitutional position of non-German Germans, where the Committee's phraseology ensured that the very first clause of the Basic Rights draft would come in for long and searching scrutiny. As both the young left-Hegelian Wilhelm Jordan and the old right-wing jurist Maximillian Grävell pointed out, now that the constitution included no explicit statement of German citizenship being understood to apply to members of all national groups within Germany's borders, the wording adopted by the Committee in the first paragraph could easily be misunderstood by non-German-speaking populations.[3] "Every German," the clause in question read, "possesses the general German citizenship." Thus, just as Wiesner had moved at the Pre-Parliament that the election regulations be changed to read "every citizen" rather than "every German," numerous deputies made essentially the same proposal with regard to the Constitutional Committee's Basic Rights draft. As the Upper Austrian official Johann Fritsch remarked, he preferred the expression "Angehörige" in Paragraph 1 "because it is generic and can be applied to any native inhabitant of German federal territory." Without it Slavic residents might fear their exclusion from the rights and freedoms of Germans as they had before the Mareck proclamation.[4] Unlike at the Pre-Parliament, however, on this occasion the assembled nationalists opted to retain the original formulation.

As many delegates at the time were well aware, the whole debate served to highlight just how perplexing, problematic, and crucial was the answer to the seemingly trivial question, "Who is a German?" As Georg Beseler noted in the Constitutional Committee regarding the need for a naturalization law, "We must answer the question of what 'a German' actually is."[5] By virtue of the *Vormärz* understanding of nationhood as a tapestry interwoven of political warp and cultural woof, a German could not be so by birth or speech alone, but neither could the name be construed as applying to members of some culturally neutral territorial state. The problem was one of definition. As deputies such as the liberal Catholic official Johann Osterrath, the Protestant historian Friedrich von Raumer, and the radical poet-politician Wilhelm Jordan all pointed out, one had to arrive at some definition of "German" that would not include Germans (by speech or descent) living in the United States or Russia nor exclude non-German-speakers living within the borders of the new Reich.[6] Yet at the same time, as representatives including the leftist Jakob Venedey and the moderate Georg Beseler argued, such a constitutional definition of the German citizen, particularly as regards the position of non-German-speakers, could not be allowed to call into question the nation's "political unity."[7]

Even very recent studies of such issues of German citizenship and national self-definition have tended to highlight the historical differences between the two principal systems of citizenship ascription, by place of birth (*jus soli*) and by birth to parents who are citizens (*jus sanguinis*). Germans have been seen as relying more exclusively on *jus sanguinis,* an observation taken to reflect a fundamentally ethnocultural understanding of nationhood in the so-long stateless nation of Germany. In this respect Germany seems to differ from the more ethnically inclusive approach of a nation such as France, with its blend of the *soli* and *sanguinis* principles and its ostensibly more civic and territorial conception of nationality. Particularly in terms of its naturalization policy, as ultimately codified nationally in the *völkisch*-exclusionary citizenship law of 1913, Germany is said to have long prioritized ties of blood. Other recent scholarship, however, has questioned the centrality of the principle of descent in pre-Wilhelmine citizenship doctrine, emphasizing the principle of residence or *jus domicilium* instead. Yet even if one accepts that descent did play a significant role in *Vormärz* thinking about citizenship, the assumption remains questionable that a romantic Pan-German blood-based vision of nationality somehow shaped German self-understanding in this period, while government officials with essentially statist views of nationhood and of *jus sanguinis* codified the citizenship laws.[8]

There is, after all, general agreement that these state laws were all framed in a basically ethnically neutral context. They were largely concerned with hometown, bread-and-butter issues of poor-law administration and communal citizenship, all the more so as the German states were generally so small, intermingled, and, be it noted, ethnographically homogenous. Whether by *soli, sanguinis,* or *domicilium,* the legal citizen ideal remained that of a population living within a state's territorial limits and knowing its laws and customs.[9] In the end, after all, each system of citizenship ascription was designed to grant citizenship on the assumption that most persons were born within a state of parents themselves citizens of that state. Only in the relatively rarer boundary cases of citizens' children born outside the state territory or of foreigners' children born inside it was any real distinction made.[10]

The 1848 National Assembly ultimately chose not to formulate a naturalization law, preferring instead to follow the suggestion of the Constitutional Committee rapporteur Georg Beseler that such a measure be left to subsequent Reich parliaments rather than written into the constitution itself. This omission did not, however, prevent several deputies from touching on these questions in revealing ways. Most discussion of citizenship at the parliament still centered around *Heimatsgesetz* and poor-law issues, yet delegates also cast some light on their general conceptions of nationhood when they delved into the more fundamental question of whether Reich citizenship would enjoy priority over individual state citizenship, or indeed whether it would become the only legal form of citizenship. The more centralist deputies such as the North Germans Georg Beseler, Georg Waitz, and Johann Tellkampf generally emphasized national over state citizenship in the interests of national unity. Others such as the Württemberger Robert von Mohl and the Viennese Eugen Megerle von Mühlfeld wanted citizenship in the individual states to convey general German citizenship.[11] In neither case was the issue of the non-German nationalities of immediate concern.

More interesting for the present study, several representatives concurred with Beseler on the need for a naturalization law to settle the details of citizenship but disagreed with his desire to put the measure off until a future Reichstag. In a proposal that casts further doubt on the significance of the *soli/sanguinis* distinction for national identity in this period, the leftist Saxon official Julius von Dieskau introduced the equally fundamental notion of *jus domicilium* and defined as German "whoever essentially resides in Germany and has received citizenship in no other state." Fellow leftist Julius Fröbel had offered a somewhat similar scheme just the year before in his *System of Social Politics,* where in a draft constitution he had included the very cosmopolitan provision that "domicile alone" should determine citizenship and that through five years' residence "every foreigner living on our territory" should become "*de facto* a full citizen with us."[12] From a less radical position, the Saxon philosophy professor and publicist Karl Biedermann suggested using the word "native" or "Eingeborene" to denote the potential citizen. The conservative Prussian jurist Maximillian Grävell for his part demanded that the questions "What is Germany?" and "Who is a German?" be answered. Neither Dieskau's nor Biedermann's proposal did so sufficiently clearly. In the case of Dieskau's *domicilium* idea, Grävell wanted some distinction made between "real" and "feigning" residents, while in that of Biedermann's "native" solution he desired an answer to the question, "Children of foreigners, for example, who are born in the country—do they thereby possess citizenship?"[13]

While Grävell could be seen as casting doubt on the proposition that foreign children be eligible for German citizenship, two other deputies came out quite strongly in favor of that principle. The Protestant, left-liberal professor of political science Tellkampf proposed that "every man is a German citizen who is born and grows up within the territory of the German federal state." For Tellkampf education formed the crucial criterion, in order that "only those be able to exercise our political rights who have lived among us and know well our interests and rights."[14] But the most powerful statement of this ideal of the citizen by education rather than by mere ties of blood, one that resonates perhaps even more movingly today than it did in 1848 amid the ongoing controversy over citizenship policy in Germany, fell from the lips of the Catholic, left-liberal attorney Johann Peter Werner of Koblenz. He proposed that upon their majority, children of foreign parents born in Germany could officially settle in a German state and acquire citizen status. Werner implored the assembled delegates, "why should not the child who was born on German soil and has grown up among Germans, and has formed manifold ties with the German—why should not this child too have the expectation of German citizenship?"[15]

(handwritten margin note: Germaness can be acquired)

For Werner as for Tellkampf, the quality of Germanness was not strained by the accident of foreign parentage—it could be acquired.

Although Werner showed that he was no adherent of unqualified *jus soli* by his support of Dieskau's view that children of Germans born abroad should also be eligible to become citizens, it remains the case that familiarity and territory rather than family and blood formed the basis of Committee and amendment drafts alike.[16] What conditions would have been attached to naturalization in a Reich citizenship law it is impossible to say, but willingness to become patriotic Germans would likely have kept the door open for non-German nationals. How deputies might have reacted to large numbers of foreign immigrants such as the Second Empire confronted in the Poles and Jews streaming in from the East, or such as Germany faces in the new millennium with the *Gastarbeiter*, it is difficult to speculate. Some would assuredly have remained open-minded and welcomed the added manpower for German economic and military might, while others would equally surely have pointed to the rural immiseration in the German Southwest and asked why non-German immigrants should be welcomed when thousands of Germans were languishing in Atlantic ports on their way to far-off America. History not being an experimental science susceptible to controlling variables, the difficulty of determining the balance of opinion in an era that did not face such a predicament remains insuperable. If for no other reason, feelings about citizenship were simply different in a land where the problem was emigration more than immigration. All that can be said is that in those aspects of the citizenship issue upon which the Assembly did pronounce judgment, namely those concerning the fate of the present inhabitants of the federal territories, the ethnographic variable led only to inclusive results. Whether one wrote "every German" or "every citizen," the words implied citizenship and liberty for all men regardless of speech, religion, customs, or any of the other qualities associated with the *Vormärz* conceptual amalgam that was nationhood.

The common denominator to all such drafts of Paragraph 1 and its definition of German citizenship was that the nation be understood as a political concept. Declaring himself wholly in favor of the Constitutional Committee's decision to use "every German," the Schleswig legal historian Andreas Michelsen explained the notion more clearly than anyone else when he argued that in a constitution for all of Germany, "it is not nationality in its natural sense, but rather nationality in its political sense that is

(handwritten margin note: Germ citi = pol. concept)

under discussion, and therefore it is definitionally entirely correct to say 'jeder Deutsche.'" Taking France and Belgium as examples, the rapporteur Georg Beseler essentially agreed and gave it as the Committee's opinion that in future, and in line with German national development and the construction of the Basic Rights, "citizenship and nationality will be considered as coinciding."[17]

In probably the most famous and robust expression of the "political concept" of nationhood, the Prussian Young Hegelian Wilhelm Jordan took the notion of historical development further in the Hegelian direction of the transition from *Naturvolk* to *Staatsvolk*. The concept "Nation," Jordan explained, "has altered completely, nationality is no longer limited by descent and language but is rather entirely determined through the political organism, through the state." Citing the examples of the multinational British and North Americans, Jordan perorated, "All who live in Germany are Germans, even when they are not Germans by birth and language. We decree them so, we elevate the word 'German' to a higher meaning, and the word 'Germany' will be henceforth a political concept [politischer Begriff]." Even the more conservative Mühlfeld, an Austrian who generally tried to defend Austrian and Slavic interests, paid homage to the political conception of nationhood when he rebutted those citizenship centralizers such as Waitz and Beseler who would put Reich citizenship above that in the individual states. As he observed in the Constitutional Committee, "if 'a German' is to become a political concept, it can only do so on the basis of citizenship in one of the German states; only through Austria can the Bohemians learn to count themselves in Germany."[18]

Eventually, despite all warnings of the potential for Slavic misunderstanding and fears of exclusion or oppression, the Assembly chose to let considerations of national unity at both the lexical and the political levels prevail and to keep intact the wording of the Constitutional Committee draft. Paragraph 1 thus appeared in print with the phrase "every German." Beseler, in his capacity as rapporteur, reassured delegates as to the legal status of non-German-speaking minority groups with a reference to the Mareck linguistic protection measure: "the development of their nationality [Nationalität] is supposed to be guaranteed them, and it goes without saying that all those rights that are due Germans devolve upon them." Or as the Committee's commentary to its version of the Mareck proclamation in the Basic Rights draft read, "A special explanation that under the Germans of the preceding paragraphs the German citizens belonging to non-

German-speaking peoples were also understood—did not seem to be re- *unspoken*
quired."[19] The principle of territoriality and of citizenship for all held firm, *citizenship*
if unsaid.

Nevertheless, all of this discussion about the appropriateness of the unqualified phrase "jeder Deutsche" did ultimately have some effect. Late October witnessed the hotly debated decisions in which the Assembly first posed its famous "question to Austria" regarding its intentions toward the new federal state. In the wake of these battles, pressure from the barely reconciled Austrian delegates not to include any further provisions in the constitution that would make it more difficult to incorporate their homeland must have become all the more intense. Perhaps for this reason, on November 6 the Constitutional Committee voted to insert a new Paragraph 1 before the "jeder Deutsche" formulation that had caused so much anguish four months earlier. The new introductory Paragraph 1 to the Basic Rights spelled out clearly: "The German people consists of the citizens of the states that form the German Empire." Most revealingly of all, and a tribute to the power of the territorial or "political concept" of the nation, the explanatory note to the new first and second paragraphs set forth in no uncertain terms the Committee's thinking about nationality in general and Germanness in particular. "Since the quality of being a German, through which Reich citizenship is conditioned, is not determined by nationality as tribal relationship [Stammesverwandtschaft]," the note specified, "it can only be founded thereupon, that either someone is subject to the Reich government, or to the government of an individual German state, by virtue of permanent residence within Reich territory alone or within a particular state territory."[20] In the end the advantages of defining nationality on the political basis upon which almost all were in essence agreed came to outweigh the risk that the act of definition would itself cast doubt on the nation's political unity.

While concerns about national unity played a role in determining when and how the ideal of citizenship for all national groups in Germany would be proclaimed, the ideal itself was never really questioned. Considerations *Rights w/*
of national unity also surfaced in thinking about the other main bundle of *ling/cult*
rights for non-German speakers, those dealing with linguistic and cultural *auto*
autonomy. Here too such worries never moved deputies from their basic consensus (both principled and pragmatic) in favor of nationality protections and against forced germanization. These considerations of national unity did, however, provoke more substantive debate regarding

against forced germanization

rights of cultural autonomy than they had about the philosophically distinct notion of nationality-blind civil and political rights. At any rate there was more disputation than contemporaries wanted to let on or than historians have noted since. The reformulated Mareck-Dahlmann proclamation did enter the Basic Rights draft as Paragraph 47, which guaranteed non-German-speaking populations "their national [volksthümliche] development, namely, the equal status of their languages, so far as their territories extend, in church, education, literature, inner administration, and legal affairs."[21] Yet close reading of this measure and of the debates on nationality rights generally reveals the existence of potentially quite troubling limitations on the delegates' tolerance for cultural difference, limits that left the ringing assurances of "no germanization" sounding more like self-confident expectations of partial cultural assimilation.

Motivated in part by liberal principle and in part by pragmatic considerations, and acknowledging the uninspiring record of past German governments in this regard, most deputies hastened to make clear that they shunned the notion of forced germanization and supported protections for minority languages. The Frankfurt Forty-Eighters began to speak out about nationality rights as early as April at the Committee of Fifty, and they also made them an early item of business when they convened the National Assembly in St. Paul's Church in May. Few so explicitly put the matter in the language of natural law as the Jewish-born left-liberal Moravian Leopold von Neuwall, who averred in his speech supporting Mareck's suggested proclamation at the Assembly in May that it was an issue of "men's innate rights," and that "we recognize nationality as the most sacred part of man, and that we view these: language, customs, religion, as a sanctuary upon which no one . . . would dare encroach."[22] Yet the Bohemian-Jewish publicist Ignaz Kuranda also viewed nationality protections as an aspect of "natural justice," and even Dahlmann translated the idea into his own more historicist idiom and declared such guarantees to be promised by "nature and history."[23] Statements against forced germanization or legal discrimination were just as numerous, just as much expressions of conviction. When the Austrian opposition leader Baron Andrian admonished the Fifty in April to reject forced germanization, he provided just one example of an opinion essentially unquestioned even among those not otherwise averse to the notion of greater assimilation into the German cultural sphere.[24]

However sincere these confessions of liberal principle, deputies still often ascribed to more self-serving justifications for nationality protections as well. Kuranda himself added "wisdom" to "justice" in a speech to the Committee of Fifty in April, while with his warnings about the need to spike the guns of "panslavistic agitators," Mareck spun the pragmatic line almost exclusively in supporting his own measure at the National Assembly in May.[25] Confronted with the ongoing German-Czech unrest, the all-too-successful Slavic election boycotts in many parts of federal Austria, and the specter of the fast-approaching Slavic Congress in Prague, deputies felt they had to meet the demands and fears of their non-German coinhabitants of the German Confederation not just with a fait accompli but with real concessions. The poet Count Anton Auersperg of Carniola, in addition to speaking out about the need for nationality rights guarantees at the Fifty, also took this commission further and waged a public epistolary campaign to win over his "Slovene brothers" to participation in the Frankfurt Parliament and the new Germany generally. By assuring non-German-speakers that they need fear neither political nor cultural discrimination, Andrian, Kuranda, Mareck, Auersperg, and the other engaged conciliators hoped to make the idea of inclusion in the new German state less threatening for these less evidently "German" German citizens. In his own formulation of the Mareck measure Dahlmann made this placatory targeting of the national groups inhabiting problematic border areas quite blatant. "Never on his own soil," Dahlmann movingly proclaimed, "will the Slav, or the Danish-speaking North-Schleswiger, or the Italian-speaking inhabitant of South Germany, or anyone else belonging to us but speaking a foreign tongue, have cause to complain that his national character has been stunted."[26] When policy and principle worked together, it was easy to be just.

Some deputies took the calculated aspect of such concessions further. Rather than just protecting the domestic harmony of the new German state, they hoped to use liberal linguistic and autonomy guarantees as bait to angle for future non-German participation in the new Germany from beyond the federal borders. In this context the "magnet theory" of German nationalism discussed in Chapter 1 received its due. At the Committee of Seventeen in April, one member pointed out the value of such a constitutional clause should nations like Belgium or the Netherlands ever consider joining the new state, a sentiment echoed at the rival Committee of Fifty by the Rhenish estate-owner Carl Stedmann. Even Kuranda told the Fifty that such nationality rights and such Slavic cooperation could only aid Germany and Austria in their historic mission in southeastern Europe.[27] Deputies could accustom themselves to the idea of sacrificing a little present unity for the sake of future internal peace and increased territorial extent and power.

Given the recognized need to appease and even to fear the disaffected Slavic masses, the boldness of Dahlmann's revised Mareck resolution assumes an even greater and more illuminating significance in showing how deputies were able to still their worries about national unity. Underscoring the notion that the Assembly was acting from a position of strength rather than yielding to outside pressure, Dahlmann wrote, "The henceforth united and free Germany is great and mighty enough to grant the peoples of different speech who have grown up in its lap, fully and without envy, what nature and history have promised them."[28] Such a remark might have served merely as a rhetorical ploy, to help delegates feel better about weak-kneed concessions—or it might simply have been a true reflection of German nationalists' confident frame of mind in the intoxicating early phases of the grand act of unification. In either case Dahlmann's statement points to one of the principal reasons why the deputies, as participants in the German culture of nationhood, were able to overcome any residual organicist concerns about the purity and unity of the emerging national state. With the feeling of the newly united nation's strength and power flowing through the deputies' veins and synapses, the inclusion of non-German nationalities in that nation need not have occasioned any worries over supposed attendant threats to its autonomy or to the smooth functioning of its liberal German public sphere. Public opinion would be a German public opinion much more than it ever had in the past, and the ties that bound Germany and Germans as a nation would be stronger than ever before. At such a moment any centrifugal tendencies of the non-German minorities could be all the more securely and magnanimously accommodated within the liberal constitutional structures of the nascent German federal state.

Even after this foundational moment of national power in the spring of 1848, both liberal logic and political calculation continued throughout the Frankfurt Parliament's course to assure adherence to the ideals of citizenship and cultural security for all residents of the German nation-state. After a brief debate in February 1849 the Assembly voted to retain unchanged the abridged Mareck-Dahlmann declaration that had been Paragraph 47 of the June draft of the Basic Rights, to become Article XIII, Paragraph 188 of the final constitution. In the reports on the various border conflicts too, the responsible committees continued to refer to these provisions as adequate to ensure the national development and freedom of any minorities to be incorporated within the German Reich. Both the Beisler report on Bohemia and the Stenzel report on Poznania and West Prussia, for instance, referred petitioners on behalf of the affected national groups to the Mareck proclamation. Even Turnvater Jahn insisted on the equal protection of language rights and "Volksthümlichkeit" for Poles and Germans as the essential precondition for including the whole of Poznania within the Reich.[29] Nor did the Prussian party's later desire to unshackle the new state from its Austrian connections cause it to consider driving the Austrians into rejecting the constitution by reneging on this fundamental principle of the *Vormärz* culture of nationhood and its nationality politics.

But for all that reasons both principled and pragmatic supported a broad and lasting consensus on linguistic protections, the course of these ideas into constitutional reality did not run smooth. From an early point, even before the debates on the Mareck measure and Paragraph 1, the Frankfurt parliamentarians wrestled with the issue of exactly what kind of nationality safeguards would be acceptable to both Germans and non-Germans. Unpublished debates from the Committee of Fifty in April show this struggle clearly, and just after this body had finally arrived at its nationality protection decision, the Austrian official Franz von Sommaruga brought the matter up among the rival "Seventeen Men of Public Trust" (charged with drawing up a draft constitution for the Confederation) and forced them to confront the same problem. After meeting qualified resistance to minority rights provisions from such members as the Austrian Anton von Schmerling and the Göttingen professor Heinrich Zachariä, the Badenese liberal leader Friedrich Bassermann suggested leaving out the nationality protection clause entirely, a motion accepted by eight votes to seven— only to be reversed four days later by a unanimous decision in favor of nearly the same formulation originally put forward by Sommaruga.[30]

If much remains unclear about the sketchily recorded but "not uninteresting discussion" in the Committee of Seventeen, unfortunately very little indeed is known about the "repeated discussions" in the Constitutional Committee of the National Assembly relating to the Mareck measure's reformulation. That these debates could not have involved just the rubber-stamping of Mareck's ideas of citizenship for all plus nationality safeguards in church, schools, and courts follows from the fact that they took two days of committee meetings.[31] Even the notable lack of argument about the new version of Mareck's motion presented to the Assembly on May 31 can as easily be explained by tactical considerations as by the assumption of

Assembly unanimity. Georg Gervinus's *Deutsche Zeitung*, for example, reported that the informal parties had agreed beforehand not to allow any debates in which regrettable words might be uttered that could prove offensive to the very disaffected groups they were attempting to placate. In the event, several deputies tried to rush the rostrum in order to insist on discussion, with at least one, the Bohemian democrat Moritz Hartmann, intending to oppose the proclamation, but they were preempted by the general cry of "immediate vote!" that rang out. Given that the Mareck-Dahlmann nationality rights measure passed "with a large majority" but not "unanimously," it would appear that the clubs made the correct decision if they wanted to avoid the airing of any linens that, while clean enough for in-house wear, would not bear the light of public scrutiny.[32]

Despite the rather fragmentary nature of the evidence, however, it is still possible to reconstruct the basic lines of argument. At the root of all the hemming and hawing about such an apparently universally acknowledged principle as the linguistic rights of Paragraph 47 lay the same deep concerns about national unity that had shaped definitions of the German citizen in Paragraph 1. In the Committee of Seventeen, for example, one of the chief authors of its draft constitution, the liberation-era nationalist Friedrich Dahlmann, made this concern abundantly evident. Dahlmann candidly observed, "However much I honor national feeling, still just as little do I think that we should allow ourselves to be moved from Germany's national unity; we want no oppression of the nationalities, but we also want German national unity." What Dahlmann meant by "national unity" can be partially gleaned from his subsequent remarks to the effect that the Czechs should send representatives to the national parliament and "speak German there." In public life at the national level at least, Dahlmann apparently believed there should be but one national language, the German language, in use.[33] For its part the Constitutional Committee carefully avoided the word "Nationalität" in its formulation of the linguistic protections clause, preferring instead the term "Volksstämme," which could as easily be used to refer to Bavarians or Saxons as to Czechs or Poles and need not question national unity.[34]

The difficulty essentially revolved around the problematic attempt to construct an acceptably unified nation by applying a territorial or "political concept" of nationality within the cultural and political web of the culture of nationhood. When combined with analysis of the better-recorded debates in the Assembly's predecessor bodies, close reading of the various formulations of the linguistic protection measure by Mareck, Dahlmann, and the Constitutional Committee reveals significant caveats to their apparently quite pluralist rights guarantees. In the second discussion of Sommaruga's motion among the Seventeen, for example, one of the participants observed of such linguistic protections that "'Im Innern' is supposed to indicate that it is the case within the territories of such nationalities, but not outside them," while among the Fifty the Bavarian Johann Eisenmann doggedly insisted on much the same point after it had first been suggested by the Austrian Mühlfeld. Nearly all the draft proposals for the Committee of Fifty's nationality rights proclamation included this seemingly innocuous phrase, a fact all the more remarkable given the recurrence of the language of territoriality in the various National Assembly formulations.[35] Mareck himself included the stipulation that other languages would receive the stated protections "in those districts in which a majority of the population speaks a language other than German," and Dahlmann retained this conception in the phrase offering "equal legal status of their languages, so far as their territories extend."[36] This jurisdictional circumscription of linguistic parity might not seem so weighty, since presumably only in districts with non-German populations would special care have to be taken that citizens be able to understand the language of government and public life. Still, the Assembly left the status of Poles, Italians, or Danes living in majority German districts in an unsettling state of constitutional limbo.

All of this emphasis on territorial extent may not at first seem entirely clearheaded. Part of the problem was that Paragraph 47 just did not fit with the other basic rights. It dealt not with the rights of individual German citizens but of certain groups of German citizens, a move away from establishing the generalized rule of law desired by liberal jurists. Instead, it hearkened back to the sort of corporate rights or privileges granted in feudal times. The drafters of the constitution need not have chosen such an archaic formulation—they might, for example, have stipulated that every German citizen had the right to free speech, to education, or to jury trial in any one of several recognized popular languages. This would have provided the nationality protections sought by Slavic and other minorities without any further definition of groups having partly distinct cultural and territorial national identities. Neuwall clearly had something like this in mind when he proposed that the Assembly "solemnly declare that nowhere, not even in the tiniest parcel of the entire German nation, will a single language, will the right of a single individual to his nationality and language be suppressed." Both the territorial and the group limitations fell away in this conception of nationality rights, a fact showing that at least some deputies preferred to think in more liberal-individualist categories on this point.

That delegates opted not to follow this suggestion and to adopt instead the territorial and group-oriented formulation of "the peoples of Germany speaking other languages" indicates that they must have felt the former to be the greater threat to national unity. Why they might have felt so becomes clear in showing how Dahlmann's concerns about national unity and the use of German in public life at the national level led directly to the insistence on territorial limitations. Tellingly, Mareck's original proclamation had included the offhand remark "German is, of course, the language of state," before moving on to grant parity in non-German majority areas. In Dahlmann's revision the stipulation disappeared, but this heralded no great victory for the cause of pluralist national identity. The territorial clause simply accomplished the same goal on its own. Under this provision non-German-speakers could use their native tongues in local affairs but not at the higher instances of public life. The territorial clause thus sufficiently met concerns about "national unity," particularly the focus on parliamentary monolingualism adumbrated by Dahlmann himself. Since German could be assumed to be the language of state, this, like much else regarding relations between Germans and other national groups, simply went better without saying.

The limiting intent and effect of this territorial phraseology emerged most clearly from a vituperative rebuttal by Georg Beseler in his capacity as rapporteur for the second reading of the Basic Rights in February 1849. When Paragraph 47 again came up for scrutiny, it became apparent that several deputies hoped to extend the circumference of nationality protections into areas beyond those sketched out in the first draft.[37] In two of the new motions, for example, the innocent phrase "so far as their territories extend" was omitted. None of the three amendment authors actually drew attention to the change, but the leftist Moravian functionary Alois Boczek did protest his dislike of Paragraph 47's implication that there was a "ruling people" in Germany.

Beseler erupted against such heresy. Whatever else the Assembly might be charged with, he asseverated, intolerance against the "non-German" peoples was not among them. With no trace of irony he went on to express himself astonished that someone could doubt "who the ruling people in Germany is," and he gave it as his firm opinion that "the German people consists above all of Germans, and if we grant other non-German

peoples in Germany equal rights then they must recognize it gratefully."
Beseler then arrived at the core of his displeasure with the new amendments and argued, "They speak against unity; they are not only questionable but even dangerous." Above all, Beseler asked with rhetorical fire,
"What is it supposed to mean when it is proposed to omit the clause 'so far
as their territories extend.' Do you want to let all the non-German peoples
who have equal rights with Germans speak in the National Assembly in
their own dialects?" Not doubting the answer to such a question, Beseler
concluded, "None of you want that, and yet this right would be given if
we intended to extend equal rights in Germany so far." In this way the territorial limitations, innocuous as they might seem prima facie, served both
to circumscribe the notion of linguistic parity and to buttress German's
position as the language of state and of the national public sphere.

Whether Beseler was correct in his assertion that "none" of the delegates would actually want other languages spoken in parliament would be
difficult to determine, yet many certainly bore witness to his view of the
role of German in the new German state. When Dahlmann had held up
the exclusive use of German in the national parliament as the touchstone
of national unity among the Seventeen, no one seemed inclined to contradict him. In the National Assembly the Bavarian Eisenmann defended
Hungarian language policy as perhaps overzealous but not essentially
wrong by capping his argument in Beseleresque rhetorical style: "What
have they really done? Would we allow in our Assembly that the one speaks
Polish, the other Italian? Well, the Hungarians do not want to suffer that
either."[38] Eisenmann's comments came in the course of debates on the
Austrian Question, during which several stray remarks about the "Babylonian confusion of languages" at the new Austrian Reichstag suggested that
at least some of those opposing the expansion of the new Germany to include Austria's extra-German possessions shared Beseler's, Dahlmann's,
and Eisenmann's views about the virtues of monolingualism in the sacro-
sanct precincts of a national legislative body.[39]

Significantly, even on the other side of the political fence among those
supporting the goal of the "70-million empire" that would incorporate all
the Habsburg territories, the anti-Semite Catholic Johann Sepp argued
that just as disparate national elements in the United States used English
in Congress, the new multinational Germany could equally well use German in its national parliament.[40] In the end it seems that if being a Ger-
man-speaker was not necessary for citizenship, it was still required for full
political participation in the new German state. The idea that some kind of

common language, particularly a widespread and cultivated one like German, remained essential to a nation's superstructural cohesiveness, to its political unity, and to the full operation of its public-opinion-forming public sphere still held powerful sway over the minds of mid-nineteenth-century educated Germans. Such a grail-like vision of national linguistic ties above the level of local heterogeneity shone nowhere more brightly than in the case of the national parliament, as the symbol, expression, and reality of national unity. Enmeshed in the tangle of cultural and political threads of nationality that defined their conceptions of nationhood, deputies did recognize that cultural and linguistic monism could not provide the necessary and sufficient condition for unity in a multinational state, but they still felt that a certain degree of such commonality was needed to ensure the nation's centripetal stability.

Even more directly than in the context of a linguistic and cultural autonomy that threatened to fragment the national public sphere, delegates' concerns about unity could be stimulated by perceived infringements on the German nation's territorial integrity pure and simple. The Austrian Schmerling foreshadowed this perspective on the limits of nationality freedoms in a multinational national state when he warned the Seventeen in April that the Slavic peoples secretly desired something more than merely linguistic liberty. Such worries that cultural autonomy might be taken too far in a political direction emerged more clearly in the context of Italian nationalist deputies' efforts to secure for their South Tyrolean constituents the greatest possible degree of independence from North Tyrol and Frankfurt. During the same debate in which Georg Beseler had so strenuously reinforced the need for territorial and institutional limits to language parity, the South Tyrolean democrat Carlo Esterle proposed an addendum to Paragraph 47 to the effect that "the political relations of these [non-German-speaking] peoples" should be ordered along the same lines of the "free development" of their nationality as were their linguistic relations. In what should have been familiar language to the German liberal nationalists who heard him, Esterle claimed that if a government of foreign bureaucrats were forced upon a non-German population as a form of "guardianship," then "the guarantee of nationality is an empty phrase, an empty word." Beseler, as might easily be surmised, thought there was "something hidden" lurking in that suggestion and opposed it accordingly.

Although the Freiburg professor and Catholic activist Franz Buss was among those proposing an amendment to Paragraph 47, he could not allow himself to go so far as Esterle. "However much the nationality of the non-German-speaking peoples must be granted," Buss declared, "endangering the unity of the Reich and state government still must not be permitted," something Esterle's motion would allegedly do.[41] In another context the left-liberal Bohemian railroad director Gustav Gross defended the continued adhesion of Bohemia to the German Reich with the very similar observation that so long as Slavic equal rights meant only the institutional use of their languages, he would continue to defend the idea, but "when this principle is given a broader extension in a German state, then I must declare myself against it." The coiner of the "political concept" himself, Wilhelm Jordan, pushed such discomfort with excessive nationality autonomy to extremes when in June he called for a stern policy against the Czech movement and expressed his glee that "we are finally acting in earnest against the attempts of the nationality-lets to seek an independent existence among us and, like parasitic growths, to annihilate our own existence."[42] For Buss and Gross as for Beseler, linguistic or even local institutional parity remained tolerable or even desirable up to a point, but when these extended so far as to cast doubt on national political unity, such liberties became license.

   If few took their organicist concerns with purity as far as the Young Hegelian Jordan, neither did everyone limit their adherence to the ideal of autonomy for other nationalities. The leftists Carl Nauwerck and Carl Vogt, for instance, had earlier supported an even more thoroughgoing South Tyrolean motion in favor of an administrative partition of the Tyrol that would have involved separate legislative bodies. But then again they also stated a willingness to go along with the Italians' preferred solution to the Tyrolean nationality conflict, namely, South Tyrol's full secession from the German Reich. In this endeavor the Italians and their left-wing allies met parliamentary defeat in no uncertain terms. It is true that Prussian party leaders Johann Droysen and Max Duncker proposed a peace between northern Italy and Austria that would allow Lombardy a large degree of national autonomy within the Austrian federal monarchy—yet that held good for Lombardy alone, which stood beyond the German state's territorial bounds. For South Tyrol itself they and most other deputies refused to believe that the cultural and local political autonomy of an unmodified Paragraph 47 did not satisfy the interests of Germans and non-Germans, natural justice and natural pragmatism alike.[43]

One of this study's principal lines of investigation has been the search for clear regional differences of opinion regarding relations between Germans and non-Germans. In particular, given Günter Wollstein's emphasis on

Austrians as the main proponents of a "soft" Slavic policy, were there strong differences between North Germans and Austrians in the matter of nationality rights? As a tally of delegates' positions in the debates described above reveals, representatives of each major region spoke on both sides of the issue. Among the Seventeen, the Austrian Sommaruga introduced the nationality protection clause that the North Germans Dahlmann and Zachariä attacked, yet the equally Austrian Schmerling also opposed it. The Moravian Neuwall and the Bohemian Hartmann did not share the same opinion of the Mareck measure, while the Bavarian Catholic Johann Sepp, the Schleswig Protestant Georg Beseler, and the Czech-descended Bohemian Count Friedrich Deym each held true to the idea of using German as the language of affairs in the national parliament. Mareck, of course, as a prime mover of both nationality protections and their circumscription, stood on either side of the putative divide. As a matter of practicality certain Austrians may have taken the lead in pushing for nationality rights proclamations, but the pattern of opinion on this issue was more evenly divided.[44]

In general, despite different shadings applied to the conception of nationality within a multinational state, nearly all deputies from the political community of the German Confederation showed themselves true products of the *Vormärz* culture of nationhood. They remained open to including other national groups within the German nation upon terms of some pluralist liberality, but the end product still had to meet their clear if not radically stringent notions of national unity. One scholar has recently argued for just such an open-ended view of national identity among Austrian liberals of this era and even after, one in which the notion of Germanness mainly implied adherence to the political and cultural norms and values of the German-speaking bourgeoisie and hence stood open to other national groups without sacrifice of their distinct cultural identities.[45] The argument in the present work suggests that even the supposedly more exclusionary nationalists of the rest of the German Confederation had similar notions of national identity. But the discussion should also have demonstrated just as clearly that for Austrians as for North Germans, even this relatively open sense of nationality involved a still deeper cultural norming and a much more complicated and problematic intertwining of ethnocultural and civic-voluntarist criteria for nationhood. In the Vienna Reichstag, after all, German Austrians were reluctant to admit even the translation of measures to be voted on, with some going so far as to support a German "language census" in election laws. Such positions were close not just to those of the North German Dahlmann but also to those of none other than Sommaruga, the Austrian nationality-protector among the Seventeen.[46] Pluralist rights and their normative restrictions could be found in all regions, and in nearly all minds, as an interconnected inheritance of the culture of nationhood.

That said, whereas Austrians such as Baron Andrian and Franz Schuselka had for years supported an equal-rights-based federal solution to the problem of keeping the Austrian monarchy intact, many adherents of the Prussian or "Little German" party, typically with ties to the northern parts of the Confederation, boasted a stronger track record of desiring greater cultural unity to go with strong central political, diplomatic, and military unity. The balance between tolerance and unity still held, but it was shifted in favor of the latter. In the Königsberg political scientist Friedrich Schubert's plea of 1846 for the civic and political equality of Prussia's non-German subjects, for instance, he allowed for these nationalities to continue to develop according to their "national individuality," yet he also maintained his belief in the general principle of statecraft that internal differences in nationality could lead to "inner weakness."[47] During the revolution itself the Little Germans made more frequent references than others to the Babel-like confusion of languages at the Austrian Reichstag, a circumstance they did not wish to see repeated at its German equivalent. If the defense of cultural unity was a widely held tenet, North Germans seem to have put even more stress on it.

Further, the Prussian party leaders, particularly those who had been involved with the national movement in Schleswig, did not just invent the doctrine of parliamentary monolingualism on the spur of the moment but had declared their allegiance to it in the course of the previous decade. When North Schleswig representatives of the Danish national movement attempted to introduce the use of Danish in the Schleswig Diet, two future Frankfurt deputies led the parliamentary opposition to this move: Georg Beseler's brother Wilhelm, one of the foremost Schleswig-Holsteiners in the 1840s and a vice president of the Frankfurt Parliament in 1848, and the more left-leaning Assembly delegate Jacob Gülich. Although at first only requiring those North Schleswig deputies who could speak German to do so, Beseler and Gülich later called for refusing the right to speak Danish even to those who did not possess an adequate knowledge of German; during the next elections in 1847, they declared, voters could simply see to it that they sent representatives to the Diet who did know German.[48]

Such insistence on the use of a single language for public life did not always work in favor of Germans. At the 1847 Germanist Conference, for example, the Schleswiger stalwart Dahlmann voiced his "sharp dissent" to the report of the committee on German emigrants in the United States. The report had suggested some ways the Germanists or German governments could promote the maintenance of German language, literature, and customs among the emigrants, but Dahlmann could not agree. He underscored his dislike of "half measures" and his wish that the emigrant carry out "self-consciously the sacrifice of his mother tongue. There are no German-constituted provinces, but the German finds there in the English-speaking laws, in the constitution of this political life the basis of a full existence for him and his."[49] With culture and polity locked in intimate juxtaposition in the *Vormärz* vision of nationhood, any strong desires for patriotic commonality ran the risk of more than a mild flirtation with cultural assimilationism.

The seemingly pluralist "political conception" of nationality thus not only put limits on the extent of linguistic rights and political autonomy to be enjoyed by the new Germany's disparate national elements, but it could and did verge on cultural assimilatory pressure as well. Germanization came to mean something more than just the attempt to draw together all the different language and cultural groups into some sort of transnational nationality via the liberal process of mutually reinforcing local and national patriotism and liberty. Germanization also came to mean German hopes for an at least partial acceptance of German high culture and cultural values as the spiritual coin of the realm. The paradox of the "non-German German" presented deputies with an inherently unstable situation, in which the drives toward ensuring cultural diversity and political unity were in constant conflict. When the "political conception" of the nation was a German "politischer Begriff," the same thinking on nationhood that allowed delegates to approve the incorporation of non-Germans into the German nation also facilitated the slippery notion that in becoming politically German they had to partake of some cultural Germanness as well.

Even when they understood that the German revolutionaries were not proposing to rule over them by nonconstitutional means, these other populations perceived the threat presented by the culture of nationhood and its fusion of culture and polity very clearly. On the purely political level, they knew they had the right to vote and to elect representatives of their special interests, but that as minorities within the new, predominantly Ger-

[handwritten margin note: minority votes]

man state they would be easily outvoted and overwhelmed. Hence the ringing reassurances of the leftist Moravian delegate Johann Berger in early July that the Czech "nationality will be most powerfully represented when they sit here in the Paulskirche" rang somewhat hollow outside St. Paul's Church itself.[50] Moreover, if they could not avoid what the South Tyrolean Esterle termed the position or perception of "guardianship," they would lack that feeling of honor and autonomy basic to the maintenance of "free national development" and to the existence of self-conscious, self-assertive nationality by the lights of the culture of nationhood. But above all, the leaders of the other national groups opposed the imputation that they could be German in other than a strictly political sense. As Esterle observed, "You can indeed make the Slav, the Czech, the Italian, etc. into a citizen of the German Reich, but never into a German." He then went on to put his finger on the nub of the difficulty with applying the prevailing view of nationhood in a multinational environment. "It seems a contradiction to me," Esterle noted, "when one speaks of the non-German peoples of Germany, equally so as if one tried to speak of non-German Germans."[51] Esterle saw the nature of the paradox and the threat of the "political concept" equally clearly. Germany might have been intended to become a "political concept" open to various national groupings, but it still remained in part a "cultural concept" as well.

At the time of the debates surrounding Paragraph 1 of the Basic Rights, the Moravian Alois Boczek had similarly attempted to enlighten the Assembly as to the nature of the difficulty. Boczek explained that even if the "every German" formulation did not cause Czechs to think they were excluded from German citizenship, they might still counter this nomenclature by saying, "We do not want to be Germans, we want to see our nationality preserved." In other words, the other nationalities might want to enjoy the rights of Germans but without actually having to become German even in name. All of this wrangling over the proper phraseology of Paragraph 1 was of course merely semantic—everyone agreed that non-Germans were included—yet it was semantic in a deep and revealing sense. The Moravian Karl Beidtel, for example, only provoked telling "laughter" with his admonitions to take into consideration "the Slavs, who are more than six million German inhabitants," and not to forget "that *these Slavs are Germans.*"[52] Most symptomatic of all, Jakob Venedey tried to bolster his argument in favor of the "every German" approach with reference to the example of the multinational British Isles: "In England too there are different nationalities, and yet all of these citizens know that they are English." Venedey could of course hardly have been more wrong—even in his day a Scot would have admitted to being British but never English. And in the heated nationalist atmosphere of the summer of 1848 the only potential solution to this dilemma—changing Germany's name to something like "The United States of Central Europe"—never even came up for discussion.[53] In ancient Thebes the sphinx had served up the riddle of the ages of man; in Frankfurt the political realities facing deputies posed the paradox of the "non-German German." In 1848, however, no Oedipus appeared to solve the mystery and free the polity from the heavy burden of its conceptual and political confusion.

As was the case in their handling of the Jewish Question, members of the nationalist opposition very often desired and expected some degree of germanization as the result of citizenship within the great German national state, but this assimilation in no way had to be total or radical in order to satisfy their notions of nationhood. In its mildest but still patronizing form, such germanization only involved the adoption of a certain amount of German *Bildung* and its concomitant capacity for political liberty. As a part of his Pauline epistolary efforts to spread the Committee of Fifty's gospel of nationality equal rights to the Carniolan Slovenes, for instance, Count Auersperg informed them, "You, gentlemen, fear the Germans' germanizing attempts for our Slovene people; I do not. The newer Germany has never germanized with force of arms, but rather everywhere through spiritual and moral force alone."[54] In the Assembly itself ideas of a German cultural mission to the Slavs represented a brassy leitmotif of the debates on the Austrian Question, one trumpeted by proponents of both the Little Germany and Greater Germany solutions to the constitutional dilemma. The Prussian party supporter Georg Waitz had, to be sure, opined that the German cultural mission to the Southeast had already been completed, and the Austrian Mühlfeld was willing to concede the point. "It may be that German culture and customs no longer have to be carried to the East and Southeast," Mühlfeld continued, "but the free Austria will bring liberty there, and all the more easily and surely if it exists as a federal state with equal rights for the different nationalities."[55] Germans still had something to teach the Slavic peoples about *Bildung*, even if only in terms of liberal politics.

Many deputies' notions of germanization, however, patently involved something more than just the liberal education of supposedly backward Eastern Europeans. Both Sepp and Wilhelm Jordan, for instance, postulated laws of linguistic conquest that were sure to result in the conversion of millions into new German-speakers, Jordan observing that "the power of a cultured language is irresistible."[56] For his part, in the February debates about revisions to Paragraph 47, the Freiburg Catholic Buss objected to the constitution's guarantee of the free national development of "Literatur." Literature, Buss claimed, was a "free-growing tree, which no legislative assembly can guarantee."[57] Without invoking force or demanding assimilation, Buss would clearly not have been surprised or displeased to find German "literature" growing at the expense of that of other nationalities.

A year earlier, the Austrian radical Schuselka had gone even farther and extended the argument to the whole cultural realm. Schuselka's opposition to the Fifty's language protection resolution derived, he later explained, from his dislike of Andrian's idea of a "guarantee" for the nationality and language of non-German groups. "The development of their nationality in cultivation, language, and literature must be left to their own power; it should not be hindered, but it cannot possibly be guaranteed." Millions of Slavs both inside and outside German territory had been germanized in the past, "not forcefully, but rather simply through the spiritual power of German culture," and Schuselka complained, "how is it now to be guaranteed that this will not subsequently occur with still other millions!" Or as Boczek expressed the idea during the second reading of Paragraph 47, "at best the possibility of a national development could be guaranteed," not its "definite result" or "success."[58] Putting it in more modern terms, Boczek, Buss, Schuselka, and the others were committed to an equality of opportunity, but the actual equality would have to take care of itself. Midcentury Germans of the national opposition agreed on the idea that other nationalities should in no way be legally hampered in their efforts at national cultural growth, that indeed these efforts should be constitutionally protected. Yet through this concession they hardly gave up their hopes and expectations for the continued assimilation of these politically German non-Germans into more culturally German Germans as well.

The essential quality of all these germanization ideas was that it occur peacefully, as Auersperg and Schuselka both emphasized, and naturally, in the realm of "natural necessity" as Wilhelm Jordan asserted. The legal protections would ensure that no actual injustice occurred, while Germans could then simply sit back and await results. Buss, in a probably unconscious echo of Dahlmann's original rhetorical flourish in the Mareck resolution, expressed the matter most plainly. "Germany," he perorated, "is spiritually and morally great enough to make the influence of its culture acceptable to other peoples by means of voluntarism; it does not have to force its language on them or hinder their national development."[59] Here it is possible to grasp the other part of the reason why faith in Germany's greatness could reconcile delegates to the entrance of non-German nationalities into the German national state on terms of relative equality. Without ever having been root-and-branch organicist cultural purists to begin with, they could allay any residual concerns with the comfortable knowledge that their new national state was so great and culturally potent that a few disparate elements would not distort its national development, particularly if these other groups could be brought to feel political loyalty to the nation through the ancient republican process of building patriotism from the ground up. But what gave them an even greater feeling of security was the belief that with time these national differences would be smoothed out, that when the attraction of German culture was combined with the lure of political power and patriotic sentiment, it would prove even more irresistible than it had in the past. Just as *Vormärz* Germans had not conceived of geographical borders as static and unalterable over the natural course of history, neither did they believe the boundaries between peoples as sociocultural entities to be impermeable and changeless. History to the historicists was as ever a process, and whether teleological or not, these nationally minded historicist Germans thought they knew which way that process tended.

Moreover, history comprised not just any kind of process but rather a dialectical or conflictual one. Faith in this notion derived at once from the historicist reading of history and from the liberal view of society, and it played out at the level of both individuals and nations. The left-leaning natural law professor Heinrich Ahrens made exactly this sort of analogical leap from the individual to the national level of liberal theory, and on the basis of this logic he went on to draw conclusions for the possible future of germanization in the German cultural and political watershed. Contending that the "great ethnographic process [Völkerprocess]" going on in the Austrian monarchy was not one of "dissolution" but rather one of "nestling up to one another," Ahrens argued that with the new liberty, "a friction and a struggle of forces occurs." Ahrens then continued with a telling reference to "the law of dynamics by which the stronger force defeats and rules the weaker" and explained that "when one speaks of equal rights among nations, it is with this principle as it is with that of equality before the law, which also does not exclude material and mental superiority and their consequences." The Brussels professor even drew the analogy into the arena of liberal economic thought when he added that this principle also operated in the same way as that of "free competition," in which again "the material and mental capital necessarily acquires the preponderance over the weaker."[60] Nor was Ahrens alone in seeing relations between the nationalities in terms of a competition in which Germans and non-Germans could each win, by the former teaching the latter. When Count Auersperg urged the Slovenes not to fear German "germanizing attempts," he told them, "We should rather seek than flee this honorable competition—it will bring profit for victor and defeated."[61] Once the liberal level playing field had been instituted, in other words, a sort of free trade in nationhood would commence, in which history's invisible hand would ensure that non-Germans closed the supposed gap in culture and civilization—by becoming more like the Germans themselves.

On this level playing field nations would have to rely on their "own power," as Schuselka put it in his objection to the Fifty's resolution, and this attitude expressed at once the German parliamentarians' commitment to the liberal teachings of rights, autonomy, and honor, and their sense of the precariousness of national existence within a Tennysonesque natural history. In his own objection to the notion of constitutional guarantees for national identity per se rather than simply for the relevant rights that would allow a nationality to protect itself, the Moravian radical Boczek gave even stronger witness to such a view of inter-nationality relations than had Schuselka. "Nations," he asserted, "which feel their own worth and realize their right to autonomous existence in the circle of peoples will know how to fight for this, even when it is not guaranteed them."[62] Deputies recognized other nationalities' right to fight on level ground for their autonomous development as nations, yet this very recognition left these other national groups largely on their own, exposed even to the possibility of complete dissolution.

Typically, it was the coiner of the "political concept" of the nation himself, the as-ever radical and uncompromising Young Hegelian Wilhelm Jordan, who toppled the fragile balance between the political and the cultural in that political conception of nationality and revealed its potential for a fuller assimilation of disparate elements. In his famous June speech on the new definition of nationhood in Paragraph 1, Jordan showed that he at least did not shun the implications of political nationality in a mental universe in which politics and culture hung together in uneasy suspension. Immediately upon the heels of his dramatic declaration of Germany as a higher, strictly political concept, Jordan confessed his faith that "there is no better way to bring the particular nationalities that are still so powerful among us to a gradual and quiet disappearance." The thought of the new united German state's greatness, which had comforted Dahlmann and Buss and given them confidence that Germany's unity and power would not be too sorely tried by the admission of nationally distinct elements into its constitution, now served Jordan as the means to "bring this particularistic nationalism to silence."[63] When applied to the realm of nationhood, the liberal ideal of the self-made man could spell doom for the independence of the ostensibly less capable competitor. In the next chapters it will become clear how such ideas played out not just within the accepted limits of the projected independent German national state but also in the determination of those national boundaries and in the establishment of that independence during the border conflicts of the revolutionary year.

It's ok to bring
other nationalities into
germ b/c they will take
up germ cult anyway.

5 | Setting Boundaries for the New Germany

Despite certain reservations and conditions the Frankfurt parliamentarians clearly made allowances for and even desired the inclusion of non-German Germans within the new state. But which non-Germans were to be so incorporated—where on the map of Europe were the nation's borders to be etched, and why precisely there? Past historians of the Assembly and its border-drawing activities have generally emphasized either its adherence to the territorial limits of the existing German Confederation or its opportunistic propensity to employ any and every argument that might advance Germany's claims on ever more land. In the first scenario deputies remained closer to a western political ideal of nationhood; in the second they had recourse to arguments from ethnocultural nationalism, power politics, and even territoriality as the occasion demanded.[1] Still other scholars find ideological patterns in the border-drawing criteria, with left and right preferentially favoring either political or cultural, power-political or humanist approaches to national identity.[2] Each explanation has its merits. Delegates certainly harbored enough human frailties to abandon or at least temporarily shelve certain ideals when perceived national interests tempted them to do so. Yet many deputies also continued to express their understanding of the new Germany as a "political concept," not just in extending citizen rights and linguistic safeguards to non-German-speakers but also in restricting the new state's bounds to the territorial limits of the Confederation. And to the extent that democrats and moderates at times found themselves at loggerheads in dealing with border issues, above all in the Polish case, they did invoke differing interpretations of nationality.

However revealing these explanations may be, they still tell only part of the tale. Opportunism and rhetorical flights could have borne these parliamentarians much farther in their hunger for land than they actually did, yet despite keeping largely to the federal boundaries in defining the new nation, they did deviate from those previously established borders when they felt it just and necessary. And for all that opposing ideological factions deployed divergent border criteria in certain contexts, this was chiefly a tactical consideration, pointing not to any clear left-right division in national identity but rather to strategic manipulation of potentialities within the common culture of nationhood. Closely analyzing the border criteria adduced in the course of Assembly debates on several key issues, including the Schleswig, Poznanian, and Austrian questions, ultimately uncovers a partial pattern behind many of the seeming inconsistencies, a template upon which German parliamentarians of all political persuasions could trace their compound conceptions of national identity and carve out boundaries for the new state that at once maintained its German national character and incorporated significant non-German minority populations within it. A given province need not even have had a German numerical majority to qualify as German, and therefore as a welcome component of the new Germany. The Frankfurt deputies only had to be satisfied that its administrative superstructure, high culture, and general will were sufficiently German-oriented to bestow upon it an overall German national character. Once these marvelously plastic criteria were met, such educated Germans assumed, they need not fear any over-powerful non-German influences that might disrupt Germany's future independent "national development." As with the parliamentarians' scholarly analyses from the *Vormärz*, or with their grants of rights to Jews and non-German-speakers during the revolution itself, their notions of nationhood adhered neither to a purely cultural "nationality principle" nor to a culturally neutral "political conception" of nationality but rather to a fruitful if problematic fusion of the two.

As for the charges of being opportunists in the determination of Germany's borders, the Frankfurt deputies of 1848 were by no means spotless. They deployed a battery of arguments to support border revisions in Schleswig, Poznania, and Istria that went beyond the old federal boundaries, but they certainly never acknowledged the force of similar arguments in order to give territory away. Indeed, several delegates, including the conservative General von Radowitz, the moderates Carl Welcker and Friedrich von Raumer, and the leftist historian Wilhelm Zimmermann, all somewhat cynically pointed out that there was no sense ceding territory in accordance with the so-called nationality principle when it was so patently foolhardy to expect other nations to respond in kind by surrendering their culturally German areas.[3] Moreover, as in the debates on northern Italy and on the location of the demarcation line between the to-be-partitioned "German" and "Polish" portions of Poznania, some speakers unabashedly cited strategic necessity and reasons of state for retaining regions deemed indispensable to the national interest but hardly defensible on either a territorial, linguistic, or "national character" basis. As Günter Wollstein has rightly emphasized, liberals or no, these German representatives nursed a vision of a pacific but powerful German *Mitteleuropa* for the postrevolutionary order.[4] They were not about to let legal or principled niceties prevent them from realizing that ideal.

On the other hand, neither did the parliamentarians attempt to draw all of a supposed Central European sphere of influence within the nation's borders. Indications abound that at least some deputies would gladly have welcomed the incorporation of such historically or culturally German regions as the Baltic provinces, Alsace, Switzerland, or the Low Countries if their inhabitants had proved in future to be attracted to the newly energized German "magnet." These delegates did not, however, lay claim to them in the present of 1848 and emphatically rejected any proposals that they should. Nor did the majority resolve to bring under the constitution any extra-federal lands for which it would be clearly impossible to argue that they somehow belonged to Germany—not in Italy, not in the Kingdom of Hungary, not in occupied Jutland, not even (with certain reservations) in Poland. If it was cynical for Welcker, Radowitz, and Zimmermann to raise the possibility of some sort of nationalist territorial horse-trading, it would be no less cynically naive of the historian to look no further than opportunism for explanations of why the deputies spoke and acted as they did in these nationality- and border-related debates.

Instead of linguistic, ethnographic, or power-political criteria, deputies relied on the legal and territorial foundation for the new state provided by the Confederation as the baseline from which any deviations or revisions had to be measured. As the final constitution simply stated, "The German Reich consists of the territory of the former German Confederation." Liberals such as Georg Beseler and Johann Droysen, who always emphasized the necessity for legality in opposition politics, naturally supported the territorial definition of the German state as a means of maintaining its "legal continuity" with the Confederation and easing its way into a wary international community. Yet even those more radical Constitutional Committee members who disavowed association with the unpopular Confederation still accepted its territorial limits as a matter of practical politics.[5] In determining the border in the Habsburg lands and in seeking to lay claim to Schleswig by virtue of its constitutional association with Holstein, the Assembly resorted above all to this political or territorial understanding of nationality. And when the Saxon government's plenipotentiary in Frankfurt Oskar von Wydenbrugk, despite his theoretical support for Italian unification, rejected Italian claims in northern Italy and Tyrol as "unreasonable demands," he labeled them such not because German-speakers might fall under the sway of a foreign nationality but rather because the Italians had "even demanded that German federal territory be ceded."[6] The pragmatically simplest approach, but also the one most congenial to a body attempting to establish what it thought of as a "political conception" of the nation, was to leave that nation more or less in its present politically defined borders.

Despite these culturally neutral good intentions, however, in debates affecting sensitive border areas the qualification "more or less" occasioned recourse to nearly the full complement of criteria for nationhood seen in the scholarly and publicistic works of the delegates' pre-1848 period. Tacitean references to ancient tribal habitations mingled with voluntarist Rousseauian echoes of the general will as justifications of German rights to certain peripheral regions. Language naturally received its due, but as in the *Vormärz* it came accompanied by the broader cultural criteria of "customs," "mindset," "descent," and a general *Bildung* or "civilization." Historical rights founded in treaties found their counterparts in the romantic realms of historical and dynastic memories, while both shared the rhetorical stage with more populist interpretations of common consciousness as a general German patriotic identity. In investigating individual aspects of the different border-drawing and border conflict debates below, it must above all be borne in mind that no single clear and concrete conception of nationhood could ever stand out amid such a cornucopia of nationality criteria. It was this very protean plasticity and multivalence that, when the deputies' desires got the better of them, helped ease them down the road to opportunism. Yet behind the madness lay some method; the desires themselves hardly sprang arbitrary and Athena-like from the delegates' brows.

It was in the first major case to be examined, the debates from June through October over the question of whether all or part of the linguistically mixed Duchy of Schleswig would be incorporated into the new German state, that speakers tried most strongly to highlight the purely legalistic and politically just nature of their territorial claims. As rapporteur for the newly formed International Committee, the future Foreign Minister Johann Gustav Heckscher, for example, on June 8 gave a detailed summary of the legal and historical relations among Schleswig, Denmark, and various German states that had led up to the current dispute over alleged rights of dynastic succession in Schleswig and of indissoluble union between Schleswig and Holstein (and hence between Schleswig and Germany through federal Holstein, Schleswig itself lying outside the Confederation).[7] In so doing Heckscher trod in the dusty archival footsteps of Schleswig party historians of the prerevolutionary period, several of whom, including Droysen, Georg Waitz, Friedrich Dahlmann, Andreas Michelsen, and Georg Beseler, sat in the Frankfurt Parliament. During the debates themselves Dahlmann, Michelsen, the Hamburg historian Christian Wurm, and the Schleswig-Holstein Provisional Government's plenipotentiary Carl Francke each invoked Germany's historical rights as the basis for claiming Schleswig in its entirety.[8] Where two rival national movements competed for sovereignty over a linguistically divided province, it was only to be expected that arguments from international law would carry more weight than those hewn with the ideological double edge of cultural nationality. A historical and territorial understanding of nationality would (German nationalists hoped) leave Schleswig intact and in Germany.

Heckscher pushed the boundaries of the notion of "history" and prefaced his long disquisition on four hundred years of Schleswig diplomatic relations with the remark that the duchy had been inhabited by "German peoples" since "as far back as history reaches," a contention in which he would later be supported by no less a scholarly luminary than the father of Germanists Jacob Grimm.[9] Grimm did not, however, rely solely on the misty reaches of a near-mythic past in order to support his claims to Schleswig in its entirety. When he argued that the "principal reason" why Schleswig should be annexed was that "Schleswig has declared its desire always to be and to remain with Germany," Grimm introduced the chief supplement or alternative to justifications based on what the radical Carl Vogt contemptuously termed the "yellowed parchment" of historical rights, namely the voluntarist impetus from the general will.[10] Michelsen, the Jena Germanist formerly of Kiel, similarly debouched from claims grounded in historical rights into those following from what he called "natural rights," by which latter he meant both the southward orientation of the province's "popular mind" and the alleged firmly declared opposition of the "popular will" in all parts of Schleswig to any separation from the German state to the south. The Schleswiger Francke adopted much the same dual approach and referred not just to the historical side of the issue but also to antipartition petitions from North Schleswig.[11] Right-leaning liberals though these men may have been, they still operated with established liberal patterns of thought and saw the popular will as crucial in driving the ancient republican process of mutually reinforcing patriotism and liberty. Territorial adherence demanded popular allegiance.

By relying so heavily on the right of self-determination for the German cause in Schleswig, deputies of course laid themselves open to charges of inconsistency if they failed to acknowledge the possible equivalent claims of the Danish-speaking minority in the duchy's northern marches. But while it is true that most continued to maintain Germany's claims to the whole duchy, previous accounts have underestimated the extent to which even Schleswig party delegates stood willing at least implicitly to allow the application of the self-determination principle to the North Schleswig minority. They did not desire partition, and they continued to claim that the North Schleswigers did not want that solution either, but the possibility hovered in the background to many of the various aggrandizing pronouncements. By choosing to cite petitions opposing partition, the moderate Francke implicitly conceded validity to similar pro-Danish statements of opinion. The same can be said of Michelsen, who asserted North Schleswig's desire to stay with Germany in no uncertain terms: "It should not surprise you when I declare, as a North Schleswiger and in the name of a Danish-speaking population: We do not want to become Danes." Even Dahlmann, in his emotionally laden speech of June 9 defending Schleswig-Holstein's historic rights and the honor of Germany, hinted that border concessions based on the preferences of the inhabitants were not unthinkable. He simply claimed never to have met a single North Schleswiger who desired separation from Schleswig-Holstein.[12] Dahlmann's fellow historian and Schleswiger Georg Waitz, both in correspondence to Droysen in April and before the Assembly in June, even more clearly held out the possibility of some sort of plebiscite to settle the matter, a position in which he received the support of the pragmatic future Reich Minister Anton von Schmerling of Austria.[13]

By the time of the September debates over the much-despised Malmö armistice, even the all-or-nothing radicals of the left had recovered their footing upon the grounds of self-determination. Jakob Venedey, Carl Vogt, and the youthful Trier firebrand Ludwig Simon all expressed their support for hearing the opinions of the affected populace on the matter of partition, while the strongly nationalist, left-leaning Bavarian liberal Johann Eisenmann stated clearly, "I was never of the opinion that, even when the Schleswigers do not come to us willingly, we should be bent on acquiring North Schleswig."[14] On the chamber's right, among those pre-eminently in favor of accepting the Malmö terms as at worst a lesser evil than civil war with the Prussians, the new Foreign Minister Heckscher alluded to a possible division of Schleswig "according to the free choice of nationality," while Rhenish estate owner Carl Stedmann declared as rapporteur for the International Committee minority that he would not put his name to a peace treaty in which "even when North Schleswig did not want to, all of Schleswig would come into the German Confederation."[15] Many deputies remained aware that at least in principle they had to support the ideal of the popular will as standing equal or even superior to the juridical-territorial approach in determining national boundaries. Even in the Schleswig affair opportunism had its limits.

In 1919 self-determination went hand in hand with linguistic self-consciousness to define the so-called "nationality principle" and serve as the basis both for border revisions and for national movements and their claims to political autonomy. If the obviously important criterion of self-determination bore the same implication in 1848, then the depiction here of a more open-ended fusion of cultural and political aspects of nationhood among midcentury Germans could stand in jeopardy. It was in this context of late nineteenth- and early twentieth-century linguistic nationalism, after all, that such scholars as Hans Kohn and Carlton Hayes began studying and categorizing nationalisms. That contemporaries were aware of a potential relationship between self-determination and linguistic nationalism is clear enough—the radical Giessen zoologist Vogt formulated his preference for "self-determination" over historical arguments by expressly equating it with the "principle of nationality." The Schleswigers should, he maintained, have all along referred to the fact "that Schleswig is largely German, and it should have been said from the outset that we do not want to annex the whole of Schleswig, but rather leave it its self-determination in a peace treaty."[16] At least in theory the nationality principle adumbrated by men such as Ernst Moritz Arndt, Jacob Grimm, and Paul Pfizer, and attested to by men such as Droysen or Vogt, revolved around an assumed link between language and voluntarist nationhood. And as a theoretical option the notion did play a role during the revolution.

Nevertheless, some of the same deputies who invoked the notion of self-determination in the Schleswig case made it clear that the "nationality principle" did not at all rely so heavily on language as the signpost to national allegiance. In the same way that most delegates were prepared to concede that Alsatians were hardly clamoring to return to Germany and give up the cultural, political, and economic benefits of life as citizens of France, they thought that members of other language-based national groups could still opt for admission into a newly liberal German nation-state. If a clearly expressed "popular will" was good enough to justify the inclusion of German Schleswigers in the German state, then so long as Danish-speakers could be convinced of the latter's political and material benefits, it would serve well enough for them as well.

The legal historian Michelsen even went so far as to deny the premise that language and nationality enjoyed any special and necessary relationship. Such a "mix-up," Michelsen warned, occurred all too frequently in contemporary politics and could easily be exploited by this or that political interest. "Language," Michelsen then proclaimed quite clearly, "is not nationality; it is an important element, a distinguishing feature of nationality, but not the only one." Michelsen then gave a capsule treatment of linguistic relationships in Schleswig designed to illustrate how such a statement held all the truer in a land where most spoke neither High German nor High Danish but rather various dialects merging gradually into one another.[17] If deputies chose not to use arguments based on language in this instance, it was not only from a desire to ensure the largest possible acquisition of territory for the new Germany but also because they simply did not see that language or other more broadly cultural criteria could by themselves suffice as guidelines for a new era of liberal international politics.

Yet for all that language could not be the cosmological elephant's back upon which the liberal nationalist world reposed, language and language policy had formed one of the two main planks of the Schleswig-Holstein movement's platform during the 1840s. As shown in the preceding chapter, it was above all influential Schleswig-Holsteiners such as Dahlmann and the brothers Beseler who pressed for restrictions on parliamentary minority linguistic rights. How then can these apparently contradictory statements about the roles of language and culture in nationality politics be reconciled? The answer follows from the recognition that while a region had to have a German national character in order to be admissible into a German national state, that criterion actually said comparatively little about whether the numerical majority of household heads in a given area spoke German by their firesides. German national character devolved not from the simple spoken word of the peasant farmer but from the less easily ascertainable or quantifiable predominance of a German "Cultur," above all but not only in the public realm. Consequently, there was a strong tendency to apply this national character to the whole of the territory in question rather than seeking further for potentially equitable partition lines.

In order to see how such a scheme worked, it is best to retreat briefly into the world of Schleswig-Holsteiner politicking during the *Vormärz*. As part of their agitation against the royal Danish language rescript of May 1840, Schleswigers such as the future Assembly delegates Wilhelm Beseler and Jacob Gülich called for reversal of the Schleswig Diet's 1838 decision to allow the conditional use of Danish in its debates and in administration. One of their principal arguments was that the 1838 Diet had failed to consider the grave legal implications of allowing Danish to be enforced as the language of court and administration in those North Schleswig areas where it was already the language of church and school. Gülich and others saw the rescript as endangering the duchy's German legal "superstructure," on which its claims to constitutional autonomy within the Danish monarchy were based. This superstructural national character applied to the whole duchy; as Wilhelm Beseler pointed out in an 1842 analogy, the presence of an Italian-speaking minority did not prevent Tyrol from being considered a German province, and neither did that of a Danish-speaking minority for Schleswig.

The key, as Gülich attested in the 1840 Diet debates, was that German served Schleswig as the language of culture, the language of the urban educated and economic elites. What the rural masses may have spoken, or thought, did not matter nearly so much.[18] Dahlmann and Michelsen for their part placed such superstructural arguments from German high culture in the historical context of the peaceful linguistic conquest of Schleswig during the medieval and Reformation eras, a conquest that had left the Diet conducted in German and the scripture-reading North Schleswiger with the Luther Bible.[19] Moreover, given that German continued to make impressive gains in its slow northward advance as the spoken and written language of Schleswig, losing its privileged status over a Danish language suddenly artificially protected by the Danish king and his Eiderdane supporters could bar the way to further peaceful germanization. An important consideration in all these border conflicts remained the German liberal's belief in a conflictual march of history in which progress seemed to stride alongside German national interests—German national character was a creature of the future as much as of the present or the past.[20]

This brief foray into the prehistory of the Assembly debates on Schleswig makes it easier to discern the chords of the German-as-superstructure theme that underlay the more vocal assertions of historical rights and self-determination there. It was again Michelsen who, in his depiction of Schleswig linguistic relationships, provided the best introduction to this idea in the Frankfurt debates. Danish-speaking North Schleswig, Michelsen explained, was divided into two parts, one where German served as the "language of culture" or "Cultursprache," and one where Danish performed that role. And even in those latter areas where Danish might seem to prevail among the educated, the languages and peoples in fact mingled to a large degree: "the larger property-owners, the officials are German; German culture is widespread there, to the border and beyond." Above all in the cities and towns, German culture had slowly moved northward until it predominated, and many people commanded both tongues. In other words, where it counted, among the educated political elites and in the urban areas all the way to Jutland, German gave the land its distinctive character.

Michelsen's Schleswig colleague Francke added his own link to this liberal chain of argument. He conceded that one area of North Schleswig did indeed speak Danish and had little sympathy for Germany but then followed this admission with the avowal that "directly next to it in all towns the most vibrant German life yet makes itself known, and wherever you find the intelligentsia [Intelligenz] it is of pure German race [Race]!"[21] Schleswig might contain a Danish minority, but as long as the political and literate classes preserved their German national character and allegiance, Schleswig as a whole must count as German. A plebiscite, Francke, Michelsen, and others felt, would surely show this.

Strange as these plastic notions of national character might seem in an age where ethnic or linguistic censuses and plebiscites have come to seem natural, such ideas fit comfortably within the mid-nineteenth-century liberal worldview. For present purposes the most crucial aspect of mid-century conceptions of nationhood to bear in mind is their focus on middle- and upper-class rather than plebeian benchmarks, on high rather than low culture. Despite historiographical preconceptions about romantic nationalism, a love of peasant folksongs did not deflect most liberal nationalists of the 1840s from concentration on the modernizing world of urban politics and culture. This focus encouraged, for example, a tendency to as-

[handwritten margin note: high cult more imp. man low cult.]

sign true nationhood and the right to national independence only to those groups large enough to sustain the requisite cultural, economic, military, and consequently political strength, as in the old saw that defined a language as a dialect backed by a sufficiently large army. Both the size of the group in question and its stereotyped status among the "civilized" nations came into play in this regard. Italians, Hungarians, and occasionally the Poles could grace the honor roll of such acknowledged nationalities, but for other groups, such as the Czechs, the assumption was more problematic.

Moreover, although the *Vormärz* and revolution can rightly be seen to mark the emergence of mass political culture in Germany, this development remained in its early stages. When liberals claimed to speak for "the people" or "das Volk," they meant educated and propertied individuals like themselves. Public opinion implied educated public opinion, and if the lower orders wanted to participate in the national public sphere, they had to adopt bourgeois social and cultural norms. Among these norms was national identity itself; outside the larger population centers the "nationality" of public life was at best weakly developed, with older nonnational, nonlinguistic forms of political, confessional, and socioeconomic group identity still central—on both sides of the linguistic divides.[22] Hence it made sense that Frankfurt deputies should look to the predominantly urban world of industry and trade, but above all to the educated world of print culture, for definitions of nationhood and the labeling of geographic areas according to nationality. One of the core articles of faith in the midcentury liberal worldview was, after all, a belief in progress, which in this instance meant the progressive advance of elite culture and values into ever broader reaches of society. Since this process seemed to bring with it the transformation of rural linguistic minorities into full-fledged participants in the ruling public sphere, such an ascription of nationality made all the more sense. If an area were not yet fully German, it could still become so. Thus, in an interesting twist on the uses of exclusion in the construction of national identity, the bourgeois liberal slighting of the rural lower classes led to a more inclusive, multinational national identity. For midcentury liberals, self-determination and linguistic nationality combined in curious ways.

[handwritten margin note: nat. ID = bourg. ID]

In contrast to the Schleswig affair with its legal, historical, and superstructural arguments, the debates on Poznania have often been cited then and since as the greatest deviation from the territorial principle of national border-drawing that seemed to guide the Assembly in so many other instances. Leftists such as Robert Blum and Franz Schuselka pointed out with a certain relish that the moderate majority cleaved faithfully to historical arguments and the territorial principle in the Schleswig or Tyrolean questions, but when it came to Poznania they suddenly performed a volte-face and began prating about the rights of (German) nationality.[23] And it is true that many deputies agitated for the possibly even forceful inclusion of Danish-speakers in an undivided Schleswig and of Italian-speakers in an undivided Tyrol, while in the case of Poznania the majority broke with existing territorial boundaries and rejected both its complete exclusion from the new Reich and its complete incorporation within it. Instead, they called directly for partition rather than just holding open the vague possibility of it as in Schleswig. Such behavior might seem to support the conclusion that the linguistic nationality principle did after all find some use along the eastern borders with Poland. It might also seem to undermine the central contentions presented here, that the Confederation's territorial boundaries constituted the basic outline for the new state, and that those borders and any deviations from them were justified according to certain malleable notions of regionwide German national character. As should become clear, however, the Poznanian debates did not diverge so widely from the delegates' core conceptions of nationhood.

Speakers supporting the inclusion of the German portions of Poznania certainly chose to make much greater use of arguments from cultural nationality than had those in the more legalistic Schleswig debates. That Germans lived there and were thought of as German served ultimately as the principal motivation for annexing sections of Poznania into the Confederation, or for that matter for bringing in the twin provinces of East and West Prussia. Despite having been left outside the German Confederation in 1815, all of these lands were still deemed German, and the diplomatic scandal could be rectified. It could be rectified all the more easily given that the territories in question lay within Prussian jurisdiction and could be claimed on the basis of their alleged cultural Germanness without nearly the same danger of provoking foreign governments and peoples as would have been the case in, say, Alsace or the Russian Baltic provinces. The Breslau historian Gustav Stenzel, as rapporteur for the International Committee in the July Poznanian debates, thus felt free to invoke the Poznanian German party's potent combination of "language" and "descent," and to employ census figures setting out the numerical relations between Poles and Germans in the Grand Duchy. Although these figures left the ascription of nationality seeming entirely concrete and unproblematic, they were based solely on spoken vernacular or religious affilia-tion, not self-identification. Other deputies also cited these census num-bers, while the young Westphalian liberal Julius Ostendorf picked up on the genealogical and linguistic aspects of Stenzel's proofs and urged the inclusion of German Poznania by noting, "That a large part of Poznania is German by descent and language has already been sufficiently explained to you."[24]

As usual, however, language did not hold the field uncontested as the signpost of nationality. The moderate Poznanian doctor Adolph Goeden, for example, added to language the more broadly cultural "customs." Goeden also drew in "geographic situation" as a factor in the Poznanian-German equation, while the radical Wilhelm Jordan, apostle of the "politi-cal" conception of the nation, in this instance chose to couple German "language" with "cultivation" or "civility."[25] Even more noteworthy, as in the Schleswig case arguments based on self-determination and the general will formed a strong phalanx supporting the incorporation of an extra-fed-eral territory into the new Reich. Just after his remarks on Poznania's lin-guistic and genealogical Germanness, for instance, young Ostendorf ap-pended, "It is by will as well." Goeden for his part injected an even greater element of Rousseauian natural right in contending that "we are Germans and belong to the fatherland because a rational, lawful, a sovereign will drives us to it, a will determined above all . . . by our German mindset and our love of the fatherland." Nor did Stenzel neglect the proposition that the Poznanian Germans were "genuine Germans" in part because they simply wanted to be.[26]

It is important to keep the issues at stake in the various debates and votes clearly in mind before drawing conclusions as to the dominance of the principle of linguistic nationality in the Assembly's handling of the Poznanian matter. Many Poles, after all, would have been incorporated into so-called German Poznania, and under the proposed demarcation line at the time of the July debates, they would actually have comprised the majority of its population. Hence the mostly right-of-center supporters of partition could hardly rely on the nationality principle alone as a means of persuasion or justification. The Poznanian leader Samuel Kerst actually re-jected the whole notion of linguistic nationality as a determining factor there. Stenzel for his part took a more moderate stance and admitted the nationality principle's justice while still maintaining that it made a weak reed on which to build a national politics. Pointing out that all large states possess inhabitants of differing nationality from that of the "primary people," Stenzel concluded that this held equally true for Germany, that "we have . . . foreign nationalities among us; they have belonged to us for centuries, and we do not want to part them from us. We are thus, even if we make the principle of nationality paramount, not of the opinion that this principle can be adhered to in all details of border-drawing." Or as the Poznanian entomologist Hermann Löw more vividly expressed this reservation, "If every little village were to be excised where 10 or 20 who speak a different language live together, one would obtain a map like a sieve, more colorful than the map of the Holy Roman Empire ever was."[27] The liberal Saxon philosophy professor Karl Biedermann, who accepted the April 22 demarcation line as including only the primarily German areas yet rejected that of May 2 as unjustly infringing on largely Polish territory, remained a relatively isolated voice on this issue.[28]

If the majority moderates did not fully toe the linguistic line in the Poznanian affair, neither did the left hold firmly to the territorial ideal as a means of defending Polish interests in the matter (a fact often overlooked). Gustav von Struve's original call at the Pre-Parliament for the restoration of Poland, after all, came coupled with the demand that German Poznanians be included in the elections for the National Assembly, and he was supported in this by the influential Cologne leftist Franz Raveaux. Even at the Frankfurt Assembly itself, Carl Vogt and Carl Nauwerck each expressed support for the admission into the new Reich of the majority-German portions of the Grand Duchy, and while Schuselka refused to follow suit he yet held out the possibility of negotiations over this point when Poland had become a sovereign state again.[29] Despite the fact that voting followed party lines quite closely on July 27, the relatively recent political fissures among the former members of the national opposition had hardly had time to reorient fundamental notions of nationhood to such an extent that their views on Poznania would become so diametrically opposed. Democratic leader Robert Blum's proposal for a Poznanian fact-gathering commission can thus be interpreted either as a mere time-wasting ploy or as an attempt to negotiate what its supporters felt would be an acceptable compromise with their Polish confreres. That the Poznanian question had become a party question, in which each side adopted the political line suggested by the (Polish or German Poznanian) local interest group with whom they were allied, did not necessarily alter greatly what the Assembly might have done if left in isolation.[30] With a large German population resident in ethnographically mixed Poznania, the question almost automatically revolved not so much around whether the Prussian Grand Duchy would be incorporated but rather how much of it would be. Consequently, new arguments beyond those of simple nationality or territoriality had to be sought. As the Schleswig case has already shown, these were not far to seek.

One of the most prominent such justifications for annexing both German-settled and Polish-settled land into the new Reich was also one of the most unanswerable: the claim of strategic necessity. In order to secure Germany's eastern borders against its threateningly large neighbor the Russian Empire, the Prussian general Radowitz and the flamboyant Prince Felix Lichnowsky pointed out, the fortress city of Poznań had to be kept as an integral part of the defensive network running from West Prussia to Silesia. "If we did not have the fortress Poznań," Prince Lichnowsky went so far as to claim, "then we would have to conquer it."[31] Although Radowitz and Lichnowsky occupied perhaps somewhat suspect positions on the Assembly's right wing, they in fact merely picked up on arguments already introduced by the more liberal Stenzel and originally formulated by the Prussian government. Since the city of Poznań included a pro-German German and Jewish majority, it would not have stretched the bounds of the self-determination ideal to claim it on that basis. The difficulty arose from the fact that to make the fortress militarily viable, the partitioned territory had to include the hinterlands and certain vital transportation lines—or so the self-proclaimed experts assured the interested deputies. This in turn entailed the incorporation of populous Polish-speaking districts within the ostensibly German portion of Poznania. The national interest of national defense thus helped fill the practical breach between supposedly competing territorial and linguistic border-drawing theories. Or as Stenzel put it, German claims to these sections of Poznania rested not on "nationality" but on "Germany's interest," not on "right" but on "necessity."[32]

For present purposes, however, by far the more interesting justifications for annexing parts of Poznania involved the notion of historical rights. In the Schleswig case long discourses on the dates and documents leading to the legal tangle of Schleswig-Holstein inseparability and Danish succession law had predominated, but the complex Poznanian situation also offered numerous if different opportunities for the use and abuse of historical scholarship. Most frequently invoked as the basis for German historical right to portions of Poznania was the medieval *Ostkolonisation* period of Germanic settlement in the eastern forests. Such recourse to the deeper medieval past put the issue squarely in the realm of history seen as a process rather than simply as a succession of contracts. Without having to pay homage to Hegelian notions of logical historical necessity, deputies could still depict the German occupation and transformation of sections of Poland as part of a natural historical process. Without trying to deny the injustice of the eighteenth-century partitions, deputies could set German possession of Poznanian lands in the context of history's grand design. This allowed them to present their case in a perspective at once morally neutral and morally legitimating in its removal from the purely human world of individual decision-making and free will. In the liberal view of history the German presence in Poznania could be made to appear the most natural, and hence most just, thing in the world.

Yet such arguments opened up ominous new approaches for the handling of nationality conflicts in Poznania or elsewhere. Denigratory chauvinist nationalism obtruded sharply from such remarks, which simultaneously helped domesticate a conscienceless view of history and politics. Wilhelm Jordan's famous speech on Germany's need for a "healthy national egoism," in which an aggrandizing theory of natural history finally triumphed over a sense of natural justice, stood in the vanguard of such tendencies, but it hardly exhausted them.

In terms of pejorative Polish stereotypes, deputies did not have to look far for forerunners. Contrary to some depictions of Polish-German friendship and cooperation during the *Vormärz,* support for the Polish cause did not at all preclude an unflattering portrait of Polish political and cultural values and achievements. Most typically, observers liked to retail the truism that without excusing bloodless diplomatic intrigues, the Poles had to bear a fair share of the blame for the partitions. Friedrich von Raumer's famous publicistic work *Poland's Fall* praised the Poles for their patriotism, bravery, and love of independence but also reminded readers that Poland's decay had internal causes such as disunity and the restriction of these very virtues to the nobility. Hence it should come as no surprise that Raumer picked up in 1848 where he had left off in 1832, pointing out that the Poles, like the Italians, bore some responsibility for their lack of statehood and might well still be too disunited to restore a national state any time in the near future.[33] Stenzel had adopted an even more negative view of Polish cultural and political capabilities in his 1830 *History of the Prussian State,* and although in Frankfurt he declared himself unwilling to tread too nearly upon another people, he still explained that Poles could exist more easily under German rule than vice versa. Poles, he contended, were bold and powerful, "as if made for war," but the rule-bound and reflective Germans proved much better in the longer times of peace.[34]

More important for the present argument, as in his prerevolutionary scholarship, Stenzel focused on medieval German city-building achievements as an element in the superiority of the German way of life over that of the Poles. City life, Stenzel maintained, had always been foreign to Poles; it was only the Germans and German Jews who had brought trade and urban settlements to Poland and then preserved them. The historian Max Duncker of Halle went even further and observed that the eastern colonization "was the natural course of things. Our people was more numerous and powerful, its nature [Art] and ability superior, its culture earlier and more mature." It was this superiority rather than the partitions that had won parts of Poland for Germany, and the results could not be undone.[35] Although disclaiming "hatred between nations" as a "barbarism incompatible with the civilization of the nineteenth century," the ever-blunt Wilhelm Jordan apparently did not include contempt as part of such hatred and carried the negative image of the Poles to its greatest extreme of the debates. Jordan commented that the "superiority of the German people over most of the Slavic peoples, with the possible exception of the Russian," was a fact, and it was one of "the facts of natural history" at that. Moments later he broke out in a tirade against the sloth of the Polish nobility, allegedly patriotic but actually irresponsible and lacking any of the vaunted German industriousness. He finally dismissed them slightingly as mere "charming Mazurka-dancers."[36]

In Jordan's speech, one of the longest and probably the most famous of the entire Frankfurt experience, he as usual carried his auditors along on a wave of rhetorical ebullience without necessarily being fully representative of their more moderate if not qualitatively different views. This rule held good both for his chauvinistic stereotyping, which earned him hisses from the left and a rebuke from President Heinrich von Gagern, and for his deployment of a Hegelian historical scheme to explain why the Poles, as a dead nationality, could not be resurrected and could not claim German Poznania as part of a new Polish state. In making this latter argument, Jordan attempted to draw the Poznanian situation and the German conquests into the scientific realm of "natural necessity" and "natural laws," as when he claimed that "one of those [natural laws] states that a people does not through its mere existence have the right to political autonomy, but rather only through the power to assert itself as a state among others." Hence the partition of Poland did not represent "the murder of a people" but

Germ justified in taking parts of Poz.

rather only the "proclamation of an already accomplished death," one it would be foolhardy to attempt to reverse.[37]

If this proved a bit too much for most deputies to take, many, naturally including Duncker and Stenzel, could have followed him in his conclusion that different native characteristics helped explain and justify the German "conquest" of Poland in previous centuries, and that this conquest gave Germans the right to deem parts of Poznania German rather than Polish. As Jordan stated early in his oration, for him the demarcation line did not at all represent a new "partition" of Poland but rather simply showed "how far German language and civilization had victoriously advanced." Somewhat later, he added that the Germans possessed German Poznania "by the right of the stronger, the right of conquest," which in this instance meant "not so much conquests by the sword as conquests by the plow-share." Young Ostendorf picked up on this remark and compared it favorably to the American displacement of Native American populations, while Stenzel sagely observed that land was not like money—it could not just be refunded years later because the people living there had changed and it was no longer the same land.[38] Within the presuppositions of such arguments the Poles found themselves sunk beneath notice and without claims to the rights of a civilized nation.

Views like these lend credence to the idea that the chauvinistic nationalism of such deputies as Stenzel and Jordan performed a negative strategic function in destroying Polish claims and sympathies more than a determinative one in showing where the demarcation line should lie.[39] Yet as in the Schleswig case closer examination of the arguments advanced by Stenzel and Jordan reveals an interesting new dimension, in which similar views on the ascription of territorial German national character come to the fore. Although the legal and constitutional complications of keeping German as the official language did not play the role they had for Schleswig, the emphasis placed by both men on the slow penetration of German urban commercial life and of urbane German culture, language, and civilization into lands previously having an entirely different national character set the matter squarely in the German-bourgeois context so integral to deputies' ideas of nationhood. As the Poznanian deacon Ernst Nerreter pointed out in June, the situations in Poznania and Schleswig were not so very different after all. Explaining how he came to this conclusion, Nerreter cited both the will of the Schleswig population and "the real reason, that in Schleswig a German population resides, had become native there and in the course of time had won the upper hand." Nerreter followed these remarks with an early version of the argument that would form the core of Stenzel's and Jordan's critiques of Polish claims to nationhood, namely that they lacked an "urban middle class, this fundamental condition and basis of our political well-being," a circumstance that had led to an imperfect conjunction of the Polish upper and lower classes.[40]

In this same connection it is crucial to highlight the centrality of Stenzel's and Jordan's critique of the Polish aristocracy to their ideas of the role of urban middle-class German *Bildung* in setting its national stamp on Poznania. Despite all the emphasis on high rather than folk culture in determining nationality, Stenzel and Jordan sought to undermine Polish claims to nationhood with the accusation that only the nobles possessed the Poles' vaunted patriotism, that in fact the aristocracy and the peasants made up "two different nations."[41] As Nerreter's less scholarly but still fairly consistent views have already foreshadowed, deputies thought that unlike the German middle class, the Polish nobility could not truly bind all classes into the overarching harmonious whole that was the liberal national ideal. In the German case cities and the bourgeois societal element served as a bridge between rural aristocracy and peasantry and eased the assimilation of each into the modern bourgeois social and cultural order. In the Polish case Stenzel, Jordan, and Nerreter all pointed to the lack of a strong middle class as a factor inhibiting the development of a truly national Polish nation.

This alleged deficiency of the Polish nationality in fact opened up the possibility that continued germanization could prove to be the Poles' salvation. Further exposure to Prussian administration in the newly created autonomous Polish province of Gnesen, Stenzel thought, could help accelerate this historical process of creating a potentially durable Polish nation and state, "a Poland not for the nobles, but for the peasants." Or, making the role of an emergent urban sector more apparent, Stenzel later articulated his desire for "a Poland for the burgher and peasant, who should preferentially be able to develop themselves." For Stenzel such indirect germanization involved only political education and sociocultural emulation. He explicitly called for the creation of institutions to stimulate the growth of Polish "national feeling," and he stipulated equally clearly that Poles left in German Poznania would not be ruled by Germans alone or be forced to become Germans.[42] For Wilhelm Jordan, Max Duncker, Heinrich Wuttke, and the Poznanian Samuel Kerst, on the other hand, germanization would probably have meant the slow transformation of

Poles in German Poznania, and perhaps in Gnesen as well, into what would essentially be cultural Germans bearing Polish surnames.[43] As in Schleswig part of the attraction of the whole argument for a connection between German national character and the urban bourgeois world of high culture and a dynamic public sphere was its apparent promise that with time the civilizing process would also entail germanization. Belief in the historical and social progress of *Bildung* also led to belief in the progress of specifically German *Bildung* among non-German peoples.

Of course, for all the similarities between the underlying assumptions and arguments in the Schleswig and Poznanian cases about what made a territory nationally German, the fact remains that in the former case the majority might have allowed but certainly did not favor partition while in the latter it positively desired it. Proposals to incorporate the whole of Poznania into the Reich were made but met with little success. In July the Catholic party proposed the inclusion of both the German and Polish "brothers" of Poznania into the new Germany, and even the venerable Turnvater Jahn argued that since partition could not be accomplished without injuring one or the other nationality, it would be better for all concerned to enjoy legal and linguistic protections within the Reich. Both motions, however, were firmly rejected by the Assembly, nor were Nauwerck and the leftist minority any more successful in reviving the proposal on behalf of their Polish allies in February of the new year.[44]

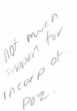

Several considerations lay behind this refusal to annex the whole of Poznania. Not least among them was the Prussian government's promise of a nationally just reorganization of the province, which had already set the terms of debate from an early stage of the revolution. Nor could the local patriotic and historical urge to keep intact a province only recently cobbled together in 1815 from the remnants of several other Prussian and Polish lands have been as great as in the case of centuries-old Schleswig. Suspicion of a potentially nationally minded Polish majority also played a role, above all given the tendency to borrow arguments from German Poznanian publicists to the effect that aggressive Polish nationalism and the eruption of violence between the two groups made it impossible for them to coexist under the same (henceforth Polish majority) administration. Finally, deputies such as the moderate Stenzel, the liberal Christian Wurm, and the leftist Jakob Venedey almost certainly meant it sincerely when they proclaimed their hopes that even the pitiful rump province of Gnesen would prove the nucleus of a future Polish national state. If the original *Polenfreundschaft* had not remained as purely polonophile as sometimes thought, neither did it disappear utterly in the wake of the inter-nationality violence in the spring of 1848.[45] The dismissive opinions of that undertaker of nationalities Wilhelm Jordan remained extreme. The bourgeois liberal notions of territorial national character would be applied to the Polish-settled parts of German Poznania but not to the whole province.

When the Assembly turned to confront the issue of Austria's future territorial and political relationship to the new German national state, delegates faced a situation very similar to that found in Poznania. True, provinces such as Bohemia, Moravia, and Carniola belonged to the German Confederation, a circumstance that certainly predisposed deputies to adhere to the territorial principle rather than to yield land on purely theoretical nationality grounds. On the other hand, these provinces all contained Slavic majority populations intermixed with more urbanized German settlement areas. As in the Poznanian case it became an important consideration in these debates not just to establish a German legal or ethnographic claim to these lands but instead to assert their prevailing German national character as demonstrated by the predominance of German culture where it counted—in the more modern and progressive forms of economic and cultural life.

First, however, all of the various justifications for the adherence of "German" lands offered in the cases of extra-federal Schleswig and Poznania went on to make oratorical curtain calls in this federal context. Gabriel Riesser was the Constitutional Committee rapporteur for the draft constitution's controversial Paragraphs 2 and 3, the "personal union" clauses that seemed to some to impede Austria from joining the new Reich, yet he still invoked the hallowed refrain of Arndt's famous song "The German's Fatherland," with its uplifting assertion of the linguistic principle of border-drawing: "As far as the German tongue resounds / . . . It must be the whole Germany!" Nor were Arndtian allusions lacking among the speeches of those insisting on the inclusion of all the Habsburg federal provinces in the new Reich.[46] Historical rights also received their due, in Arndt's and Ignaz Kuranda's references to the Bohemian "great-grandsons of the Marcomanni," and in the assurances of the Austrian oppositionists Eugen Megerle von Mühlfeld and Baron Viktor von Andrian-Werburg that historical, political, and dynastic ties would bridge differences in "tribe and language" among the federal Austrian nationalities.[47] Particularly with regards to Tyrol and Bohemia, strategic considerations of national defense against the enemies to the east claimed a share of Assembly attention and credence.[48] But above all in this question, deputies proclaimed their adherence to the territorial principle and declared their refusal to yield any federal lands at all. Neatly summing up all the various midcentury German criteria for nationhood, the minor Austrian official Johann Fritsch averred that the lands of German Austria had acquired the right to remain connected to Germany "through origin, descent, customs, habit, common experiences, many, yea innumerable wars carried on together, and through innumerable interests that they have defended with one another." Adding then "ancient treaties" and the Vienna settlements to his list, the moderate Fritsch concluded with perhaps his strongest argument: "Finally we also possess this right through the common popular will."[49]

Amid the welter of potential nationality criteria, however, the basic outlines of the liberal notion of national character as conferred by an economic and cultural elite still stood out. As it had for Schleswig and Poznania such a perspective left a territory's national character relatively independent of the presence of rural non-German populations. In arguing for the inclusion in the new Reich of the federal—but only the federal—parts of the Habsburg Empire, the Upper Austrian mining official Camillo Wagner invoked nearly all the above nationality criteria to show that in these lands "all is German." He conceded the existence of sizable Slavic populations in federal Austria but dismissed them as for the most part peripheral and scattered. Shoring up this line of reasoning with reference to the German realm of urban culture, Wagner concluded, "In general, German-Austria is thoroughly German territory that belongs to Germany with its citizenry [Bürgerthume], with its culture [Bildung] and all its sympathies."[50]

Other deputies looked even more specifically to the liberal realm of German *Bildung* and economic life for proofs of the predominantly German character of even the majority-Slavic parts of German Austria. To support his published contention that Bohemia was not just a Slavic province but would remain bound to Germany, the Bohemian radical Franz Schuselka adduced both the thousand-year connection between his home province and Germany and the supposed fact that "the country's most beautiful and significant districts, precisely those for whose rural and industrial culture [Kultur] Bohemia is today most renowned, possess a pure German population of nearly two million people."[51] Fellow Bohemian Ignaz Kuranda made much the same point in June, only more fully and tellingly.

Freely admitting that Czechs outnumbered Germans in Bohemia by more than half a million, Kuranda still contended that the German minority greatly outweighed the Czechs in other respects. As had Schuselka, Kuranda stressed that the main sites of efficient agriculture and industry lay in the pure German crescent-moon area of Bohemia. Giving mines as an example, Kuranda asked rhetorically, "Who built them up? German hands, German industry. Who founded the city-life, the middle class in Bohemia, the industrious, prosperous middle class by which Bohemia distinguishes itself from Poland, Croatia, and other half or entirely Slavic lands?"[52] And with a coy reference to the German origins of higher education and culture in Bohemia, Kuranda completed this encapsulation of midcentury educated German notions of wherein lay the true German national character of a province that in other, allegedly less significant respects was more Slavic. In terms of the broader debate on borders, all this meant that just as the presence of linguistic minorities in Schleswig and Tyrol did not alter deputies' impression of them as nationally German, not even the presence of a Slavic majority in provinces such as Bohemia or Moravia prevented their being claimed as integrally German in character.

The Austrian Question proved to be one of the keys to the 1848 revolution's success or failure, and, most important for larger interpretations of that event, the attitudes of the Assembly majority suggest that there was not so great a divergence of opinion on where the new Germany's borders should lie as might be imagined from the usual depictions of the Little Germany/Greater Germany distinction. For reasons of both territoriality and plastic notions of nationality, most deputies on both sides seem to have desired the federal borders in Austria. In other words, it was for the most part not in the border-drawing aspects of the culture of nationhood that one must seek for the contestation in national identity that ultimately helped doom attempts at revolutionary unification in 1848.

Throughout the Austrian debates contention revolved primarily around constitutional arrangements rather than borders per se. The conditions under which federal Austria would enter the new state, and not the prior concern of whether or how much of it should do so, formed the point of departure for most treatments of the issue. Considerations beyond the delegates' underlying conceptions of nationhood thus played a large role. Politically, for example, many deputies opposed the plans of the Little German or Kaiser party simply because they could not accept the notion of a Prussian kaiser, or even of any emperor at all, lording it over what was

If Klein-Dt.

don't want
Prus. kaiser

*

Religious
tension

Prus. would
dom Free
Trade

Austria =
not liberalized

supposed to become a free and united Germany. Similarly, the Prussian party's emphasis on greater government centralization offended the more federal or particularist sensibilities of many representatives from smaller states.

Special interests also proved important. Catholic members of the Assembly often preferred the former federal boundaries for the new state as a means of ensuring a Catholic majority, whereas a Little German solution would potentially leave them at the mercy of an often anticlerical, anti-Catholic mass of Protestant liberals. Beyond religious concerns many from the smaller German states feared a polity dominated by Prussia without the Habsburg counterweight. Austrians and Prussians themselves, of course, often simply rallied round the banner of their respective dynasties and made of the Austrian debates just one more chapter in the long annals of Austro-Prussian rivalry. Finally, more pragmatic interests also influenced opinions. Many South Germans, for instance, worried that Prussian dominance meant the apotheosis of Manchesterite free trade policies, while Assembly economic pundits from across Germany feared that a rancorous constitutional split could put paid to their hopes of complete access to the markets of the great Central European economic watershed. Given a fairly general accord that Germany's borders should by and large remain those of the Confederation, a view held among most Prussian party and Greater German adherents alike, explaining the differential willingness to deviate from those borders focuses attention preeminently on the realm of factors exogenous to basic thinking on nationality.

The contention that Little Germans like Greater Germans shared both a desire for the federal borders and many of the same assumptions about nationality might seem strange. During the *Vormärz*, after all, individuals including Georg Gervinus and Johann Droysen, but above all Paul Pfizer and Friedrich Dahlmann, had undeniably and forcefully argued that with the coming ascendancy of liberal government and the nationality principle, the multinational Austrian monarchy would be unable to sustain itself. The German portions of Austria would naturally fall into the arms of the larger German fatherland, and the long-standing Austro-Prussian dualism in Germany would reach its end with the assumption of leadership by Prussia. There was, of course, an alternative—if Austria successfully resisted liberalization it might yet manage to retain control over its diverse, far-flung populations. But if that occurred, as those such as the brothers von Gagern believed, the Habsburg Empire would be forced to withdraw from anything more than a close treaty of alliance with the liberal, Prussian-led German national state. In any event, these prognosticators apparently foresaw a future in which linguistic nationality would determine national allegiance. The German nation-state would for the most part be just that—German.

This portrait of such early Prussian party perspectives seems clear enough, and since it fits with the party divisions between Little and Greater Germans in the winter and early spring of 1849, there might not appear to be much need to explore further. Yet if the above contention as to the primacy of federal borders is true, and if most deputies tended to assign German national character to territories in such a way that the whole of Schleswig or even Bohemia was seen as a predominantly German province, then something must be missing from the picture. When Prussian party adherents such as Dahlmann and Droysen spoke of the German parts of Austria coming into the Reich, did they envision ethnographic partitions of Austria's federal provinces, or did they simply think each province would quite naturally be included in its entirety? Paul Pfizer, although one of the most categorical of all the early proponents of a Prussia-centered Germany, had left a loophole (previously noted in Chapter 1) in his supposedly hard-and-fast rule as to the impossibility of multilingual states in a just liberal society. Any minute inequality or injustice practiced against one of those national groups would be enough to justify secession—but without that inequality or injustice, a secessionist movement was not justified.[53] In general these theoretical and programmatic texts were simply too schematic to be able to tell what their authors might have been thinking about the situation of, say, the Slovenes in Carniola, a fact that leaves Pfizer's caveat with only suggestive significance. Galicia and Lombardy would almost certainly have joined with their respective national states in the new order, but the political futures of the Czechs and Slovenes, under conditions of protected linguistic rights, were hardly as clear.[54]

If in the *Vormärz* pundits could afford to be circumspect or hazy in their predictions, during the revolution they had to declare precisely what they meant. When that happened, it became much easier to see that at least during the revolution's first few months, many among even the Prussian party stalwarts thought the federal borders were still an attainable goal. Georg Waitz, associated with Dahlmann, Droysen, and other Prussian or "Hereditary Kaiser" party colleagues, on several occasions stated his belief that Austria would fall apart along nationality lines in the emerging period of liberalization. He nevertheless frequently stated his equally strong support for the maintenance of the former federal borders in Austria. Waitz even specifically hoped that the Bohemian and Moravian Czechs might elect to combine with Germany rather than with the Hungarians.[55] Pfizer and Droysen each worked for the institution of a Prussian hereditary emperor in the new Germany, but at least through the early summer months they continued to think of the possibility that Austria's "German" lands might indeed find their way into the German federal state. And Heinrich von Gagern, though one of those convinced earliest of the unlikelihood and even of the undesirability of Austria's breakup and entrance into the new Reich, still acknowledged the right of national self-determination—for Polish Galicia and northern Italy but not for the other nationalities, who as "satellites" in the German "solar system" lacked a solid claim to sovereign independence.[56] In general the Prussian party seems to have been no more apt to interpret the nationality principle in European politics in "one nation/one state" terms than were the supporters of Austria. They simply had other political priorities that trumped the question of borders in the construction of the new nation.

Moreover, the Little Germans, even later when basing their politics on the assumption of Austria's nonentrance into a Prussian-led Reich, still often believed that a time would come when German Austria would be able to rejoin the German national state. Georg Beseler, Friedrich Bassermann, Hermann von Beckerath, and Georg von Vincke were but some of those who thought the Little German approach might yet prove to be only a temporary expedient, awaiting the day when the Austrian monarchy could no longer constrain its constituent nationalities. Such a conviction certainly eased Carl Welcker's and Oskar von Wydenbrugk's transitions from *Grossdeutsche* to *Kleindeutsche* in March, as did the knowledge that they would not be alone among their recent former opponents in thinking so. As Wydenbrugk quaintly expressed the idea, since the new Austrian constitution held out no great prospects of lasting success, voting for the personal union paragraphs in the Frankfurt constitution (which the Austrian government would likely find unacceptable, thus preventing Austrian participation in the new German state) would merely constitute an "Auf Wiedersehen!" to the Austrian delegates, not a farewell.[57] In this respect too the federal borders continued to form the basis of most deputies' thinking on national borders, even in the spring of 1849.

One aspect of the debates, however, emphatically did cast a discriminating light on notions of the extent and boundaries of German nationality—the treatment of the 70-million Reich concept. Although originally put forward by the Bohemian estate owner Count Friedrich Deym, the idea of including all the Habsburg lands in a new German federal state was taken over by the new Habsburg emperor's Schwarzenberg Ministry in its various proposals for a directorial form of government in a merely reformed Confederation. While some Prussian party adherents admitted the allure of Deym's grand Reich idea of October, they still elected to oppose it as impractical or irreconcilable with their understanding of nationhood. The notion of accepting the Austrian government's plan of a loose federal structure coupled with such a very large non-German minority, however, roused their vigorous and unqualified opposition. Significantly, the Austrian Schmerling and his Greater German or Directorial party found the idea no more to their taste.

Quite obviously Deym, Karl Möring, Johann Sepp, Moritz Mohl, and the others who envisioned the formation of a German state extending into the depths of southeastern Europe must have strained the bonds between the cultural and political elements of nationality to near or beyond their limits. Whether Deym and his fellows truly thought the liberal political process would create a new national sentiment on the basis of a multilingual, multicultural society remains uncertain, although Mohl at least felt that citizenship and parliamentary participation for these groups would have the same nationality-reconciling, patriotism-inducing effect that possession of French citizenship did for the Basques, Bretons, and Alsatians of France. Möring too, though with more emphasis on the federative nature of the process of national identity-building, still seems to have looked forward to a day when Rumanians and Rhinelanders, Hungarians and Hanoverians would sit together in the same parliamentary body.[58] More intriguingly, Deym himself did not hesitate to invoke high cultural considerations in his plea for a Germany to the Black Sea that would rule over 70, 80, or even 100 million souls. He urged deputies to recall that to the borders of Bukovina and to the Dalmatian coast, "every educated person speaks German; it is only the German element that everywhere brings civilization to the Slavic and Magyar lands." Deym therefore implored the Assembly not to yield "land saturated with German culture" simply to satisfy certain notions of constitutional propriety.[59] If imperialist dreams of German size and strength supplied the heart of the 70-million approach, it was nourished by the ideational blood of an especially open-ended interpretation of the liberal culture of nationhood.

While still remaining within the bounds of the culture of nationhood, members of the Kaiser or Little German party took the association of the cultural and political aspects of nationality in a more exclusionary direction and let concerns for the nation's cultural and political unity determine their strong objections to the construction of a super-Germany in the midst of the European continent. They earnestly desired that the new German national state possess a German national character, and their requirements for meeting that stipulation could by no means match Deym's for malleability. The quality of being German did not depend wholly or even primarily on language or culture, nor did it have to be total in terms of the populations living in a given territory. Germans did not even have to constitute an absolute majority for a region to be dubbed German. Still, the quantitative relationship did matter. The Westphalian Vincke observed, for instance, that with the 70-million ideal, "whether the thing is practical or not, you will never call it a *German state.*" Against the counterargument that if Prussia was allowed to sweep its extra-federal territories into the Reich under its wing, Austria should be granted the same privilege, Gabriel Riesser offered an amusing analogy that made clear the importance of scale in ensuring Germany's German national character. "And then, because I took my brother with his family into my house, and among them there was an adoptive child," Riesser asked with rhetorical bite, "have I thereby made my house into an open hall, into which foreign throngs may enter as they please, without my consent?"[60] The Kaiser party supporters remained willing, even eager at times, to accept the entrance of millions of non-Germans into the German national state, yet when it came to the tens of millions of "barbaric or half-barbaric" non-Germans in the plains and mountains of Hungary, they hoped to bar the constitutional door.[61] Not all Germans had to be German, but Germany itself and all its provinces had to be predominantly so.

The Little Germans particularly focused on two points in their campaign to maintain a certain limited cultural and constitutional purity for the German national state: the avoidance of parliamentary multilingualism and the notion that Germany had to pursue an independent "German politics" insulated from the possibility of an overweening non-German influence. As for the latter, many Prussians and other North Germans did not want to expose themselves to the weight of 28 million non-Germans with special interests of their own that might prove powerful enough to deflect Germany from its national interests. Hence one of their main arguments in favor of a Prussian as opposed to an Austrian kaiser was that even in a Reich with the federal borders, Austria and its Habsburg rulers would still be subject to a large degree of (primarily Slavic) non-German influence from outside those borders. As Gervinus contended in the *Deutsche Zeitung* in May, Austria would always have to satisfy its Slavic inhabitants and turn a large share of its attention to the east, thus attenuating its German character and leadership qualifications. Or as Georg Beseler put it more bluntly in committee in December, "Austria is not a German power, it only has German components." Prussia, on the other hand, was according to Beseler "entirely German."[62] Such non-German influence the Kaiser party could not accept. As Riesser's March report for the Constitutional Committee stated, no constitution that left "Germany's development dependent upon a predominantly non-German influence" could be acceptable to the German people.[63] Such considerations had all along informed the Prussian party's desire for constitutional restrictions on the conditions under which federal Austria could join the new Reich and the federal borders be achieved.

Arst no purely germ (Pruss. is)

As for Prussian party adherents' views on multinational parliaments, they may be guessed quite easily from their somewhat restrictive treatment of language rights in Schleswig during the 1840s and in the formulation of the Mareck nationality protection measure during the revolution itself. Too much multilingualism at the level of the national parliament simply would not work, they thought, and could well endanger the nation's essential cohesiveness and character. The Austrian government's proposal for a Directory on March 4, 1849 actually recognized this fact and would have deprived the reformed Confederation of a true "Volkshaus," or popularly elected parliament, in part to accommodate the new non-German territories. This lack of a parliament was a circumstance of special odium to Little and Greater German liberals alike. The Prussian party in particular took it as an object lesson in the dangers of over-diluting nationality. A nation had to have a House of Representatives, but it could not have too many nationalities represented in it. Vincke and Gustav Rümelin each thought such a construct would be a "monstrosity," Vincke sneeringly observing that delegates would have to take instruction from "all the language teachers in the world" in order to understand its deliberations. The Jewish-rights crusader Riesser for his part opined that while a multinational parliament was not impossible, nations already had enough internal divisions to overcome without adding the potentially schismatic factor of nationality.[64]

against multinat parl (single nat) Parl needed to maintain germ character

Still, much the same language of nationality incompatibility as came from the Little Germans could be heard from the Greater Germans, and

WANT FEDERAL BORDERS!

with the same result—a preference for the federal borders. Among left-leaning liberals, for example, the Bavarian Johann Eisenmann seemed to be among the foremost in desiring Germany's decoupling from Austria's non-German elements, yet careful attention to the non-German groups he cited reveals them all to be among those outside the Confederation: Poles, Italians, Croats, Slovaks, and Hungarians.[65] Similarly, even as the Jena leftist Gottlieb Schüler complained of lack of recognition for the nationality principle in the bloodless negotiations of the Assembly and the diplomats, his own Germany retained all of federal Austria: "if Italy, Hungary, Poland are not lost for Austria, then Austria will be lost for Germany, and which do you prefer—would you rather give up Austria, or should Austria rather give up Italy and Poland?"[66] Although the leftists Vogt and Ludwig Simon held out some hope for a transnational parliament of freely federated nationalities, they generally agreed with assessments of the difficulties involved in multinational parliamentary and constitutional arrangements. The liberal Heinrich Ahrens shared these concerns, while his Greater German colleague Welcker thought an Austrian politician would have to be "crazy" to want a multilingual Reichstag.[67] The conviction that a fully constitutional regime could not deal with the problems of too-many-million non-Germans ran stronger and deeper among the Kaiser party, but it grew out of a basic shared vision of nationality.

For their part, if Austrians were not to give up all faith in the continued existence of their homeland, they naturally had to maintain a greater belief in the potential for successful multinational government. Several Austrian oppositionists, including the leftist Anton Wiesner and the more conservative Eugen Megerle von Mühlfeld, insisted that on the basis of "nationality equal rights" as opposed to the pure linguistic nationality principle, the Austrian monarchy would prove able to strengthen a sense of national belonging among its various constituent nationalities. Neither, it should be noted, wanted to amalgamate all Habsburg possessions with Germany, but their arguments demonstrated the extent to which Baron Andrian's and Schuselka's *Vormärz* ideas for the liberal reform of the monarchy lived on in both moderate and radical circles in Austrian politics.[68] Equally, the Austrian official Fritsch followed his long list of factors proving the link between Germany and federal Austria with one nearly as long demonstrating the "organic" nature of the connection between the latter and the rest of the Habsburg monarchy. "Language" and "descent," of course, remained notably absent from the second list, where material, political, and historical interests made up the ties that bound. Whether by wish or by

link b/w Germ/Aust

worldview, most Austrian deputies seem to have had greater faith in Austria's constitutional future. Austrians and North Germans all still tended to operate with the main principles of the culture of nationhood, yet different political and cultural contexts had lent distinct nuances to their construal of them.[69]

Whether supporters of the 70-million Reich or Greater German concepts, Austrians still shared concerns about German national character and unity with Prussian party adherents. Many may not have felt their liberal countryman Franz Unterrichter's animus against the idea of federal Austrians sitting in the same Reichstag with representatives of the nationalities from extra-federal Habsburg lands, but as seen in the last chapter, they were not notably more eager to see other tongues invade the hallowed space of a German parliament, in Frankfurt or in Vienna. Tellingly, even Count Deym thought Germany and the Habsburg monarchy would require two separate parliaments with some kind of overarching appointed upper house to provide unity, otherwise a thousand-delegate, multilingual parliament would become a true "Babylonian confusion." The Austrian leader Schmerling, however much he too wanted to preserve intact the Austrian monarchy, still attested his unwillingness to follow Prince Schwarzenberg's plan and deprive Germany either of a true *Volkshaus* or of its German character—and this in private correspondence to his superior in the Austrian government, Prince Schwarzenberg. As he told the prince in an echo of the Prussian Vincke's words, "It could not possibly be the *German* federal state that would be so formed," and he had difficulty imagining Rhinelanders and Ruthenians sitting together in parliament.[70] Further, Austrian deputies desired a vigorous German national policy and worried about the dangers of non-German influence just as their northern neighbors did. The difference was simply that, short of jettisoning much of their homeland, the most effective way to ensure German greatness was to transform the German Confederation into the Greater German Reich. Even if many Austrian delegates held more sanguine opinions on the practicality of multinational constitutional government than did their North German counterparts, the sort of concerns seen in the last chapter about German national character, above all in the representational realm of the national parliament, remained fairly general.

All of this lends credence to Günter Wollstein's notion that there was no such great difference between the Austrian debates of October and January–March as has traditionally been assumed, primarily because there was in fact not such a great difference between the Little and Greater German groupings. Each shared the same basic assumptions about the need for a strong, German-dominated *Mitteleuropa,* in which it was a matter of secondary concern whether that leadership was split between the Austrian monarchy and Prussian-led Germany or simply derived from a federal Germany in which the extra-federal Habsburg lands still felt the force of German influence. Constitutional arrangements, not borders, formed the crux of debate. On October 27 a vote took place on Paragraphs 2 and 3, which set out the restrictive governmental provisions under which nonfederal lands could remain associated with federal territories. This vote saw large majorities of 340–76 and 316–90 pass the two "personal union" paragraphs, and an even larger one reject the 70-million Reich. At this time the multinational (but not too multinational) federal borders held almost complete sway over Assembly delegates' minds.

By January, however, support for Paragraphs 2 and 3 and for Gagern's new pro-Prussian party Reich Ministry had become razor-thin and ultimately uncertain. The big shifts of opinion had come among Austrians, South Germans, Catholics, and leftists, particularly once it became clear how closely linked the issues of kaiser, Prussian kaiser, and personal union were. The Austrians and their allies on the right pushed for some kind of looser arrangement that would allow the monarchy to remain intact but within the German federal structure, while their sometime allies on the left joined in opposing the Prussian kaiser and the associated abandonment of German Austria, yet still hoped to see the collapse of the reactionary Austrian monarchy as well. The Prussian party theoretically maintained its hopes for the federal borders in Austria yet expected and in many cases even preferred that Austria remain closely allied but not constitutionally joined to the German federal state.

The question, of course, is whether any of these dramatic shifts in parliamentary alliances and positions involved or occasioned transformations of national identity in terms of opinions on national boundaries and multinational nationalism. The Austrians and some of the leftists had changed their views on Paragraphs 2 and 3, thus perhaps showing some preference for incorporating "all" of Germany within the federal borders, even at the expense of certain elements of constitutional unity. And at least some on the left may have been growing more consequent in their application of the nationality principle in the course of the revolution, at least insofar as they seem to have accepted that even if the Czechs could be brought to accept membership in Germany (as opposed to their earlier talk of forcing them to it with the edge of the sword) they would have to be granted a great deal of federal autonomy to make it work.[71] But for the most part it would be difficult to argue that either the leftists or the Austrians had changed their basic opinions on nationhood and national boundaries. The language and argumentation deployed did not change greatly in the course of the revolutionary fall and winter. Both Austrians and leftists pursued their own political goals, which happened still to coincide in maintaining the federal borders, but each group was also willing to compromise those borders if its own political conditions could not be met—just like the Prussian party.

For the latter, on the other hand, some shift toward a more exclusionary preference for national homogeneity and unity over set, territorially defined national borders may have taken place. It was not so much that the justifications for a purely German (Prussian) leadership had changed. Rather, in the new context of the increasing unlikelihood that the Austrian parliamentarians or government would agree to acceptable conditions of entry, these antipluralist proofs began to take on greater logical rigor and rhetorical strength as well as a different resonance. In July even the well-connected Prussian party theorist and organizer Droysen could still speak of his hopes for bringing the German lands of the Habsburg monarchy into the new Reich, but by December it was clear to Droysen and his fellows that after Prince Schwarzenberg's Kremsier Program of November 27, no federal state with both a hereditary kaiser and Austrian participation would be possible.[72] Gagern's October view that German policy would have to reckon on the maintenance of a strong Austrian monarchy to serve as an ally against France and Russia had, by December, prevailed over those of Dahlmann, Waitz, and the others who had thought of German Austria separating from the rest of the Habsburg lands.

After the Kremsier Program, when Prussian party spokesmen adverted to the problems of multinational, multilingual politics, their persuasive efforts applied to the Little German 32-million Reich, which was much more purely German in its national character than the 45-million version with the federal borders had been. A left-liberal newcomer to the Kaiser party camp, the Darmstadt attorney Theodor Reh, already accustomed from his efforts on behalf of both Poles and Germans to argue on the basis of the nationality principle, now contended that only the "pure German being" in Germany should be united—the Reich had no need to force into its hesitating embrace the millions of Slavic "enemies" living in federal Austria.[73]

* * *

Some of the conceptual ballast inherent in the existence of millions of Austrian Czechs and Slovenes, whom even Prussian party adherents had expected to become part of a rejuvenated German Reich, had now been cast overboard. Such conceptual freighting had helped keep the culture of nationhood open-ended, its propositions allowing the admission of non-Germans into German nationalists' "imagined" national community. But with the seemingly definitive end to hopes for a new Reich that would incorporate as much of the old one as was politically feasible, they no longer had to combine the old multinational ideal of the Holy Roman Empire with newer liberal political ideas to create that inclusive union of the cultural and the political in the national. No longer would they have to rely on their liberal faith in the course of history and in the politically mediated, patriotism-generating process to allay their worries about the crystallization of national identity. Instead, Germans could allow the linguistic and self-determinative elements of the nationality principle to run to their seemingly logical conclusions, all the more so as the other, in part linguistically defined national movements had proved so unwilling to subordinate themselves to a German national state. The compound would proceed slowly toward one of its potential logical extremes: a sense of nationality as both cultural and political but with the cultural and political boundaries completely overlapping. Exclusivity would become the defining moment of the liberal political process. German citizens would in future come under increasing pressure to show themselves German by both culture and allegiance—and eventually by birth.

Still, even this post-October shift among Kaiser party stalwarts did not spring from an ideological vacuum but rather followed as an extension of the above-noted preexisting differences between North Germans and Austrians on such notions as federal autonomy and multinational parliaments. Potentialities already present *in nuce* within the culture of nationhood were simply drawn in different directions in response to the course of events, as delegates tailored their rhetoric and logic to suit a changing political and social matrix during the fall and winter of 1848–1849. By the period of Bismarckian national unification of the 1860s and after, these differences of emphasis had had time to grow more pronounced. The union of cultural and political aspects of nationality had been compressed into the full doctrine of the nation-state seen in the work of historians such as the later Droysen or, later still, Friedrich Meinecke. Moreover, notions of culture and politics themselves had not remained frozen but had been altered to suit the increasingly democratic and positivist tendencies in German intellectual, social, and political life. Above all in the Habsburg dominions, as the century wore on rural schooling and linguistic censuses increasingly displaced emphasis on the world of urban civility in nationality definitions and nationality politics. In 1848 debate was still emphatically not about the construction of a culturally homogeneous nation-state, but the conceptual elements out of which that doctrine would later be compounded could be seen in a process of distillation and development. The oddly, often egocentrically elastic notions of German national character and of broad-based criteria for nationality generally would eventually funnel into the confining flask of a much more exclusivist and assimilatory ideology.

6 | National Honor, National Conflict: Germany's International and Historical Role

Not least as a result of the Frankfurt Assembly's border-drawing activities described in the previous chapter, the new Germany soon found itself mired in numerous nationality conflicts. The question naturally arises as to why the *Völkerfrühling* spirit of international fraternity so quickly yielded to an inflamed atmosphere of competing national interests. Many commentators have remained content with observing that nationalism harbors an inherent tendency toward aggression and the naked pursuit of national interest, while others have focused the blame for chauvinist-aggressive manifestations of nationalism on either the Frankfurt democrats or liberals. Chapter 5, however, has already shown that neither opportunism nor doctrinaire territoriality was able to displace certain deeply held, constraining beliefs about national boundaries and national identity in the Assembly's border-drawing policies, beliefs that spanned political and geographic divides. This conclusion suggests the need to probe deeper into the midcentury German nationalist mentality for more context-specific explanations of Assembly bellicosity. Even noting the desire for glory, power, and national honor after decades of political impotence, while it takes the investigation further, ultimately just multiplies the questions.

The present chapter therefore reexamines the border-drawing debates from this new perspective in order to determine how elements of the culture of nationhood might have predisposed deputies to engage so readily and passionately in certain kinds of national conflict. First it looks at how the notions of national honor and autonomy described in Chapter 2 unfolded such explosive power during the revolutionary year. Then it explores the related implications for Assembly policy of the delegates' dialectical historical consciousness. In general the present chapter traces the ramifications of this second structural component of the culture of nationhood for relations among nationalities and for domestic politics, as Assem-

174

bly deputies tried to define the new Germany's role as an actor on the world-historical stage during the 1848 Revolution.

Certainly many delegates hoped to see the new Germany realize the old post-Kantian liberal dream of a *Mitteleuropa* capable of enforcing peaceful order on the Continent. But this vision of a Frankfurt-led *Pax Germanica* only seemed so attractive in light of the lessons of history within the culture of *Bildung*, in which peace and stability did not figure prominently. History, like the natural world in general, instead rolled onward as the seat of a dialectic of war and conflict, of rises and falls, of glory and ignominy. Borders could change, perhaps radically, and Germany had to be in a position to defend or even expand its own if it were to maintain its European prominence. Through a forceful self-assertiveness the new Germany had to harness the patriotic strength of its free citizens in order to ground its claims to the international recognition and respect that alone comported with its rights and honor.

Moreover, it was in this arena of international conflict that the cultural component of the nationality alloy carried perhaps its sharpest edge, not just in the sense of a mighty, distinctly German civilization, but also in that of a larger Teutonic association of peoples standing in opposition to correlative conglomerates of Europe's Romance and Slavic peoples. Only in the context of such a competitive world of national and even racial conflict, where a nation's borders and stability rested only on its physical and moral hardihood, can the full implications of the debates over Schleswig, Poznania, and Austria be grasped. In this context alone does it become possible to see how crucial to the Forty-Eighters' national identity and national politics were their interconnected notions of personal and national honor, autonomy, unity, liberty, and power. Each of these qualities mutually built upon and upheld the others, hence all seemed equally necessary attributes of a nation that hoped to withstand its confrontation with the slowly but inexorably grinding wheel of history. Yet in the historical scenario of the 1848 Revolution, attempts to construct a durable national edifice on the basis of such ideas ultimately collapsed under the weight of internal contradictions, international mistrust, and the resurgence of the dynastic governments and their standing armies, all through the very nationality conflicts that the honor- and strength-conscious Frankfurt parliamentarians helped provoke.

The rhetoric of national honor is often taken by historians to be nothing more than a tawdry mask for aggressive national interest.[1] As the discussion in Chapter 2 indicated, however, the invocation of national honor did not merely reflect bellicosity but in certain situations actually helped motivate it. Thinking in terms of national honor was not just a justification for adopting an aggressive stance toward neighboring nationalities but was rather deeply formative of the Forty-Eighters' understanding of politics. During the revolutionary period the ideas of personal honor and autonomy that were so central to the early nineteenth-century culture of *Bildung* carried over into the realm of nations as moral and juridical personalities just as they had before 1848.

While "national honor" did not degenerate into the jingoistic if emotionally resonant rallying cry in 1848 that is sometimes claimed, the concept did undergo a certain adulteration and association with ideas more typically encountered in the realm of Machiavellian power politics. In Assembly parlance the phrase "national honor" did tend to become coupled with that of "national interest," above all on the Assembly's right. Even in the Schleswig debates, in which Friedrich Dahlmann so powerfully moved the Assembly to declare the affair one of national honor, speakers such as General von Radowitz could argue that Germany fought not just for the "rights" of treaties but for the "honor" and the "interest" of the fatherland as well. Similarly, the historian Max Duncker observed later on that the Schleswig question touched not merely on issues of rights or nationality but on those of Germany's future, of its fleet and colonization.[2]

Speakers also sometimes placed the notion of honor in the realm of military glory, the other of the twin aspects of national honor often taken to exhaust its cultural meanings for the nineteenth century. Although references to the glory of the fatherland were not actually that numerous, several deputies both left and right did speak of how German "military honor" or "Waffenehre" had been pledged on the battlefields of Schleswig and Jutland.[3] And if the word "glory" was lacking, the expressions "greatness," "dignity," and "prestige" were often coupled with "honor," amply filling its role and suggesting that Assembly deputies definitely held notions of honor somewhat different from the bourgeois-shopkeeper conceptions purportedly prevalent since the days of Lessing and Kant. The notion that the Assembly or the German nation it represented could become the object of foreigners' contempt burned ulcer-like within these fledgling national politicians.

For all this increased tendency to link the idea of Germany's national honor with its national prestige or even its naked national interest, however, more than enough evidence remains to point up the continued prev-

alence of a mixed or intermediate conception of honor. Between the ideal-
ized, purely internal bourgeois type of honor and the aristocratic-military
form associated with the preservation of fragile reputations through the
code of the duello lay an almost religious belief in the near identity between the sphere of honor and the sphere of rights, a belief and an identity
manifested in the preservation of personal, or national, autonomy. Much
of the idolatrous fascination held by notions of national honor and reputation for nineteenth-century liberal nationalists derived, as often noted,
from the transference of dynastic and aristocratic ideals onto the integu-
ment of democratic politics in the wake of the French Revolution. Yet as
argued above for the *Vormärz*, the centrality of ideas of national honor to
liberal national politics emerged much more simply and directly from the
legal theory and ethical philosophy underlying the culture of nationhood.

For the revolutionary period itself this theory found its clearest application in the series of debates over Schleswig. The issue of who possessed the
duchy was, after all, first and foremost cast in terms of historical rights, of
legal and constitutional claims founded in treaties. If contract and rights-
theory notions of honor were to be invoked, this would be the place for it,
as a close reading of arguments both for and against the aggressive and
bellicose German policy in Schleswig confirms. For as Carl Welcker had argued in the prerevolutionary period, if there were no rights, there was no
honor, and if there was no honor, then neither could there be any lasting
claim to rights. Or as the Young German publicist Ludolf Wienbarg had
compactly and pungently put the idea in the motto to his 1846 work *The
Danish Gauntlet*, "Where our right is undefended, / Our manhood is
without honor."[4]

Assembly deputies continued to cast the question in terms of the rights-
honor connection in 1848. The Schleswiger legal historian Andreas
Michelsen, for example, followed his remarks of June 9 on Schleswig dialects and national character with the argument that if a peace were concluded in violation of Schleswig's right to remain whole and bound to
Holstein, "that would be a peace that injured Germany's honor . . . that
contains an obvious injury to its rights." The decision passed by the Assembly that same day also set up an equation between "the rights of the
duchies Schleswig and Holstein and the honor of Germany" in that it required the guarantee of both in any eventual peace to emerge from the ongoing negotiations with Denmark.[5] During the September crisis over approval of the unsatisfactory Malmö armistice, the leftist Holstein delegate
Arnold Engel followed this line of reasoning even more closely and de-

clared the rights of Schleswig-Holstein and the honor of Germany to be "one and the same."[6]

Moreover, the emotional lading taken on by legal or rights-based arguments through association with ideas and feelings of honor helps explain why so many in the Assembly seemed reluctant to compromise on the issue of partition. Michelsen's June remarks in this context have just been noted, but the left-leaning Holstein representative Heinrich Claussen made the implications of the rights-honor connection even clearer in his speech on July 10, after reports of unfavorable armistice conditions had begun to filter into the German press. Claussen contended that if the reports were true, "the rights of the duchies as well as the honor of Germany have been injured in the most disgraceful way." Arguing that North Schleswig enjoyed no separate status in international law from that of the rest of the duchy, Claussen perorated, "if we are in the right, gentlemen, we must put everything behind it, for Germany's honor demands that the right be protected to the utmost extremity and that no title of it be yielded."[7] Where honor entered in, even the finest point of rights had to be defended as if it were the greatest. Compromise began to seem compromising.

Similarly, some of the pressure felt in September to defend Schleswig's ostensible rights in their entirety must have derived from the fact that pledges to that effect having been given previously, it became difficult to retreat from them without injuring one's honor and losing face in the realm of public and international (or even private) opinion. This held true both for the corporate honor of the Assembly as the perceived representative of the nation and for the personal honor of the deputies within it. After all, the Pre-Parliament, the reformed Federal Diet, the Committee of Fifty, and the National Assembly itself had each made solemn proclamations in the revolution's heady early months, and backing away from them would certainly have involved a crucial loss of prestige. The liberal Holsteiner Carl Esmarch, the leftist Stuttgart historian Wilhelm Zimmermann, and the centrist Hamburg historian Christian Wurm all trumpeted variations on this theme to try to bring delegates to a sense of their duty, of what they owed the Schleswigers, the nation, and not least the Assembly itself. As the oratorically gifted Austrian radical Karl Giskra admonished with reference to all these previous decisions, "We have given our word to keep Schleswig-Holstein entirely with Germany . . . and we must redeem that word like men of honor." Even if they failed and fell in the attempt, Giskra concluded, they would at least fall with the knowledge, "All is lost, but not honor!"[8]

It has been observed that such rhetorical flourishing of national honor generally played much better on the left than on the right.[9] If one's criterion for success requires that the rhetoric advanced actually persuade and effect a change of opinion, this certainly holds true. The September crisis, at least, saw the converse occur—a slim majority in favor of delaying fulfillment of the conditions of the Malmö armistice on September 5 shrank through the defection of predominantly right-leaning deputies until on September 16 it became a slim minority in favor of rejecting the accord entirely. In large part, the use of arguments from national honor and national right, particularly as the crisis neared its resolution, remained the province of the Schleswig-Holsteiners and their leftist allies, and this rhetoric did not enable them to maintain their majority.

More noteworthy for present purposes, however, is the extent to which those who opposed rejection of the Malmö agreement felt they had to meet such latter-day Catos of national honor on their own ground and advance alternative interpretations of how notions of rights, honor, and prestige should be applied to this question. It is a sterling example of the manipulation of a shared "political language" by ideological opponents. For like conceptions of nationhood themselves, those of personal and national honor enjoyed a certain useful malleability, itself in part the product of the whole doctrine's mixed juristic and military, bourgeois and aristocratic heritage. In October, for example, when the moderate Schleswiger Esmarch adjured the Assembly that "right and duty" required annexing Schleswig in Paragraph 1 of the constitution, and that "honor" required keeping that promise before the eyes of the world, Georg Beseler responded that here honor meant keeping the pledge not to break the recently accepted Malmö accord by a unilateral proclamation of Schleswig's entrance into the Reich.[10] Reich Minister Hermann von Beckerath, fresh from his attack on the institutions of military caste honor in the 1847 Prussian United Diet, stayed true to his beliefs in the Schleswig case and advised that it comported much better with the honor of a great people to leave the sword in its sheath rather than draw it in what might become a bloody civil war with Prussia. The Austrian opposition aristocrat Eugen Megerle von Mühlfeld brought out the allegedly more bourgeois aspects of the rights-honor thesis even more compellingly when he observed that in his opinion, "honor rests and must rest upon a moral foundation. Truth in words, honesty in deeds, faithfulness in promises above all give the reputation of honor."[11]

But if opponents of an overly aggressive stance in the Schleswig affair stressed alternative potentialities within the theory of honor, they worked with the same set of axioms. Defending one's honor "before the eyes of the world" still occupied an important place in their value systems—they simply denied the premise that the conditions of the Malmö armistice constituted an affront to Germany's or the Assembly's honor. Beckerath, for instance, acknowledged that if the accord were truly dishonorable, "then I would probably not be the last to vote for risking everything to keep every insult far from the nation." But Beckerath, like Mühlfeld, and even the normally radical and honor-conscious Wilhelm Jordan, thought that however unsatisfactory and disadvantageous the document might be, it still did not encroach too nearly upon the nation's honor. The legal and political theorist Sylvester Jordan, eminently qualified to speak on such a subject, for his part maintained that an injury to national honor could only come from having an "insulting condition forced upon us," which had not been the case in the Malmö accord.[12] Foreign Minister Johann Heckscher argued even more clearly on the basis of the rights-honor connection. Injury to honor, he asserted, could only come from the infringement of "clearly recognized rights," something Germany's claim to the whole of Schleswig could not as yet be considered.[13] Whatever their disagreements in applying the theory to the Schleswig question, the opposing sides spoke the same language of rights, honor, and respect. As with the culture of nationhood generally, ideological contestation in the language of honor revolved more around its interpretation within that language's bounds than around efforts to challenge those bounds themselves.

Although this conclusion might not seem so weighty outside the realm of pure cultural history, it actually provides an underappreciated explanatory context for the ideas of midcentury German liberals on both foreign policy and domestic constitution-making. Deputies' notions of honor and respect provided a framework for their conceptions of how a nation should be constructed internally and how it should act externally. The above-noted association of honor and "greatness" did not merely indicate a certain thirst for glory and national pride during the intoxicating days of the founding of a German state. Rather, it underscored the extent to which deputies thought the quest for international respect and the autonomy that was both its cause and consequence had to rest on the solid base of national power, or *Macht*. As Julius Fröbel had observed in his political treatise of 1847, however difficult "Nation" might be to define, it certainly bore connotations of "greatness and power."[14] In the *Vormärz* the desire to gain that kind of respect for Germany, and mediately for oneself, had helped drive the formation of national feeling and the desire for a national state. This power, in turn, had to be achieved through the mutually reinforcing liberal institutions and patriotic unity that formed the marrow of national sentiment.

Understood as part of such unified institutions, of course, was the establishment of a national diplomatic representation and a national army of sufficient strength to make foreign powers take respectful notice of the new state. Later in Sylvester Jordan's attempt to dissuade the Assembly from an over-fine sense of its national honor, for example, he argued that only when Germany finally emerged "forcefully" and "unified by one constitution, has one army at its command, and is prosperous through business and trade; then can Germany truly confront other nations as a great people and step forth in the dignity that Germany deserves." Two dimensions stand out here: the sense of a prior need for inner "strengthening" and the notion that such new strength, as a "thorn in the eye" of foreign powers, spelled the onset of a fully national German foreign policy.[15] Examining each dimension further will help give a fuller appreciation of Assembly conceptions of nationality. In the deputies' minds these two spheres of nationhood, the inward and the outward, intersected much more than tangentially.

Although the present work cannot even attempt to offer a full treatment of the Frankfurt parliamentarians' views on foreign and military policy, a few pertinent observations should help elucidate their opinions on the value of honor, unity, autonomy, and power in national existence. Günter Wollstein, for instance, has duly noted that for Dahlmann, introducing the language of honor into the Schleswig debates served as a clarion call for the pursuit of a sovereign "power-political upswing" and "national interest politics."[16] Toward the end of his famous speech of June 9 declaring the Schleswig affair a matter of Germany's national honor, Dahlmann made such interconnections abundantly clear. Urging deputies to lend no ears to foreigners who complained that the annexation of Schleswig would disrupt the European balance of power, Dahlmann proceeded to tell them what would knock it askew: "For of course the previous balance of power in Europe will be shifted when our Germany arises from a weak, sunken communal life, from an association little valued abroad to dignity, honor, and greatness." After a pause for a hearty "Bravo!" from the Assembly, Dahlmann soared near the empyrean or apocalyptic heights of the nation's future and insisted that Germany wanted that disruption and would maintain it "until the last drop of blood has streamed out of us."[17] Unity and the honor-bound will to insist on and defend the nation's rights would bring that greatness. Failure to do so, as this new Elijah assured deputies in even more blistering and prophetic tones during September's high-voltage debates on the Malmö armistice, would doom the national effort forever. Not just Schleswig but Germany's national unity itself was at stake: "If we submit in face of the foreign powers at the first test, faint-hearted at the outset, at the first sight of danger, then, gentlemen, you will never be able to lift your once-proud head again . . . Never!" As the leftist Wilhelm Zimmermann argued soon thereafter, "if Germany's honor is given up in this way, then a Germany only just awakened from a deathlike sleep would be dead, dead before the eyes of Europe, because its honor would have died."[18]

Yet if the invocation of honor often led to a simple bellicose sloganeering or a more complex and telling but equally disturbing imagery of death and blood, it did not exhaust itself in these. As in the examples of Dahlmann and Zimmermann just above, honor and the power to enforce it stood revealed as essential qualities for a nation to be accepted as such among its fellows. Without honor and respected acceptance, a nation could never fulfill its moral and political missions. The appeal to honor reinforced the tendency to take a maximalist stand in defense of Germany's perceived rights, not only because it was simply honorable to do so but also because it provided the only means of achieving greatness and acquiring respect "before the eyes" of those other powers the German representatives earnestly hoped to emulate. All such foreign policy interventions in the name of Germany's national honor helped put flesh on the bones of the International Committee's official report by Oskar von Wydenbrugk on the guiding principles of the new state's foreign policy, at the head of which stood the guarantee of its "honor and rights."[19]

Carl Mittermaier's official commentary to the draft constitution brought out an equally crucial aspect of thinking on international affairs and the interconnections among unity, honor, respect, and power. It reiterated that only when Germany confronted the other three powers "as a great power" and as "*one* state" could it take up its "due position" and "win independence and the respect of the other states."[20] The key point here follows from the introduction of the term "Selbstständigkeit": "indepedence" or "autonomy." The striving for autonomous action was the basis of the *Vormärz* ideal of personal honor as of the underlying culture of *Bildung;* as such autonomy was the object of profound devotion. And during the revolution as before, conceptions of personal identity car-

ried over into the realm of national identity. Wilhelm Beseler brought all
the component terms of this language together when in March he proclaimed that "it is the paramount right [Ehrenrecht] of a free people,
namely, to determine its destiny itself," and followed this statement with
the injunction that, if Germany wanted to be "a great, independent nation," influential and "self-active," then it must always stand ready "to defend its freedom and its honor." To do so, it needed a strong, unified state
that would have "enough power to protect its freedom and to establish
the new glory of the German name." Rights and honor, greatness and autonomy, unity and power: Beseler showed their interrelations more clearly
and concisely than most, but for all that he expressed a basic political truth
among Forty-Eighters. Similarly, at the head of his famous motion calling
for the immediate adoption of the Frankfurt constitution in face of Austrian recalcitrance, the rights-and-honor theorist Carl Welcker declared
foreign influence on Germany's nascent constitution an infringement of
"the most sacred original right of free peoples," against which the German
nation would rise up "and defend its honor as one man."[21] After years of
experiencing Germany as the "plaything of European politics," Assembly
delegates wanted to play the game themselves and pursue an entirely independent political line.

Such inclinations toward autonomous political action could be taken
quite far and helped determine Assembly attitudes toward numerous aspects of foreign policy. Many speakers, as in the debates on the Wydenbrugk report, shunned the idea of alliance, if not of diplomatic communication and problem-solving, as unnecessary and indeed unworthy of a
strong, free people. A nation, they thought, should be able to maintain its
integrity on its own behalf, without sacrificing independence through reli-
ance on another people. Being swayed from doing what was right as a consequence of listening to the opinions of foreign powers similarly counted
as a "disgrace."[22] Deputies even employed such arguments from autonomy to urge the incorporation of German Poznania into the Reich. After
all, if one of the most frequently given reasons for why Germany should
desire a strong restored Poland was that it could serve as a bulwark against
the despotic eastern common enemy, then opponents of the idea found it
easy to counter that Germany needed no such external aid, that, in Wilhelm Jordan's words, Germany was "alone man enough to let every attack
on its integrity shatter powerlessly against it."[23] Finally, it is in this context
that liberal denials of other, smaller or weaker nationalities' rights to sovereign independence must be understood. If independence could not be

achieved through a nation's own independent efforts, it simply did not possess the same value, particularly if it came tied to foreign influence in its process of national development. However harsh and utilitarian, such reasoning at least did not emerge from hypocrisy alone—this was a standard Germans of the national opposition were also prepared to apply to themselves.[24]

Such emphasis on autonomous power, dignity, and even prestige did not spend its entire force in the realm of foreign policy but rather bore additional implications for the constitutional framework of domestic politics. Once again, liberalism and nationalism came together in deputies' political thinking. As the discussion of the *Vormärz* culture of nationhood has shown, in the liberal ancient republican tradition strength and liberty comprised mutually necessary and interlocking supports, each nourished by and nourishing a patriotic love of country. Running in the one direction, a certain measure of unity in the sense of governmental centralization and executive authority (above all in military and diplomatic affairs) was clearly required in order to guarantee the nation's self-assertive strength on the international scene. At the same time, national patriotic commitment would be necessary to support that effort, and since such feelings grew best amid free institutions, some balance between authority and liberty would have to be sought. Moreover, nearly all deputies remained aware of the need to encourage citizen participation and patriotism at the state and local levels in order to produce men who would also be strong and committed citizens nationally, hence the wide support for communal *Selbstverwaltung* or "self-government" and for the *Bundesstaat* or federal form of constitution. Here too some dynamic equilibrium was required.

In the commentary to the draft constitution Johann Droysen expressed this reciprocal relationship between strength and liberty in terms of that between "unity" and "freedom," or "Einheit" and "Freiheit," which far from being mutually conflicting categories were rather mutually supportive. "The German people," Droysen claimed, had now come to the realization "that both are only possible with one another and through one another; the imperial constitution guarantees respectively the one through the other." The more left-centrist Mittermaier also invoked such ideas in his portion of the draft commentary and underscored the need to encourage patriotic service at both the state and national levels, something that only the federal solution would allow. For both, however, it was clear that patriotism and freedom had to exist not just nationally but also on the

Einheit +
Freiheit

smaller scale closer to the citizens' lives, where one experienced the "development of our powers" and where a more dynamic society led to "more capacity for living" and "more enjoyment of liberty," each tied to greater concern for "the interests of the common fatherland."[25] Or as the Hessian deputy Friedrich Schulz observed, local self-government was "the basis of all healthy civic life, the best school of genuine political virtue and capability," and it would guarantee the "liberty and power" of the nation as a whole.[26] Citizens had to grow into that role through independent-minded debate, decision-making, and active involvement, starting locally and moving up from there.

All of this consensus about the role of *Selbständigkeit* or autonomy in the lives of individuals and nations (separately and reciprocally) did not, of course, prevent a great deal of partisan debate about constitutional provisions and the proper social extension of citizen participation. Even on almost universally accepted principles such as the federal form of constitution and the need for local self-government, democrats and moderates found plenty to disagree about, with the left striving for a stronger federal government as a way of trimming the powers of monarchical state governments, yet also wanting a weaker federal presence locally. Issues such as suffrage qualifications and the definition of the head of state sparked still greater disagreements. Disputes over the meaning of "Selbständigkeit" or "independent status" as a criterion for voting rights comprise a fascinating case study in the ideological contestation of a political language, while those over the balance of political centralization and political liberty in choosing between a monarchical and a republican form of unified national government were naturally some of the sharpest disputes of all. Even within the moderate monarchist camp opinion divided between those deputies who wanted a broader franchise with indirect voting and those who preferred greater restrictions under a system of direct elections, or between those who wanted a unitary head of state and those who believed it necessary that some corporate entity fulfill that role.[27] But above (or underlying) all of these ideological battles, the basic scheme of a mutually reinforcing chain of autonomous strength and liberty, running from individuals through communities and states to the nation itself, remained intact.

Disagreements

still agree on underlying ideals

Moreover, if it was clear that a strong federal state required strong citizens and communities, and that this could only come about through free institutions, it was just as widely believed that the strength of these free institutions required a powerful, self-assertive federal government capable of instilling respect in other nations and patriotic pride in the citizens of its

need assertive/ powerful federal gov

own. As Mittermaier expounded the virtues of the federal form of constitution he also paid tribute to this side of the reciprocal relationship, noting
how the willingness to engage in patriotic "sacrifice" would be stimulated
by "the feeling of enthusiasm in belonging to a fatherland respected and
feared by foreign nations." The old radical nationalist Turnvater Jahn, in
arguing for broad citizen participation in the life of both community and
nation, echoed such views, couching them not just in the language of
power and respect but also of honor. This belief in the necessity of power
to guarantee liberty was of course in part just a truism about the need for a
strong national defense in military and diplomatic terms, but as the above
examples attest it was a psychological concern as well. Again invoking the
language of national honor, Reich Minister Beckerath expressed this relationship quite clearly when he observed that when a nation did not have
the requisite power, this was a "humiliation" for it. "The first requirement
of a great, civilized nation," Beckerath argued, "is that of power; it wants
to be externally honored and powerful, and on this condition also depends
its internal liberty, which rests upon its self-confidence."[28] As with the
connection between rights and honor, that among honor, liberty, and
strength held true for nations as much as for persons. This was so not just
through the process of analogical reasoning from individuals to nations as
collective personalities, but also because a circuit of mutually reinforcing
cause and effect bound these two levels together in the ideological space
where domestic and foreign policy met.

Beckerath made his remarks during the debates on the so-called "Question to Austria" contained in Paragraphs 2 and 3 of the constitution, and
he was by no means alone in unleashing such arguments there. This circumstance hardly owed much to chance, for if in the previous chapter it
became clear that the Austrian Question spun more around the axis of
constitutional and political issues than around that of national borders, it
now becomes more apparent why this was the case. In determining Germany's borders and relationship with Austria, as in settling certain aspects
of its constitutional framework as a unified, federative constitutional monarchy, issues of German power and status were crucial. As Georg Waitz
told the Assembly in October, "Circumstances cannot force us to give up
what we have recognized to be necessary for Germany's unity, strength,
and dignity; they can never force us to allow an unclear mixed relation, in
which *one* German army and *one* German policy are not possible, not feasible." Or as Gabriel Riesser stated a week later in his capacity as spokesman

for the Constitutional Committee majority on this question, "The stand-point of the Constitutional Committee, its basic principle, was entirely and only that which would further the power and unity of the federal state we want to establish."[29] The insistence on the personal union clauses; on a strong diplomatic and military centralization; and, for many, on a heredi-tary kaiser to serve as the single will directing the new national state and its national policy: all of these considerations entered into the thinking of Prussian party affiliates as they tried to force through the constitutional provisions deemed necessary to establish a federal state capable of acting firmly and autonomously in the international arena on a basis of internal strength, honor, and unity. Leadership by an Austria too much under Slavic influence, parliamentary association with millions of non-Germans in Habsburg extra-federal territories, and the degree of constitutional lax-ity that would be required to incorporate part or all of the Austrian lands in the new state seemed equally unappealing, even monstrous or traitor-ous, to the Kaiser party faithful. National power, liberty, and unity be-longed together, as Georg Beseler observed in his own take on these themes, for they alone gave the possibility of a "national politics," some-thing that "we want to have, because we must have it, if we want to remain a nation."[30]

Moreover, these more practical, purely political considerations of power and unity intermingled with the concerns for a certain degree of purity touched on previously as reasons for the Prussian party's acquiescence in the Little German solution and for its fierce opposition to the 70-million Reich idea. Many deputies still felt as did the Königsberg political scientist Friedrich Schubert that all other things being equal, the more nationally pure state had the advantage in strength over the more diverse. Or as the German Jew Riesser opined in a remark noted in the previous chapter, while it was by no means impossible that different nationalities should combine in the enjoyment of a representative national constitution, there were already enough opportunities for disunity arising from consider-ations of party and interest in a nation without adding potentially schis-matic nationality divisions as well.[31]

Perhaps the young Rhenish Prussian Catholic official Wilhelm Wich-mann made the juxtaposition of concerns about purity and autonomy clearest in his wonderfully revealing if brief speech during the October de-bates. Rejecting comparison with the United States on the grounds that the young republic encompassed a much less drastic diversity of language, descent, customs, and above all levels of civilization than would be the case in a proposed 70-million Reich, Wichmann argued that the always victorious "German element" would necessarily lose something "if it is bound through a thousand considerations to foreign peoples. Alliances are always dangerous for him who is strong enough to assert himself alone. 'The strong man,' says Schiller, 'is strongest, when alone.'" With reference to the dangers presented by powerful neighbors to the east and west, Wichmann then put the argument even more clearly in the ominous context of the value of ethnographic purity. If hostilities broke out, Wichmann contended, Germany could only withstand those neighbors "if out of the great crystallization of peoples underway in Europe we emerge as a clear crystal, through the excretion of as many foreign components as at all possible." Only in this way could Germany establish a national policy that would allow it to "assert itself with honor in the assembly of nations."[32] As Wichmann's words showed, concern for the purity of the German national state combined easily with an intense desire for pure autonomy, in each case shunning foreign influence and interference. Both were bound up with notions of the causal interrelationships among unity, liberty, strength, and honor. With political and cultural aspects of nationality so intertwined, purity at one level almost necessarily implicated purity at the other. But as usual these arguments functioned only within the porous confines of a national identity still partly open, as the result of that plastic and fruitful threading of political and cultural filaments of nationhood. At least in October the Prussian Wichmann still argued for the federal borders, not for Little Germany.

Of course, as the *grossdeutsch* Würzburg law professor Carl Edel reminded the assembled deputies in late January, he and his comrades wanted the "power," the "independence," and the "greatness of Germany" just as much as Prussian party adherents did. They simply had different ideas as to how this was to be achieved. Even the eccentric Catholic classicist Ernst von Lasaulx, in speaking for the establishment of a 70-million Reich if at all possible, expressed his agreement with the notion that liberty and power stood in an unbreakable causal loop, while the Austrian Johann Perthaler desired the formation of a "German" foreign policy with fully as much ardor as Wichmann or the Beselers.[33] The Austrians and their supporters vehemently denied that the parts of a divided Germany could somehow emerge separately stronger because more internally unified. For them, ensuring Germany's stature meant maximizing its size instead, at least to the federal borders, as Heinrich Ahrens pointed out in explaining the true meaning and sources of national power or *Macht,* but perhaps even beyond.[34] With Germans as the leading element of a federative empire of nationalities, the Greater Germans believed, such diversity would be given a sufficient degree of unity and patriotic national feeling to support Germany's role as the Central European hegemon. Where the Kaiser party stressed qualitative strength and unity in the constitution and in the population, the Directorials simply emphasized the quantitative factor of power in terms of both territory and population.

All aspects of the midcentury educated German conceptions of nationhood discussed thus far—the central role of honor and the defense of rights, the requirements of national unity and power as essential for the nurture of both individual and national honor and liberty—could be deemed simply self-aggrandizing, opportunistic, destabilizingly dangerous. And indeed to some extent they were all those and more. Yet to make sense of these interconnected ideas at a deeper level, to understand the psychological environment in which such notions could germinate and flourish as natural-seeming outgrowths of a healthy understanding of the world the delegates lived in, those ideas have to be juxtaposed with deputies' visions of human history as an arena for conflict and competition among nations. If points of honor and right had to be defended so firmly and immaculately, it was because people and nations existed in a world in which they could be wrested from the unwary or unassertive individual. If power and prestige compulsorily emerged as the *raisons d'être* of national politics and *raison d'état*, it was because only they could ensure the maintenance of liberty in the world of international politics. Midcentury Germans did not necessarily see history as horrifically Hobbesian, but neither did they envision it as comfortably Condorcean. Progress followed as the day the night, but only through the dialectical play of forces neither light nor dark but simply natural and remorseless.

Those deputies unconvinced of the necessity or at least of the utility of restoring a partitioned Poland, for instance, had little trouble finding reasons why such a Polish state and the new Germany would almost inevitably tumble into conflict. Invoking notions of both natural borders and national power, several observers, including Heinrich Laube, Julius Ostendorf, Gustav Rümelin, and above all Wilhelm Jordan, asserted their belief that a reunified Poland would be forced to attempt annexation of the Baltic coast in West Prussia. No nation in the modern age, they thought, could possibly survive as a "Binnenvolk," or landlocked people.[35] They and others also doubted that a Polish nationalist movement aiming at restoration of the 1772 borders, which included large sections of Prussian and Austrian territory, would be able or willing to avoid disputes with a German nationalist movement insistent on the German national character of a sizable portion of these once Polish lands. Whatever expectations of peaceful relations might have sprouted in the March sunshine of the "Springtime of the Nations" could hardly have survived the divisive Polish-German rhetoric and violence clouding the Poznanian borderlands. Moreover, such expectations may not ever have risen quite as high as one would suspect from a traditional interpretation of the prerevolutionary *Polenfreundschaft*. At least in the eyes of Gustav Stenzel prior to the revolution and of Gustav Rümelin during it, antipathy between Pole and German seemed at once ancient, natural, and very much alive.[36]

Even more than conflict with the Poles, members of the resurgent national opposition looked forward with trepidation or euphoria to a final reckoning with the foreign power they held most responsible for Germany's political woes: Russia. Even—or above all—those who still hoped for a fraternal alliance with Poland harbored expectations of a revolutionary war against the czar. Such a conflagration might be sparked from the tinder lying abundantly on the ground in Poland, or it might jump from the flames already scorching the earth of Schleswig. In any case, during the revolution's early months it seemed almost certain that war would come, for surely the Russian autocracy could not sit immobile while a revolutionary transformation of European politics occurred on its western borders. At the Pre-Parliament, for example, the moderate Heinrich von Gagern invoked the danger of a war with Russia as a good reason not to engage in abstract republican experiments when concrete defensive measures should be the order of the day, while on the other end of the political spectrum the radical Friedrich Hecker adduced the same fear in support of his motion to declare the Pre-Parliament a permanent assembly in the tradition of the 1792 French Convention.[37] Some deputies continued to expect and even to welcome such a war. As Droysen remarked in March of 1849, he had never thought the Germans would escape without a "baptism by blood," and he felt sure that "only a healthy war can restore the nation's morality." Droysen's party colleague Rudolf Haym felt much the same way at the time, as did the conservative Catholic Lasaulx. If in the context of the September crisis the would-be left-centrist Prime Minister Friedrich von Hermann did not embrace war, he still thought it potentially bracing for German national feeling.[38]

In an atmosphere in which apocalyptic images of war alternately weighed on or buoyed up deputies' spirits, it should occasion no surprise to discover that when they dealt with the several very real conflicts in which Germans found themselves entangled during the revolutionary year, the language chosen fully reflected the intensity of the emotions aroused. In the June debates on Schleswig, for instance, the left-liberal Moravian Giskra cried that the Danes would be "hounded out of the German borderlands, back where they belong," while the North Schleswiger Michelsen informed his eager auditors that his constituents needed to be secured from the "vengeful terrorism of the Danes." And in September Dahlmann asked the Assembly, "Can we deliver our countrymen, our own flesh and blood, over to certain ruin, to the vengeance of their hate-filled Danish enemies?"[39] Heated, even purple rhetoric, to be sure, but not so out of place amid the crisis mentality of wartime, and among those raised in a period and a social milieu that fostered robust diction and full-blown oratory. It serves as a bellwether for the near-religious exaltation that gripped deputies and rendered their judgment suspect at this dramatic crisis point in the Frankfurt revolutionary experience, but little more.

Much the same sort of language could be heard from the supporters of the German Poznanians as they attempted to secure the National Assembly's backing for their cause, yet there it reached heights, or depths, unmeasured in the Schleswig case. Although they also predicted disaster and bloodshed for their countrymen, this time at the hands of the Poles, these delegates also introduced the added dimension of the "race-war," of the "war of annihilation" or even of "extermination," into their discourse. No one on either side actually advocated such a thing—they simply shared a deep fear that such desires for a total solution to the quarrels and violence lurked within the minds of their opposite numbers in the Polish or German camps. If such total solutions had not yet entered the realm of thinkable policy, they had, disturbingly, entered the realm of the thinkable per se. Early in the debates Adolph Goeden of Krotoszyn reminded his listeners that hatred of Germans formed part of the "Gospel of the Pole," that "extermination" had been one of the goals of the 1846 Polish nationalist conspiracy, and that a "true war of annihilation against Germans" had actually been underway in Poznania before the Prussian army stepped in to pacify the situation.[40] The only Polish nationalist present in the Assembly at the time, the Catholic cleric and professor Jan Janiszewski, for his part accused Germans of promoting not just the "annihilation of this [Polish] nationality" but also a full-scale "war of annihilation against Poles," while immediately afterward the Poznanian leader Samuel Kerst spoke of the "most frightful war of extermination against Germans" carried out by the Poles during the spring. And Wilhelm Jordan, in his masterful if radical contribution to the debate, enunciated his belief that the Poles would eventually find their way to the Russians and join forces in a "life-and-death struggle" against the Germans.[41]

Jordan often found himself well out in front of the rest of the Assembly in the extremity of his opinions, yet on this occasion he merely voiced a commonplace among his fellows, that the Polish question formed part of a larger Slavic question in which life-and-death issues were at stake. The Poznanian entomologist Dr. Hermann Löw, who also feared that blood would flow in his homeland, elevated the discussion to near-mythic proportions of paranoid defiance when in July he remarked, "Slavism, gentlemen, comes bearing arms and knocking upon our door from more than one side—let it resound in the house as it did in the Trojan horse!"[42] The leftist leader Jakob Venedey, who by contrast supported both the restoration of Poland and the exclusion of the German Poznanian delegates from the Assembly, also adverted to the danger posed for Germans by the "Slavic question" and warned his listeners that "if we do not make the right decision soon, they will be right on top of us!" Even more troubling, Venedey seemed to believe such a war to be almost inevitable, with the main point of acting justly being to ensure that when war came it would be a just one for the Germans. The usually cosmopolitan Young Hegelian philosopher Arnold Ruge, also arguing from the pro-Polish standpoint in July, worried that failure to meet Polish demands would allow Russia "to unleash upon us the hatred of the entire Slavic element, of this monstrous family of peoples."[43] With such talk of extermination and of broader consequences among the Slavic peoples, the Poznanian question somehow scraped across a particularly sensitive nerve in this parliamentary body.

The race-war concept surfaced not just in the Polish context but also in others where German-Slavic relations were concerned. Venedey, for example, only days after his speech of June 3 on the Poznanian question, held up the specter of a potential "Raçenkrieg" in Bohemia, while the Austrian representatives Johann Berger, Ernst Schilling, and the ever-fiery Giskra each alerted the Assembly to the dangers of a "general bloodbath and national war of extermination" against Germans there.[44] Significantly, such race-war imagery emerged solely in the context of Slavic-related debates. This fact suggests that deputies' usage more nearly reflected the modern notion of race as applying to large groups of purportedly related peoples, rather than the other contemporary sense of the term as indicating merely a single group, such as the British or French races.

Such racial terminology could never have found the same resonance in the struggle with the Danes over Schleswig. The Danes, whatever their misdemeanors in the eyes of Germans, still formed part of the great community of Teutonic peoples. This meant not only that the rhetoric arising from that dispute could never ascend to the fateful peaks of racial conflict, but also that in some senses the conflict seemed wrong, counter to the larger interests of both parties, even unnatural. *Vormärz* Germanists had established a fine tradition of calling for some sort of alliance with the Scandinavian nations against the common Russian menace, while others had alluded to the possibility of an even closer union.[45] During the June debates, for instance, Jacob Grimm qualified his remarks about the former Jutes being a Germanic as opposed to a Scandinavian people with the telling reservation, "insofar as we may be permitted to oppose Germanic peoples to the Scandinavian."[46] Teutonic peoples might differ and have differences but only as brothers differed—they were still part of the same family.

Such notions of deeper cultural and ancestral affinity encouraged deputies to think in terms of potential alliances even during moments of conflict. In particular they helped ease the transition of some Schleswig-Holsteiners to acceptance of the Malmö armistice in September. The old nationalist historian Ernst Moritz Arndt, for instance, made this ramblingly clear when on September 14 he urged that there was still hope that "the Danes will more and more come to the fraternal feeling they owe us, and the Swedes too, that they will come to feel that they are the brother people of one stock, and that they must be a brother people with us so that no eastern barbarism and savagery now threatening us from all Slavic and Gaulish peoples can force its way in."[47] Similarly in the brief October debate on the territorial extent of the German Reich, Georg Beseler averred: "I have always regretted the struggle between the Danes and the duchies, namely because I saw here in enmity Germanic peoples who have a common enemy, against whom they should stand together in association."[48] Seemingly pressured from the East, deputies felt a counterpressure to cease hostilities with their Germanic confreres to the North and join with them instead.

Following his observations on Schleswig's intricate mesh of dialects, the Germanist scholar Andreas Michelsen made a further point of potentially clarifying but ominous significance. "Between the German and the Danish language," Michelsen stated, "there is no such difference and opposition as between the Slavic and German language."[49] Michelsen's words came just after his assertion that language and nationality were not the same

thing, which latter claim made rhetorical sense in the context of his argument to include Danish-speakers in the German nation on the basis of various nonlinguistic criteria drawn from the conceptually rich mix of the
culture of nationhood. Michelsen's additional observation regarding the
relationship between German and Slavic languages did not, however, involve a non sequitur but rather served to spotlight all the more dramatically the extent to which many deputies thought of Europe as divided not
just into nations but also into larger cultural entities. If language and nationhood were distinct, language affinity provided all the more useful a
marker of these grander, protoracial divisions, Pan-Slavic and Pan-German. The more strictly cultural elements of the compound conceptions of
nationhood found their most unrestricted field of application in the comparatively untrammeled imaginative realm of such transnational associations rather than in that of the much more confined, concrete, and politically valenced one of nations themselves. For this reason the chauvinistic
arguments from ethnography, and above all the racially inspired fears of
population-destroying wars of annihilation, could not take hold in the
context of the seemingly fratricidal conflict raging in Schleswig. Given
the broader picture of long-term historical developments and population
shifts in Europe, the Danish war became an aberration, while the struggles
with the Poles and Czechs seemed only too natural. Historians typically
underscore the dangers of ethnic thinking in nationalism; among the
Forty-Eighters these dangers were clearly greater when considering these
larger ethnographic groupings.

This recourse to ethnic transnationality bears an even deeper significance for understanding both German national identity and the nationalist politics that derived from it. For the already demonstrated tendency
of midcentury educated Germans to weave together cultural and political skeins of nationality into the colorful patterns of nationalist ideology
played out with equal if not greater facility in their thinking about the relationships among the transnational groupings than it did in that about nations themselves. In the lines of these cultural divisions many deputies
thought to augur Europe's future political and historical development. In
his 1848 *History of the German Language,* Jacob Grimm was already spec-
ulating about the future division of European hegemony among the three
great transnational groupings: Teutonic, Slavic, and Romance. Even the
relatively level-headed businessman and Reich Finance Minister Beckerath
assumed that countries such as Switzerland, Holland, the United States,
and England would form Germany's future natural allies, natural by virtue

of their belonging to the same great Teutonic lineage. And going in the other direction, in rejecting proposals to establish an offensive-defensive alliance with the French Republic, Beckerath referred to the fruitful historical "friction" between the Romance and Teutonic peoples.[50] From the perspective of the culture of nationhood the perception of cultural ties powerfully suggested the establishment of political ties as well. In the cause of seeking better Germanic relations, deputies were sometimes willing to shelve their insistence on fully, isolatingly autonomous foreign relations.

Frankfurt delegates advocated such broader ties above all because they thought the transnational groupings were almost destined to come into conflict. Hegemony might be divided among the three main groups, but this would involve no static balance of power. Rather, the different clusters of peoples would sooner or later band together and attempt to overpower their rivals by force of arms or simply by moral, mental, and economic force. In the Poznanian case, for example, Wilhelm Jordan and others assumed that the Poles and Russians would be drawn by their cultural commonalities into some kind of anti-German political and ultimately military union. The "magnet theory" behind German liberal visions of a dynamic future *Mitteleuropa* should also be considered in this context, with Germany acting as lodestone for the coalescence of the continent's Germanic elements against the encroaching power of the Slavic nations. In its intertwining of cultural and political affinities such transnational thinking offered both the dangerous serpent of Pan-Slavism and the inspiring infant Hercules of Pan-Germanism for the deputies' contemplation.

Perhaps the clearest and most forceful exposition of this theory of "supranational camps" or "Völkerlager" came from the oppositionist Austrian officer Karl Möring, who both in print and in speeches to the Assembly painted an epic mural of grand transnational unions and competition for the European future. During the debates of July 22 on the International Committee's foreign policy report, Möring detailed his ideas of the "three great national camps" and engaged in a bit of demographic cost-accounting to assess the relative strength of each. If the Germans were not to be overwhelmed by the 70 million Latins or the 80 million Slavs, Möring reckoned, they would have to band together into a 65-million-strong *Mitteleuropa* incorporating Austria's extra-federal lands. Going geographically even further afield, Möring then proposed the broadening of such an association to include the cooperation of the United States, Britain, Scandinavia, Holland, and Switzerland, a union giving the grand total of nearly 130 million souls, able "to legislate for the whole world."[51]

Striking in Möring's visions is the fact that once again cultural considerations led to political conclusions, which then depended on the basic fusion of nationality concepts to produce a polity culturally diverse in the interests of political strength. Starting from notions of Pan-Slavic and Pan-Germanic transnational affiliations, Möring arrived at the creation of a "German" Central Europe including millions of those who theoretically should have been accounted in the opposing camp. Thinkers like Möring deemed the pull of "national sympathies" great enough to pose both a Pan-Slav danger and a Pan-German opportunity, yet not so great as to preclude the establishment of fully "national" political structures that transcended such purely cultural affinities. Through ties of history and *Bildung* within the Habsburg Empire and the German Reich of which it was to form such a prominent part, the "Völkerlager" danger could be circumvented, and millions of potential enemies turned into very real helpmeets.[52]

The *Mitteleuropa* Möring described essentially mirrored not just Count Friedrich Deym's 70-million Reich idea but also the later Greater and Little German concepts of a Central Europe at once stabilizing for peace and striving for dynamic expansion. Such a notion was manifested particularly vividly in Heinrich von Gagern's proposal for a close alliance between a unified Prussian-led Germany and a reinvigorated Habsburg monarchy. As argued above, of course, the adherents of the Prussian party had different notions about how much non-German participation in a German national state might really prove to be helpful than did their *grossdeutsch* or 70-million Reich counterparts, yet each group found it necessary to devise a means of strengthening Germany by including at least some non-Germans. Moreover, each of these concepts must be set into the same context of a Europe seen as fissioning along generally ethnographic lines and heading for some kind of large-scale contest among the associations so formed. As the Slavic background to the Poznanian and Bohemian debates had already foreshadowed, the Austrian Question would provide the venue for renewed concerns about full-fledged "race-wars" between the westward-looking Slavs and the eastward-looking Germans. As the originator of the Little Germany concept Paul Pfizer had remarked several years previously, the great Migration of the Nations had not yet reached its climax. During the revolution it seemed even more likely that, as the Austrian Franz Schuselka had observed at about the same time as Pfizer, Eastern Europe was about to become the "theater of world events."[53] These events German nationalist politicians had to prepare the nation to confront.

In all of these debates on the Austrian, or indeed on any of the Slavic questions, a degree of fear crept in that could not be heard in any other connection. It was not simply because Poles, unlike Danes, lacked a good Teutonic heritage, for the German reaction to the Slavs differed in kind and not merely in quantity from that to, say, the Romance French or Italians. Numbers of course played a role, for Denmark could hardly pose the same sort of threat as Russia. Yet France too had the resources to launch a powerful campaign against the Germans, and many were the delegates who could have attested from personal experience both to that fact and to the hatred of the French that had been so prevalent not so long ago. Yet the French and Italians belonged to the larger "western" cultural sphere, to a western civilization seen as "Germanic" in a significant sense, in a way that the Slavs to the east did not. As an editorial in Georg Gervinus's *Deutsche Zeitung* noted, the Slavs, even the Poles and those living in Austria, had yet to prove that they were of the Occident rather than the Orient. In the early 1840s the leftist Heidelberg professor Karl Hagen had pointed out that the French stood much closer to German *Bildung* than did the Russians, and the conservative Lasaulx still felt the same way in 1848, when in the Constitutional Committee he contested the claim that giving up the left bank of the Rhine would be a greater act of treachery than ceding Austria to the Slavs. Lasaulx flatly denied this, for as he put it, "The French stand nearer to us in civilization [Bildung], yes, in nationality [Volkstümlichkeit] than do the Slavs to whom these Germans would be betrayed."[54] When there was mention of Slavic peoples, the image of a race of men dangerously different, uncivilized and potentially savage, hovered very near the Frankfurt consciousness. Despite the folkloric efforts of Jacob Grimm or the Austrian poet Count Anton Auersperg, any small Slavophilic sloop floated frailly upon a surging Slavophobic sea.

Such fears took on all the more portentous an aspect in that, as had been the case before 1848, the oft-noted liberal optimism did not always carry over into the realm of international or interracial relations. The classic statement of historical pessimism on this point must remain that of the romantic Lasaulx, who on December 12 told the other members of the Constitutional Committee that his ideas of Germany were "entirely hopeless." Comparing the German urge to recreate kaiser and Reich both to a flame that flickers before it dies and to a dying man's senile memories of youth, Lasaulx went on to conclude that "the Slavs will gobble us up, as in

Austria."[55] In his pungent speech on Poznania, of course, Wilhelm Jordan had endorsed the Hegelian notion of peoples who outlive their time upon the world-historical stage and thereby essentially cease to exist. If in this instance it was the Poles and not the Germans who received Jordan's last rites, his "life-and-death struggle" between the possibly superior Russians and the Germans would by no means necessarily end in favor of the latter—as indeed Hegel himself had wondered whether the Slavic peoples might not bring their own successor stage of development into world history. The radical Giessen life-scientist Carl Vogt for his part conceded Jordan's point as to the existence of doomed peoples, even as he denied that the Poles could be deemed such. Vogt's biographer has dismissed this admission as an aberration, yet it seems to comport with the overall Vogtian vision of a pre-Darwinian natural and human history continually transforming under the impact of cataclysmic forces and events.[56] Not surprisingly then, late in the debates of March 1849 on the Austrian Question, a somewhat desperate and despairing Vogt called for a "politics of the sword" to reclaim German Austria from the forces of reaction and thus begin the unavoidable "war between the civilization of the West and the barbarism of the East."[57] Even if not all deputies shared these moments of enervating pessimism, they certainly believed in the dictum about the Lord and those who help themselves. They knew the price of autonomy was armed preparedness.

Lest it be argued that figures such as Vogt, Lasaulx, and Jordan were hardly the most representative of representatives, and their ideas of the German future suspect, a look at some of the many other iterations of fears of a general "national war," or "race-war," or Slavic assimilation of the Germans in the East should make it clear how such thoughts haunted many in the Assembly from beginning to end of the revolutionary experience, and how they helped shape thinking on the Austrian Question itself. In his later account of the debates and negotiations concerning Austria, for example, the Hamburg liberal Christian Wurm acknowledged that the Greater German left at least had one legitimate reason for its stance, namely, fear for the fate of the Germans in Austria if left to the hands of the Slavic majority.[58] The moderate Breslau Catholic Julius Ambrosch uneasily speculated as early as October that if Austria's German provinces later tried to break away on their own, "a monstrous war of nationalities between Germans and Slavs" might well result. For his part the Prussian party leader Droysen waited in fatalistic expectation of the coming "race-war" over the lower Danube region between Germans and Russians, a battle that had to be fought but that would redound to the "salvation of our children."[59]

Against this backdrop of racialist ideas and almost apocalyptic fears, all the various approaches to answering the Austrian Question begin to reveal a deeper commonality. The new Germany had to be strong and honored not simply to fulfill the dictates of an overweening and long-repressed sense of pride (although that played its part), but rather because it faced what many deputies thought to be a powerful threat of world-historical proportions. Although having somewhat different ideas of nationality and national strength, supporters of each of the three concepts for German unification—Little German, Greater German, and 70-million Reich—sincerely believed they held the secret to Germany's future power and defensive-offensive capacity against the threats presented by western economic and military giants and by the Slavic colossus and its potential satellites to the East. As Günter Wollstein has convincingly shown, in practical terms the differences between these groups hardly amounted to as much as often thought. Many followers of the Gagerns and the Beselers still hoped to preserve German influence over the Slavic peoples through the intermediary Austrian monarchy, while many of the Austrians and their allies simply strove for the more direct influence of federalist rule.[60]

Moreover, each of these alternative solutions involved more than just preparation for an exercise of raw power against a Russo-Slavic military foe. Instead, many deputies seemed to expect or at least hope that the battle would be fought out on the grounds of cultural and spiritual resources rather than strictly martial ones. For if prepared to acknowledge physical power and strength of numbers on the part of the Slavic peoples, and even a certain youthful vigor in their cultural achievements, most Germans tended to think of their own German-western civilization as superior in the sense of being more highly developed and therefore offering better chances of success in the coming competition between these two transnational groupings. While a bellicose and fatalistic Dahlmann could tell members of the Constitutional Committee that political doctrines typically required "bloody sanctions" before they could become fully established, many liberals at this time tended to think more in terms of economic and cultural competition in the free play of the marketplace and the public sphere. Or as Waitz had responded to another of Dahlmann's apocalyptic outbursts in committee, the times of peace would outweigh the times of war.[61] Such peace would still be a scene of continuous struggle, conflict, and competition, yet these would be peaceable.

As seen in previous chapters, the combination of a tightly wound cul-

tural-political conception of nationhood and a view of history as a conflict-driven process led to an ideologically motivated assimilatory urge. These assimilationist expectations were directed not just at non-German inhabitants of the Confederation and the future Reich (as seen in Chapter 4) but potentially at non-German populations living in German-ruled extra-federal lands and even beyond. The negative image of Poles and Czechs as somehow less civilized and less capable of full participation in modern liberal political life became even darker-hued for the predominantly Slavic peoples of the Habsburg Empire's Hungarian possessions. As the pro-Directorial Franz Buss remarked in March 1849, Austria's new constitution could have been more liberal, but it had to make allowances for the lower level of civilization in areas like Croatia. The perceived need for germanization was thus even greater for these extra-federal lands than for those lying within the borders of the old Confederation. Buss observed in this regard that relations between Slavs and Germans were "Austria's wound," but they could be healed with time and German effort.[62] As noted in earlier contexts, one of the deputies' most widely held beliefs was that Germany had a great world-historical mission to carry out in southeastern Europe. Waitz and some of his fellow Prussian party adherents warned, to be sure, against funneling too much of the nation's energies in this direction while neglecting developments at home and in the Atlantic world of the North and West. Yet even Waitz acceded in the somewhat Jordanesque notion that Germany still could and would make cultural conquests in the East.[63] In this respect too the typical liberal faith in a general civilizing process translated into hopes for a pivotal and expanding German role in it.

Such notions of germanizing cultural conquests primarily involved bringing the benefits of western, German civilization to the benighted East. At least some delegates, however, dreamed of a germanization that would transform the territories in question by making over their non-German inhabitants into fully fledged Germans. To a degree this could occur by means of actual colonization, a move that would allow Germany to strengthen its position vis à vis the Russians in the East rather than see its national human resources drain away into the Atlantic. But for the most part deputies simply assumed that the backward peoples of southeastern Europe would recognize the superiority of German culture and economic prowess and adopt them accordingly. In both respects their image of the medieval *Ostkolonisation* served as a model for future events. As the earlier eastern colonization had involved the transplantation of German populations into the forests and marshes of Poland, Germans would follow their

Saxon forbears into the Balkans. As the eastern colonization had involved the often voluntary introduction of German laws, cities, and commerce, and even agricultural practices, the same would occur in this new drive to the East. And as large tracts of what before the thirteenth century had been Slavic lands were almost totally assimilated into the German cultural sphere, their inhabitants adopting German ways and speech, that too would come to pass once more.

The Bavarian Catholic activist Johann Sepp argued such a view strongly and to the discomfort of at least some in the Assembly as part of his speech of January 12 in favor of a 70-million Reich. Had a personal union clause such as the Prussian party envisioned for the Frankfurt constitution determined the relations of the Dukes of Brandenburg, Sepp contended, the duchy might yet be Slavic. Instead, the dukes promoted immigration and civilization in their lands and transformed them into a *"new Germany."* Similar events, Sepp prognosticated, could still occur in the Habsburg lands. "Can we wish," he asked, "that the close tie linking the Slavs to Germany be severed, or rather more that the peaceful preparation for the gradual transformation of these foreign states into Germanic ones continue, that the tie of German culture and civilization be made even closer?" Sepp seemed to lose much of his audience, however, when he urged that a multinational but monolingual parliament in the 70-million Reich would serve as the most efficacious means of promoting "the quick and peaceful expansion of the German language, to secure our hegemonic realm in *Mitteleuropa*."[64] For Sepp notions of German rule and germanization came inextricably linked, foreshadowed by a medieval precedent and furthered by ideas of the peaceful conflict of liberal political, cultural, and economic life.

As usual, it was Wilhelm Jordan who expressed these ideas in their most extreme form, while at the same time putting them most securely into the context of *Ostkolonisation*. Referring back to the regrets expressed by Waitz in October about the difficulty of determining Germany's eastern borders, Jordan could not have disagreed more. He saw instead a grand opportunity in the spectacle of a region unbounded in space or history. Depicting the Germans as a two-thousand-year-old but still youthful people, Jordan went on to draw deputies into the romantic depths of organic imagery. He envisioned Prussia and Austria as two branches of a great German tree, expanding victoriously into the East with "German civility, language, and science." In deciding the Austrian question the Assembly would have to be guided by the expectation "that in the same way that true Prussia once became a German land from a predominantly non-German one, and has now become a land entering into Germany, in the same way the whole of Austria—hear me well, I say the *whole* of Austria . . . will also reach the point in time where it can decisively proclaim its entrance into Germany."[65] As he had argued for the incorporation of German Poznania on the basis of its past transformation into a German land, the Prussian party adherent Jordan now held out the hope of Austria's future triumphant return into a German state extending to the Black Sea—an Austria and a German state made German in more than simply political terms. Jordan went beyond most deputies in the range and completeness of his assimilationist visions, but others may also have been able to reconcile themselves to a Little German present in the hope that German *Mitteleuropa* might someday come.

With the adumbration of a potential thoroughgoing germanization of Eastern Europe, one that would extend German influence to the Black Sea, it becomes easier to see the complex interrelationship between notions of national boundaries and of national strength within the context of the culture of nationhood and its concomitant theme of processual, dialectical historical change. Mutually reinforcing power, honor, unity, and liberty provided the impetus for maintaining or even expanding Germany's national borders in a perceived world of constant conflict, while the same cyclical process reassured deputies that a sense of patriotic common consciousness would promote the construction of a shared national identity within those linguistically multinational borders. Nations had to do more than just be; they had to act. For midcentury Germans the experience of nationhood involved not just the mental or political act of defining the nation spatially and formally, but instead just as centrally entailed the construction of its internal cultural-political content and its external political behavior. Germany had to be put on the map in both the literal and metaphorical senses of the term. Only then could the nation truly be said to exist as a well-defined, individual historical actor, with its own autonomous character and qualities.

In the context of the Austrian debates this requirement for self-assertive action meant that the Assembly's two main groups drew differing approaches to assuring national strength and unity from differing emphases within the common culture of nationhood. The Prussian party chose to emphasize a qualitative degree of unity greater at once in political and in cultural respects, while the Austrians and their allies preferred to stress the powerful possibilities of sheer size. Moreover, given both the gravity of the seemingly approaching struggle and the rising fortunes of the reactionary powers, the two opposing camps in part differed simply (but sharply) in their diametrically opposed assessments of which solution to the constitutional problem stood the greatest chance of becoming constitutional reality in the near future. All these considerations of power, struggle, and political reality help explain the emotional intensity with which the Kaiser and Directorial parties, despite broadly similar national goals and national identities, carried on the constitutional fight.

In this process neither the cultural nor the political aspects of nationality could be elevated to predominance within the educated German's image of nationhood. For reasons of national strength, and of national identity as the consciousness of a quite broadly defined and multistranded commonality, the nation was not limited to the linguistic community but could theoretically extend far beyond. Expectations of future assimilation among neighboring nationalities, inside or outside those borders, allowed these already loose limits to be stretched even further. At the same time, while nations could be defined and constructed as "political concepts," imputing cultural differences between nationalities drove potentially deep crevices between such linguistic, descent-based, and culturally diverse groups. In theory, or even in practice during more peaceful times, the German nation could be imagined as a multinational entity. During a period of political, sociocultural, or ideological crisis such social and psychological lines of fracture could easily widen and be exploited for rhetorical and political effect. The mere act of defining nationality partly in cultural (or in modern parlance ethnic) terms proved the first dangerous step down the road to forgetting the common underlying humanity and the potential for national coexistence among peoples. National difference led to racial, and racial difference to the potentially self-fulfilling prophecies of world-historical struggles ending in loss of identity or even extinction. In the course of the revolutionary upheaval of 1848–1849 such a sense of multivalent crisis did prevail, and deputies did exploit these divisions in ways that began to expand and later to crack the conceptual parameters of the culture of nationhood. The nationality conglomerate began to crumble along its composite lines of fracture, leaving the parliamentarians to confront their vision of history, a history as red in sword and plowshare as ever nature was in tooth and claw.

Conclusion: The German Culture of Nationhood in Comparative Perspective

The preceding chapters have described how, as the revolutionary flood-waters of 1848 washed over the old contours and boundaries of the European political landscape, the Frankfurt parliamentarians toiled at their vexing task of constructing a German national state on the basis of the culturally multinational German Confederation. In stepping back to examine the present work's findings in broader historical perspective, this concluding chapter offers both a concise summary and some speculative comparative observations. The summary surveys the central structural elements of the prerevolutionary German culture of nationhood, their reinforcement by other pillars of the delegates' belief systems, and the application of these cultural predispositions to the various nationality-related issues confronted in Frankfurt. The comparative section tenders a few suggestions as to how this study's conclusions might alter some of the received wisdom on the relationship between German and other European variants of nationalist ideology. For by challenging the oft-employed dichotomy between cultural and political forms of nationalism, the present analysis also calls into question the associated typology of nationalisms according to their location in Eastern or Western Europe.

To say that liberalism and nationalism were closely related in the nineteenth century, or that German nationalist ideology stood intermediate along the cultural-political spectrum, partaking of both French-style emancipatory and native romantic cultural definitions of the nation, is not novel. What is new here is to have excavated a mound of prerevolutionary publications by a broad swath of representative educated Germans, including but extending beyond future Frankfurt deputies, in order to establish precisely how and why these men combined liberalism and nationalism, or cultural and political approaches to the problem of national definition.

205

Particularly in its careful attention to the boundary criteria of nationality the present work has broken new ground. Analyzing the words of mid-century educated Germans in this way reveals that just as they loaded the terms *Volk* and *Nation* with both political and cultural connotations, they interwove cultural and political elements into their conceptions of nationhood in several important respects. First, they generally recognized that no single cultural or political marker could define nationality. For these thinkers neither state borders nor laws and constitutions, neither customs nor religion, neither historical memory nor even biological descent or language could alone satisfactorily demarcate the boundaries of the thing called nation. Nationhood instead encompassed a variable mixture of these elements. But, second, in this protean context the future deputies did more than simply join political criteria for national boundaries with cultural ones. At a much deeper and more significant level they construed such categories as law, religion, and constitutional predilections so as to explode barriers between culture and politics as realms of thought.

What has usually been viewed as a cultural form of nationalism thus turns out to have been inextricably intertwined with political categories and referents, an entanglement revealed in a third, equally fundamental way. The parliamentarians conceived of the nation not as a static entity to be given a hieratic legitimacy by having its boundary criteria abstracted and frozen as lines on a map but rather as a process in which the nation had to be continually reborn in the consciousness of those belonging to it. Identity was not stasis but rather an active process among the members of the nation: remembering shared experiences, ancestors, or heroes; exchanging words and deeds; recognizing one another as members of the same living community. Where liberalism met nationalism, national identity could only develop as the result of consciousness-raising practices within the public domain of a free press, associations, festivals, and widely available education for the nation's citizens. When nationhood came to involve such ostensibly cultural realms as religion or law, and above all when it came to rely on the apparatus of the public sphere as the locus of identity, the various conceptual elements of nationality congealed into an alloy of the cultural and political that was both message and medium of nationhood. So malleable was this alloy that future parliamentarians could even find room for the inclusion of culturally "non-German Germans" within the longed-for national state.

That the accretion of national identity must occur as the result of a certain public process in a liberal political framework made ample sense to educated contemporaries in light of what has been revealed here as the other bastion of their views of nationhood, their dialectical historicism. The future deputies believed that all knowledge, all identity, all progress in the world arose through dialectical confrontation among individuals and ideas to expose a higher union and meaning. The historical consciousness and even the epistemological convictions of the Forty-Eighter generation powerfully suggested the essential flux of existence, in which both individual and national identities could only be the result of developmental processes rather than static essences, and processes moreover that operated best in an open political and cultural environment. Not just in the boundary criteria, then, but also in the political means and ends potentially distinct cultural and political perspectives on nationality were joined together. The most recent historian of cultural nationalism has emphasized both that cultural nationalists believed in a world of struggle and that they had a politics of their own. Yet even he overlooks the extent to which ostensibly cultural nationalists might pursue a liberal politics very similar to that of supposedly political nationalists, and that they might thereby veer from a strictly cultural form of national identity in their boundary criteria as well.[1]

Given this basic conflictual view of history, Germans schooled in the culture of *Bildung* also believed that only constant striving, constant exertion of inner strength, could secure a place within the charmed circle of those in the progressive forefront of the civilizing process. For individuals this Heraclitean, confrontational view of life meant maintaining honor as the sole guarantor of one's rights, and defending those rights as the only means of upholding honor. The right to rights had to be demonstrated in no uncertain terms. Only then, only when the rational individual had through his own inner strength carved out an autonomous space in which to act and assert himself, could he begin to fulfill the moral vocation almost universally believed to underlie social and political life.

For early nineteenth-century German liberal nationalists, the same held true for nations, which they conceived as moral individuals or personalities in the sphere of law and politics. Nations too had to possess honor and autonomy in order to secure the rights-based realm of activity in which the national will could assert itself in pursuit of its own moral vocation and historical mission. Without that honor, and without the inner strength, character, and self-confidence upon which it reposed, a nation could never resist the moral force of its competitors in the international arena. With its borders whittled away and its native culture supplanted, a nation without honor and independence would succumb, becoming just another in the long succession of peoples who had come and gone in the annals of human history. The same public process that bolstered the communal sense of national identity also helped nourish a nation's spiritual resources for this ongoing struggle, and in both cases it was the social and psychological mechanisms of liberal politics that engaged the patriotic gears so powerfully. In a dialectically historicist world, nations had to steel themselves in that cultural and political alloy of national identity in order that they might strive against other nations and avoid the fate of history's weak and forgotten.

The present investigation has shown then that midcentury educated German national identity was constructed around the twin notions of the nation as broadly based community and as historical actor. These linked ideas of nationality helped define a German "culture of nationhood." This culture of nationhood was by no means monolithic. As revealed in examining nationalist efforts to synthesize a national past, for example, there was no commonly accepted "master narrative" of German history before 1848. The similarities in such proposed national narratives emerged more at the level of deep structures and broad patterns than in detail. If the compulsion to produce such narratives was widespread, the competing versions of the national past were widely varied. Yet certain fundamental constraints deriving from the culture of nationhood did promote deep commonalities in the Forty-Eighter generation's historical consciousness. Moreover, the same balance between underlying parameters and higher-level diversity seen in the case of historical narratives applies to many of the other tendencies described here, from the role of honor and autonomy to the lack of any fully "ethnic" or "cultural" construal of the nationality principle in this period.

That the concept of a "culture of nationhood" deserves this appellation rather than simply that of a "nationalist ideology" follows from the fact that nationhood, as a mental construct, lay embedded in the surrounding cultural matrix, at once shaping it and shaped by it. These relationships, reciprocal and often rather remote, were too complex and too deeply rooted for complete conscious control by nationalist ideologues bent on the cultural work of inventing traditions and spinning master narratives. A great deal of self-aware manipulation took place, but there were limits to it, firmer if wider in the case of nationhood than in more purely political contexts. In the one direction, the concept of the nation served as an increasingly fundamental category of German thought in the early and middle decades of the nineteenth century. Not just in politics, but in art, philosophy, history, science, and economic life as in many other fields of human endeavor, the nation played a leading, even tautological role in framing and interpreting the phenomena of human existence. More relevant here, however, is the extent to which other, independent aspects of the surrounding culture helped mold concepts of nationhood. Outside that broader cultural context, German ideas of the nation cannot be fully understood. Rights-based legal theory and liberal politics; the romantic mode of historicizing and seeking for both social and personal wholeness through the harmonic resolution of conflicting forces; the epistemological transition to dialectical thinking among post-Kantians of all stripes: all of these broad intellectual and cultural trends influenced the ways in which educated Germans conceptualized and lived the experience of nationhood.

Feeding all these cultural streams, the deep underlying wellspring of the culture of *Bildung,* like the culture of nationhood it also helped nourish, was itself the confluence of broader social and cultural currents. In part a response to fears of onrushing social change in the era of the French Revolution, the culture of "self-formation" offered a way to break down or at least redefine and broaden old elites while creating a new one, as well as a way to ameliorate the tensions of modern life.[2] Its neoclassicizing, neo-humanist educational philosophy served as a benchmark for social distinction, while at the same time it encouraged honorable self-assertion as the key to self-realization in the higher interests of humanity, as the elixir that would reconcile the demands of individual and community. In national terms the culture of *Bildung* meant an immersion in classical sources that reinforced the conflation of the cultural and the political in nationhood. Those texts presented an image of community based on numerous criteria, from physical appearance and language, to laws and customs, to an ancient republican civic humanism that mirrored the active creation of patriotic common consciousness in liberal and nationalist theory and offered yet another means of reconciling individual and community. This translation of classical modes of thought into modern parlance also reinforced notions of conflictual history and national transience through exposure to cyclical theories of history and to narratives punctuated with waves of barbarian invaders. At least in part, the specific elements of the culture of nationhood and its associated nationalist ideologies represented unintended consequences of the larger cultural decisions and deeper cultural trends manifested in the German culture of *Bildung.*

*   *   *

This culture of nationhood provided the educational incubator for delegates to the Frankfurt National Assembly of 1848, who during that disorienting year of revolution drew on its tenets for guidance as they tried to "put the German nation on the map." The amalgamation of cultural and political criteria of nationhood ensured that in their border-drawing policies the new Germany's representatives adhered closely but by no means undeviatingly to the territorial limits of the German Confederation, neither striking out far afield in quest of a union of all linguistic or ancestral Germans nor seeking to exclude certain populations from membership in a German national state on the basis of language. Similarly, when the deputies confronted that most basic of constitutional questions—Who is a German?—they adopted what Wilhelm Jordan termed the "political conception" of nationhood and defined as German any resident of the German states. There was never any question that non-German-speakers would receive the same civic and political rights as other German citizens. Such civic equality resulted in part from a simple sense of natural justice, but it was also seen as the essential precondition for creating and maintaining a patriotic German national identity among these groups. Through the exercise of their rights in the liberal public sphere, the non-Germans' strong sense of local patriotism and identity might be expanded to embrace the German national level as well.

If this cycle of mutually reinforcing local and national patriotism were to operate fully among Germany's non-German citizens, the liberal grants of civic rights would also have to extend into the cultural realm. This was the seemingly paradoxical flip side of welding together culture and politics in constructions of nationhood. If speaking German or being of German descent was not to be a requirement for German citizenship, then the enjoyment of non-German culture and speech should be as free as possible. Under the so-called Mareck proclamation of May 1848, duly adopted into the constitution as Paragraph 188, the Assembly freely recognized the right of other nationalities within the new Germany to use their own languages in schools, church, courts, and local administration.

Much the same reasoning seen in the case of the non-German-speaking nationalities grounded the Assembly's firmly stated decision to grant full civic, political, and religious equality to German Jews (or to any other recognized religious denomination). For Johann Sepp and Moritz Mohl, who at once opposed the introduction of allegedly unassimilable Jews into the German body politic and dreamed of incorporating millions of Habsburg Hungary's Slavic inhabitants into that same body, the Jewish Question remained sui generis, not soluble according to the principles applied in the case of nationality. For most other deputies, however, the readiness to vote for a Jewish emancipation that was not conditional upon the sacrifice of Jewish religion or cultural community should be seen at least partly in the context of the culture of nationhood. If many delegates still shared the anti-Jewish stereotypes all too common then, they also believed that German Jews would become good German citizens when given the requisite freedom and equality. Contrary to some prevalent historiography on midcentury German liberal and Protestant attitudes toward Jews and the Jewish Question, this sample of prominent liberals neither applied racial or religious reasoning to argue for the exclusion of Jews from public life nor demanded the eradication of Jewish identity through full assimilation as the price of Jewish emancipation. Instead, religious, particularly Catholic, conservatives were the chief proponents of religious- or at times nationality-based anti-Judaism, and even they either converted to emancipation or kept a politic silence on the issue while in Frankfurt. While by no means generally philo-Semitic, the Assembly delegates cannot be considered radically anti-Semitic either. Whatever may have been the case later, for them the Jewish Question did not constitute the negative focus of German national identity.

At the same time, it cannot be denied that deputies expected a certain amount of assimilation to result from Jewish participation in German public life. Many probably even silently hoped for the full-scale religious conversion of Jews and their subsequent integration into the (Protestant or Catholic) German nation—this was, after all, still an age of sincere religious conviction and proselytizing. Most, however, would probably have followed their colleague Heinrich Laube in pointing to a man such as Assembly Vice President Gabriel Riesser as the ideal of the assimilated Jew—thoroughly at home in German culture, a worthy professional, and patriotically serving his nation in public life, he remained unrepentantly Jewish. Regarding the Orthodox Jewish communities of the rural west or the eastern shtetls, many parliamentarians remained uncomfortable and prejudiced. Yet once launched freely and equally into the stream of German national life, they hoped, time and the progressive dialectical triumph of enlightened ideas over those allegedly tainted relicts of former times would eventually ensure the proper degree of Jewish assimilation into self-professedly progressive German culture.

Much the same time-delayed Damoclean threat that hung over separate Jewish identity also dangled above the various non-German nationalities of the nascent Reich. Again, except for a few more radical thinkers, most delegates probably did not require a future complete loss of Czech or Danish identity as the mortgaged assimilatory cost of admission into the German national state. Becoming its patriotic citizens and adopting its political values as their own would have sufficed. Yet the possibility, and in some cases even the hope or expectation, that with time the non-German nationalities would come to see the benefits of integrating more fully into ostensibly superior German culture as into German political life still loomed oppressively. Moreover, the seemingly liberal guarantees of nationality linguistic rights themselves revealed significant reservations not immediately visible at the time or noted since. If the Assembly delegates had not set out to destroy particularist identities, neither did they desire to see them become too prominent a presence on the national scene. Other groups were free to speak their languages in a variety of public settings but only within the confines of their native territories. Above all in the symbolic space of the German national parliament, only German would be admissible. The cultural and political amalgam that was German national identity, while allowing the incorporation of non-German-speaking populations on conditions of apparent equality, simultaneously led to pressure on these groups to acculturate. While not wholly cultural, neither was nationality wholly political.

All of this discussion of German nationalist attitudes toward Jews and non-German-speakers obviously has important implications not just for older portrayals of German nationalism as xenophobic but also for those newer ones that emphasize the central role of exclusion and Othering in the formation of national identity. For whether it was the French as the external point of reference, or the various subaltern groups in Germany, newer scholarship influenced by poststructuralist theories has essentially translated the older view of German nationalism into a new idiom. The main difference now is that the processes of exclusion and Othering are no longer seen as the products of German nationalism alone but as intrinsic to the experience of nationhood. The present work does not attempt to overturn such ideas of the role of alterity in the formation of group consciousness, but it does enjoin caution in applying them. Exclusion did play a role, but it was not Jews or non-German-speakers, nor even Catholics, who were to be shut out from full membership in the German nation, at least not in this period. While these groups were subjected to forces of cultural norming, it was through inclusion, not exclusion, that German liberal nationalists attempted to foster a national identity among these groups and among themselves. Stating the cultural and political norms expected of these new Germans of course had the effect of reaffirming Germans' own identity, even as it put pressure on that of the others, but exclusion from the nation was not prominent here, neither rhetorically nor institutionally.

Where exclusion did play a dramatic role in the construction of national identity was in the case of women. Gender roles and the doctrine of the separate spheres, as establishing the Othered mirror by which male citizens could learn to recognize themselves, were the primary locus of exclusionary identity politics in 1848 as in the years preceding. Exclusion from public life was not complete, not even in theory, and women found ways to manipulate the language of nationalism so as to expand their public roles even further. Yet the exclusion was deep and functionally significant in the formation of national identity. For that matter, it provided yet one more way in which German nationalists transversed the categories of the cultural and the political in this period. For while of course culturally German, at times even the purest representation of Germanness, women were part of the political nation chiefly through their exclusion from it.[3]

For all that in their dealings with other national groups the Assembly delegates attempted to tailor the constitution in inclusively political and territorial cloth, in border-drawing as in nationality rights the parliamentarians failed to keep the German cultural stitching from showing through. All of the various potential criteria for nationality current during the prerevolutionary period, not just the political, found expression in the boundary debates of 1848: descent, language, customs, historical rights, historical memory, self-determination. If arguments from self-determining popular will facilitated the incorporation into the new Reich of the Prussian territories lying outside the Confederation, namely East Prussia, West Prussia, and parts of Poznania, the presence in those provinces of large contiguous populations considered German by descent and language remained one of the prime motivations for doing so. Given the contested nature of Germany's territorial claims on Schleswig, the cultural component of the Assembly's insistence on annexing at least the majority-German portions of the duchy kept pace with the self-determination, historical, and territorial justifications adduced. That the Assembly did not reach out its grasping hand even farther to demand linguistically German territories historically associated with the Holy Roman Empire simply helps demonstrate the fact that their beliefs led deputies to draw the boundary lines of nationality on a mixed cultural and political basis rather than according to some single criterion.

Similar reasoning largely explains why the Assembly did not promote the annexation of Austrian territories lying outside the Confederation in the same way it had Prussia's. Although even Little German or Prussian party adherents remained willing, often eager, to incorporate Austria's federal lands with their millions of Czechs and Slovenes, only a small minority of delegates stood ready to stretch the cultural weft of conceptually interwoven nationhood even further in the direction of multinational inclusivity. Most parliamentarians still wanted to think of the future Reich and its component provinces as in some sense nationally German, something they could not convince themselves of in the case of the far-flung, predominantly Magyar and Slavic lands of the Crown of St. Stephen. They did, certainly, construe nationality in a peculiarly liberal way, as above all a matter of *Bildung*. In their search for German culture they looked not to the hearthside words of the peasant farmer but to the busy urban world of print media and economic life, a maneuver that allowed deputies in the debates over borders in Schleswig, Poznania, and Austria to claim as nationally German regions that were non-German in terms of the predominant spoken vernacular. Still, for most not even this hubristic sense of nationality as bourgeois "high culture" could be applied to areas almost totally lacking in such a German cultural presence.

The Austrians of the Paulskirche did not typically extend German nationality to those areas either, but with their pronounced Catholic and multinational imperial traditions, they still possessed a more plastic sense of national identity in this regard than most North Germans. Such already-present regional divergences within the overarching culture of nationhood formed points of departure for the later Little German, Greater German, and Greater Austrian groupings of the 1860s, all the more so once it had become clear by the late fall of 1848 that the Austrian government would never allow the entrance of any of its territories into the German state on terms acceptable to a Frankfurt majority. The 1848 Revolution and its associated political and national conflicts played a crucial role in beginning the fragmentation of the midcentury culture of nationhood. But it was only a beginning, and a slow one. Although the sort of organicist intolerance of cultural difference associated with the germanizing policies of the post-1871 *kleindeutsch* Kaiserreich could be glimpsed *in nuce* during the Frankfurt debates, to come to fruition it had to undergo an extensive process of development in the intervening decades. Even the Little Germans preserved the latent openness of the culture of nationhood's definition of nationality. The Assembly's inclination toward passive (almost never active) germanization continued to owe more to cultural arrogance than to cultural aggression.

Presaging national confrontation not just in this measured cultural form but also in more dramatic political or military fashion, the conflictual nature of the *Vormärz* culture of nationhood provided a stormy backdrop for delegates' thinking during the revolution. If the hopes for harmony and cooperation that led to the euphoric "Springtime of the Peoples" in March of 1848 were no less real, the ominous image of a "war of the peoples" threatened to blot out the peaceful spring sunshine. Through their historicizing educations many deputies had come to believe that conflict was the world's modus operandi, and that a nation was only as secure as its internal strength could make it. National honor as both source and signifier of that strength stood at the center of their political worldviews, and above all in the Schleswig affair, but generally as well, the oft-sounded theme of national honor served deputies as rhetorical polestar. Only by insisting on Germany's national rights could they uphold its national honor, and only by means of the latter could they present the German nation as an international force to be reckoned with, a body capable of defending its borders both spiritually and physically against encroaching neighbors. The liberal nationalist dialectic established a sort of free trade in nationhood. It offered the potential gains of progressive germanization, but at the same time it held out the possibility that, if Germany did not maintain its national strength and integrity better than it had in the past, the German nation's international rivals could outcompete it in that marketplace.

Similarly in the Austrian debates, the desire to be bigger and stronger externally while still patriotically united internally shaped the thinking of both Prussian and Austrian party adherents, and it also ensured that constitutional questions rather than different definitions of "Germany" would form the crux of this long, bitter struggle. Both parliamentary groupings harbored some notion of a German-led Central European hegemon in which Germans would exercise power in cooperation with non-Germans, just as both tended to favor maintaining the old federal borders in Austria for the new German state. It was over the constitutional framework that would allow such Austrian and non-German participation that unresolvably contested visions of the German future ultimately arose.

Moreover, in this case too the dialectical historicist outlook and expectations of partial or even total assimilation of non-German-speakers helped reconcile deputies to one solution or the other as mere staging posts on the road to fulfilling Germany's national mission. In the search for national power in a German-dominated *Mitteleuropa*, germanization did not even have to stop at the borders of the Reich but could make impressive territorial gains for the German nation in the fertile lands of Eastern Europe. Yet just as surely, many feared, the eastward thrust of the western "Teutonic" peoples would be met with a powerful counterpressure from the "Slavic" East, in which context the quest for national unity and power took on an even darker-hued necessity. Recast in racial terms, the notion of national conflict became all the more dangerous in the form of racial conflict, considered partly as a cultural phenomenon but above all as a potentially catastrophic "war of annihilation" or "war of extermination." The radical border shifts and mass migrations associated with the period of the crumbling Roman Empire cast a haunting shade over the future as well as the past. Those informed by the culture of nationhood and its underlying culture of *Bildung*, though typically optimistic, even arrogant about Germany's future, still could not guarantee that Germany would be the chosen nation to carry on the future civilization of Europe. Slavic writers such as Jan Kollár and Adam Mickiewicz, after all, believed just as firmly that their own peoples were destined to usher in world civilization's final phase.[4]

Everything said so far has focused on the Frankfurt parliamentarians and their German contextual counterparts in the culture of nationhood. As the reference to Slavic nationalists attests, however, the question also arises as to how the fresh perspectives offered here on the formative phases of the German national movement might relate to the study of national ideologies elsewhere in nineteenth-century Europe. Appending at least a few comparative remarks becomes all the more imperative given that in its original formulation the cultural-political typology of nationalisms came attached to an East-West dichotomy as well.

Although the East-West dichotomy has certainly not gone unchallenged since the days when Hans Kohn first established the notion in the 1940s, it still represents an important point of departure in the literature, particularly for Eastern European nationalism. Lawrence Orton, for example, in his study of the 1848 Slavic Congress in Prague, still operates within this East-West framework. Orton sees western nationalisms as modeled after the French, in which the political nation represented by the inhabitants of the preexisting French state became the primary unit of nationality. In the East, however, German or romantic nationalism, with its emphasis on language as the sole determinant of national community, purportedly presented an alternative model for nationalism among the frequently stateless nationalities there. Similarly in his study of the national ideologies of the "little peoples" of Eastern Europe, Peter Brock retains the distinction between a French-style political nationality and a German-style cultural variety.[5] Even the authors of the modernization or sociological school of nationalism studies, while replacing the East-West typology with some functionalist form bearing on the relationships between the national movement and the established state powers, effectively retain certain aspects of it. A vernacular linguistic definition of nationality becomes part of the effort to carve a place in the modern world of print culture for one's own in-group in either the unification or secessionist forms of nationalism endemic to East-Central Europe, while romantic longing for organic community is redefined as lack of respect for the individual rights central to the western bourgeois liberal tradition.[6] The relative social, economic, and political "backwardness" of Eastern Europe simply does surrogate duty for Kohn's original ideological distinction.

Still, several authors have pointed out exceptions to this sharp delineation between national movements in the established national states of the West and those in the multinational empires of the East. Andrzej Walicki and Piotr Wandycz, for example, have both noted that by continuing to push for the restoration of Poland's historic 1772 borders the members of the Polish national movement maintained a political rather than a linguistic definition of nationality—they were fully aware of the presence of potential Ruthenian, Lithuanian, and even Kashubian nationalities within the *soi disant* Polish state.[7] For the Hungarian case Laszlo Deme has argued that Magyar nationalism was hardly so romantic or illiberal as its reputation suggests. Even Brock has admitted the Poles and Magyars to be exceptions to the East-West rule, while Orton has noted that when Czech activist Karel Havlíček turned from Pan-Slavism to Austro-Slavism, he repudiated the strictly cultural definition of nationhood in favor of a more broad-based and inclusive one.[8] Risto Alapuro accepts Kohn's dichotomy but concludes that the Finnish national movement was a mixture of the two types while, more generally, Anthony Smith, Peter Alter, and Jiří Kořalka have each observed that ethnic and political perspectives alike formed important components of most European nationalist ideologies, East and West.[9]

To point to political nationalisms in Eastern Europe, or even to coexisting cultural and political elements of nationalism, however, is not the same as following through on the present argument that the cultural and the political as categories of thought were not separable at this time, and then exploring the implications of that thesis for nationality politics. Polish nationalists did incorporate political and territorial aspects to their national identity, yet since they also stressed the superiority of civilized Polish culture and claims to nationality above those of the Ruthenians and Lithuanians, as had the Germans regarding the Czechs or the Poles themselves, their brand of nationalism also seems to have fused cultural and political concepts of the nation. The Magyars had no intention of creating an exclusive Magyar-only nation-state, but whether they would have allowed their Slavic compatriots actually to form part of a liberal Hungarian nation without significant cultural sacrifices remains uncertain. The Austro-Slavs, on the other hand, particularly Czechs like Havlíček, definitely seem to have employed modes of thought not so very different from the Germans and Poles. As the Poles claimed their historic multinational borders, the Czechs also desired the restoration of the mixed Polish-German-Czech Bohemian crownlands, quite possibly with the addition of the emergent Slovaks as well. They also maintained a strongly Austrian component to their national identities, thus making it possible to be at once fervent Czechs and ardent supporters of a multinational, liberal Habsburg federation. As the Frankfurt delegates for the most part eschewed the notion of a too-Slavic 70-million Empire, Austro-Slavs such as František Palacký abhorred the idea of becoming but a small portion of a greater German national state in 1848. Each group could accept cultural heterogeneity within a polity, but it could not stretch that acceptance indefinitely.

It is even possible to detect signs that early Slavic nationalists of the stateless peoples may have spun a similarly two-stranded ideological cocoon rather than relying solely on that of culture. Certain groups, such as the Sorbs and Slovaks, do seem to have focused almost entirely on the vernacular language as the center of national identity while retaining dynastic loyalties as an entirely separate matter. On the other hand, the Ruthenian national awakener Ivan Vahylevych adopted a definition of nationality resting on the twin stanchions of polity and culture. "A nation," Vahylevych claimed, "is a people which, having entered upon political life, has acquired a specific character," and he went on to add that it was self-evident that every nation should have, or have had, a political existence since the latter was "the external form of internal being." Culture was crucial for Vahylevych too—language above all, but coupled with the more general "customs and manners" familiar from the German context. Also noteworthy is that in 1848 Vahylevych entertained the possibility of cooperating with the Poles in forming a multinational Polish nation, not because he remained somehow mired in an unpolitical nationalism, but because he remained inspired by a miscible form of national identity allowing political unity and cultural heterogeneity to coexist within a liberal polity.[10]

In an era and region where linguistic and territorial boundaries rarely converged, those who followed the Slovenes of 1848 in their proposal to redraw borders on ethnographic lines remained atypical.[11] Like their liberal German counterparts, early Slavic national awakeners could and often did stand aloof from cultural revival in language groups perceived as being too small or backward to support the burdens of modern public discourse. A Sorb such as Jan Petr Jordan, a Slovak such as L'udovít Štúr, and a Slovene such as Jernej Kopitar could all promote the creation of literary languages from selected peasant vernaculars, yet they met opposition from those such as Pavel Šafařík, Kollár, Palacký, and even Jordan (!), who followed the Slavicist doyen Josef Dobrovský in preferring to limit the number of Slavic literary languages to a few populous and historically grounded groups such as the Czechs and Poles.[12] Considerations of national strength and sustainability influenced Slavic nationalists too and led to similar pressure to overlook purely linguistic differences and to incorporate or even assimilate other potential Slavic nationalities, just as they might cooperate with Germans as Austro-Slavs in a liberal Greater Austria. The year 1848 had not yet seen the advent of the hotly contested linguistic censuses of the later nineteenth century, when national identity seemed to be wholly rooted in the defense and propagation of the standardized language nearest to one's own mother tongue.[13] The hard-nosed political mass nationalism of the later Habsburg Empire required a quick and dirty means of defining and quantifying nationality, and popular language fit the bill. For the earlier period this was not so clear. Indeed, the collapse of minority aspirations and hopes for cooperation in 1848, coupled with the rejection of the Kremsier constitution, helped bring about the transition. Many of the observations made in the present work about the nature of German national identity and nationalism at least bear consideration in describing the situation in pre-1850s Eastern Europe as well.

That the Hungarians and Slavic peoples should have shared some of the often hubristic assumptions of German liberal nationalism need not surprise. After all, the claim has always been that men such as Kollár and Šafařík were influenced by what they learned of romantic nationalism in Germany.[14] If the present work is correct in its more nuanced portrayal of a German culture of nationhood in which organicist "culture" (particularly language) did not comprise the whole of nationality, then it makes perfect sense that its early Slavic interpreters likewise might not have come to place such exclusive emphasis on language as the seat of nationality. A more mixed, inclusive sense of national identity, bearing with it a certain arrogant expectation of partial cultural assimilation in the interests of liberal progress, could have been the result of such influence. As even among the adherents of the Little German party, the day of the full exclusionist fusion of cultural and political elements of nationality in the mature nation-state ideology of the later nineteenth century had not yet dawned. The narrow survey of non-German sources undertaken here can hardly prove such a statement, but it might well suggest the efficacy of posing the question.

Those who have pointed to the existence of western political nationalism in the East among the Poles and Magyars have typically explained this by adducing the greater, or at least earlier, inspiration afforded by the French Revolution-style political nation than by the later German romantic version. This Jacobin influence is undeniable, but it still begs the question of whether the French or British models were themselves so purely political in their definitions of nationhood. The assumption that British and French national identities were preformed in the political context of homogeneous monarchical states is, after all, patently false. French identity, like France itself, represented a multiethnic, multilingual historical accretion of peoples and territories by no means complete in 1789, or even 1815. British identity in turn has only too often been conflated with English identity, ignoring the fact of the kingdom's continued multinational, multicultural structure.[15] And in both cases, the French and the British, the construction of national identity did not take place in a vacuum but rather involved the definition of the self in opposition to the character ascribed to its "Othered" archrival. British identity involved strong anti-French sentiments, while increasingly after 1789 French nationalists told themselves they were everything that perfidious Albion was not.[16] In all these senses the British and French structured their national identities around the twin poles of culture and polity.

This should be obvious to any student of British or French history, yet it is only in the past few years that French cultural nationalism and British nationalism of any sort have received much historiographical attention. Most scholars still treat revolutionary French nationalism as an exclusively political movement bent on social leveling, but Eugen Weber has recently pointed to debates about the national ancestry of the French as significant in the construction of a French identity and of a French national history capable of trumping local particularist identities and historical narratives. Another scholar has similarly noted the increasing sense of "Frenchness" involved in the construal and granting of French citizenship over the period 1789–1793.[17] Moreover, the "linguistic terrorism" of the Revolution's Jacobin phase, for all that it can be deemed purely political or utilitarian in nature, still presupposed the necessary connection between patriotism and cultural assimilation, political unity and cultural homogeneity. This assumption's "nationalist" implications could be seen distinctly enough among the Jacobins Bertrand Barère and Louis Saint-Just, the latter stating in 1793 that it was no longer possible to be "German in language and patriotic in heart."[18] While the less centralist British never went to quite the same active lengths in assuring the cultural supremacy of the English language, many still desired that the process of assimilation continue in order to produce a more unified British (English!) identity. Further, just as France had its Abbé Sieyès, Augustin Thierry, and Henri Martin, Britain had its Walter Scott and John Pinkerton to stress the importance of racial genealogy for national character.[19] And as easily in the West as in the East, racialist notions could be taken to racist extremes. L. Perry Curtis, Jr. has portrayed the disturbing British dehumanization of the "simian" Celtic Irish, while Léon Poliakov and others have revealed the more modern forms of anti-Semitism latent within the Enlightenment thought of Voltaire and the West as in that of Kant or Bruno Bauer in the German lands.[20] Broadly construed culture and ethnicity enjoyed a similar centrality in western as in eastern conceptions of nationhood.

Insofar as racialist genealogical speculations in both Britain and France remained tied to concurrent nationalist debates over class relationships and the necessity for a new kind of patriotic union of state and people (the "nation"), they serve to show how interconnected the cultural and political facets of nationality also were in the minds of westerners. The historical battles between Gallo-Romans and Franks, or Normans and Saxons, continued to rage just as fiercely centuries later in the new context of burgeoning nationalist ideological warfare.[21] Race, religion, morality, constitutional theory, customs and manners, and in general what came to be called "national character": all these represented partial aspects of national identity in Britain and France as they did in Germany. Broadly conceived and partly interchangeable notions of race, culture, and political culture were united in all three lands to create the conceptual amalgam of nationhood.

Similar observations on the convergences among European national ideologies of East and West in this period apply just as strongly to their essentially dialectical and conflictual understanding of historical and social processes as to the compound nature of national identity. Partly as the result of Herder's harrowing prediction that the Magyars would be overwhelmed by the more numerous Germanic and Slavic peoples, Hungarian nationalists such as Lajos Kossuth adopted a sort of siege mentality and conceived of the national mission as the defensive consolidation of the Crown of St. Stephen in the form of a magyarized national state.[22] Slavic nationalists in turn directed their cultural and national revival efforts to fending off incipient germanization and magyarization, not to mention frequently promoting the "-ization" of smaller Slavic groups in the interests of powerful consolidation. Placing ostensibly "cultural" Slavic nationalism in this conflictual context even goes some way toward suggesting another dimension of its politicization, at least by the 1830s. The scholar Šafařík, for instance, in good Dahlmannian style stirringly informed the assembled delegates to the 1848 Prague Congress of the alternatives between liberation or germanization and magyarization, honor or death and glory. And even in Kollár's carefully worded avoidance of political claims for Slav "reciprocity," the poet and publicist still thought in terms of the strength, honor, and dignity of the Slavic nation, key words that ought to be familiar from the German case.[23] A latter-day Diogenes searching in this era for a truly unpolitical Slavic nationalist might well have required sturdy boots and a well-fueled lantern.

In Britain and France such a competitive streak was at least in part an inheritance from the diplomatic and military rivalry of the dynastic states, but this aggressive competition was joined in the cultural sphere as well, with each society striving to achieve cultural supremacy over its rival. Even the internationalist Jules Michelet shared the low French opinion of British character, and while espousing hopes for a utopian era of European peace he continued to believe in the lasting and beneficial nature of national distinctness and rivalries.[24] As noted above in the context of western racialism, figures such as Scott and Thierry deemed racial conflict a dominant historical theme, one destined to resonate in British and French political discourse for some time to come. National or even racial conflict, whether military or simply cultural, remained an important component of conceptions of nationhood both to the east and west of the German lands, as it did there.

There is no need to search too far afield for an at least tentative explanation of these similarities. While the distinct blend of neohellenism, romanticism, and idealism that made up the German culture of *Bildung* remained the authentic recipe of the Germanophone world, an analogous mixture of pedagogical classicism, Enlightenment liberalism, and dialectical historicism also flavored the educational experiences of generations of other Europeans. Speaking the language of ancient republican civic humanism, the Scot Adam Ferguson espoused the virtues of competition and conflict among both individuals and nations in public life, and if Michelet followed Vico more than Herder in his romantic historicism, his romantic and liberal sense of progress as the resolution of inner and social dissonance into dynamic harmony was still quite similar to that of the Weimar-inspired Germans.[25] The notion of the rational but passionate individual at the root of the German idea of *Bildung* did not differ as much as often claimed from that of western liberalism, while the fundamental tensions among self, community, and universal divinity in organicist German romanticism also set basic parameters for discussion and creativity in the countries across the Rhine. And to the east, of course, the educational common ground trod at Jena by Kollár, Šafařík, and Wilhelm von Humboldt, or in Carniola and Vienna by Kopitar and Count Auersperg, lay closer still.

Similar remarks on root European congruences in the tropes of nationality could be made for the criteria of national identity. All over Europe reflective individuals searching for group identity linked religion, mores and customs, laws, climate, and race with the historical bonds knit by political coexistence. In part the result of imitation of one's nationally minded neighbors, this tendency to compress political and broadly cultural facets of identity into the single prized gem of nationhood could only have received added impetus from common exposure to the classical historians and geographers, who made much the same distinctions. Above all, the ideas of race and ethnology in any given nation cannot really be understood apart from their European context. Investigators the continent over not only drew on a common classical heritage of ethnographic depictions and physiognomic and humoral schemes, but they also simply represented a community of scholars who read each other's works: Prichard, Camper, and Blumenbach; Lavater, Coombe, and Gall. This sharing of ideas did not prevent national differences of opinion. The first half of the nineteenth century, for instance, saw a greater receptivity to materialist interpretations of race in France than in Britain or Germany. Yet such intellectual contacts served as at least a series of drawbridges across the moats that surrounded national cultures.[26]

All of the preceding remarks taken together suggest that the East-West dichotomization of nationalisms might as well be dropped as admitting too many exceptions to prove any rule. Kipling notwithstanding, East and West may have met in this instance. They shared certain points of contact in their notions of national identity and international relations, with the western lands retaining strong cultural elements in their national ideologies and the eastern often continuing to operate within political modes of thought in their own versions of nationalism. Moreover, the very cultural-political dichotomy on which the East-West typology rests has proven inadequate to explain the nuances of early German nationalism and might well also fail to do so for other European national movements. Only further study upon the basis of a much wider array of sources could answer this broader question. In the meantime the newer functional typologies suggested by members of the modernization school such as Anthony Smith, Eric Hobsbawm, or John Breuilly still offer the best approaches to the subject. Even if there was a tendency to interweave cultural and political strands of identity in the eastern national movements as in Germany and the West, this could proceed more fully among the "historical" peoples with state traditions than among those minorities slowly defining themselves as nations while waging a battle against the domination of foreign state authorities. Still, no typology should entirely lose sight of the ideological dimension, for it is there that structural similarities in the national movements could most readily transcend the functional categories thus partitioning them. Even where a shared idea was adapted to a different use in a new functional context, the ideological ancestry and analogy can be illuminating. The East-West typology facilitates neither analytical approach.

In neither case, not for the East-West typology and especially not for the more general issue of the cultural-political dichotomy, has the present work attempted to eclipse all that has come before. Older perspectives emphasizing ideas and newer ones highlighting the structural contexts of polity, society, economy, and cultural practice all help to provide a rounded view of this very complex subject. On the other hand, this study does represent a novel attempt to reconstruct the early German culture of nationhood from within and from the ground up, partly by relating it to broader intellectual, social, and cultural trends. Certain previously held notions about the relationship between the cultural and political realms of thought and experience in the construction of national identity and ideology during the first half of the nineteenth century, at least in the German context and possibly among its neighbors as well, thereby reveal themselves to be at best misleading, at worst mistaken. Even when interpreted in their proper cultural and intellectual contexts, ideas of race, language, and history alone did not a nation define. The so-important nationality principle, oft cried and oft decried, was by no means as simple as it seemed—then or since.

Even the cultural-theoretic focus on exclusion and Othering in the construction of national narratives and national identity requires nuanced handling before it can be applied to the German case of the first half of the nineteenth century. Exclusion did play a role in liberal nationalism, partly with regard to class norming and above all with regard to gender roles and stereotyping. Yet tolerance for alterity at the level of race and ethnicity was much greater than supposed, and while normative expectations also surfaced in the context of nationality relations, it is still crucial to grasp that the mixed cultural-political constructions of national identity turned not on exclusion but on inclusion, and a nonforceful inclusion with guaranteed rights of citizenship and cultural autonomy at that. Moreover, with the loss of the cultural-political and East-West dichotomies, those aspects of the *Sonderweg* thesis pertaining to the specially pernicious German brand of nationalism lose much of their impetus for the period leading up to the 1848 Revolution. Just as bourgeois liberal influence in German society and culture seems to have been greater than previously thought when measured against a looser western model, liberalism and the culture of nationhood also seem to have been intricately interlaced, above all in the 1830s and 1840s, but throughout the period examined here. The dangerous coin of racialist and chauvinist aggression was certainly current then in Germany, but the German ideological mint held no monopoly on it. Only later would that debased coinage of narrowly construed, exclusionary national identity displace the ideals shared by the large majority of the Frankfurt parliamentarians and thus obscure the potential for a more tolerant, inclusive definition of German nationality that still existed in 1848.

Notes

Abbreviations

BA F, DB	Bundesarchiv, Frankfurt Aussenstelle, Deutscher Bund
Droysen, *Verhandlungen*	*Die Verhandlungen des Verfassungsausschusses der deutschen Nationalversammlung, Teil 1.* Vaduz: Topos, 1987 [orig. Leipzig, 1849].
1846 Verhandlungen	*Verhandlungen der Germanisten zu Frankfurt am Main am 24., 25. und 26. September 1846.* Frankfurt a. M., 1847.
1847 Verhandlungen	*Verhandlungen der Germanisten zu Lübeck am 27., 28. und 30. September 1847.* Lübeck, 1848.
Hübner, *Aktenstücke*	Johann Droysen. *Aktenstücke und Aufzeichnungen zur Geschichte der Frankfurter Nationalversammlung aus dem Nachlass von Johann Gustav Droysen.* Ed. Rudolf Hübner. Stuttgart: Deutsche Verlags-Anstalt, 1924.
HZ	*Historische Zeitschrift*
JHI	*Journal of the History of Ideas*
JMH	*Journal of Modern History*
Jucho, *Verhandlungen*	Friedrich Jucho, ed. *Verhandlungen des deutschen Parlaments, Offizielle Ausgabe, Mit einer geschichtlichen Einleitung über die Entstehung der Vertretung des ganzen deutschen Volkes.* Frankfurt a. M., 1848.
LBIYB	*Leo Baeck Institute Year Book*
OffBer	*Offizieller Bericht über die Verhandlungen zur Gründung eines deutschen Parlaments.* Frankfurt a. M., 1848.
StB x:y (vol.: p.)	Franz Wigard. *Stenographische Berichte über die Verhandlungen der deutschen konstituierenden Nationalversammlung zu Frankfurt a. M.* 9 vols. Frankfurt a. M., 1848–1849.

StLex   Carl von Rotteck and Carl Welcker, eds. *Das Staats-*
                     Lexikon: Encyklopädie der sämmtlichen
                     Staatswissenschaften für alle Stände. 15 + 4 vols.
                     Altona, 1834–1848.

Introduction

1. Friedrich Nietzsche, *Beyond Good and Evil: Prelude to a Philosophy of the Fu-*
   ture, trans. R. J. Hollingdale (Harmondsworth: Penguin, 1990 [orig. 1886]),
   174.
2. Günter Wollstein, *Das "Grossdeutschland" der Paulskirche: Nationale Ziele in*
   der bürgerlichen Revolution von 1848/49 (Düsseldorf: Droste, 1977). Although Wollstein avoids calling the Frankfurt parliamentarians "forerunners of
   Hitler" as do Lewis Namier, *1848: The Revolution of the Intellectuals* (Garden
   City, N.Y.: Anchor, 1964 [orig. 1944]), and Roy Pascal, "The Frankfort Parliament, 1848, and the Drang nach Osten," *JMH* 18 (1946): 108–122, his
   views do have roots in these treatments. For the politicized debate over
   whether the liberals or democrats were to blame for the chauvinist nationalism
   that helped vitiate chances for the revolution's success, see Veit Valentin as a
   defender of the democrats, *Geschichte der deutschen Revolution von 1848–49*
   (Berlin: Ullstein, 1930); as defenders of the liberals see Wilhelm Mommsen,
   Grösse und Versagen des deutschen Bürgertums: Ein Beitrag zur Geschichte der
   Jahre 1848–1849 (Stuttgart: Deutsche Verlags-Anstalt, 1949), and Frank
   Eyck, *The Frankfurt Parliament 1848–1849* (London: Macmillan, 1968).
3. Wollstein, *Grossdeutschland,* 221.
4. For a survey of the social-historical literature, see the review essays by Dieter
   Langewiesche, "Die deutsche Revolution von 1848/49 und die vorrevo-
   lutionäre Gesellschaft: Forschungsstand und Forschungsperspektiven," *Archiv*
   für Sozialgeschichte 21 (1981): 458–498, and "Teil 2," *Archiv für Sozial-*
   geschichte 31 (1991): 331–443.
5. Jonathan Sperber, "Festivals of National Unity in the German Revolution of
   1848–1849," *Past and Present* 136 (1992): 114–138, is a fine example of the
   ways in which this methodology can produce thought-provoking statements
   about early nineteenth-century German nationalism. Sperber reveals the popular "discourse of the nation," different from its elite counterpart, which
   emerges from study of the revolutionary festivals in the Rhineland. He shows
   how these festivals of unity usually turned on the exclusion of some particular
   religious or social group.
6. Friedrich Meinecke, *Cosmopolitanism and the National State,* trans. Robert
   Kinder (Princeton: Princeton University Press, 1970); Hans Kohn, *The Idea of*
   Nationalism: A Study of Its Origins and Background (New York: Macmillan,
   1946), esp. 329–331 and 351. Kohn also makes a related distinction between
   the phases of eastern cultural nationalism, as either purely cultural in its goals
   or as pursuing the political end of sovereign statehood. By focusing on a pe-

riod in which German nationalism was already avowedly political in that sense, challenging this second dichotomy does not form so large a part of the present study's aims.

7. See Anthony D. Smith, *Theories of Nationalism* (New York: Holmes and Meier, 1983), 195–199 for the mixed critique and acceptance of Kohn's typology, and 16–17, 21 for the "core doctrine" of nationalism and the German version; Eric Hobsbawm, *Nations and Nationalism since 1780: Programme, Myth, Reality* (Cambridge: Cambridge University Press, 1992), 37–38, 102–103; Liah Greenfeld, *Nationalism: Five Roads to Modernity* (Cambridge, Mass.: Harvard University Press, 1992), esp. 14–17 and ch. 4.

8. Charlotte Tacke, *Denkmal im sozialen Raum: nationale Symbole in Deutschland und Frankreich im 19. Jahrhundert* (Göttingen: Vandenhoeck & Ruprecht, 1995), esp. 35–36, 73–74. Tacke argues that the dichotomous national identities do not indicate any essential difference between the nations but rather reflect their construction as distinct "collective national stereotypes" in the realm of cultural self-representation. For the two recent studies, see Matthew Levinger, *Enlightened Nationalism: The Transformation of Prussian Political Culture, 1806–1848* (New York: Oxford University Press, 2000), esp. ch. 5 and 223–225; and Panikos Panayi, *Ethnic Minorities in Nineteenth and Twentieth Century Germany: Jews, Gypsies, Poles, Turks, and Others* (Harlow: Longman, 2000), 1–3 and ch. 2.

9. Karl W. Deutsch, *Nationalism and Social Communication: An Inquiry into the Foundations of Nationality* (Cambridge, Mass.: MIT Press, 1966), set the tone for the concrete, sociological analysis of the phenomenon of nationality. From Deutsch stem the fundamental concepts of "nation-building" and "social communication" that help explain the construction of nationhood during the industrial era. Besides Smith and Hobsbawm above, other notable contributions to the sociological school of interpretation include Benedict Anderson, *Imagined Communities: Reflections on the Origin and Spread of Nationalism* (London: Verso, 1991); Ernest Gellner, *Nations and Nationalism* (Oxford: Blackwell, 1983); and for Germany, above all the work of Otto Dann. While all of these authors fit into the sociological mold, this by no means implies monotone treatments, Anderson in particular overlapping with anthropologically based cultural studies approaches.

10. Gellner, *Nations,* 123–127, suggests that individual thinkers are "hardly worth analyzing"—it is the social communication of mass media itself, not its message, that constructs national consciousness. Hobsbawm, *Nations,* 24, does sketch out a liberal theory of the nation that takes into account criteria of nationhood. He simply points out that this was never central to liberal discourse since the idea of the nation was considered "obvious."

11. For a general survey of the newer literature on nationalism, see Geoff Eley and Ronald Grigor Suny, "Introduction: From the Moment of Social History to the Work of Cultural Representation," in Eley and Suny, eds., *Becoming National: A Reader* (New York: Oxford University Press, 1996), 3–37; for Ger-

many, see Dieter Langewiesche, "Nation, Nationalismus, Nationalstaat: Forschungsstand und Forschungsperspektiven," *Neue Politische Literatur* 40 (1995): 190–236, esp. 212–219. A fine recent work that engages both cultural studies and sociological approaches is Jörg Echternkamp's *Der Aufstieg des deutschen Nationalismus (1770–1840)* (Frankfurt a. M.: Campus, 1998).

12. For two interesting efforts to negotiate the middle ground between historical transparency and opacity in dialogue with F. R. Ankersmit's reflections on the relationship between postmodernism and historicism, see Chris Lorenz, "Historical Knowledge and Historical Reality: A Plea for 'Internal Realism,'" *History and Theory* 33 (1994): 297–327, and John H. Zammito, "Ankersmit's Postmodernist Historiography: The Hyperbole of 'Opacity,'" *History and Theory* 37 (1998): 330–346.

13. For Ideas in Context, see the contributions by Quentin Skinner, esp. "A Reply to My Critics," in James Tully, ed., *Meaning and Context: Quentin Skinner and His Critics* (Princeton: Princeton University Press, 1988), 231–288, and Tully's introduction, "The Pen Is a Mighty Sword: Quentin Skinner's Analysis of Politics," 3–25. The historicist recovery of intended meaning from within texts located in specific historical contexts, going beyond the canon, dealing with pragmatic political choices, and considering institutional power relations, can all be found in this approach. Skinner developed the model on the basis of the later Wittgenstein and of J. L. Austin's speech-act theory, where every statement is an action intended to have an effect within a specific field of social conventions (its "illocutionary force").

14. John Breuilly, *Nationalism and the State* (Manchester: Manchester University Press, 1993), 3; on 12–13 Breuilly admits that doctrine matters but maintains that the only basis for a typology is political (unification, separatist, reform), not doctrinal (ethnic, linguistic, liberal, or romantic). Such a typology is, however, less useful in dealing with the problems of minority rights and border-drawing of concern here.

15. Shifting attention to the boundary markers and ideational content of nationhood has received some support from scholars dissatisfied with the at times confining sociological approach to the subject. Anthony Smith's more recent revisionist writings, for example, argue for an understanding of nations as partly cultural rather than purely conscious inventions. Peoples in his view possess a surprisingly durable core of values, images, and symbols ("ethnicity"), which are subsumed into the later constructions of nationalism ("nations"). Smith, *The Ethnic Origins of Nations* (Oxford: Blackwell, 1986).

16. As Wilhelm Mommsen warned, more than one interpretation of the revolution has faltered through neglecting the profound changes in opinion that occurred as early as 1849. *Grösse*, 10. In France, Count Gobineau's culturally pessimist theory of racial inequality developed in response to the 1848 February Revolution. Michael D. Biddiss, *Father of the Racist Ideology: The Social and Political Thought of Count Gobineau* (London: Weidenfeld & Nicolson, 1970), 59–100. Among Assembly deputies, the radical Julius Fröbel similarly

turned to racialist and *Realpolitik* doctrines in the revolution's aftermath. Rainer Koch, *Demokratie und Staat bei Julius Fröbel 1805–1893: liberales Denken zwischen Naturrecht und Sozialdarwinismus* (Wiesbaden: Steiner, 1978), 240–255.

I. The *Vormärz* Culture of Nationhood

1. See Hans Kohn, *The Mind of Germany: The Education of a Nation* (New York: Scribner, 1965), for his fullest account of German nationalism.
2. I owe the idea of the coherence of early romanticism and idealism in the Jena circle of Fichte, Schleiermacher, the Humboldts, and the Schlegels to Cyrus Hamlin of Yale University. For a fine brief treatment of these continuities, see Robert C. Solomon, *Continental Philosophy since 1750: The Rise and Fall of the Self* (New York: Oxford University Press, 1988), ch. 3, esp. 44–48.

1. Defining National Boundaries

1. Reinhart Koselleck, "Lexikalischer Rückblick," part of the entry "Volk, Nation, Nationalismus, Masse," in *Geschichtliche Grundbegriffe: Historisches Lexikon zur politisch-sozialen Sprache in Deutschland* (Stuttgart: Klett, 1992), 7: 380–389, here 382; Bernd Schönemann, "Frühe Neuzeit und 19. Jahrhundert," in ibid., 281–380, esp. 284.
2. Julius Fröbel, *System der socialen Politik* (Mannheim, 1847), 1: 241–242.
3. Carl Welcker, "Völkerrecht," in *StLex*, vol. 15 (1843), 731; for the "Nation, Nationalität" cross-reference, vol. 11 (1841), 154. Such overlapping diction could occur even in the same sentence, as in the radical Gustav von Struve's use of both *Volk* and *Nation* in a political context in one paragraph, while a few pages later he put the two words next to each other to refer to blood relationships. *Grundzüge der Staatswissenschaft* (Frankfurt a. M., 1848), 4: 188–189, 196. For a conservative example, the school of historical law theorist Friedrich Stahl typically used "Volk" when he meant the population of a state but occasionally used "Nation" for variety's sake, while at other times Stahl oscillated between the two words' prepolitical sense. *Philosophie des Rechts nach geschichtlicher Ansicht* (Heidelberg, 1830–1837).
4. Struve, *Grundzüge*, for example, employed *Nationalität* and *Nation* as synonyms for prepolitical groups, which was the most common understanding (vol. 4, pp. 206–207), while at other times he used *Nationalität* to mean a "strong feeling of nationhood" (ibid., 188–189).
5. F. C. Dahlmann, *Die Politik, auf den Grund und den Mass der gegebenen Zustände zurückgeführt* (Göttingen, 1835), 3–4.
6. Hanno Beck, *Carl Ritter, Genius der Geographie: Zu seinem Leben und Werk* (Berlin: Reimer, 1979), 25, emphasizes the Napoleonic context to Ritter's and Humboldt's researches.
7. See E. M. Arndt, *Versuch in vergleichender Völkergeshichte* (Leipzig, 1844),

205, for the Dauphiné; see also Günther Wiegand, *Zum deutschen Russland-interesse im 19. Jahrhundert: E. M. Arndt und Varnhagen von Ense* (Stuttgart: Klett, 1967), 33–35, which contends Arndt remained true to the idea of "to each people its ocean" while waffling on the relative merits of language versus rivers and mountains as national boundaries.

8. B. G. Niebuhr, *Vorträge über alte Länder- und Völkerkunde,* in M. Isler, ed., *Historische und philologische Vorträge* (Berlin, 1851 [orig. 1827–1828]), 284–285, 597; Georg Wilhelm Friedrich Hegel, *Vorlesungen über die Philosophie der Weltgeschichte. Band 1: Die Vernunft in der Geschichte,* ed. Johannes Hoffmeister (Hamburg: Meiner, 1968), 195–196.

9. Friedrich Ludwig Jahn, *Deutsches Volkstum* (New York: Olms, 1980 [orig. 1813]), 41–44. Even in 1833 Jahn maintained that mountain ranges were natural national borders. *Merke zum Deutschen Volksthum* (Hildburghausen, 1833), 137–140.

10. Georg Friedrich Kolb, "Natürliche Grenze," in *StLex* (1841), 11: 155–157.

11. Ernst Moritz Arndt, "Des Deutschen Vaterland," in *Gedichte* (Berlin, 1860), 233–235, quote at 234; Kolb, "Natürliche Grenze," 157.

12. Johann Gottlieb Fichte, *Reden an die deutsche Nation,* ed. Fritz Medicus (Hamburg: Meiner, 1955), 61; a view shared by Arndt, as for example, *Völkergeschichte,* 396, where he praised German as an "Ursprache" as opposed to a "Mischsprache."

13. *1846 Verhandlungen,* 11; Fröbel, *System,* 1: 239–240.

14. Wilhelm von Humboldt, "Latium und Hellas, oder Betrachtungen über das classische Alterthum," in Albert Leitzmann, ed., *Wilhelm von Humboldts Gesammelte Schriften* (Berlin, 1904), 3: 136–170, here 166.

15. For Herder's views of language and influence in linguistic thought, see R. H. Robins, *A Short History of Linguistics* (London: Longman, 1990), 166–168, 190; Fichte, *Reden,* 61.

16. Most recently on these connections, see Jörg Echternkamp, *Der Aufstieg des deutschen Nationalismus (1770–1840)* (Frankfurt a. M.: Campus, 1998), 305–306.

17. Stephen K. Land, "Universalism and Relativism: A Philosophical Problem of Translation in the Eighteenth Century," *JHI* 35 (1974): 597–610, downplays the extent of Enlightenment universalism and suggests that thinkers from Locke onwards were fully aware of the translation difficulties occasioned by differing national paths of historical development that left languages with differing conceptual lexica.

18. Wilhelm von Humboldt, *Ueber die Verschiedenheit des menschlichen Sprachbaues und ihren Einfluss auf die geistige Entwicklung des Menschengeschlechts* (1835), in *Gesammelte Schriften,* 7: 1–344, here 55–65 for the general connection between speech and thought, esp. 60 and 64–65. For Humboldt's linguistic philosophy, emphasizing his epistemological originality, see Jürgen Trabant, *Traditionen Humboldts* (Frankfurt a. M.: Suhrkamp, 1990), esp. 37–55, and ch. 8 on the centrality of dialectics. For similarly seminal thinking

on the dialectical, hermeneutical roots of knowledge and the soluble problems of mutual national comprehension, see Friedrich Schleiermacher, *Hermeneutik und Kritik,* ed. Manfred Frank (Frankfurt a. M.: Suhrkamp, 1977), esp. 76–84, 91–92, 169–170, and "Appendix," 361–370 (essay of 1805/ 1806).

19. Again Humboldt expressed the thought most powerfully, as for example in *Verschiedenheit,* 36–38, and especially as quoted from *Kawi-Werk,* 3: 427, in Alexander von Humboldt, *Kosmos: Entwurf einer physischen Weltbeschreibung* (Stuttgart, 1845), 1: 385–386 and note pp. 492–493: "More than anything else in man, language embraces the entire race. Precisely in its nation-separating quality it unifies the differences of individualities." This idea follows from one of the most basic idealist and romantic tropes, the attempt to reconcile the polarity "unity" and "diversity."

20. Jacob Grimm, *Geschichte der deutschen Sprache* (Leipzig, 1848), 169–170; Schleiermacher, *Hermeneutik,* "Appendix," 423–424 (1831 ms); Jakob Philipp Fallmerayer, *Welchen Einfluss hatte die Besetzung Griechenlands durch die Slaven auf das Schicksal der Stadt Athen und der Landschaft Attika?* (Stuttgart, 1835), 53–54. On the early comparative linguists, see Robins, *Linguistics,* 187–201.

21. Kolb, "Natürliche Grenze," 157.

22. See Ludwig Uhland, *Sagengeschichte der germanischen und romanischen Völker,* ed. A. V. Keller, in *Uhlands Schriften zur Geschichte der Dichtung und Sage* (Stuttgart, 1868), 7: 3–4, for a classic programmatic statement. Grimm was famous then and now for his collections of German fairy tales and folkways, and for the impetus he gave to such studies elsewhere in Europe.

23. See Jahn, *Deutsches Volkstum,* ch. 7, for national costume and festivals; Friedrich Theodor Vischer, *Aesthetik oder Wissenschaft des Schönen* (Reutlingen, 1847), 2: 295–297, for his general complaint against homogenized modern fashions, and "Aus einer griechischen Reise," in Vischer, *Altes und Neues* (Stuttgart, 1882), 9–37, 28–29, and esp. 35–37, for his feeling of inward "tornness" at the sight of Greeks in frock coats, a feeling also ascribed to modernity in general.

24. Georg Waitz, *Deutsche Verfassungsgeschichte* (Kiel, 1844), 1: 49; Arndt similarly determined the Franks' degree of kinship with the Saxons and Alemanni by comparing their settlement patterns even more than their languages. *Völkergeschichte,* 198.

25. Struve, *Grundzüge,* 4: 197–198.

26. Friedrich Carl von Savigny, *Vom Beruf unsrer Zeit für Gesetzgebung und Rechtswissenschaft* (Heidelberg, 1840 [orig. 1814]), 8–11, quote at 8.

27. Georg Beseler, *Volksrecht und Juristenrecht* (Leipzig, 1843), 59ff.; *1846 Verhandlungen,* 64. The Hessian jurist Sylvester Jordan, who like Mittermaier had absorbed aspects of both the older natural law and newer historical law traditions, also thought the sphere of customary law closest to popular attitudes, which further suggests the extent of such ideas beyond the historical school

of law as such. *Lehrbuch des allgemeinen und deutschen Staatsrechts* (Kassel, 1831), 1: 42.

28. *1846 Verhandlungen*, 74. These statements occurred in the course of a debate over the place of Roman law in modern German courts.

29. G. A. H. Stenzel, *Geschichte des preussischen Staats* (Hamburg, 1830), 1: 72. F. M. Barnard attacks Kohn's dichotomy from much this direction in a path-breaking essay that argues that both cultural and political "types" of nationalism were attempts to expand the notion of culture, itself embedded in nature, to include political relations and thereby legitimate them as natural. "National Culture and Political Legitimacy: Herder and Rousseau," *JHI* 44 (1983): 231–253.

30. Anton Christ, *Ueber deutsche Nationalgesetzgebung. Ein Beitrag zur Erzielung gemeinsamer für ganz Deutschland gültiger Gesetzbücher und zur Abschaffung des römischen und des französischen Rechts insbesondere* (Karlsruhe, 1842): 46.

31. See Stahl, *Philosophie des Rechts*, 1: 36, on Greek ideas of fate, but the principle applied generally. The Freiburg Catholic law professor and future deputy Franz Buss closely echoed Stahl on this point in his *Geschichte der Staatswissenschaft* (Freiburg i. B., 1839), 1: lix.

32. Siegfried Peetz, *Die Wiederkehr im Unterschied: Ernst von Lasaulx* (Freiburg i. B.: Alber, 1989), 351, from a fully-quoted Lasaulx letter of 1829, and see 202, where Peetz makes the autonomous spin-offs point for Lasaulx; see also Hegel, *Weltgeschichte*, 124–137, for the primary importance of religion in the *Volksgeist*.

33. See Wolfgang Hock, *Liberales Denken im Zeitalter der Paulskirche: Droysen und die Frankfurter Mitte* (Münster: Aschendorff, 1957), 93–101; and Raymond G. Gettell, *History of Political Thought* (London: Allen, 1924), ch. 19, for the moral and ethical overtones in liberal politics.

34. Herder, Friedrich Schlegel, and the future Assembly delegates Carl Welcker and Friedrich Vischer are other notable examples of this tendency.

35. See Gustav von Struve, *Handbuch der Phrenologie* (Leipzig, 1845), 293–294, for the German-Protestant connection, as also Jacob Grimm, *Deutsche Mythologie* (2d ed., Göttingen, 1844), xliii–xlvi, where Roman Catholicism seemed like a corrupt interruption of the continuity between pure German paganism and Protestantism; Jakob Philipp Fallmerayer, "Marquis de Custine: La Russie en 1839" (1843 review), in Georg Martin Thomas, ed., *Gesammelte Werke* (Leipzig, 1861), 3: 20–56, esp. 22–23. The Catholic conservative Görres Circle shared Fallmerayer's religious view of the Russo-German difference. Frank Reuther, "Das Russlandbild der 'Historisch-politischen Blätter für das katholische Deutschland' im Vormärz," *Jahrbücher für Geschichte Osteuropas* 39 (1991): 177–198, here 183.

36. See Wilhelm von Humboldt, *Prüfung der Untersuchungen über die Urbewohner Hispaniens vermittelst der vaskischen Sprache,* in *Gesammelte Schriften* (orig. 1821), 4: 57–232, here esp. 182; Carl Ritter, *Die Vorhalle Europäischer Völkergeschichten vor Herodotus* (Berlin, 1820); Karl Otfried Müller, *Geschichte*

hellenischer Stämme und Städte, vols. 2 and 3: *Die Dorier* (Breslau, 1824), esp. vol. 2, pp. IX–X and 199–214, but also note his use of mythology to distinguish between the aboriginal Pelasgians and Hellenes as nations, ibid., 13–14; Julius Ambrosch, *Studien und Andeutungen im Gebiet des altrömischen Bodens und Cultus* (Breslau, 1839), esp. viii, xvi–xvii, 169–173, 191–192.

37. See Grimm, *Geschichte,* 161 for a general statement, 231–233 and 236 for the Scythian case; Uhland, *Sagengeschichte,* 548–554 for comparisons of Germanic and Persian mythology to establish a genealogical relationship; Kaspar Zeuss, *Die Deutschen und die Nachbarstämme* (Munich, 1837), esp. 21–49 for the Indo-European dimension, and 285–290 for the Scythian-Persian connection against Niebuhr's Mongol thesis; B. G. Niebuhr, "Untersuchungen über die Geschichte der Skythen, Geten, und Sarmaten," in Niebuhr, *Kleine historische und philologische Schriften* (Bonn, 1828), 352–398, esp. 362 for religious rites among other customs as supporting the Scythian-Mongol connection. In general, Niebuhr placed least emphasis on religion as a guide to national affinity, Uhland and Grimm more but well behind language, while Zeuss relied as heavily on mythological as on linguistic evidence.

38. See *Herodotus,* trans. A. D. Godley (Cambridge, Mass.: Harvard University Press, 1938), bk. IV, esp. §§59–81, 106–109, for ethnographic categories applied to the Scythians; *Tacitus on Britain and Germany: A Translation of the "agricola" and "Germania,"* trans. H. Mattingly (Harmondsworth: Penguin, 1948), 101–140, for *Germania.* In general, see Klaus E. Müller, *Geschichte der antiken Ethnographie und ethnologischen Theoriebildung: Von den Anfängen bis auf die Byzantinischen Historiographen* (Wiesbaden: Steiner, 1972–1980), 1: 94–131, for Hekataios and Herodotus; and 2: 80–107, for Tacitus.

39. Klaus von See, *Deutsche Germanen-Ideologie von Humanismus bis zur Gegenwart* (Frankfurt a. M.: Athenäum, 1970), 9–13, 15–16; see, for example, Heinrich Luden, *Geschichte des teutschen Volkes* (Gotha, 1825), 1: 12–14, 448–454, for his emphasis on original German purity. But Luden recognized Celtic mixing in the population of southern Germany and refused to speculate whether a migration from Asia might have taken place at some point in the distant past; see 9–10 for Celts, 13–14 for migration. Both Grimm and Uhland also disputed Tacitus's claim of German aboriginal status: Grimm's *Geschichte* accepted the Indo-European Asian migration theory, as did Uhland, *Sagengeschichte,* 477–479.

40. See James Q. Whitman, *The Legacy of Roman Law in the German Romantic Era: Historical Vision and Legal Change* (Princeton: Princeton University Press, 1990), x–xiv, for his general thesis that classical and in particular Roman law scholarship exercised a previously unrecognized influence on the German legal community and inspired a native brand of "ancient constitutionalism" tied to Holy Roman Empire traditions. For ethnography, Martin Braun has pointed to the formative role of the Greek and Tacitean ethnographic tradition in the thought of Georg Forster, although he stresses continuities in western philosophy over direct encounter with the classics. *"Nichts Men-*

schliches soll mir fremd sein"—*Georg Forster und die frühe deutsche Völkerkunde vor dem Hintergrund der klassischen Kulturwissenschaften* (Bonn: Holos, 1991), 1–37, and esp. note 25, p. 180. In addition to the classics, another probable source of attitudes toward nationhood was the Old Testament, as in Hans Kohn, *The Idea of Nationalism: A Study in Its Origins and Background* (New York: Macmillan, 1944), ch. 2, esp. p. 36, but more research is needed on this point.

41. Niebuhr, "Skythen," 361. Alexander von Humboldt, *Kosmos,* note 10, pp. 491–492, opposed Niebuhr's view, as did Zeuss, *Die Deutschen,* 284–285. Fallmerayer, *Einfluss,* 48–49, and Vischer, "Reise," 31–32, both relied to some extent on facial features as a guide to ethnic affinity in their attempts to settle the question of the modern Greeks' Hellenic heritage.

42. Niebuhr, *Völkerkunde,* 329, noted how Arndt had drawn his attention to the sharp differences remaining among ancient populations in the French, Italian, and German Alps as seen in physiognomies and customs, while Arndt, *Völkergeschichte,* 313 and 355–356, tried to deduce ancient ethnic affinities from current physical features for the Russians and Walloons. See Struve, *Phrenologie,* 292, for the basic stability of European populations since ancient times. Karl Bernhardi more authoritatively expressed the notion that the ethnographic map of Europe had changed little in the past two millennia. *Sprachkarte von Deutschland* (Kassel, 1844), 1–2.

43. See Léon Poliakov, *The Aryan Myth: A History of Racist and Nationalist Ideas in Europe,* trans. Edmund Howard (New York: Heinemann, 1974), ch. 9, for the Aryan theory in the late eighteenth and early nineteenth centuries.

44. Karl Salomo Zachariä, *Vierzig Bücher vom Staate* (Heidelberg, 1839), 2: 158–159; Friedrich Schlegel, *Philosophie der Geschichte,* in Jean-Jaques Anstett, ed., *Kritische Friedrich Schlegel Ausgabe* (Munich: Schöningh, 1971 [orig. 1829]), 9: 151; Alexander von Humboldt, *Kosmos,* 384; Fröbel, *System,* 1: 239–240. See also Grimm, *Geschichte,* 5.

45. Struve, *Phrenologie,* esp. 293–294; Fröbel, *System,* 1: 452–454. Fröbel also reserved a slot for the mixed "Romance" race made up of Celtic, Germanic, Iberian, and Italic remnants. Fröbel used the language criterion much more religiously than Struve as part of his attempt to fulfill Alexander von Humboldt's plan of breaking up the unwieldy three- or five-race classificatory systems into smaller, more natural groups. Fröbel, ibid., 1: 254–259; Humboldt, *Kosmos,* 382–383.

46. See, for example, Humboldt's famous letter to Goethe on the "Musée des petits Augustins," in *Gesammelte Schriften,* 2: 345–375. Vischer has already been mentioned in connection with his sketches of Greek and Slavic physiognomies, but see also *Aesthetik,* 2: 206–213, where he attacked phrenology as "charlatanism" but accorded some value to physiognomy; Carl Vogt, *Ocean und Mittelmeer* (Frankfurt a. M., 1848), 2: 202–204; and Wiegand, *Russlandinteresse,* 26–28 for Arndt's use of national physiognomies, and 61–62 for his distrust of Lavater's general approach. Poliakov, *Aryan Myth,* 328, makes the

point that the anticlerical liberal left tended to welcome such new materialistic ideas more readily, which holds true fairly well here.

47. See J. G. Spurzheim, *Outlines of Phrenology* (Boston, 1832), 11–14, for restriction to individuals, with examples of application to nations at 18–19, 29–30, 70; Johann Caspar Lavater, *Physiognomische Fragmente zur Beförderung der Menschenkenntniss und Menschenliebe* (Winterthur, 1787), 3: 85–127, esp. 85–89 and 126–127; Struve, *Phrenologie*, 292. Humboldt hoped to use physiognomy as a basis for his planned "Characterology of the Eighteenth Century," intended to describe the main Western European national characters. See "Das Achtzehnte Jahrhundert," in *Gesammelte Schriften*, 2: 1–112.

48. Wulf D. Hund more strongly points the finger at Kant's racism. See Hund, *Rassismus: die soziale Konstruktion natürlicher Ungleichheit* (Münster: Westfälisches Dampfboot, 1999), 87–88, 119–126, quote at 124 (from Kant's essay of 1788, "Über den Gebrauch teleologischer Prinzipien in der Philosophie").

49. Arndt, *Völkergeschichte*, 11–12; Struve, *Phrenologie*, 291–292; Fallmerayer, "August Bürck: Die Reisen des Venetianers Marco Polo im dreizehnten Jahrhundert" (1845), in *Werke*, 3: 80–112, here 80; Vischer, *Aesthetik*, 2: 175–176; Gervinus, "Ueber Schlosser's universal-historische Uebersicht der alten Welt und ihrer Cultur," in *Gesammelte kleine Schriften*, vol. 7 of *Historische Schriften von G. G. Gervinus* (Leipzig, 1839), 333–382, here 363–364; also "Historische Briefe. Veranlasst durch Heeren und das Archiv von Schlosser und Bercht," in ibid., 1–134, esp. 24–25.

50. Fröbel, *System*, 1: 160–164 (bk. 3 generally sets out the "negative elements" of reality to be treated as means in achieving the overall moral purpose); Arnold Ruge, *Der Patriotismus* (Frankfurt a. M.: Insel, 1968 [orig. 1846]), 30–31, 40–41; see also Ruge, *Polemische Briefe* (Leipzig: Zentralantiquariat der DDR, 1976 [orig. 1847]), 279–280, for an echo of the Hegelian idea of German philosophy's creation of a "second nature" of freedom as opposed to the deterministic first nature.

51. Hegel, *Weltgeschichte;* see also G. W. F. Hegel, *Phänomenologie des Geistes,* vol. 3 of Eva Moldenhauer and Karl Markus Michel, eds., *Werke* (Frankfurt a. M.: Suhrkamp, 1970), 233–257 on physiognomy and phrenology, esp. 243–244.

52. See Friedrich Schiller, "Ueber Anmut und Würde," in Karl Goedeke, ed., *Sämmtliche Werke* (Stuttgart, n.d. [orig. 1793]), 14: 5–57, here 26, where Schiller deemed the "mute features" "not empty of meaning" but less telling than the "mimetic" or "speaking" ones; Vischer, *Aesthetik*, 2: 213; Joseph von Radowitz, "Physiognomie," in *Gesammelte Schriften* (Berlin, 1853), 5: 253–255.

53. Wilhelm Jordan, *Geschichte der Insel Hayti und ihres Negerstaats* (Leipzig, 1846), 1: 3; Georg Friedrich Kolb, "Racen der Menschen," in *StLex* (1842), 13: 389–408, quote at 408. Such examples could be multiplied, as with the opposition jurist Sylvester Jordan's remarks in his *Lehrbuch*, 1: 29–30, 101–102, or the professor of natural law Heinrich Ahrens's powerful plea for recog-

nition that despite an unequal degree of development all races possessed the same rational capacities and could fulfill the same rational, civilized functions. *Das Naturrecht oder die Rechtsphilosophie nach dem gegenwärtigen Zustande dieser Wissenschaft in Deutschland,* trans. Adolph Wink (Braunschweig, 1846), 166–167.

54. See Fröbel, *System,* 1: 14–25, for the general argument, where he pointed to the ability to learn other languages or to modify an existing one as evidence for "general capacity for civilization," and 257–259 for the Humboldt quote; see also Alexander von Humboldt, *Kosmos,* 385–386, for the original context.

55. As George Stocking has argued, the whole thrust of early nineteenth-century ethnological research lay in demonstrating the common origin of mankind as depicted in the Mosaic account. Without steering in the direction of Biblical literalism, the great majority of figures examined here upheld a belief in both monogenesis and moral progress toward *Humanität.* Stocking, *Victorian Anthropology* (New York: Free Press, 1987), ch. 2. For a rare example of a future deputy opposing monogenesis, see the left-liberal J. G. A. Wirth, *Die Geschichte der Deutschen* (Stuttgart, 1846), 1: 206–207.

56. See Lavater, *Physiognomische Fragmente,* 3: 128–144, esp. 131–136, in which emotions and the imaginative powers of the mother play such a large role that children of a second marriage can acquire the facial expressions of a beloved first husband (!), and 142–144, where some sort of "seed" from both parents is obviously involved but again with much room for affective influence during and after conception. See also Struve, *Phrenologie,* 274–275, where parental "bodily and mental forces" at the moment of conception, or indeed the mother's moods during gestation, affect heredity; Vischer, "Reise," 24–25.

57. Fröbel, *System,* 1: 175–177. In general, Stocking, *Victorian Anthropology,* 63–64, 106, notes the Lamarckian heredity of acquired characteristics and the consequent overlap in early nineteenth-century ideas of race and culture, ideas thus much different from those scientifically current today.

58. Dahlmann, *Politik,* 4–5; Jakob Friedrich Fries, *Handbuch der praktischen Philosophie oder der philosophischen Zwecklehre* (Heidelberg, 1818), 145–146. Carl Welcker similarly placed less emphasis on descent in the modern period as part of a gradual transition from "sensuality" to "morality" ("Sinnlichkeit" to "Sittlichkeit") in human society. Brigitte Theune, *Volk und Nation bei Jahn, Rotteck, Welcker und Dahlmann* (Berlin: Ebering, 1937), 63–65.

59. H. K. Hoffmann, "Volk, Volksthümlichkeit, etc.," in *StLex* (1843), 15: 727–731, 727 (quote), 731 (Jahn's influence); Fröbel, *System,* 1: 240.

60. See Hegel, *Weltgeschichte,* 60; Günter Birtsch, *Die Nation als sittliche Idee: Der Nationalstaatsbegriff in Geschichtsschreibung und politischer Gedankenwelt Johann Gustav Droysens* (Cologne: Böhlau, 1964), 36–38, 51–53. See also Fichte, *Reden,* Speech 8, for the placement of the *Volk* in the divine realm but emphasizing the necessity of patriotic enthusiasm and education; Peetz, *Lasaulx,* 351, for Schelling's pupil Lasaulx on the *Volk* as "common consciousness" ("gemeinschaftliches Bewusstsein"), expressed in language and religion.

61. See Savigny, *Beruf,* 9–12, for the conscious element of the law-*Volksgeist* connection, leading to jurist control of customary law in higher cultures; Beseler, *Volksrecht,* 59, for reiteration of Savigny's views, 5 on the need for "conscious national unity," and 65–67 for the more liberal interpretation in opposition to "jurists' law." The conservative Stahl, *Philosophie des Rechts,* vol. 2, pt. 2, pp. 21–23, also emphasized the conscious element in conjunction with and going beyond descent in creating national unity.

62. See Fries, *Handbuch,* 141, 143; Hock, *Droysen,* 49–54, for Droysen and several other liberals; Theune, *Volk und Nation,* 60–61, for Welcker; Roland Feldmann, *Jacob Grimm und die Politik* (n.p., 1969), 262–263.

63. From Kant's "What is Enlightenment?" essay onwards, the demand for freedom of discussion was very nearly the sine qua non of liberalism, making it otiose to enumerate its adherents among the Forty-Eighters. Carl Welcker was but *primus inter pares.*

64. See the Austrian Baron Viktor von Andrian-Werburg, *Oesterreich und dessen Zukunft,* pt. 2 (Hamburg, 1847), 105–106, including the "Pflanzschule" and "Erziehungsanstalt" quotes, and 110–111. For varied examples of a quintessentially liberal notion, see the Bavarian Catholic natural law theorist Conrad Cucumus, *Lehrbuch des Staatsrechts der konstitutionellen Monarchie Baierns* (Würzburg, 1825), 257, where self-government is the citizen's "preceptress for constitutional freedom"; the Germanist historical law professor Beseler, *Volksrecht,* 159–160, 177; and Struve, *Grundzüge,* 3: 169–173.

65. See Paul Nolte's suggestive article, "Bürgerideal, Gemeinde und Republik, Klassischer Republikanismus im frühen deutschen Liberalismus," *HZ* 254 (1992): 609–656. Thinkers of the eighteenth-century Scottish Enlightenment had already been able to forge an acceptable compromise between the demands of civic virtue and commercial society, which allowed for a partial fusion of the civic humanist and rights-based traditions among neohumanist German liberals in the period studied here. For the Scottish example, see J. G. A. Pocock, *The Machiavellian Moment: Florentine Political Thought and the Atlantic Republican Tradition* (Princeton: Princeton University Press, 1975), ch. 14.

66. See Baron Viktor von Andrian-Werburg, *Oesterreich* (Hamburg, 1843), vol. 1, esp. pp. 186–187 and 201–203, for a process that was to have worked all the more smoothly in the context of a free public sphere and a national representative body seated in Vienna, as on 197–198; Franz Schuselka, "Ist Österreich deutsch?" (two excerpts) in Madeleine Rietra, ed., *Jung Österreich: Dokumente und Materialien zur liberalen österreichischen Opposition 1835–1848* (Amsterdam: Rodopi, 1980 [orig. 1843]), 217–223, here 220; Count Friedrich Deym, *Drei Denkschriften,* (Karlsbad, 1848 [orig. 1847]), 7–8, 12–13.

67. See Hermann von der Dunk, *Der deutsche Vormärz und Belgien 1830/48* (Wiesbaden: Steiner, 1966), for a fine study of such thinking, especially for that of future Assembly delegates Arndt, Grimm, Karl Biedermann, Gustav Höfken, and Ignaz Kuranda, who ran the gamut of ethnic, historical, strategic,

and economic motives for their Pan-German politics. See also Günter Wollstein, *Das "Grossdeutschland" der Paulskirche: Nationale Ziele in der bürgerlichen Revolution von 1848/49* (Düsseldorf: Droste, 1977), 56, 319 ("magnet
theory").

68. See Tom Garvin, "Ethnic Markers, Modern Nationalisms, and the Nightmare
of History," in Peter Krüger, ed., *Ethnicity and Nationalism: Case Studies in
Their Intrinsic Tension and Political Dynamics* (Marburg: Hitzeroth, 1993),
61–74, esp. 69–72. Ethnic markers could themselves attain the status of
mythemes within the collective memory, given that a central element of such
national tales involved telling who the nation was and where it came from.

69. See Otto Dann, "Das alte Reich und die junge Nation. Zur Bedeutung des
Reiches für die nationale Bewegung in Deutschland," *Jahrbuch für die Geschichte Mittel- und Ostdeutschlands* 35 (1986): 108–126, where he also points
to basic problems with the whole *Kultur/Staatsnation* dichotomy.

70. See Paul Pfizer, *Gedanken über Recht, Staat und Kirche* (Stuttgart, 1842), 1:
287–288, a key passage; Struve, *Grundzüge*, 4: 206–207, for the emigration
option; and Gustav von Struve, *Briefe über Kirche und Staat* (Mannheim,
1846), 121–122, for a list of the new Germany's provinces. As noted above,
the radical Badenese Germanist and future deputy Anton Christ was much like
Pfizer in appending a telling footnote on the possibility of multinational government to his own strong statement of the nationality principle. *Nationalgesetzgebung*, 45–46.

2. The Nation as Historical Actor

1. Most recently, see Jörg Echternkamp, *Der Aufstieg des deutschen Nationalismus (1770–1840)* (Frankfurt a. M.: Campus, 1998), esp. 203–213 for the romantic conservatives and 306–336 for the liberal nationalists. See also Wolfgang Altgeld, "Deutsche Romantik und Geschichte Italiens im Mittelalter," in
Reinhard Elze and Pierangelo Schiera, eds., *Italia e Germania. Immagini,
modelli, miti fra due popoli nell'Ottocento: il Medioevo/Das Mittelalter. Ansichten, Stereotypen und Mythen zweier Völker im neunzehnten Jahrhundert:
Deutschland und Italien* (Bologna: Il Mulino, 1988), 193–220. An earlier
source for the romantic versus liberal distinction is Walter Schieblich, *Die
Auffassung des mittelalterlichen Kaisertums in der deutschen Geschichtsschreibung von Leibniz bis Giesebrecht* (Berlin: Ebering, 1932). Insofar as
Schieblich notes the extent to which liberals were also often attracted by romantic notions and captivated by the medieval era, his work comes closer to
the views outlined here.

2. J. G. A. Wirth, *Die Geschichte der Deutschen* (Stuttgart, 1846), vol. 1, esp.
pp. 32ff.

3. Jakob Venedey, *Römerthum, Christenthum und Germanenthum und deren
wechselseitigen Einfluss bei der Umgestaltung der Sclaverei des Alterthums in die
Leibeigenschaft des Mittelalters* (Frankfurt a. M., 1840). Welcker did not posit

the medieval period as ideal, but he refused to dismiss it as a "dark age" and found much to admire in an era of robust self-help and self-government. "Deutsche Staatengeschichte, Deutschland, Deutsche, Germanen, deutsche Standesverhältnisse, deutsche Kaiser und deutsche Grundgesetze," *StLex* (1837), 4: 281–337, here 317–318.

4. Gustav Stenzel praised the Saxon and Salic periods. *Geschichte Deutschlands unter den Fränkischen Kaisern,* 2 vols. (Leipzig, 1827–1828). Schieblich, *Auffassung,* 101, notes the popularity of the Hohenstaufen era as cultural and political highpoint, above all through Friedrich von Raumer's *Geschichte der Hohenstaufen und ihrer Zeit,* 6 vols. (Leipzig, 1823–1825). Ludwig Uhland also emphasized the Hohenstaufen. "Aus den Vorlesungen über Geschichte der deutschen Poesie im Mittelalter I.," in *Uhlands Gesammelte Werke* (Stuttgart, n.d. [orig. 1830]), 4: 127–235, here 139. The Swabian Uhland's case suggests the extent to which geographic origins, not just political allegiances, might influence the patriotic choice of golden age.

5. Wirth, *Geschichte,* 2: 16, 142ff. On cities as a general medieval point of attraction for liberals, including Carl von Rotteck and Heinrich Luden, see Echternkamp, *Aufstieg,* 332–333, 335.

6. Arndt did laud the Teutonic *Vorzeit* but still found much to praise in the medieval period, from the flourishing cities to the cultural glories of Christian art and the Crusades. He even identified the period from 1000–1500 as Germany's true highpoint. *Ansichten und Aussichten der Teutschen Geschichte* (Leipzig, 1814), 128. Again, both critique of the Teutons and admiration for the Middle Ages spread well into the ranks of the liberal or *Burschenschaft* nationalists.

7. Welcker, "Deutsche Staatengeschichte," 302–304, was among the fans of Charlemagne. Wirth, Arndt, and August Friedrich Gfrörer were among his many detractors: Wirth, *Geschichte,* 1: 512–514, 539–541; Arndt, *Ansichten,* 165–166; and August Friedrich Gfrörer, *Geschichte der ost- und westfränkischen Carolinger vom Tode Ludwigs des Frommen bis zum Ende Conrads I. (840–918)* (Freiburg i. B., 1848), 1: 3–4, 19, 27, 65. Echternkamp, *Aufstieg,* 120–121, also notes Charlemagne as an example of the difficulties involved in selecting a national hero. On Barbarossa, see Altgeld, "Deutsche Romantik"; and Arno Borst, "Barbarossas Erwachen—Zur Geschichte der deutschen Identität," in Odo Marquard and Karlheinz Stierle, eds., *Identität* (Munich: Fink, 1979), 17–60.

8. See Echternkamp, *Aufstieg,* 120–121, on Frederick the Great as disputed hero. Joseph had Austrian admirers such as the poet Moritz Hartmann, but others found him similarly too close to Enlightenment rationalism.

9. Paul Pfizer, *Das Vaterland* (Stuttgart, 1845), 15; George Phillips, "Das Denkmal des Arminius," in *Vermischte Schriften* (Vienna, 1856), 1: 163–177; Moritz Hartmann, "Deutsche Monumente," in *Moritz Hartmann's Gesammelte Werke* (Stuttgart, 1874), 1: 24–26; Arndt, *Ansichten,* 46–64, 115; Wirth, *Geschichte,* 1: 336–337.

10. On Germania, see Lothar Gall, *Germania: Eine deutsche Marianne? Une Marianne allemande?* (Bonn: Bouvier, 1993). On how the use of the female figure of Germania underlined the role of women's exclusion in cementing both feelings of liberal national identity and masculinity among German males, see Patricia Mazón, "Germania Triumphant: The Niederwald National Monument and the Liberal Moment in Imperial Germany," *German History* 18 (2000): 162–192. Echternkamp, *Aufstieg*, 206–207, 315, also emphasizes that liberal nationalist historians focused on the *Volk* more than individuals as the maker of the nation's history.

11. Karl Salomo Zachariä, *Vierzig Bücher vom Staate* (Heidelberg, 1839), 2: 114–115. It is important to note here the contemporary usage of "culture" and "civilization" as processes, neither yet bearing the sense of a static property they would come to imply later. See Norbert Elias, in Michael Schröter, ed., *The Germans: Power Struggles and the Development of Habitus in the Nineteenth and Twentieth Centuries,* trans. Eric Dunning and Stephen Mennell (Cambridge, England: Polity, 1996), 123–129.

12. See Friedrich Schiller, "Ueber die ästhetische Erziehung des Menschen," in Karl Goedeke, ed., *Schillers sämmtliche Werke in sechzehn Bänden* (Stuttgart, n.d. [orig. 1793]), 14: 100–196, here 116–118 for modern alienation, 108–109 for totality of character as necessary for freedom, and 162 for the definition of aesthetic as harmonizing diverse "powers" with respect to the "whole."

13. For the idealist tradition of revolutionary dialectical change, see Bernard Yack's fine study, *The Longing for Total Revolution: Philosophic Sources of Social Discontent from Rousseau to Marx and Nietzsche* (Princeton: Princeton University Press, 1986), which also emphasizes the role of the Jena post-Kantian left, including Schiller and Fichte. For the historians, see Georg Iggers, *The German Conception of History: The National Tradition of Historical Thought from Herder to the Present,* (Middletown, Conn.: Wesleyan University Press, 1968), which highlights Humboldt and Ranke plus the Assembly figures Droysen, Gervinus, and Dahlmann, to which for a conservative Catholic historian add Siegfried Peetz, *Die Wiederkehr im Unterschied: Ernst von Lasaulx* (Freiburg i. B.: Alber, 1989).

14. Elie Kedourie perceptively emphasizes the idealist-derived centrality of personal and historical struggle in the nationalist view of the world but from a somewhat different angle, with Kant, Fichte, and Herder the principal sources of this secular theodicy. See Kedourie, *Nationalism* (London: Hutchinson, 1961), 30, 51–57.

15. Karl Heinz Schäfer, *Ernst Moritz Arndt als politischer Publizist: Studien zu Publizistik, Pressepolitik und kollektivem Bewusstsein im frühen 19. Jahrhundert* (Bonn: Röhrscheid, 1974), 126–128; Gustav von Struve, *Handbuch der Phrenologie* (Leipzig, 1845), 97, 100; Paul Pfizer, *Gedanken über Recht, Staat und Kirche* (Stuttgart, 1842), 1: 93–94.

16. See Johann Gustav Droysen, *Geschichte Alexanders des Grossen* (Hamburg, 1833), 1 for "creation" quote, and 205 for the Hegel-like sentiments on jus-

tice and history; Wilhelm Jordan, *Geschichte der Insel Hayti und ihres Neger-staats* (Leipzig, 1846), 1: 13, for his remarks on the tragic fate of the aboriginal Haitians as they encountered the "triumphal chariot of the world-conquering culture" of Spain, and 244 for the quote in the text.

17. Johann Gottfried Herder, *Ideen zur Philosophie der Geschichte der Menschheit,* in Martin Bollacher, ed., *Werke* (Frankfurt, a. M.: Deutsche Klassiker Verlag, 1989 [orig. 1784–1791]), 6: 690–696; Georg Wilhelm Friedrich Hegel, *Vorlesungen über die Philosophie der Weltgeschichte,* ed. Johannes Hoffmeister (Hamburg: Meiner, 1968), 4: 758–759; Friedrich Schlegel, *Philosophie der Geschichte,* in Jean-Jacques Anstett, ed., *Kritische Friedrich Schlegel Ausgabe* (Munich: Schöningh, 1971 [orig. 1829]), 9: 258–260; Carl Welcker, "Natürliche Grundlagen der Staatsverhältnisse und aller gründlichen gesunden Staatswissenschaft," in *StLex, Supplemente* (1847), vol. 3, esp. pp. 804–805; Sylvester Jordan, *Lehrbuch des allgemeinen und deutschen Staatsrechts* (Kassel, 1831), 106–107; Venedey, *Römerthum, Christenthum und Germanenthum.* Venedey defended himself (313–314) against charges of overzealous German patriotism by claiming that practically all of "civilized Europe" was Germanic or germanized, and that his patriotism was therefore very nearly cosmopolitanism! See also Heinz Gollwitzer's uniquely valuable "Zum politischen Germanismus des 19. Jahrhunderts," in *Festschrift für Hermann Heimpel,* ed. Mitarbeiter des Max-Planck-Instituts für Geschichte (Göttingen: Vandenhoeck & Ruprecht, 1971), 282–356, here 287, note 12, for the extent to which Germans of Fichte's period considered the Romance peoples to be of Germanic extraction.

18. See Gustav Stenzel, *Geschichte des preussischen Staats* (Hamburg, 1830), 4ff., while in his *Geschichte Deutschlands,* 1: 726, Stenzel even refers to Slavic settlements west of the Elbe; Raumer, *Geschichte der Hohenstaufen,* 1: 365–372; Friedrich Christoph Dahlmann, *Geschichte Dännemarks* (Hamburg, 1840), 1: 189–190, 332–333; Georg Phillips, "Beiträge zur Geschichte Deutschlands vom Jahre 887 bis 936," in *Abhandlungen der Historischen Classe der Koeniglich Bayerischen Akademie der Wissenschaften* (1842), 3: 3–124, here 33–34, 48–61.

19. Karl Bernhardi, *Sprachkarte von Deutschland* (Kassel, 1844), 6–12, esp. 8.

20. See Herder, *Ideen,* 790–791; Grimm, *1846 Verhandlungen,* 14 for language, 16, 71, 81 for law.

21. Georg Waitz, "Ueber das germanische Element in der Geschichte des neuern Europa," *Allgemeine Zeitschrift der Geschichte* (1848), 9: 59–71, esp. 68–69. Examples of this trope could be multiplied, as in Stenzel, *Geschichte Deutschlands,* 1: 745. For the connection of such a stance to the Forty-Eighters' experience of neohumanist education, see Friedrich Welcker (Carl's brother), "Ueber die Bedeutung der Philologie," in his *Schriften zur Griechischen Literatur dritter Theil* (Bonn, 1861), 4: 1–16, esp. 4.

22. Phillips, "Beiträge," 49–50, a view shared not surprisingly by Arndt himself: E. M. Arndt, *Versuch in vergleichender Völkergeschichte* (Leipzig, 1844), 369–

370. For Stenzel, see especially his lecture on Silesian germanization at the 1847 Germanist Conference, *1847 Verhandlungen,* 171–179, where Stenzel also mentions *connubium* as an aspect of the germanizing process, 177. The Königsberg historian and political geographer Friedrich Schubert spoke just afterwards on the germanization of Prussia, ibid., 179–181. Bernhardi, *Sprachkarte,* 11, left open the question of German survival in the Slavic East but tended to the view that the Germanic population had not entirely succumbed during the Migration Period.

23. See Max Vasmer, *B. Kopitars Briefwechsel mit Jakob Grimm* (Cologne: Böhlau, 1987), esp. vii–xi, xv–xxvii, for Grimm's Slavistic interests; Ludwig Uhland, *Sagengeschichte der germanischen und romanischen Völker,* ed. A. V. Keller, in *Uhlands Schriften zur Geschichte der Dichtung und Sage* (Stuttgart, 1868), 7: 9–10; Anton Auersperg, *Volkslieder aus Krain,* in Eduard Castle et al., eds., *Anastasius Grüns Werke* (Berlin, 1909), 5: 9–37, for Auersperg's preface and the editor's introduction; Herder, *Ideen,* 696–699; Jakob Philipp Fallmerayer, "Blick auf die untern Donauländer," in Georg Martin Thomas, ed., *Gesammelte Werke* (Leipzig, 1861 [orig. 1839]), 2: 3–18, here 13, for the positive evaluation; Fallmerayer, *Welchen Einfluss hatte die Besetzung Griechenlands durch die Slaven auf das Schicksal der Stadt Athen und der Landschaft Attika?* (Stuttgart, 1835), 4–5, 53–54, for the central question of whether the New Greeks, as of Slavic and Albanian descent, would be able to launch themselves into the progressive mainstream of western culture.

24. See, for example, Stenzel, *Geschichte des preussischen Staats,* 10–12, 71–79, as the strongest such judgment; Arndt, *Völkergeschichte,* 312–313, on their political capabilities; Karl Hagen, "Russland und das Slaventhum," in *Fragen der Zeit* (Stuttgart, 1843), 1: 315–366, esp. 322–327, 348–353; and Frank Reuther, "Das Russlandbild der 'Historisch-politischen Blätter für das katholische Deutschland' im Vormärz," *Jahrbücher für Geschichte Osteuropas* 39 (1991): 177–198, for disparaging views from the conservative Catholics of the Görres Circle.

25. Not just Hegel-inspired radicals like Ruge or liberals like Droysen polemicized against a static view of history and of historical rights—even historical law professors such as Beseler did. See James Q. Whitman, *The Legacy of Roman Law in the German Romantic Era: Historical Vision and Legal Change* (Princeton: Princeton University Press, 1990), which if it underestimates the strength of German liberalism among jurists, still argues convincingly for the conservative Savigny's reformist bent.

26. F. C. Dahlmann, *Die Politik, auf den Grund und den Mass der gegebenen Zustände zurückgeführt* (Göttingen, 1835), 5; Paul Pfizer, *Vaterland,* 297.

27. See Viktor von Andrian-Werburg, *Oesterreich und dessen Zukunft* (Hamburg, 1843), 1: 196; Franz Schuselka, *Deutsche Volkspolitik* (Hamburg, 1846), 184, for his emphasis that germanization was to be peaceful and only at the level of high culture—other nationalities' identities would not be threatened; Jordan, *Hayti,* 247–248.

28. See Hermann von der Dunk, *Der deutsche Vormärz und Belgien 1830/48*

(Wiesbaden: Steiner, 1966), esp. ch. 3; *1846 Verhandlungen,* 41 for Dahl-mann, 55 for Michelsen; see also Schuselka on the future of German *Bildung* in Denmark, *Deutsche Volkspolitik,* 37.

29. See Ignaz Kuranda, "Die jüngsten Poeten. Erster Brief," *Die Grenzboten* 6, no. 1 (1847): 1–14, here 7, for the Czechs' "quälenden Dilemma"; similarly Count Friedrich Deym, who like Kuranda tended to see the path of historical development working against the Czechs and others in this respect: Deym, *Drei Denkschriften* (Karlsbad, 1848 [orig. 1847]), 20–22. See also Kuranda, *Belgien seit seiner Revolution* (Leipzig, 1846), 110–114.

30. See Georg Wilhelm Friedrich Hegel, *Grundlinien der Philosophie des Rechts,* ed. Johannes Hoffmeister (Hamburg: Meiner, 1955), 280–281 (§324) for Hegel's remarks on war as promoting the "moral health of nations," and 282–283 (§328) on the virtues of modern depersonalized warfare as emphasizing the connection of the individual to the collectivity. Pfizer, *Gedanken,* 1: 93–94, is probably the strongest echo of such ideas among the future parliamentarians, though he was alive to the evils of war as well.

31. See Franz Schuselka, "Ist Österreich deutsch?" (two excerpts), in Madeleine Rietra, ed., *Jung Österreich: Dokumente und Materialien zur liberalen öster-reichischen Opposition 1835–1848* (Amsterdam: Rodopi, 1980 [orig. 1843]), 217–223, here 219–220; Gustav von Struve, *Grundzüge der Staatswissenschaft* (Frankfurt a. M., 1848), 1: 91–92, where having to acquire natural resources from another nation was seen as "paying tribute."

32. See Gangolf Hübinger, *Georg Gottfried Gervinus: Historisches Urteil und politische Kritik* (Göttingen: Vandenhoeck & Ruprecht, 1984), 147–148; Struve, *Grundzüge,* 4: 152, where he went so far as to liken a nation without a fleet to a bird without wings; Arndt, *Erinnerungen aus dem äusseren Leben* (Leipzig, 1840), 344–345, whose desire for a fleet also promoted his desire to bring Holland and Belgium back into the Reich. Eric Hobsbawm, *Nations and Nationalism since 1789: Programme, Myth, Reality* (Cambridge: Cambridge University Press, 1992), 29–31, highlights size, strength, and overall viability as part of the liberal criteria for nationhood.

33. Such views need not have classical referents alone—Gustav Stenzel savagely praised medieval hardihood over modern weakness as resulting precisely from the self-reliant attitude fostered by an era of small, often self-governing government. *Geschichte Deutschlands,* 1: 755.

34. Friedrich Schiller, "Ueber Völkerwanderung, Kreuzzüge und Mittelalter," in Goedeke, ed., *Werke,* 13: 7–16, here 12–13; Hegel, *Grundlinien,* 291 (§347). Hegel, of course, saw the Germans as the final link in the chain of world-historical peoples, but not everyone could achieve such Olympian confidence.

35. See Pfizer, *Gedanken,* 2: 89–90; Welcker, "Natürliche Grundlagen," 756–760 for the scheme and his acknowledged debts to the ancient Greeks, and 806, 810 for the hopes of avoiding senility; Struve, *Grundzüge,* 1: 12–16, and *Phrenologie,* 328–329. Both Welcker and Struve made clear the biologistic, organicist context to such thinking about nations and history.

36. Karl Hagen, "Ueber die angebliche Entartung und Hoffnungslosigkeit

unserer Zeit" (orig. 1838), in Hagen, *Fragen der Zeit* (Stuttgart, 1843), 1: 47–72, here 56–60; Peetz, *Lasaulx*, 328–330.

37. For Slav-German antipathy as natural, see Arndt, *Völkergeschichte*, 314–315; Stenzel, *Geschichte des preussischen Staats*, 12; and Struve, *Grundzüge*, 4: 196. The idea that Russia anchored the conservative Holy Alliance and impeded German liberal and national development was a commonplace at this time.

38. Jakob Philipp Fallmerayer, "Marquis de Custine: La Russie en 1839" (orig. 1843), in *Werke*, 3: 20–56, 25–29, and "Donauländer," 3–4; Arndt, *Völkergeschichte*, 314.

39. See Arnold Ruge, *Polemische Briefe* (Leipzig: Zentralantiquariat der DDR, 1976 [orig. 1847]), 303; Hagen, "Russland und das Slaventhum," 355–356 for the fears of Pan-Slav propaganda, 358 for Hagen's conviction that if Germany were a "free, united, powerful nation" there would be no doubt of victory.

40. See Pfizer, *Vaterland*, 56–57 for "Vernichtung," 101 for the Slavs as a new "Nationalfeind" to join the French; Schuselka, "Ist Österreich deutsch?" 222 for "Schauplatz von Weltereignissen," *Deutsche Volkspolitik*, 13–14 for "Weltkampf" and "Geschichtskatastrophe." Droysen, *Geschichte Alexanders*, 1–3, saw an ongoing historical struggle between Occident and Orient; Fallmerayer, "Donauländer," 8, also deemed the Russian "Slavic empire" the culmination of an ancient East/West struggle. By the later 1840s Droysen had come to see the Schleswig affair as the first stage of the coming "great struggle" with Russia. *Johann Gustav Droysen Briefwechsel*, ed. Rudolf Hübner (Stuttgart: Deutsche Verlags-Anstalt, 1929), 1: 355 (April 22, 1847).

41. Eberhard Kolb, "Polenbild und Polenfreundschaft der deutschen Frühliberalen: Zu Motivation und Funktion aussenpolitischer Parteinahme im Vormärz," *Saeculum* 26 (1975): 111–127, focuses on the Russophobia of the 1820s, but it was still thriving in the 1840s. The millenarian quality to such thinking needs to be seen in the context of the increasing general expectation of revolutionary change in Europe, whether social, political, or military.

42. See Ulrich Scheuner, *Der Beitrag der Romantik zur politischen Theorie* (Opladen: Westdeutscher Verlag, 1980), and the older but still important Paul Kluckhohn, *Persönlichkeit und Gemeinschaft: Studien zur Staatsauffassung der deutschen Romantik* (Halle: Niemeyer, 1925).

43. Dahlmann, *Politik*, 4; Adam Müller, *Die Elemente der Staatskunst*, ed. Jakob Baxa (Vienna: Wiener Literarische Anstalt, 1922), 1: 37. For the extent of romantic and organicist ideas beyond the movement itself, see Kluckhohn, *Persönlichkeit*, 102–104; and Klaus von See, *Die Ideen von 1789 und die Ideen von 1914: Völkisches Denken in Deutschland zwischen Französischer Revolution und Ersten Weltkrieg* (Frankfurt, a. M.: Athenaion, 1975), where Dahlmann, Grimm, Uhland, Gervinus, Arndt, Jahn, and Niebuhr are all included under this rubric.

44. Raymond G. Gettell, *History of Political Thought* (London: Allen, 1924), 400–401, presents such a view of Ahrens; Conrad Cucumus, *Lehrbuch des*

Staatsrechts der konstitutionellen Monarchie Baierns (Würzburg, 1825), 29. Cucumus also explicitly linked the idea of "personality" to "Organismus" there, and, indeed, the whole concept of the state's "personality" or "moral personhood" often bore an intimate relation to the romantic, organicist ideal of reconciling "diversity" and "unity." Friedrich Julius Stahl, for example, joined natural and historical law ideas when he equated the unifying idea of the organic with personality itself, all ultimately derived from God. *Philosophie des Rechts, nach geschichtlicher Ansicht* (Heidelberg, 1830–1837), vol. 2, pt. 1, pp. 53–54.

45. E[duard] A[lbrecht], "Recension" of Romeo Maurenbrecher's *Grundsätze des heutigen deutschen Staatsrechts,* in *Göttingische gelehrte Anzeigen* (1837), 3: 1489–1504 and 1508–1515, esp. 1491–1492 and 1498–1499; Georg Beseler, *Volksrecht und Juristenrecht* (Leipzig, 1843), 173. Both Albrecht and Beseler were taking a middle position here between radical views of popular sovereignty and conservative ideas of the state personality as residing solely in the person of the monarch or in the legal status of the state fiscus. See Anke Borsdorff, *Wilhelm Eduard Albrecht, Lehrer und Verfechter des Rechts: Leben und Werk* (Pfaffenweiler: Cerberus, 1993), pt. 2, ch. 3, pp. 319–321, for the deep influence Albrecht's review had on later German legal theorists.

46. Without minimizing the importance of ideas of duty associated with rights or of community with individuality, the views on liberalism presented here differ from those in the tradition of Leonard Krieger on the extent of German commitment to versions of natural-law, rights-based liberalism within the idealist and historicist intellectual milieu. For a short corrective to this older literature, see Diethelm Klippel, "The True Concept of Liberty: Political Theory in Germany in the Second Half of the Eighteenth Century," in Eckhart Hellmuth, ed., *The Transformation of Political Culture: England and Germany in the Late Eighteenth Century* (New York: Oxford University Press, 1990), 447–466.

47. See Pfizer, *Gedanken,* 1: 14 for the quote, 13–14 for a preparatory definition of a legal subject or "Person" as whoever can demand recognition of his free will, and 41 for the definition of honor.

48. Carl Welcker, "Infamie, Ehre, Ehrenstrafen . . ." in *StLex* (1839), 8: 310–350, here 314 for "possibility," 318 for "injury"; on 312 Welcker defined a "Person" as "a moral personality with moral dignity and freedom," and the essence of *"true honor"* as "realized and recognized free moral individuality."

49. Among nondelegates, Rotteck, Fries, Kant, and to some extent Hegel and Stahl were all influential legal and political theorists who operated within this congeries of ideas surrounding personhood, autonomy, and their social and legal recognition as the bases of fulfilling the individual's and species' moral missions. Again, natural law ideas survived well into the historicist and idealist period.

50. See Cucumus, *Lehrbuch,* 2; Heinrich Ahrens, *Das Naturrecht oder die Rechtsphilosophie nach dem gegenwärtigen Zustande dieser Wissenschaft in Deutschland,* trans. Adolph Wink (Braunschweig, 1846), 162–165, 164, for both

quotes. Personality was again the basis for the status of legal subject in Ahrens's thought.

51. Ahrens, *Naturrecht*, 149, argues that for both individuals and nations progress can only result from autonomy. See Beseler, *Volksrecht*, 254, for both the connection between rights and honor and his objection to "Vormundschaft." On 151 Beseler also bemoaned the loss of honor penalties in judicial sentencing, with the consequent decline of the importance of honor in German public life.

52. The honor-rights connection formed part of both Roman and old Germanic legal traditions, hence the ease with which scholars immersed in the ancient and medieval sources could work with these ideas in the German schools of both natural and historical law. See Welcker, "Infamie, Ehre," 314–315. Here, too, educated Germans bore the stamp of their classicism. The scholar of historical law Georg Phillips, while not explicitly making honor the basis of German law, still followed Albrecht in setting "Wehrhaftigkeit," or the ability and willingness to bear arms in defense of oneself, at the root of German civil law and of the right to liberty generally. *Grundsätze des gemeinen Deutschen Privatrechts mit Einschluss des Lehnrechts* (Berlin, 1846), 1: v–vi, 264–265.

53. For a classic statement of the bourgeois versus noble redefinition of honor thesis, see George Fenwick Jones, *Honor in German Literature* (Chapel Hill: University of North Carolina Press, 1959), esp. 123–192; for the imperial feudalization thesis, see both Norbert Elias, "Dueling and Membership of the Imperial Ruling Class: Demanding and Giving Satisfaction," in *The Germans,* 44–119, and Kevin McAleer, *Dueling: The Cult of Honor in Fin-de-Siècle Germany* (Princeton: Princeton University Press, 1994), esp. 197–208. See also Ute Frevert, *Ehrenmänner: Das Duell in der bürgerlichen Gesellschaft* (Munich: Beck, 1991).

54. See Stahl, *Philosophie des Rechts*, 2: 290–291, where, while arguing that some inequality in honor must be retained, he still considered that an overarching "human dignity" should be the primary definition; Hegel, *Grundlinien*, 205–206 (§§253–255), where he did disapprove of the code's "barbarism" as being too sensitive and not distinguishing between degrees of injury; Radowitz, *Gesammelte Schriften* (Berlin, 1852–1853), 4: 14–20. Frevert, *Ehrenmänner,* 90–99, discusses the debate on military courts of honor at the 1847 Prussian United Diet, in which several future Frankfurt deputies led the charge against the extension of military honor-court jurisdiction into civil politics, but for her this indicates not rejection of the feudal code of honor but simply a lesser degree of commitment to it than would be the case fifty years later.

55. See Ernst Moritz Arndt, "Der deutsche Studentenstaat," in Arndt, *Schriften für und an seine lieben Deutschen* (Leipzig, 1845 [orig. 1815]), 2: 235–292, here 284–287; Günther Jahn, *Friedrich Ludwig Jahn: Volkserzieher und Vorkämpfer für Deutschlands Einigung* (Göttingen: Muster-Schmidt, 1992), 22; and Franz Schuselka, *Deutsche Fahrten vor und während der Revolution* (Vienna, 1849), 1: 166–167, where he approved of Jena student duels as helping to nurture a generation of men ready to risk their lives for honor rather than

"patiently suffer slaps and kicks like dogs." As Friedrich Vischer remarked in his autobiography, in the general effort to make students more earnest, the *Burschenschafter* wanted them to take duels more seriously as well. *Altes und Neues* (Stuttgart, 1882), 3: 261. For a minority voice opposing nearly all student duels, see Friedrich Wilhelm Carové, *Entwurf einer Burschenschafts-Ordnung und Versuch einer Begründung derselben* (Eisenach, 1818).

56. Welcker, "Infamie, Ehre," quote at 349; defense of duels at 323–330; 312 and 315–316 set out his definition of "true honor" as both internal and external in opposition to schools of thought insisting on one type or the other. The key link between inner and social honor was the belief that a healthy feeling of self-worth required both liberty and recognition. See Stahl, *Philosophie des Rechts,* 2: 229–230, where he defined true honor as internal rather than "good reputation" but still insisted on the necessity of its freedom and recognition by others in the rule of law. These explanations go some way toward clarifying the historiographical ambiguity surrounding liberal, bourgeois notions of internalized honor in this period.

57. Frevert, *Ehrenmänner,* 57–58, makes a similar point about the role of duels in healing the sense of alienation diagnosed by Hegel.

58. See Geoffrey Best, *Honour among Men and Nations: Transformation of an Idea* (Toronto: University of Toronto Press, 1982), esp. lectures 1 and 2, with a brief statement of the thesis at xi–xii.

59. Carlton Hayes, "Nationalism and Militarism," in *Essays on Nationalism* (New York: Macmillan, 1926), 156–195, nearly equates national rights, interests, and honor, seeing each as promoting militarism and a sense of unrestrained autonomy, but with national honor as both the "ultimate concept of nationalism" and "in plain English, national prestige" (183). See also Friedrich Zunkel, "Ehre, Reputation," in *Geschichtliche Grundbegriffe: Historisches Lexikon zur politisch-sozialen Sprache in Deutschland* (Stuttgart: Klett, 1975), 2: 1–63, here 52–53 and 56–61. The discrepancy in the standard picture between bourgeois ideas of personal honor as internalized virtue and of national honor as militarist prestige never seems to have disturbed historians of the subject.

60. Hegel, *Grundlinien,* 278 (§322) and 284 (§331); see also 286 (§334), where it becomes clear that Hegel allows nations much more readily than individuals to declare their honor, that is, their sense of infinite worth, to be involved in even minor affairs. Jakob Friedrich Fries, *Handbuch der praktischen Philosophie oder der philosophischen Zwecklehre* (Heidelberg, 1818), quote at 339; see also 378, where he argues that autonomy and war are the first concerns of a nation and its honor.

61. See Pfizer, *Vaterland,* 55, 61, and 62 for the long quote, where Pfizer made it clear that Germany's ability to be a mover in world progress depended on the external respect it could claim; see also *Gedanken,* 1: 215–219, where Pfizer assigned inalienable rights of life, liberty, and honor to the state collective person as to individuals; Carl Welcker, "Injurie, Majestätsbeleidigung und durch

beide begründete Pressvergehen, Ehrbeleidigungen gegen Völker," in *StLex* (1839), 8: 350–376, quote at 357.

62. Pfizer, *Vaterland,* 176; Welcker, "Infamie, Ehre," 322–323; Beseler, *Volksrecht,* 254.

63. As Best, *Honour,* 45–46 notes, nations seemed to acquire the honor of the "swaggering squireen" and the "instant readiness to fight" of the duello code with its points of honor.

64. Theodor Schieder, for example, points out how in the prerevolutionary decades the whole notion of "state sovereignty" that followed from the collective personality theory fell ripely into the hands of liberal particularists, not just of nationalists, but he goes on to see this as a staging post on the road to nation-state ideals in the 1840s. "Partikularismus und nationales Bewusstsein im Denken des Vormärz," in Otto Dann and Hans-Ulrich Wehler, eds., *Nationalismus und Nationalstaat: Studien zum nationalen Problem im modernen Europa* (Göttingen: Vandenhoeck & Ruprecht, 1991), 166–196, esp. 181ff.

65. Hans Kohn, *The Mind of Germany: The Education of a Nation* (New York: Scribner, 1965), 51.

66. Conversely, however, the almost religious faith in a human progress that would spell the end to personal, social, and national alienation also gave these prerevolutionary nationalists their characteristic confidence that in the end their goals would be met and their claims recognized abroad.

67. Arndt, *Erinnerungen,* 352; Frederick von Raumer, *England in 1841,* trans. H. Evans Lloyd (London, 1842), 75.

68. *1847 Verhandlungen,* 4–20, quote at 18.

69. See Peter Wende, *Radikalismus im Vormärz: Untersuchungen zur politischen Theorie der frühen deutschen Demokratie* (Wiesbaden: Steiner, 1975), 195, for Ruge, Struve, and Fröbel; Günter Birtsch, *Die Nation als sittliche Idee: der Nationalstaatsbegriff in Geschichtsschreibung und politischer Gedankenwelt Johann Gustav Droysens* (Cologne: Böhlau, 1964), 135; Sylvester Jordan, *Lehrbuch des allgemeinen und deutschen Staatsrechts* (Kassel, 1831), 29–30, 51.

70. See Pfizer, *Gedanken,* 2: 138; Ahrens, *Naturrecht,* 98–99, "Gleichgewicht" being both the diplomatic term for "balance of power" and the scientific term for "equilibrium."

71. One can find such views in figures as different as Julius Fröbel, *System der socialen Politik* (Mannheim, 1847), 1: 251, and Dahlmann, *Politik,* 5–6, where states were seen to be but "preliminary stages" to the "great common work of humanity."

II. Nationhood and Revolution in Germany, 1848–1849

1. See Dieter Düding, *Organisierter gesellschaftlicher Nationalismus in Deutschland (1808–1847): Bedeutung und Funktion der Turner- und Sängervereine für die deutsche Nationalbewegung* (Munich: Oldenbourg, 1984), 323, for how crucial the organized movement was in 1848, at which point the various

men's choral, gymnastic, and shooting societies boasted nearly 200,000 members in 2,000 local branches.

3. The German Nation and the German Jews

1. For revisionist perspectives, see the still standard Eleonore Sterling, *Judenhass: Die Anfänge des politischen Antisemitismus in Deutschland (1815–1850)* (Frankfurt a. M.: Europäische Verlagsanstalt, 1969), ch. 4; Léon Poliakov, *The History of Anti-Semitism: From Voltaire to Wagner*, trans. Miriam Kochan (New York: Vanguard, 1975), 3: 237–244, and 389; and Jacob Katz, *From Prejudice to Destruction: Anti-Semitism, 1700–1933* (Cambridge, Mass.: Harvard University Press, 1980), ch. 12. See also Rainer Erb and Werner Bergmann, *Die Nachtseite der Judenemanzipation: Der Widerstand gegen die Integration der Juden in Deutschland 1780–1860* (Berlin: Metropol, 1989), 28–36; Paul Lawrence Rose, *German Question/Jewish Question: Revolutionary Antisemitism in Germany from Kant to Wagner* (Princeton: Princeton University Press, 1992), esp. ch. 5 and pp. 181–184. For Badenese liberals, see Reinhard Rürup, "Die Emanzipation der Juden in Baden," in *Emanzipation und Antisemitismus: Studien zur "Judenfrage" der bürgerlichen Gesellschaft* (Göttingen: Vandenhoeck & Ruprecht, 1975), 37–73, esp. 46–67; and Dagmar Herzog, *Intimacy and Exclusion: Religious Politics in Pre-Revolutionary Baden* (Princeton: Princeton University Press, 1996), chs. 2, 4.

2. Much of the revisionist argument rests on Sterling's and Rürup's analyses of Badenese liberal resistance to emancipation from 1831–1845, while Katz, *Prejudice*, ch. 12, similarly mentions the influential Badenese rationalist theologian Heinrich Paulus, but beyond him only a relatively narrow range of voices.

3. David Sorkin, "The Genesis of the Ideology of Emancipation: 1806–1840," *LBIYB* 32 (1987): 11–40.

4. Poliakov, *Anti-Semitism*, Sterling, *Judenhass*, Rose, *German Question*, and most clearly of all Katz, *Prejudice*, each emphasize the connections between older Christian and newer nationalist-organicist forms of anti-Judaism. Rose, however, stresses more strongly that the emancipation debate in early nineteenth-century Germany revolved around the question of Jewish "national character." See also Wolfgang Altgeld's fine study, *Katholizismus, Protestantismus, Judentum: Über religiös begründete Gegensätze und nationalreligiöse Ideen in der Geschichte des deutschen Nationalismus* (Mainz: Grünewald, 1992), 36–42, where he argues that however true the continuity of Christian elements in modern anti-Semitism, one should still not overlook its anti-Christian and *völkisch* tendencies.

5. See Poliakov, *Anti-Semitism*, chs. 5 and 6 for the Enlightenment in France and Germany; also Katz, *Prejudice*, chs. 2, 3, and 5.

6. See, for example, Altgeld, *Katholizismus*, 53–57, 115–116 on the Rousseauian connection, Rousseau himself not having turned these ideas against the Jews,

and 102–107 on Dohm; and Rose's discussion of Dohm, *German Question*, 70–79, where, like Altgeld, he stresses the degree to which Dohm, and following him later German thinkers, considered the Jewish Question more a national than a religious issue. Ibid., 74–77.

7. Both Rose, *German Question*, 40–43, and Altgeld, *Katholizismus*, 57, overstate the significance of the German-Jewish dichotomy for German national identity. The Jewish Question's lesser centrality in early German nationalism even applies to Arndt and Jahn, who Poliakov concedes were only opportunistic anti-Semites, not going out of their way to agitate against German Jews. *Anti-Semitism*, 300.

8. For Welcker on usury, see Rürup, "Baden," 56 and 152, note 133, while on "contempt" and "theocratic state" see Gabriel Riesser's account of the debates in his periodical *Der Jude* (Altona, 1832–1833), 43 and 86 respectively; for Itzstein, see Riesser, 166, including the radical leader's observation that the sight of a cow to be sold "works upon [Jewish traders] with a magic power, they leap after it by the dozens."

9. See Sylvester Jordan, *Lehrbuch des allgemeinen und deutschen Staatsrechts* (Kassel, 1831), 404, note 5; and Conrad Cucumus, *Lehrbuch des Staatsrechts der konstitutionellen Monarchie Baierns* (Würzburg, 1825), 220–221, note 3, where he argued that before laws could do any good one had "to free the Jews from their national prejudices, to have them adopt those ideas making up the age's common property."

10. F. C. Dahlmann, *Die Politik, auf den Grund und den Mass der gegebenen Zustände zurückgeführt* (Göttingen, 1835), 328. See also Anton Springer, *Friedrich Christoph Dahlmann* (Leipzig, 1870), 1: 357–360, for the severe limitations Dahlmann placed on Jewish emancipation in the Hanover Diet's debates of the early 1830s. Like Cucumus, Dahlmann believed Jewish equality could only occur slowly, through a policy of rewarding improvements in Jewish character and patriotism with corresponding enhancement of their political and legal status.

11. See Poliakov, *Anti-Semitism*, 417, for Ruge; Friedrich Theodor Vischer, *Aesthetik oder Wissenschaft des Schönen* (Reutlingen, 1847), 2: 231–232.

12. See Anton Auersperg, "Fünf Ostern" (12th ed., 1869 [orig. 1835]) in *Anastasius Grüns Werke*, ed. Eduard Castle (Berlin, 1909), 1: 256–275, here 265–268, ll. 305–428, where note especially the biological element of an unchanging physiognomy and complexion in both northern and southern latitudes: 266, ll. 361–368; 268, l. 419 for the quote; and 267, ll. 381–384 for Jewish usury, a crime with which Auersperg also charged Christians, even if they were less skillful at it. See also Cucumus, *Lehrbuch*, 220, note 3; Franz Schuselka, "Deutsche Worte eines Österreichers" (excerpts), in Madeleine Rietra, ed., *Jung Österreich: Dokumente und Materialien zur liberalen österreichischen Opposition 1835–1848* (Amsterdam: Rodopi, 1980 [orig. 1843]), 298–305, here 304, where the radical Schuselka thought the "nobility of birth" at least had more redeeming qualities than the "nobility of money,

which makes the Kingdom of Israel supreme and makes all Christian kingdoms including the Papal States its debtors"; Karl Möring, "Nur eine Bitte," in Rietra, 411–421, 413, provides a similar diagnosis of Jewish financial power.

13. See Heinrich Laube, *Die Krieger*, vol. 2 of *Das Junge Europa: Roman in drei Büchern*, in Heinrich Hubert Houben, ed., *Heinrich Laube's gesammelte Werke* (Leipzig, 1908), vol. 1, esp. pp. 10–24 and 290–291 for the relative worth of money and persons beyond the family, 24 for "Habichtsnase"; Laube, "Einleitung des Verfassers" to *Struensee*, in Houben, ed., vol. 24, pp. 123–145, esp. 130–132, quote at 130.

14. For solutions to the Jewish Question, see Welcker and Itzstein in Rürup, "Baden," 56–64; Dahlmann, *Politik*, 328; Cucumus, *Lehrbuch*, 221; Laube, "Einleitung," 130–132; Jordan, *Lehrbuch*, 404; and for Schuselka's call for full emancipation, "Die deutschen Juden," in *Deutsche Volkspolitik* (Hamburg, 1846), 314–320.

15. Dohm's general idea was that Jews had been degraded by centuries of Christian oppression, hence the problem lay in the Christian states rather than in the Jews themselves. Consequently, good legislation and the end to such denigrating exclusion from broader progressive society could gradually help educate and "better" the Jews. On Dohm, see David Sorkin, *The Transformation of German Jewry, 1780–1840* (New York: Oxford University Press, 1987), 23–28, and (with some caution) Rose, *German Question*, 70–79.

16. Friedrich von Raumer, *Geschichte der Hohenstaufen und ihrer Zeit* (Leipzig, 1825), 5: 315; Gustav Stenzel, *Geschichte Deutschlands unter den Fränkischen Kaisern* (Leipzig, 1827), 1: 566, 731; Jordan, *Lehrbuch*, 404; Auersperg, "Fünf Ostern," 266, ll. 341–344, 369–376, and esp. 351–352. Laube, *Krieger*, 287–288, showed how the novel's main Jewish figure, the noble Joel, despairingly gave up trying to be "a man . . . among men" and decided to become a peddler, and at ibid., 290–291, revealed the sharper past rejection and disappointment of Joel's father, Manasse. See also Laube, "Einleitung," 130, for Jewish incorrigibility over the past two millennia, with the implication that emancipation could cure the problem. Stüve cited in Uwe Eissing, "Reform der Rechtsverhältnisse der Juden im Königreich Hannover (1815–1842)," *Niedersächsisches Jahrbuch für Landesgeschichte* 64 (1992): 287–340, here 316–317.

17. See Paul Pfizer, *Gedanken über Recht, Staat und Kirche* (Stuttgart, 1842), 1: 235, for restrictions on Jewish office-holding and the even fuller exclusion of women and the uneducated poor from political rights; Dahlmann, *Politik*, 328, with Quakers and Mennonites also in mind.

18. See Sylvester Jordan, *Versuche über allgemeines Staatsrecht* (Marburg, 1828), 439–440, for a clear, strong statement of freedom of conscience, which still stipulated that a religion could not endanger the continued rule of law, as also 445–454. Pfizer, *Gedanken*, 2: 29–30, pointed to polygamy and antinomian doctrines in this context, while in a speech supporting Jewish emancipation at the 1847 Prussian United Diet, future Frankfurt deputy Erdmann von Gott-

berg limited the state's legitimate checklist to monogamy and monotheism. Karl Biedermann, *Geschichte des ersten preussischen Reichstags* (Leipzig, 1847), 368–369. Unlike Jordan, Dahlmann upheld the virtues of a publicly tolerated but legally restricted status for sects holding views incompatible with statehood, as here the Quakers or, implicitly, the Jews. *Politik*, 319. Dahlmann hoped this intermediate status would pressure such sects into mending their ways.

19. See Laube, *Krieger*, 294–295, for the Jewish need to let go of the past and "die"; "Einleitung," 130 for the "Barbaren" and "radical" emancipation quotes, and 132 for Auerbach and Riesser. Rose, *German Question*, ch. 12, esp. pp. 211 and 218–220, points to Laube as calling for the eradication of Judaism and Jewish identity, and as influential in the "revolutionary anti-semitism" of nineteenth-century Germany through his direct influence on Wagner. Rose's view relies partly on a mistaken notion (213, 220) that Joel died in some kind of redeeming "symbolic suicide" in *The Warriors* (he did not). According to Laube's summing up of *Young Europe*'s cast of characters in their later lives, "Joel, the beautiful heart, peddles because the cruel world will have it so." *Die Bürger*, 146, vol. 3 of *Das Junge Europa*. On Riesser and Auerbach, see Sorkin, *Transformation*, ch. 7.

20. Jordan, *Lehrbuch*, 404. The Brunswick opposition leader Karl Steinacker set out the general idea clearly with his argument that "continuing *Bildung*" would prune Jewish religion of many climatic, political, and chance elements, adding that it would not matter so much if the process did not fully remove them "so long as a complete agreement of all men in their views is not demanded as a precondition of public welfare." "Emancipation der Juden," in *StLex* (1837), 5: 22–52, here 46.

21. Jordan, *Versuch*, 439, gave a clear statement of this truism, accepted either from the objective fact that one could not know and therefore control what another was thinking or from the Kantian metaphysical notion of legality as lying below the level of conscience and duty, which were binding in the realm of moral freedom but not enforceable in the mundane world of laws.

22. For representative views, see two articles in Georg Phillips and Guido Görres, eds., *Historisch-politische Blätter für das katholische Deutschland:* Ignaz Döllinger, "Die jüdische Frage," in vol. 2 (Munich, 1838): 377–397, and the anonymous "Nationen und Nationalität," in 19 (1847): 440–445, which in attacking the notion of national purity among European nations asserted that there was only one pure nation, the Jewish.

23. See Dagmar Herzog, "Anti-Judaism in Intra-Christian Conflict: Catholics and Liberals in Baden in the 1840s," *Central European History* 27 (1994): 267–281, 273–274, 276 on Buss; on von Linde, see note 60 below; on the Görres Circle, see Karl-Thomas Remlein, "Der Bayerische Landtag und die Judenemanzipation nach der Revolution 1848," in Harm-Hinrich Brandt, ed., *Zwischen Schutzherrschaft und Emanzipation: Studien zur Geschichte der mainfränkischen Juden im 19. Jahrhundert* (Würzburg: Freunde Main-

fränkischer Kunst und Geschichte, 1987), 139–203, here 172–175, including prerevolutionary attitudes; for Sepp, see Erb and Bergmann, *Nachtseite,* 38, note 79, where Sepp argued in 1842 for the need for Jews to free themselves from the Mosaic laws and their "national-religious autonomy" before they could be emancipated. See also James F. Harris, *The People Speak! Anti-Semitism and Emancipation in Nineteenth-Century Bavaria* (Ann Arbor: University of Michigan Press, 1994), 56–58, for Döllinger's 1846 speech against emancipation, in which he argued that it would not alter Jewish character and that Christians still needed protection from Jewish economic depredations.

24. Radowitz, "Reden welche in dem Stände-Saale zu Berlin nicht gehalten worden," in *Gesammelte Schriften* (Berlin, 1852–1853), 3: 235–252. See also his earlier (1836) remarks for similar ideas on the relationship between Christianity and Judaism, including the nationality-religion connection, the call for corporate rights as an alternative to emancipation or persecution, and the notion that while individual Jews could convert, the whole of Jewry never could. "Judenthum," in *Schriften,* 5: 93–95. In the 1847 Prussian United Diet's House of Lords Lichnowsky dismissed the proposal that Jews receive the right of election to provincial diets, asking sarcastically whom they were supposed to represent there—"certainly not the Christians." Biedermann, *Geschichte,* 396.

25. For Arndt's ideas see his 1843 letters to the demagogic anti-Semite Heinrich Marcard, in Ernst Moritz Arndt, *Briefe,* ed. Albrecht Dühr (Darmstadt: Wissenschaftliche Buchgesellschaft, 1975): 97–98 for humane treatment of German Jews, and 108–109 for assimilation through conversion. The connection between these two ideas only became explicit in an 1847 editorial letter cited in Annegret Brammer, *Judenpolitik und Judengesetzgebung in Preussen 1812 bis 1847 mit einem Ausblick auf das Gleichberechtigungsgesetz des Norddeutschen Bundes von 1869* (Berlin: Schelzky & Jeep, 1987), 83 and its endnote 45a at 430. Although often considered among the forerunners of racist anti-Semitism, Arndt's ideas clearly comported more closely with those of other Christian-state religious conservatives.

26. Katz, *Prejudice,* 149. Taking this critique farther, Erb and Bergmann chide the politically responsible classes of Germany during this period for setting both prejudice and casual discussion of extreme solutions to the Jewish Question on the way to becoming a "cultural norm," an attitude that accustomed German society to a degree of intolerance boding ill for its ability to resist the realization of such radical slogans in times of crisis. See *Nachtseite,* 62–63, for a passage highlighting the continuities if not identities between *Vormärz* and Nazi extreme solutions.

27. This growing liberal support for principled emancipation and opposition to anti-Judaism has not gone unnoticed. Even studies emphasizing liberal ambivalence on the Jewish Question have pointed to it, as for example Rürup, "Baden," and Herzog, *Intimacy and Exclusion,* on the Badenese opposition's transition from its 1830s antiemancipation stance to its support for the process in 1846–1849, with Rürup dating the change from the later 1830s, Herzog

from about 1845–1846. Dietmar Preissler, *Frühantisemitismus in der Freien Stadt Frankfurt und im Grossherzogtum Hessen (1810 bis 1860)* (Heidelberg: Winter, 1989), 141, has noted the declining virulence and frequency of anti-Semitic arguments in Frankfurt am Main. Anton Keim, *Die Judenfrage im Landtag des Grossherzogtums Hessen 1820–1849: Ein Beitrag zur Geschichte der Juden im Vormärz* (Darmstadt: Hessische Historische Kommission, 1983), 199, 234–235, has seen a similar shift in the Grand Duchy of Hesse, and as Rürup does for Baden, he highlights the increasingly doctrinaire human rights basis of liberal calls for equality.

28. Moshe Zimmermann, *Hamburgischer Patriotismus und deutscher National-ismus: Die Emanzipation der Juden in Hamburg 1830–1865* (Hamburg: Hans Christians Verlag, 1979), quote at 125. On the Prussian Rhineland, see Dieter Kastner's "Einführung" and the relevant documents in Kastner, ed., *Der Rheinische Provinziallandtag und die Emanzipation der Juden im Rheinland 1825–1845* (Cologne: Rheinland Verlag, 1989), introduction, 1: 7–85.

29. For Jordan's role, see Riesser, *Jude* (1833), 122; for Reh, Keim, *Judenfrage*, 154, 208–209 (quote).

30. See Zimmermann, *Hamburg*, 130–131, 135 for Wurm; Schuselka, *Deutsche Volkspolitik*, 314–320. Kuranda covered emancipation politics in his influential periodical *Die Grenzboten;* Hartmann movingly depicted a wounded German Jewish soldier in the politically resonant poem "Bei Waterloo." *Gesammelte Werke* (Stuttgart, 1874), 1: 33–34. The Badenese list was compiled from Rürup, "Baden," and Herzog, *Intimacy and Exclusion,* plus the 1848 Second Chamber debates on emancipation, where Brentano's motion of February 14 preceded the revolution, while the later debates were part of the general March demands of both radicals and liberals. See Werner Schubert, ed., *Verhandlungen der Stände-Versammlung des Grossherzogthums Baden in den Jahren 1847 bis 1849* (Vaduz: Topos, 1989), 3: 135 for Brentano's motion; 4: 50–51, 61–64, 72–75, and 108–114 for the March debates.

31. Friedrich Wilhelm Schubert, *Handbuch der Allgemeinen Staatskunde des Preussischen Staats* (vol. 1), vol. 6 of *Handbuch der Allgemeinen Staatskunde von Europa* (Königsberg, 1846), 478–479; Biedermann, *Geschichte*, 374–375, 379 for Vincke, 371 for Beckerath. Joseph Hansen, *Gustav von Mevissen: Ein rheinisches Lebensbild 1815–1899* (Berlin, 1906), 2: 281–283, 307–315, includes Mevissen's letters and speeches on this "question of humanity" (315); for Beckerath's crucial role in the Rhineland, see Kastner, "Einführung," 53–61. Beckerath and Mevissen are the two main examples of the "true believer" category of emancipation supporters in Shulamith Sharon Magnus's fine 1988 Columbia dissertation, "Cologne: Jewish Emancipation in a German City, 1798–1871," 363–371.

32. See Beckerath's speech in Kastner, ed., *Rheinland,* 684–690, 685, and 690 for the longer quote. This time reciting from a Jewish catechism, Beckerath argued similarly at the 1847 United Diet. Biedermann, *Geschichte*, 371. For Beckerath's speech to the 1845 Rhenish Diet, see Kastner, 913–915.

33. See Biedermann, *Geschichte*, 374–375, for Vincke; Hansen, *Mevissen*, 2: 308–310. Similarly, Friedrich Schubert expected Prussian Jews to meet emancipation with an end to that "obstinacy in holding on to customs and opinions" that made a closer "social union between Christians and Jews" more difficult in the present day. *Handbuch*, 6: 478–479.

34. See Schubert, ed., *Verhandlungen*, 4: 73 for Brentano, 112–113 for Hecker and Metz, the latter including a plea for Jews to turn to crafts and agriculture. It should be noted that Christian Kapp (113–114) disputed the Jew-usury connection. Mathy is cited in Michael Anthony Riff, "The Anti-Jewish Aspect of the Revolutionary Unrest of 1848 in Baden and Its Impact on Emancipation," *LBIYB* 21 (1976): 27–40, 38.

35. See Rürup, "Baden," 60 and 152, note 133 for Welcker's change in 1833, pp. 65 and 159, note 182 for Hecker's about-face in 1845.

36. Magnus, "Cologne," 339–344, emphasizes a change from an educated to an entrepreneurial elite in the Rhenish liberal leadership; Preissler, *Frühantisemitismus*, 141, note 3, briefly notes the increasing influence of an educated jurist elite in Frankfurt as a factor in the decreasing political weight of the artisan-based antiemancipation group there.

37. Keim, *Judenfrage*, 234–235. As argued above, natural law liberalism in Germany was never so dead as some would claim, but the July Revolution did help popularize such ideas and bring men who held them into prominence.

38. See Herzog, *Intimacy and Exclusion*, esp. 75–81, where 80–81 make clear that opposition to Catholicism more than commitment to equality motivated the liberal change of opinion—this is too strong a statement except for a few such as the radical Hecker. The question of dates is plagued by the fact that 1837 also marked the incipient rise of liberalism's general fortunes and strength as it recovered from the persecution of 1833–1834 and as it responded to the Göttingen Seven scandal in 1837 itself.

39. See Magnus, "Cologne," 297–303, 332–339 for the decreasing hometown mercantilist fear of Jewish economic competition and upward mobility as liberal economics began to incorporate a more dynamic vision of an economy offering enough for all.

40. See Hübner, *Aktenstücke*, 76–77, for the debate approving "equality of all religious groups in civil and political rights," with the Jewish situation not mentioned but rather only worries about Jesuits.

41. See Droysen, *Verhandlungen*, 8–9 for all remarks except Schüler's; 15 for the latter. While I concede a certain lack of enthusiasm among the speakers, Droysen's stenographic reports are not verbatim, hence one should be careful not to put too much weight on phrases such as "im Prinzip" or "he has nothing against it." For the Committee's *Grundgesetz* draft of Article III on religion, see StB 1: 683, 685.

42. It should be emphasized that it was Moritz and not his brother Robert who made this speech, a fact often strangely missed. Harris, *Bavaria*, 39, and Altgeld, *Katholizismus*, 193, for example, both identify Robert as the speaker.

43. See StB 3: 1754–1755 for Mohl's speech. Mohl praised the 1828 law of his native Württemberg, which gave considerable political rights to Jews but also included economic restrictions intended to promote agricultural and craft occupations among them. Ibid., 1754.

44. See StB 3: 1784 for Gfrörer; 1949–1950, quote at 1950, for Saltzwedell. The Enlightenment anticlericalism of leftists like Carl Vogt and Carl Nauwerck, as well as of the embittered Josephine Catholic Sylvester Jordan, could also apply to the Jewish temple organization, Jordan explicitly including "rabbis" in his denunciation of clerical hindrance to freedom of conscience. See ibid., 1646–1648, quote at 1647; 1668–1670 for Vogt's famous speech; and 1692–1695 for Nauwerck. Such attacks, however, generally focused on Catholics, particularly Jesuits, thus reinforcing Altgeld's view that anti-Catholicism proved a more potent force than anti-Judaism among the nationalist Protestants of nineteenth-century Germany. *Katholizismus,* 4–5.

45. StB 3: 1750–1751, here 1750.

46. See StB 3: 1755 for Riesser, "Stammestrennung"; 2017 for Mittermaier. Franz Tafel of Zweibrücken also thought mixed marriages would promote "more unity between Christians and non-Christians," and he quoted Saint Paul to the effect that the Christian man sanctified the non-Christian woman. Ibid., 1656. Riesser alone mentioned the provision for children of such unions, but Robert Blum's "Emancipation der Juden" article in Blum, ed., *Volksthümliches Handbuch der Staatswissenschaften und Politik: Ein Staatslexikon für das Volk* (Leipzig, 1848), 1: 318–321, attested to radical support for that aspect of civil marriage as well. Ibid., 319.

47. See StB 3: 1752–1753, here 1753, for Barth's "Nationalunterschied" comment, which was in no way framed to cast any aspersions but simply to ensure German Jews a full, practical legal equality.

48. Rose, *German Question,* 183, argues that intermarriage is just as bad as baptism and takes Riesser's support for mixed marriages as evidence for his assimilationist tendency toward the "destruction of Jewish identity." This would seem to be a restrictive definition of that identity.

49. See StB 3: 1756 for Riesser; 1758 for Linde's subsequent remarks, including an echo of Riesser's quip that if conversion lowered all barriers between these groups, a difference of nationality could not be involved.

50. StB 3: 1755. Schuselka later unleashed a similar argument against opponents of Jewish emancipation in the Austrian Reichstag, observing that if they truly considered Jews a separate nationality they should be consistent and apply their avowed principle of nationality equal rights to them. Schuselka reiterated that he did not believe the Jews were a separate nationality. *Deutsche Fahrten vor und während der Revolution* (Vienna, 1849), 2: 323–324.

51. See StB 3: 1756 for Riesser and the "voices"; 1762 for Beseler. It is worth noting the correspondence between the voices' timescale for the shift in "public opinion" and that established here for the liberal opposition who claimed to represent that public opinion.

52. See Preissler, *Frühantisemitismus*, 221, or Sterling, *Judenhass*, 132–134, on the lack of "conviction" with which the revolution-inspired liberals went about emancipation. For a study of Baden, one of the prime venues of anti-Jewish riots, see Riff, "Unrest," where he recounts among other events the rowdy reception of Brentano by some of his constituents, unhappy with his pro-emancipation motion in the Diet's session of 1848 (38–39).

53. StB 3: 1750. Welcker in Baden and Erdmann von Gottberg in Prussia had made similar arguments about the need to combat public opinion when it was simply prejudice in disguise. Rürup, "Baden," 63; Biedermann, *Geschichte*, 368–369.

54. See StB 3: 1757 for Osterrath, arguing also in favor of certain exemptions for Mennonites.

55. See StB 3: 1634 for Jürgens, "Weltanschauung"; 1637 for Grävell; 1638 for the motion by Riesser and other centrist liberals; 1632 for the Committee draft, where Paragraph 13 bore the crucial if unstated implication in favor of Jewish equality. The old Bavarian natural law jurist Wilhelm Behr provided a classic statement of the liberal theory of religious freedom and its potential application to the claims of German Jews when he argued that if the "Israelite church" did not contain doctrines incompatible with "the general rule of law," it deserved not just toleration but full legal equality. Behr did not say here whether Judaism included such doctrines, but he had promoted emancipation as far back as 1819 when his official support for it helped spark the anti-Jewish "Hep! Hep!" riots in Würzburg. See StB 3: 1725–1726; Katz, *Prejudice*, 98.

56. See StB 3: 1670–1672 for Jürgens; 1780 for Lasaulx. In fact, the only practical use to which some delegates might have liked to put the right of state oversight of religious and civic duties applied to sects like the Mennonites who refused military service and might therefore be refused full equality. Though himself a Mennonite, the Jewish emancipator Beckerath, for example, wanted no special exemptions from the Committee's rule made for his coreligionists, a view that met with both positive and negative reactions. See Beckerath, ibid. at 1753–1754, with the Danzigers Heinrich Martens, 1751–1752, and Johann Osterrath, 1757–1758, speaking in favor of Mennonite exemptions.

57. See StB 3: 1752–1753 for Barth; 1757–1758 for Osterrath; 1758–1759 for Linde; StB 1: 985 for Schuselka, who feared "horrible scenes" if popular "prejudice" reacted against Jewish attempts to settle in small towns. As Linde pointed out, if the desired political and legal equality did not really come to pass, freedom of conscience could not truly be said to exist. StB 3: 1758.

58. StB 3: 1764.

59. See StB 3: 1733–1734 for Reichensperger, who used the example of certain monastic orders; 1734–1735 for Linde, who referred directly to Judaism. The Catholic party's proposed amendment to Paragraph 12, in which crimes committed in the course of worship could be punished solely according to the general penal code, basically had the effect of a "no exceptional laws" clause. Ibid., 1637. The moderate Bavarian Catholic historical law jurist Karl von Arndts

conceded the conditions attached to religious freedom, citing as examples the sixteenth-century Anabaptists and polygamy, but similarly spoke against the state's right to judge doctrine as opposed to punishing a crime like polygamy according to the general legal code. Ibid., 1738–1739.

60. See Justus von Linde, *Staatskirche, Gewissensfreiheit und religiöse Vereine. Ein Beitrag zur Betrachtung der neuesten kirchlichen Ereignisse aus dem Standpunkte des Rechts und der Politik* (Mainz, 1845), 49–50, 70–71, and 88–89, for his proofs that the Federal Constitution's religious freedom clause applied to the three recognized Christian confessions alone, not to the Jews (or anyone else). See especially 88–89, where his arguments showing that full religious freedom did not exist for the Jews would be used in 1848 to support the extension of such religious freedom to them.

61. See StB 3: 1688–1692, 1688–1689 for the remarks on Christianity; 1691 for the "Ungetaufte" argument for church independence.

62. StB 3: 1695–1697, quote at 1696–1697. Georg Phillips, for example, argued that since Jews and Christian sectarians would now enjoy perfect religious freedom and independence, the Catholic Church should receive the same privilege in the interests of equality and fairness. "Die Katholiken und die deutsche Bewegung," *Historisch-politische Blätter für das katholische Deutschland* 21 (1848): 448.

63. See Sepp [anon.], *An das Volk von Oberbayern* (Munich, 1848), 31, where he admitted he had previously thought that Germans needed to be emancipated from the Jews more than the reverse; Remlein, "Bayerische Landtag," 163–164 for the quote. In general for these debates, see also Harris, *Bavaria,* 69–77, where Döllinger, like Sepp, appears among the emancipation opponents who considered Jews an economic threat and unassimilable without conversion. Yet Döllinger was still willing to let Jews hold state offices and to end most discriminatory measures in civil law. Ibid., 73; Remlein, 165, 170–171. Döllinger's acquiescence to emancipation in 1848 thus may not have been wholly feigned.

64. See Michael Brenner, "Zwischen Revolution und rechtlicher Gleichstellung," in Brenner and Michael A. Meyer, eds., *Deutschjüdische Geschichte in der Neuzeit* (Munich: Beck, 1996), 2: 287–325, 295–296, for the sudden end to traditionalist opposition to emancipation in the 1848 Revolution. See also Meyer, "Jüdische Gemeinden im Übergang," in ibid., 96–134, 105–106, and 132–134, for traditionalist resistance to emancipation, and Meyer, "Jüdisches Selbstverständnis," also in ibid., 135–207, 145–154, for a treatment of the various strands of opinion on the best ways to accept emancipation and German identity while remaining Jewish.

65. Werner E. Mosse, "The Revolution of 1848: Jewish Emancipation in Germany and Its Limits," in Mosse, Arnold Paucker, and Reinhard Rürup, eds., *Revolution and Evolution: 1848 in German-Jewish History* (Tübingen: Mohr, 1981), 389–401, quote at 401. Mosse's general deemphasis of the role of the Assembly's religious equality decision in the broader process of German Jewish emancipation, on the other hand, stands on firmer ground.

4. Citizenship and Nationality Rights

1. *OffBer*, 28–29. Just the day before Wiesner had broken a lance against fellow leftist Wilhelm Schulz of Darmstadt for daring to question whether universal manhood suffrage would be possible in Austria, with its "millions of Slavic peasants." Slavic participation was almost never questioned, but not never. *OffBer*, 14 for Schulz; 14–15 for Wiesner.

2. See Jucho, *Verhandlungen*, 67, for the Fifty's proclamation. The Austrians Baron Viktor von Andrian-Werburg and Ignaz Kuranda both took care to emphasize this aspect of the measure, Andrian referring to the "full and unconditional equality" Austria's non-German citizens were to enjoy. Ibid., 56–57 for Andrian; 59 for Kuranda. In his publicistic efforts among the Slovenes, Count Auersperg drove home the same point of political equality. Anton Auersperg, *Anastasius Grüns Werke*, ed. Eduard Castle et al. (Berlin, 1909), 6: 130–143. See StB 1: 118 for Mareck's motion; 183 for Dahlmann's revision.

3. See StB 1: 736 for Grävell; 737 for Jordan. The Hessian Wilhelm Wernher disagreed, saying Paragraph 47 did make citizenship rights clear through the accompanying commentary. Ibid., 741.

4. See StB 1: 682 for Paragraph 1; 733–734 for Fritsch; 727–731 and 754–755 for the fourteen relevant motions.

5. Droysen, *Verhandlungen*, 31.

6. See StB 1: 707 for Osterrath; 737 for Jordan; see also Friedrich von Raumer, *Briefe aus Frankfurt und Paris 1848–1849* (Leipzig, 1849), 1: 165, for his similar comments.

7. See StB 1: 738 for Beseler's "politische Einheit" remark; 739 for Venedey.

8. For the now-standard French-German *soli-sanguinis* distinction, see Rogers Brubaker, *Citizenship and Nationhood in France and Germany* (Cambridge, Mass.: Harvard University Press, 1992). Brubaker correctly points to the prevalence of *sanguinis* provisions in the citizenship laws of *Vormärz* and pre-Kaiserreich German states, and to the role of conservative officials in codifying them, yet he still stresses the ostensibly romantic, blood-based sense of nationality underlying them. Most recently, Andreas Fahrmeier has questioned whether descent even played much of a role in the interstate treaties he takes to be the core of citizenship codes in this era. "Nineteenth-Century German Citizenships: A Reconsideration," *The Historical Journal* 40 (1997): 721–752. His emphasis on the residence criterion, however, seems to apply more to the case of citizenship acquisition by naturalization than to citizenship ascription at birth (an important but not always heeded distinction in dealing with this subject).

9. By giving a distinctly *völkisch* twist to the notion of *sanguinis* so as to apply it not merely to the body of existing German citizens and their lineal descendants but also to the considerably less well-defined worldwide population of ethnic Germans, that approach has blighted the hopes of many an aspiring citizen of Germany. In addition to Brubaker, *Citizenship,* and Fahrmeier, "Reconsideration," see Rolf Grawert, *Staat und Staatsangehörigkeit: Verfassungs-*

geschichtliche Untersuchung zur Entstehung der Staatsangehörigkeit (Berlin: Duncker & Humblot, 1973), pt. 2 for general context, and 195–199 for the Frankfurt debates; and Mack Walker, *German Home Towns: Community, State, and General Estate 1648–1871* (Ithaca: Cornell University Press, 1971), chs. 9 and 11 for discussion of the *Heimatsgesetz* context.

10. Often the systems operated in combination, granting citizenship as the United States does today, to those born on a state's territory or to its dependents when abroad.

11. See Droysen, *Verhandlungen,* 31–33, for these Constitutional Committee discussions.

12. See StB 1: 729 for Dieskau's motion; Julius Fröbel, *System der socialen Politik* (Mannheim, 1847), 2: 294, and 118 for the theory behind the provision. It should be added that *Vormärz* naturalization laws generally allowed for acquisition by combined residence and special declaration anyway. Fahrmeier, "Reconsideration," 738.

13. See StB 1: 732–733 for Biedermann; 736–737 for Grävell. Whether Grävell intended to exclude children of long-term residents rather than the merely chance-born is uncertain.

14. StB 1: 740. Tellkampf also included naturalization as another means of citizenship acquisition.

15. StB 1: 761. Werner generally hoped to correct for those long-term residents who neglected to naturalize. Ibid., 760.

16. See StB 1: 761 for Werner's motion.

17. See StB 1: 741 for Michelsen; 738 for Beseler.

18. See StB 1: 737 for Jordan; Droysen, *Verhandlungen,* 31–32 for Mühlfeld.

19. See StB 1: 741 for Beseler; 687 for the "Motive."

20. See Hübner, *Aktenstücke,* 695, for the new Paragraph 1 and "Note"; see also the entry for November 6, which states that §2 and the note were accepted without discussion. Ibid., 189.

21. See StB 1: 684 for the formal Committee draft of Paragraph 47 of the Basic Rights.

22. See StB 1: 119 for Neuwall's "Heiligthum" analogy; 121 for "angeborene Rechte."

23. See Jucho, *Verhandlungen,* 57–58 for Kuranda; StB 1: 183 for Dahlmann.

24. Jucho, *Verhandlungen,* 57. See also Theodor Schieder, "Typologie und Erscheinungsformen des Nationalstaats in Europa," in Otto Dann and Hans-Ulrich Wehler, eds., *Nationalismus und Nationalstaat: Studien zum nationalen Problem im modernen Europa* (Göttingen: Vandenhoeck & Ruprecht, 1991), 65–86, here 77–78, on the near-total support for linguistic and minority protections among midcentury liberals.

25. See Jucho, *Verhandlungen,* 57–58 for Kuranda; StB 1: 118–119 for Mareck, who emphasized his intention of appealing to the many Czech and Slovene leaders who under the proper conditions, he claimed, would prefer to remain with Germany and Austria rather than join a "South Pan-Slavic Reich."

26. See StB 1: 183 for Dahlmann; Auersperg, *Werke*, 6: 130–143. Droysen's diary entry on the Committee meetings for the Mareck measure tellingly referred to it as the "Slav motion." Hübner, *Aktenstücke*, 813.

27. See Hübner, *Aktenstücke*, 90, for the Seventeen; Jucho, *Verhandlungen*, 58, for Kuranda. Not unlike Gustav Stresemann seventy-five years later, Kuranda also argued that by supporting nationality freedoms within Germany's borders, Germany would obtain leverage in bargaining for the same freedoms on behalf of Germans living under foreign rule. Stedmann hoped for the future inclusion of Swiss and Belgian French- and Italian-speakers. BA F, DB 50/8, fol. 79 (April 16); see also Günter Wollstein, *Das "Grossdeutschland" der Paulskirche: Nationale Ziele in der bürgerlichen Revolution von 1848/49* (Düsseldorf: Droste, 1977), 197.

28. StB 1: 183.

29. StB 1: 664 for Beisler report; StB 2: 1128 for Stenzel report; ibid., 1183 for Jahn's motion.

30. See Hübner, *Aktenstücke*, 78–79 for Schmerling, Zachariä, and Bassermann; 90 for the brief note about the April 25 debates and the decision to accept the clause. It had been decided to omit the explanatory commentary to the draft, which meant that the April 21 idea to leave out the constitutional clause in favor of a simple statement of good intent in the commentary had to be rethought, the result being the revival of Sommaruga's original proposal. Schmerling and Zachariä both thought the other nationalities' linguistic demands were merely the thin end of a wedge to result in "the greatest possible development of Slavic nationality" (Schmerling).

31. See Hübner, *Aktenstücke*, 813, the entries for Sunday/Monday, May 28/29; and the tantalizing "not uninteresting discussion" comment also from Droysen, in Hübner, 78. The discussions in the Constitutional Committee become all the more intriguing given that Dahlmann had introduced his version of the proposal on the first day, a fact drawn from protocols that Droysen did not include in his printed edition of 1849. BA F, DB 51/230, fols. 4–5.

32. See *Deutsche Zeitung* #153 (Frankfurt, June 2, 1848), p. 1222, for the scene on the floor of the Paulskirche, with the interjection by Hartmann and the comments on the size of the majority in StB 1: 184. For Hartmann's intent to oppose the measure as inefficacious, see ibid., 213. Droysen, BA F, DB 51/230, fols. 4–5, points to the Constitutional Committee as the origin of the recommendation to avoid further discussion.

33. Hübner, *Aktenstücke*, 77–78.

34. Grawert, *Staatsangehörigkeit*, 198–199, notes the avoidance of the word "Nation."

35. Hübner, *Aktenstücke*, 90; the adopted phraseology still bore the marks of this restriction, reading "Freedom of national development, in particular also of the non-German peoples through equal legal status of their languages in respect of schooling and inner administration." For Eisenmann, see BA F, DB 50/8, fol. 67; and for the various draft proposals, fols. 68–77. For the Fifty de-

bates, see also Stedmann's notes, BA F, FSg. 1/236, fol. 90, where the Austrian Mühlfeld seems to have been the originator of the territorial clause.

36. See StB 1: 118 for Mareck; 183 for Dahlmann. It was Dahlmann's version that was codified in the constitution as §47. StB 1: 684.

37. For all of the following brief but pregnant debates and motions, see StB 7: 5207–5210.

38. StB 4: 2778. At the Committee of Fifty in April Eisenmann had already come out against multilingual debating. BA F, DB 50/8, fol. 80v (from the unpublished April 16 debates).

39. See Hübner, *Aktenstücke,* 630, and StB 8: 5803–5804 for Carl Welcker on the "babylonische Sprachverwirrung"; StB 6: 4635 for Georg von Vincke in the same words.

40. StB 6: 4607. Count Deym, another supporter of the 70-million Reich, also expressed doubts about the "babylonische Verwirrung" of such a multilingual parliament, leading him to suggest two assemblies plus a "General Parliament." StB 4: 2882.

41. See StB 7: 5208 for Esterle; 5210 for Beseler; 5209 for Buss, who hoped with his editorial motion to secure greater local institutional autonomy for non-German-speaking districts.

42. See StB 4: 2895 for Gross; StB 1: 419 for Jordan.

43. See StB 3: 1550–1551 for Nauwerck; 1555–1557 for Vogt; 1560 for the motion from Duncker, Droysen, Waitz et al.

44. See Wollstein, *Grossdeutschland,* 216–217, 221, 321, on the Austrians' role.

45. Pieter M. Judson, *Exclusive Revolutionaries: Liberal Politics, Social Experience, and National Identity in the Austrian Empire, 1848–1914* (Ann Arbor: University of Michigan Press, 1996), 58–62, 85, 151, 269–270.

46. Franz von Sommaruga, *Oesterreichs Zukunft und dessen Stellung zu Deutschland. Ein Beitrag zur Lösung der österreichischen Frage* (Stuttgart, n.d. [November 1848]), 13; see generally Roman Rosdolsky, *Die Bauernabgeordneten im konstituierenden österreichischen Reichstag 1848–1849* (Vienna: Europaverlag, 1976), 195–202.

47. See Friedrich Schubert, *Handbuch der Allgemeinen Staatskunde von Europa* (Königsberg, 1846), 6: 443–445 for the plea for nationality and religious equal rights, 443 for the admission that "national differences" still counted when assessing a state's strength and unity. Schubert thus continued to believe what he had in 1835 in volume 1 on the Russian Empire, where on page 12 he put forth the axiom that under equal conditions the more nationally pure state would be the stronger.

48. See especially William Carr, *Schleswig-Holstein 1815–48: A Study in National Conflict* (Manchester: Manchester University Press, 1963), 154–156, 166–179, for Gülich's and Wilhelm Beseler's involvement; and Jürgen Rohweder, *Sprache und Nationalität: Nordschleswig und die Anfänge der dänischen Sprachpolitik in der ersten Hälfte des 19. Jahrhunderts* (Glückstadt: Augustin, 1976), 166, 247–251, for Beseler and Gülich.

49. See *1847 Verhandlungen,* 47, where Anton Christ supported Dahlmann's ideas. See also Heinrich von Gagern's letter of August 18, 1844, where he critiqued his father Hans Christoph's ideas on German emigration and urged that emigrants to areas with an already-established "dominant people" should "incorporate" themselves into that people rather than attempting to form a "nation within a nation," or "Volk im Volke." Paul Wentzcke and Wolfgang Klötzer, eds., *Deutscher Liberalismus im Vormärz. Heinrich von Gagern: Briefe und Reden 1815–1848* (Göttingen: Musterschmidt, 1959), 278.

50. StB 1: 674.

51. StB 7: 5208.

52. See StB 1: 741 for Boczek; StB 4: 2849 for Beidtel.

53. See StB 1: 739 for Venedey. At least one person, the Viennese pamphleteer Franz Rehmüller, had publicized the idea of such a nationality-neutral nomenclature, the "vereinigten mitteleuropäischen Staaten." Paul Wentzcke, *Kritische Bibliographie der Flugschriften zur deutschen Verfassungsfrage 1848–1851* (Halle: Niemeyer, 1911), 119.

54. See Auersperg, *Werke,* 6: 140 for "sittliche Kraft"; on 143 Auersperg made clear that the Slovenes needed to stay under German-Austrian "guidance" a bit longer before they were "fully matured."

55. See StB 4: 2787 for Waitz; 2856 for Mühlfeld. Heinrich von Gagern (ibid., 2896–2900), the Austrian official and historian Alfred von Arneth (2780), and Sepp (StB 6: 4607) are but a few of the many who sounded this theme.

56. See StB 6: 4575–4576 for Jordan, citing mixed marriages as a potent force in the process; 4607 for Sepp.

57. StB 7: 5209. Georg Beseler soon thereafter (March 2) proposed the same omission in the Constitutional Committee, a move that suggests he too may have foreseen the possible decline of non-German cultures in the face of allegedly superior German civilization. Hübner, *Aktenstücke,* 566.

58. See Franz Schuselka, *Deutsche Fahrten vor und während der Revolution* (Vienna, 1849), 2: 107; StB 7: 5209 for Boczek.

59. See StB 6: 4575 for Jordan, as part of his remarks on the advance of German as the educated language of Eastern Europe; StB 7: 5209 for Buss, where he added that Germany had no need of "forced germanization in order to impress the seal of German spirit upon the peoples yearning after it, for their blessing." Thus had Ignaz Kuranda critiqued Dutch king William I's discriminatory anti-Walloon language policy: "Why break the tree that in the natural course surely if slowly would have bent anyway?" *Belgien seit seiner Revolution* (Leipzig, 1846), 282–283.

60. See StB 7: 4811 for all of these revealing arguments.

61. Auersperg, *Werke,* 6: 140–141. In the introduction to his contemporaneous anthology of translated Slovene lieder, Auersperg carried the battle and contest imagery into the cultural realm of folksong as well. Ibid., 5: 37.

62. StB 7: 5209.

63. StB 1: 737–738.

5. Setting Boundaries for the New Germany

1. For the territorial view, see Rolf Grawert, *Staat und Staatsangehörigkeit: Verfassungsgeschichtliche Untersuchung zur Entstehung der Staatsangehörigkeit* (Berlin: Duncker & Humblot, 1973), 198; John Breuilly, *Nationalism and the State* (Manchester: Manchester University Press, 1993), 106; and Hans Rothfels, "1848—One Hundred Years After," *JMH* 20 (1948): 291–319, here 310–315. For the opportunistic view, see Günter Wollstein, *Das "Grossdeutschland" der Paulskirche: Nationale Ziele in der bürgerlichen Revolution von 1848/49* (Düsseldorf: Droste, 1977), 318; and Hans-Georg Kraume, *Aussenpolitik 1848. Die holländische Provinz Limburg in der deutschen Revolution* (Düsseldorf: Droste, 1979), 12–13. Frank Eyck, *The Frankfurt Parliament 1848–1849* (London: Macmillan, 1968), 254–255, sees most German nationalists as still attached to the old imperial territorial boundaries but ready to use historical or self-determination arguments as occasion demanded to defend them.

2. See Wolfram Siemann, *The German Revolution of 1848–49*, trans. Christiane Banerji (New York: St. Martin's, 1998), 143, with the "national democratic" left emphasizing ethnic self-determination and the "antagonistic nationalist" center-right employing historical and power-political arguments; and Karl-Georg Faber, "Nationalität und Geschichte in der Frankfurter Nationalversammlung," in Wolfgang Klötzer, Rüdiger Moldenhauer, and Dieter Rebentisch, eds., *Ideen und Strukturen der deutschen Revolution 1848*, a special issue of *Archiv für Frankfurts Geschichte und Kunst* 54 (1974): 103–123. For Faber, deputies oscillated between a Western European voluntarist, subjective definition of nationhood and an Eastern European cultural, objective one, with the left favoring self-determination arguments and moderates the historical or linguistic approach.

3. Joseph Maria von Radowitz, "Berichte," in *Gesammelte Schriften* (Berlin, 1852–1853), 3: 380; Friedrich von Raumer, *Briefe aus Frankfurt und Paris 1848–1849* (Leipzig, 1849), 1: 35, 94–95, and his report for the International Committee on the Italian situation, StB 2: 1546; Welcker in *OffBer,* 18 (Pre-Parliament); Wilhelm Zimmermann, *Die deutsche Revolution* (Karlsruhe, 1848 [1850–1851]), 785–786.

4. Wollstein, *Grossdeutschland,* 330–335.

5. See Hans-Ulrich Evers, *Alle deutsche Verfassungen* (Munich: Goldmann, 1985), 29 (Paragraph 1); Droysen, *Verhandlungen,* 314–318 for the entire September 26 discussion, with Droysen quote at 315.

6. StB 2: 1115.

7. StB 1: 246–247.

8. See StB 1: 274 for Dahlmann; 274–275 for Francke; 278–280 for Wurm; 284–285 for Michelsen.

9. See StB 1: 246 for Heckscher; 289 for Grimm.

10. See StB 1: 289 for Grimm; 288 for Vogt.

11. See StB 1: 284 for Michelsen; 275 for Francke.
12. See StB 1: 284 for Michelsen; 274 for Dahlmann. Schleswiger Carl Esmarch admitted that not all North Schleswigers wanted to join Germany but thought nearly all preferred to remain in an undivided Schleswig rather than join with the Danes, hence acceding to partition was more a recognition of diplomatic realities than of national self-determination's applicability here. BA F, DB 53/40, fols. 111–120v. Francke and the other Schleswig-Holstein delegates seem to have harbored similar views but were more ready to accept border adjustments by plebiscite. BA F, FSg 1/60, fols. 5–9 (August 1848); DB 53/40, fols. 9–18 (December 1848). Non-Schleswigers were also willing to listen to partition ideas, at least in closed session, as a relieved Raumer reported of the International Committee meetings. *Briefe,* 1: 54–56 (June 3).
13. See StB 1: 290 for Waitz; 275–276 for Schmerling. For Waitz's letter of April 18, see Johann Gustav Droysen, *Briefwechsel,* ed. Rudolf Hübner (Stuttgart: Deutsche Verlags-Anstalt, 1924), 1: 410.
14. See StB 3: 2045 for Venedey; 2093 for Vogt; 2122–2123 for Simon; 2052 for Eisenmann.
15. See StB 3: 2135 for Heckscher; 2139 for Stedmann.
16. StB 3: 2093.
17. StB 1: 284. Similarly, Carl Esmarch argued in a pamphlet that while Danish was spoken in North Schleswig, no Danish "Nationalität" was present there. *Ueber den bevorstehenden Friedensschluss mit Dännemark* (Frankfurt a. M., 1848), 6.
18. See William Carr, *Schleswig-Holstein 1815–48: A Study in National Conflict* (Manchester: Manchester University Press, 1963), 154–155, for Beseler's role in adopting the superstructural argument in the early 1840s; 165 for the Tyrolean comparison; 145 for Gülich's comments on the value of German as the vehicle of educated opinion. See also Jürgen Rohweder, *Sprache und Nationalität: Nordschleswig und die Anfänge der dänischen Sprachpolitik in der ersten Hälfte des 19. Jahrhunderts* (Glückstadt: Augustin, 1976), 278–279, on fears of the rescript as endangering the duchy's "Deutschheit" or "deutschen Charakter."
19. See especially Dahlmann's and Michelsen's contributions to the 1846 Germanist Conference, *1846 Verhandlungen,* 41 and 55 respectively. In his influential *Die Politik, auf den Grund und das Mass der gegebenen Zustände zurückgeführt* (Göttingen, 1835), 166, Dahlmann stressed the fact that Schleswig and Holstein had held parliament together and in German as the basis of their right to remain connected and bound to Germany. See also Rohweder, *Sprache und Nationalität,* 247, for the 1840 Gülich report on the language rescript, which used similar historical arguments for the natural advance of German in the duchy.
20. See, for example, Jacob Grimm, *Geschichte der deutschen Sprache* (Leipzig, 1848), 834, and Franz Schuselka, *Deutsche Volkspolitik* (Hamburg, 1846), 36–37, for such thoughts on peaceful germanization.

21. See StB 1: 284 for Michelsen; StB 3: 2054–2055 for Francke. The legend of H. Biernatzki's linguistic map of Schleswig used in the Assembly significantly bears the note, "The language of the educated in the entire duchy is regularly German." Biernatzki, "Nationalitäten und Sprachenkarte des Herzogthums Schleswig." In the copy submitted by Reich Commissar Carl von Stedmann to the Foreign Ministry, the phrase is even underlined. BA F, DB 53/29, fol. 33.

22. For a thought-provoking discussion of the bourgeois acculturation theme, see Dieter Langewiesche, "Kulturelle Nationsbildung im Deutschland des 19. Jahrhunderts," in Manfred Hettling and Paul Nolte, eds., *Nation und Gesellschaft in Deutschland: Historische Essays* (Munich: Beck, 1996), 46–64. On the late development of national identity in the Habsburg realm's rural areas, see Andreas Moritsch, ed., *Vom Ethnos zur Nationalität: der nationale Differenzierungsprozess am Beispiel ausgewählter Orte in Kärnten und im Burgenland* (Munich: Oldenbourg, 1991).

23. See StB 2: 1142 for Blum; 1160 for Schuselka. As Raumer did not hesitate to point out, the left had shown similar inconsistency in supporting both the inclusion of the Schleswig delegates and the exclusion of those from Poznania. *Briefe*, 1: 58 (June 5).

24. See StB 2: 1222 for "Sprache" and "Abstammung"; 1135–1137 and 1220–1223 in general for Stenzel; 1175 for Ostendorf.

25. See StB 2: 1138 for Goeden; 1143 for Jordan.

26. See StB 2: 1175 for Ostendorf; 138 for Goeden; and 1221 for Stenzel, who on 1222 added "sympathy" and "feeling" to language and descent as grounds for the German Poznanians' Germanness.

27. See StB 2: 1169 for Kerst; 1221 for Stenzel; 1193 for Löw.

28. See StB 2: 1239 for Biedermann's written explanation of his "no" vote on July 27. Goeden and the Poznanian Ernst Viebig both privately expressed dissatisfaction with the final demarcation line in February 1849 but voted "yes" nonetheless. BA F, FSg. 1/32, fol. 5v (Goeden); FSg. 1/185, fol. 23 (Viebig).

29. See *OffBer*, 16 for Raveaux, 18 for Struve; StB 2: 1153 for Vogt's speech, 1130–1131 for Nauwerck's motion allowing partition, 1161 for Schuselka.

30. See Wollstein, *Grossdeutschland*, 187, on the Assembly parties' lack of originality on this question; on 139 Wollstein highlights the backstage role of Kerst and Stenzel in turning the issue into a strict party question.

31. See StB 2: 1182 for Lichnowsky; 1156 for Radowitz.

32. See StB 2: 1221–1222 for Stenzel.

33. Raumer, *Polens Untergang* (Leipzig, 1832), 77; *Briefe*, 1: 246 (July 28), 318–319 (September 3). Even among the left-leaning supporters of Polish restoration, Johann Eisenmann both claimed Poznania for the Germans and blamed Polish noble disunity and exclusivity as contributing to Poland's partition. See *Aufruf zur Herstellung des Königreichs Polen* (Erlangen, 1848), 12 for the Poznanian claims, 14–16 for the Polish nobility.

34. G. A. H. Stenzel, *Geschichte des preussischen Staats* (Hamburg, 1830), 1: 11–12; StB 2: 1221.

35. Stenzel, *Geschichte des preussischen Staats,* 71, 79; StB 2: 1124–1125; Max Duncker, *Zur Geschichte der deutschen Reichsversammlung in Frankfurt* (Berlin, 1849), 28.

36. StB 2: 1145–1148.

37. StB 2: 1146.

38. See StB 2: 1143 for Jordan's "partition" remark, 1146 for "conquest"; 1175 for Ostendorf; 1223 for Stenzel.

39. Wollstein, *Grossdeutschland,* 187–188.

40. StB 1: 225. Eisenmann, *Aufruf,* 14–16, also emphasized the need for middle-class cooperation. In July Jordan contended that Polish peasants in Poznania would rather stay under the more enlightened rule of the Prussians than fall under the sway of the old Polish nobility. StB 2: 1149.

41. See StB 2: 1135 for Stenzel quote; 1146–1147 for Jordan. Stenzel had already set out this view in his *Geschichte des preussischen Staats,* 7, where he argued that the Polish nobility were the descendants of a conquering people distinct from the natives, and that even in his day the two groups bore entirely different pigmentation. For a clearer statement of Jordan's singling out the missing burgher class as the reason why Poland could not develop as a true nation, see his incidental comments in *Geschichte der Insel Hayti und ihres Negerstaats* (Leipzig, 1846), 1: 247–248.

42. See StB 2: 1136 for "peasants" and "Nationalgefühl"; 1222 for "burghers" and assurances on germanization.

43. See Duncker, *Geschichte,* 29, where he also mentioned the possibility that the demarcation line would not halt germanization; Wollstein, *Grossdeutschland,* 172, on Kerst's hopes for germanization in German Poznania. For Jordan the case is not so clear—in his Poland speech he mentioned only the Prussian service in creating a new popular Polish nationality educated in "civility and humanity" (StB 2: 1147), but in later contexts he certainly intended germanization elsewhere in the East to be more thorough, as StB 6: 4575. See also Heinrich Wuttke, *Polen und Deutsche* (Leipzig, 1848), 53–54, on the "silent advance" of "Germandom" among the Poles.

44. See StB 2: 1183 for Jahn's motion; 1202–1203 for Friedrich Thinnes on behalf of the Catholics; StB 7: 5066 for Nauwerck's motion, retracted at 5085 as a dramatic gesture.

45. See StB 2: 1135–1137, 1220–1223 for Stenzel; StB 7: 5076 for Wurm; 5072 for Venedey.

46. See StB 4: 2765 for Riesser in October. Venedey's January report included Arndtian references. StB 6: 4539, 4542.

47. See StB 1: 215, 674 for Arndt; 664 for Kuranda. See also Andrian for differences in "Stamm und Sprache," in Jucho, *Verhandlungen,* 56–57; Megerle von Mühlfeld in Droysen, *Verhandlungen,* 318.

48. Venedey's report referred to both, StB 6: 4542, with Bohemia the German "Zwingburg." Radowitz compared yielding Tyrol to giving up the door to one's house. StB 1: 666.

49. StB 4: 2772.
50. StB 4: 2850–2851.
51. Schuselka, *Deutsche Fahrten vor und während der Revolution* (Vienna, 1849), 2: 171–172.
52. See StB 1: 664–665 for Kuranda's creative and revealing use of social history; Kuranda, *Belgien seit seiner Revolution* (Leipzig, 1846), 112–113, for the "silent centuries" of germanization at the level of law and culture in Bohemia.
53. Paul Pfizer, *Gedanken über Recht, Staat und Kirche* (Stuttgart, 1842), 1: 287–288.
54. Dahlmann, for example, spoke of the Italians and Poles as likely to break off from the Austrian Empire, but he did not mention other nationalities. *Politik*, 167.
55. See StB 4: 2786–2789 for Waitz's October comments on the legitimacy of the federal borders and on the coming period of the nationality principle; StB 8: 5837 (March 19), where Waitz still maintained his stance on the desirability of the federal borders, even in Bohemia; and Droysen, *Verhandlungen*, 322, for Waitz's mention of his hopes regarding the Czechs. See also Droysen, ibid., 324, for Dahlmann's strong statement that personal union would only accelerate, not cause, the breakup of Austria along nationality lines—leaving federal Austria to Germany.
56. See Paul Pfizer, *Beiträge zur Feststellung der deutschen Reichsgewalt* (Frankfurt a. M., 1848), esp. 16; Droysen, *Briefwechsel*, 439 (July 2) for his Austrian hopes; for Droysen's already devised plan of the personal union clauses, "Denkschrift, die deutschen Angelegenheiten betreffend," in *Beiträge zur neuesten deutschen Geschichte* (Braunschweig, 1849), 41–56; for Gagern, StB 4: 2898. In January Gagern still contended Austria was welcome to join the Reich; he simply thought it could not and would not. StB 6: 4564.
57. See StB 8: 5829 for Wydenbrugk; 5804 for Welcker. Wollstein, *Grossdeutschland*, 296–297, highlights these four prominent Prussian party members on this point.
58. Interestingly, Sepp joined Moritz Mohl in preferring a parliament for the whole 70-million Reich. See StB 6: 4607 for Sepp, 4620–4622 for Mohl. For Mohl's French comparison, see BA F, FSg. 1/140, fol. 32. See also Möring, *"Entweder—oder!"* (Frankfurt a. M., n.d. [December 1848]), 6–7, 9–10.
59. StB 4: 2882.
60. See StB 6: 4636 for Vincke; StB 8: 5904 for Riesser.
61. Ernst Moritz Arndt, *Briefe*, ed. Albrecht Dühr (Darmstadt: Wissenschaftliche Buchgesellschaft, 1975), 3: 312 (24. Wintermonds [December]).
62. See Gervinus in the *Deutsche Zeitung* editorial of #128 (May 8, 1848), 1017–1018; Hübner, *Aktenstücke*, 284, for Beseler's observations before the Constitutional Committee.
63. StB 8: 5794.
64. See StB 6: 4635 for Vincke; StB 8: 5903 for Riesser; Gustav Rümelin, *Aus der*

Paulskirche, ed. H. R. Schäfer (Stuttgart, 1892), 110–111 (October 24). The Mareck measure is discussed in my Chapter 4.

65. StB 8: 5844. Eisenmann's interpellation of August 25 displays the same trend (StB 3: 1721) as does a similar one by Welcker (StB 8: 5803).

66. StB 8: 5898. On 5899 Schüler extended an invitation to the Poles, Italians, and Hungarians to enter into a federation if they so desired. Similarly, Wilhelm Zimmermann later commented that many on the left hoped for the Hungarian nationalities, Poles, and Italians to unite in a federation with Germany to fight for freedom—again presupposing a federal, multinational Germany within the context of a recognized nationality principle. *Die deutsche Revolution,* 783–784.

67. See StB 8: 5822 for Vogt, 5875 for Simon, 5852 for Ahrens; StB 6: 4765 for Welcker.

68. See StB 4: 2784–2786 for Wiesner; 2854–2857 for Mühlfeld. See above, Chapter 1, for Andrian and Schuselka.

69. See StB 4: 2772 for Fritsch. One could add Friedrich Graf Deym, *Drei Denkschriften* (Karlsbad, 1848), 7–8, 12–13, and Karl Beidtel, *Die Auflösung der staatlichen Einheit der Oestreich'schen Monarchie durch die National-Versammlung* (Leipzig, 1848), 3–4, for similar statements of faith in the power of forces other than linguistic to create a strong Austrian identity.

70. See StB 4: 2882 for Deym; Franz Unterrichter, *Ein Paar Worte über die österreichische Frage* (Frankfurt a. M., n.d. [December 1848]), 5–6, also with the Babel image. For Schmerling, March 22, 1849, after resigning as Austrian plenipotentiary in Frankfurt, see BA F, FSg. 1/73:5, #110, fols. 207–208.

71. Already in October Vogt had begun taking this line, stressing the separate constitutional provisions and parliamentary translations needed for Bohemia and its Diet, while by March the leftists were putting more weight on the idea of a federation of nations and promoting statements that no non-German peoples would be forced to join the German state. Vogt, StB 4: 2890–2891, 3130. See StB 8: 5806–5807 for the proposed proclamation, chiefly on behalf of the Italians and Poles, but now given more general validity.

72. On this point compare Droysen's letters of July 2, December 3, and December 16: *Briefwechsel,* 438–440, 486–489, and 494–497.

73. Hübner, *Aktenstücke,* 590 (March 5, 1849).

6. National Honor, National Conflict

1. Carlton Hayes, *Essays on Nationalism* (New York: Macmillan, 1926), 186–187.

2. See StB 2: 1156 for Radowitz; Max Duncker, *Zur Geschichte der deutschen Reichsversammlung in Frankfurt* (Berlin, 1849), 31.

3. For examples of references to military honor in the Schleswig debates, see StB 1: 280 for Gabriel Riesser's motion to conduct the war in a manner befitting "the honor of the German troops," and for Karl Giskra's remarks on the insult

to German "Waffenehre" in Danish possession of the "trophy" of North Schleswig. In correspondence Ernst Moritz Arndt did explicitly couple "Macht Ehre und Ruhm": *Briefe*, ed. Albrecht Dühr (Darmstadt: Wissenschaftliche Buchgesellschaft, 1975), 3: 314 (27. Hornungs 1849 [February]).

4. Ludolf Wienbarg, *Der dänische Fehdehandschuh* (Hamburg, 1846), title page ("Wo unser Recht wär' wehrlos, / Wär' unsre Mannschaft ehrlos").

5. See StB 1: 285 for Michelsen; 233–234 for the motion of June 6; and 295 for its acceptance "with a large majority" on the 9th.

6. StB 3: 1865.

7. StB 2: 818–820.

8. See StB 4: 2757–2758 for Esmarch; StB 3: 1887 for Zimmermann; 1906–1907 for Wurm; 2083 for Giskra's "Ehrenmänner" reference, and 2086 for his rousing conclusion. See also on this point Heinrich Laube, *Das erste deutsche Parlament*, in Heinrich Hubert Houben and Albert Hänel, eds., *Heinrich Laubes gesammelten Werke* (Leipzig, 1909), 37: 146.

9. Walter Bussmann, "Das deutsche Nationalbewusstsein im 19. Jahrhundert," in Werner Weidenfeld, ed., *Die Identität der Deutschen* (Munich: Hanser, 1983), 74–75.

10. See StB 4: 2757–2758 for Esmarch; 2760 for Beseler.

11. See StB 3: 1900 for Beckerath on Malmö, and 1836 for his similar views on the Limburg question; 2082 for Mühlfeld.

12. StB 3: 2063.

13. See StB 3: 1900 for Beckerath; 2042–2043 for Heckscher; 2088 for Wilhelm Jordan.

14. Julius Fröbel, *System der socialen Politik* (Mannheim, 1847), 1: 241–242.

15. See StB 3: 2065 for Jordan's argument.

16. Günter Wollstein, *Das "Grossdeutschland" der Paulskirche: Nationale Ziele in der bürgerlichen Revolution von 1848/49* (Düsseldorf: Droste, 1977), 45.

17. StB 1: 274.

18. See StB 3: 1882 for Dahlmann; 1888 for Zimmermann.

19. See StB 1: 654 for the printed report.

20. Droysen, *Verhandlungen*, 433.

21. See StB 8: 5849 and 5851 for Beseler; 5666 for Welcker.

22. See StB 2: 1206 for Giskra's objections to heeding French opinion regarding Poznanian policy, a point made with specific reference to the Wydenbrugk report's setting of Germany's "honor and independence" as the highest principle of its foreign policy.

23. See StB 2: 1144 for Jordan.

24. Friedrich von Raumer, *Briefe aus Frankfurt und Paris 1848–1849* (Leipzig, 1849), 1: 318–319, 341; Duncker, *Geschichte*, 23, 44.

25. See Droysen, *Verhandlungen*, 450 for Droysen, 424 for Mittermaier. Droysen was here justifying the balance between the federal and state constitutions and the right of limited oversight of free associations in civil society, while Mittermaier was explaining the balance in the sphere of constitutional, diplomatic, and military affairs.

26. StB 7: 5158–5159.
27. On these constitutional debates, see Manfred Botzenhart, *Deutscher Parlamentarismus in der Revolutionszeit, 1848–1850* (Düsseldorf: Droste, 1977), 641–692, esp. 663–679 on the suffrage debates and 674 on the difficulties of defining "Selbständigkeit" in an era of social and economic change.
28. See Droysen, *Verhandlungen,* 424 for Mittermaier; StB 7: 5282 for Jahn; StB 6: 4595 for Beckerath.
29. See StB 4: 2788 for Waitz; 2909 for Riesser.
30. StB 6: 4626–4627.
31. See StB 8: 5903 for Riesser's comments.
32. See StB 4: 2884 for Wichmann's telling arguments.
33. See StB 6: 4836 for Edel; 4776 for Lasaulx; Johann Perthaler, *Das Erbkaiserthum Kleindeutschland* (Frankfurt a. M., 1849), 12–14.
34. See StB 8: 5853 for Ahrens.
35. See StB 2: 1145 for Jordan; 1175 for Ostendorf; Laube, *Parlament,* 37: 126–127; Gustav Rümelin, *Aus der Paulskirche,* ed. H. R. Schäfer (Stuttgart, 1892), 49.
36. G. A. H. Stenzel, *Geschichte des preussischen Staats* (Hamburg, 1830), 1: 12; Rümelin, *Aus der Paulskirche,* 49.
37. See *OffBer,* 7 for Gagern (March 31); 34 for Hecker (April 1).
38. See Droysen, *Johann Gustav Droysen. Briefwechsel,* ed. Rudolf Hübner (Stuttgart: Deutsche Verlags-Anstalt, 1924), 1: 527 (March 10, 1849); Rudolf Haym, *Ausgewählter Briefwechsel Rudolf Hayms,* ed. Hans Rosenberg (Stuttgart: Deutsche Verlags-Anstalt, 1930), 75 (March 6, 1849); StB 3: 2060 for Hermann. See also Ludwig von Pastor, *Leben des Freiherrn Max von Gagern 1810–1889: Ein Beitrag zur politischen und kirchlichen Geschichte des neunzehnten Jahrhunderts* (Kempten: Kösel, 1912), 235–236, note 1, for similar views by the liberal Catholic Max von Gagern (Heinrich's younger brother) and his correspondent Lasaulx.
39. See StB 1: 280 for Giskra; 283 for Michelsen; StB 3: 1882 for Dahlmann.
40. See StB 2: 1137–1138 for Goeden. Even earlier in June, Ernst Nerreter had spoken of a possible "death-struggle of despair" in Poznania. StB 1: 225.
41. See StB 2: 1169 for Janiszewski; 1170 for Kerst; 1145 for Jordan.
42. StB 2: 1195.
43. See StB 1: 197 for Venedey (June 3); StB 2: 1187 for Ruge, "Völker-Familie."
44. See StB 1: 419 for both Venedey and the quoted Berger-Schilling motion; 671 for Giskra, as also for Ruge's warning of a possible "race-war" in Bohemia.
45. For various iterations see Friedrich von Raumer, *Geschichte der Hohenstaufen und ihrer Zeit* (Leipzig, 1823), 1: 365, and *Briefe,* 2: 89; Dahlmann at the 1846 Germanist conference, *1846 Verhandlungen,* 42–43; Franz Schuselka, *Deutsche Volkspolitik* (Hamburg, 1846), 34–37.
46. See StB 1: 289 for Grimm, but see also his *Geschichte der deutschen Sprache* (Leipzig, 1848), 726, 738, 794, and 837 for similar remarks on Jutland and Germany in a more scholarly context.
47. StB 3: 2050. Wollstein, *Grossdeutschland,* 319–320, notes the importance of

transethnic thinking, and on 312 its dampening effect on anti-Danish positions.

48. See StB 4: 2759 for Beseler; his fellow Schleswiger Carl Francke had used a weaker version of the argument on 2751.

49. StB 1: 284.

50. See Grimm, *Geschichte,* v–vi; StB 2: 1112–1113 for Beckerath.

51. StB 2: 1113–1114. Möring invoked both linguistic relationship and geographic situation in explaining why the groups would draw together.

52. See Carl Möring, *"Entweder—oder!"* (Frankfurt a. M., n.d. [December 1848]), 8, for his dreams of "marrying Germania and Slava."

53. Paul Pfizer, *Das Vaterland* (Stuttgart, 1845), 297; Franz Schuselka, "Ist Österreich deutsch?" (two excerpts) in Madeleine Rietra, ed., *Jung Österreich: Dokumente und Materialien zur liberalen österreichischen Opposition 1835–1848* (Amsterdam: Rodopi, 1980 [orig. 1843]), 217–223, here 222.

54. See *Deutsche Zeitung* #132 (May 12, 1848), 1049; Karl Hagen, *Fragen der Zeit* (Stuttgart, 1843), 1: 322; Hübner, *Aktenstücke,* 589–590, for Lasaulx.

55. Droysen, *Verhandlungen,* 279.

56. See StB 2: 1143 for Jordan's original statement; 1153 for Vogt's admission and doubts as to whether the Slavs would be so doomed; Hermann Misteli, *Carl Vogt, seine Entwicklung vom angehenden naturwissenschaftlichen Materialisten zum idealen Politiker der Paulskirche (1817–1849)* (Zurich: Gebrüder Leemann & Co., 1938), 206.

57. See StB 8: 5822–5823 for Vogt; and see ibid., 5834, for Wilhelm Schulz's similar remarks to the effect that he would accept a Prussian hereditary emperor only on condition of an immediate declaration of war to carry Germany to the shores of the Black Sea.

58. Christian Friedrich Wurm, *Die Diplomatie, das Parlament, und der deutsche Bundesstaat* (Braunschweig, 1849), 19–20. As examples of such *grossdeutsch* worries, see Ahrens's remarks in the Constitutional Committee on December 13, in Hübner, *Aktenstücke,* 287; and the January Venedey report itself, StB 6: 4542.

59. See Ludwig Bergsträsser, ed., *Das Frankfurter Parlament in Briefen und Tagebüchern* (Frankfurt a. M.: Frankfurter Societätsdruckerei, 1929), 38, for Ambrosch; Droysen, *Briefwechsel,* 1: 496 (December 16) for the "Rassenkrieg," and 529 (March 15, 1849).

60. This is the basic thesis of Wollstein, *Grossdeutschland.* The present study simply provides a deeper and different intellectual-cultural context for these tendencies.

61. See Droysen, *Verhandlungen,* 338 for Dahlmann; 109–110 for the Waitz-Dahlmann interplay.

62. See StB 8: 5862–5863 for both remarks.

63. StB 4: 2787–2788.

64. StB 6: 4607.

65. StB 6: 4574–4575.

Conclusion

1. John Hutchinson, *The Dynamics of Cultural Nationalism: The Gaelic Revival and the Creation of the Irish Nation State* (London: Allen & Unwin, 1987), ch. 1. Hutchinson thus revises but maintains the older dichotomy, as at pp. 12–13.

2. For this sociological aspect of educational reform, see Lenore O'Boyle, "Klassische Bildung und soziale Struktur in Deutschland zwischen 1800 und 1848," *HZ* 207 (1968): 584–608.

3. Generally on the role of gender exclusion in post–French Revolution nationalism, and for the transversal of the cultural and political dichotomy, see Glenda Sluga, "Identity, Gender and the History of European Nations and Nationalisms," *Nations and Nationalism* 4 (1998): 87–111. For a treatment of the same issue in the German case that also emphasizes women's ability to manipulate that nationalist ideology in their favor, see Ute Planert, "Zwischen Partizipation und Restriktion: Frauenemanzipation und nationales Paradigma von der Aufklärung bis zum Ersten Weltkrieg," in Dieter Langewiesche and Georg Schmidt, eds., *Föderative Nation: Deutschlandkonzepte von der Reformation bis zum Ersten Weltkrieg* (Munich: Oldenbourg, 2000), 387–428.

4. See Andrzej Walicki, *Philosophy and Romantic Nationalism: The Case of Poland* (Oxford: Clarendon Press, 1982), pt. 3, ch. 2 on Mickiewicz's "messianism"; Jan Kollár, *Ueber die literarische Wechselseitigkeit zwischen den verschiedenen Stämmen und Mundarten der slawischen Nation* (Leipzig, 1844), 65, where he proposes not full "slavicization" but rather the centrality of a new Slavic culture of humanity for Europe.

5. Lawrence Orton, *The Prague Slav Congress of 1848* (New York: Columbia University Press, 1978), 1; Peter Brock, *Folk Cultures and Little Peoples: Aspects of National Awakening in East Central Europe* (New York: Columbia University Press, 1992), 74.

6. Ernest Gellner's prototypical "Ruritanian" nationalism in the empire of "Megalomania" is an obvious eastern reference. *Nations and Nationalism* (Oxford: Blackwell, 1983), 58–62. See Anthony D. Smith, *Theories of Nationalism* (New York: Holmes and Meier, 1983), 198–199 for the emphasis on rights, and 231–236 where he makes clear the different role of language and culture in the nationalism of the multinational empires as opposed to that of Great Britain. Smith in *The Ethnic Origins of Nations* (Oxford: Blackwell, 1986), 140–141, no longer insists on a strict East-West typology but retains certain aspects of it, with Germany and Italy intermediate. See also Miroslav Hroch, *The Social Interpretation of Linguistic Demands in European National Movements* (Badia Fiesolana: European University Institute, 1994), esp. 10–11, where Hroch draws East/West distinctions within the context of differing rates of modernization.

7. See Andrzej Walicki, "National Messianism and the Historical Controversies in the Polish Thought of 1831–1848," in Roland Sussex and J. C. Eade, eds.,

Culture and Nationalism in Nineteenth-Century Eastern Europe (Columbus, Ohio: Slavica, 1985), 128–142, here 128–129, and 134 opposing Kohn; Piotr Wandycz, *The Lands of Partitioned Poland, 1795–1918* (Seattle: University of Washington Press, 1984), 148–149, on the 1772 borders; and Wandycz, *The Price of Freedom: East Central Europe in Modern Times* (London: Routledge, 1992), 137–142, for the Polish combination of Enlightenment and romantic types of national identity.

8. See Laszlo Deme, "Pre-1848 Magyar Nationalism Revisited: Ethnic and Authoritarian or Political and Progressive," *East European Quarterly* 27 (1993): 141–169, esp. 141–145 for his explicit revision of Kohn; Brock, *Folk Cultures,* 74; Orton, *Slav Congress,* 11.

9. Risto Alapuro, "Classi sociali e nazionalismo in Finlandia: uno studio comparativo," *Quaderni Storici* 84 (1993): 745–773; Jiří Kořalka, "Hans Kohn's Dichotomie und die neuzeitliche Nationsbildung der Tschechen," in Eva Schmidt-Hartmann, ed., *Formen des nationalen Bewusstseins im Lichte zeitgenössischer Nationalismustheorien* (Munich: Oldenbourg, 1994), 263–276; Smith, *Ethnic Origins,* 147–148; Peter Alter, *Nationalism,* trans. Stuart McKinnon-Evans (London: Edward Arnold, 1989), 14–17. Kořalka still accepts Kohn's cultural-political dichotomy but suggests it can describe a nationalist ideology at different phases of development, with both types successively appearing in eastern and western variants, a view similar to Hutchinson, *Cultural Nationalism,* 40–41.

10. See Brock, *Folk Cultures,* 40–41 for the extended quote, 45–48 for Vahylevych's preference for democracy over the simple preservation of Ukrainian cultural identity and his consequent stress on shared history, constitutional ideals, and fatherland with the Poles; Jan Kozik, *The Ukrainian National Movement in Galicia: 1815–1849,* trans. and ed. Lawrence D. Orton and Andrew Gorski (Toronto: University of Toronto Press, 1986), 110, for the same partial quote, where, as generally in Brock, it is used to support Vahylevych's identification of nationality with culture alone.

11. Orton, *Slav Congress,* 28, citing a petition of April 22, 1848 by the Graz Slovenija society. At both the Prague Congress (ibid., 71–72) and the Kremsier Reichstag, deputies adopted a compromise solution by retaining historical territories while creating autonomous districts within them along ethnographic lines. Robert A. Kann, *The Multinational Empire: Nationalism and National Reform in the Habsburg Monarchy 1848–1918* (New York: Octagon, 1970 [orig. 1950]), 2: 21–39.

12. See Brock, *Folk Cultures,* 77 for Štúr, 116–118 and 141, note 12 for Jordan's desire to create a Sorb vernacular while following Palacký in opposing Štúr's new Slovak creation on Slavic unity grounds; Kozik, *Ukrainian National Movement,* 9, 84 for Kollár, Kopitar, Dobrovský, and Šafařík.

13. See Eric Hobsbawm, *Nations and Nationalism since 1789: Programme, Myth, Reality* (Cambridge: Cambridge University Press, 1992), 94–100, for this context.

14. Kollár and Šafařík both learned romantic nationalism at the feet of Heinrich

Luden in Jena, where as a Lutheran Kollár also participated in the 1817 Wartburg Festival. Hans Kohn in particular emphasizes such early connections. *Pan-Slavism: Its History and Ideology* (Notre Dame: University of Notre Dame Press, 1953).

15. As welcome correctives, see Keith Robbins, *Nineteenth-Century Britain: Integration and Diversity* (Oxford: Clarendon Press, 1988); and Linda Colley, *Britons: Forging the Nation 1707–1837* (New Haven: Yale University Press, 1992).

16. Gerald Newman, *The Rise of English Nationalism: A Cultural History 1740–1830* (London: Weidenfeld and Nicolson, 1987), esp. 118–119, emphasizes the anti-French component to English cultural nationalism; Colley, *Britons,* ch. 1, esp. p. 25, stresses the Protestant, anti-Catholic aspect of British Francophobe identity. David Bell, "Recent Works on Early Modern French National Identity," *JMH* 68 (1996): 84–113, esp. 86–90, 107–110, emphasizes the civic nature of French national identity before the Revolution and insists there was no Anglophobe equivalent to British Francophobia in the eighteenth century.

17. See Brian Jenkins, *Nationalism in France: Class and Nation since 1789* (London: Routledge, 1990), 11, for France as the prototype of the political nation; Eugen Weber, *My France: Politics, Culture, Myth* (Cambridge, Mass.: Harvard University Press, 1991), 23; Norman Hampson, "The Idea of the Nation in Revolutionary France," in Alan Forrest and Peter Jones, eds., *Reshaping France: Town, Country and Region during the French Revolution* (Manchester: Manchester University Press, 1991), 13–25, here 20–22, for conceptions of "Frenchness" in citizenship.

18. Patrice L.-R. Higonnet, "The Politics of Linguistic Terrorism and Grammatical Hegemony during the French Revolution," *Social History* 5 (1980): 41–69, Saint-Just quote at 54; Martin Lyons, "Regionalism and Linguistic Conformity in the French Revolution," in Forrest and Jones, eds., *Reshaping France,* 179–192; David A. Bell, "Lingua Populi, Lingua Dei: Language, Religion, and the Origins of French Revolutionary Nationalism," *American Historical Review* 100 (1995): 1403–1437. Higonnet and Lyons both concentrate on utilitarian, egalitarian motivations and the intent to standardize French patois as well as spread French into non-French-speaking areas such as Brittany and Alsace, while Bell highlights attempts to combat religious missionizing in patois; yet in each case linguistic assimilation remains the normative presupposition behind political unity.

19. See Robbins, *Nineteenth-Century Britain,* 29–30, on the desire or assumption of many Victorians that English was or would become the language of Britain, desires expressed against Welsh (31–32), Scots (38–39), and Gaelic (41–42); Weber, *My France,* 24–31, on Thierry and Martin; Newman, *English Nationalism,* 114–119. Reginald Horsman emphasizes the first half of the nineteenth century in the growth of such racial thinking in Britain, in "Origins of Racial Anglo-Saxonism in Great Britain before 1850," *JHI* 37 (1976): 387–410.

20. See L. Perry Curtis, Jr., *Apes and Angels: The Irishman in Victorian Caricature*

(Washington, D.C.: Smithsonian, 1971), esp. 13–15 for the European context; Léon Poliakov, *The History of Anti-Semitism: From Voltaire to Wagner*, trans. Miriam Kochan (New York: Vanguard, 1975), 3: 86–99, on Voltaire; and Jacob Katz, *From Prejudice to Destruction: Anti-Semitism, 1700–1933* (Cambridge, Mass.: Harvard University Press, 1980), chs. 2 and 3.

21. See Weber, *My France,* 27–31, on the correlation between the overlapping ideological uses of the "race war" and "class war" concepts; Newman, *English Nationalism,* 116, 189–191, on the "Norman Yoke" theory; and Léon Poliakov, *The Aryan Myth: A History of Racist and Nationalist Ideas in Europe*, trans. Edmund Howard (New York: Heinemann, 1974), 24–36 (France), 46–53 (England).

22. Istvan Deak, *The Lawful Revolution: Louis Kossuth and the Hungarians, 1848–1849* (New York: Columbia University Press, 1979), 44.

23. See Orton, *Slav Congress,* 66 for Šafařík; Kollár, *Wechselseitigkeit,* 18, 90 for reflections on Slavic power and "national honor," and 71 on the need for a strong "Selbstgefühl" or sense of self-esteem to support these pretensions.

24. See Jules Michelet, *The People,* ed. and trans. John P. McKay (Urbana: University of Illinois Press, 1973), 186–189 for his anti-British stance; 193, where Britain like Germany is by "language, race, and instinct" barred from the full "Romano-Christian" democratic tradition; and 179–182 for the necessary diversity of national genius.

25. See Adam Ferguson, *An Essay on the History of Civil Society* (Edinburgh: Edinburgh University Press, 1966 [orig. 1767]), 22–24, 61–62; Michelet, *The People,* esp. 138–142 for the individual level, and 143–148 for the same scheme as the key to social regeneration.

26. See Poliakov, *Aryan Myth,* as an example of such a Europe-wide study, with the point about differing receptivity to materialism in ch. 10; see also Curtis's treatment of the ancient and European context to physiognomic studies in Britain, *Apes and Angels,* ch. 1. Tellingly, James Cowles Prichard's contribution to the 1847 Oxford BAAS meeting made clear the extremely broad source base for studies of ethnographic affinity both ancient and modern. "On the Various Methods of Research Which Contribute to the Advancement of Ethnology, and of the Relations of That Science to Other Branches of Knowledge," in *Report of the Seventeenth Meeting of the British Association for the Advancement of Science* (London, 1848), 230–253. Pointing up the international nature of these endeavors were both Prichard's references to Continental scholars and the presence of Max Müller and Baron Christian Bunsen as two of the other speakers on the panel.

Index